Converging Identities

Carolina Academic Press African World Series
Toyin Falola, Series Editor

Africa, Empire and Globalization:
Essays in Honor of A. G. Hopkins
Toyin Falola, editor, and Emily Brownell, editor

African Entrepreneurship in Jos, Central Nigeria, 1902–1985
S.U. Fwatshak

An African Music and Dance Curriculum Model:
Performing Arts in Education
Modesto Amegago

Authority Stealing:
Anti-Corruption War and Democratic Politics
in Post-Military Nigeria
Wale Adebanwi

The Bukusu of Kenya:
Folktales, Culture and Social Identities
Namulundah Florence

Contemporary African Literature: New Approaches
Tanure Ojaide

Contesting Islam in Africa:
Homegrown Wahhabism and Muslim Identity in Northern Ghana, 1920–2010
Abdulai Iddrisu

Converging Identities:
Blackness in the Modern African Diaspora
Julius O. Adekunle and Hettie V. Williams

Democracy in Africa:
Political Changes and Challenges
Saliba Sarsar, editor, and Julius O. Adekunle, editor

Diaspora and Imagined Nationality:
USA-Africa Dialogue and Cyberframing Nigerian Nationhood
Koleade Odutola

Food Crop Production, Hunger, and Rural Poverty in
Nigeria's Benue Area, 1920–1995
Mike Odugbo Odey

Esu:
Yoruba God, Power, and the Imaginative Frontiers
Toyin Falola

Converging Identities

Blackness in the Modern African Diaspora

Edited by

Julius O. Adekunle

Hettie V. Williams

CAROLINA ACADEMIC PRESS

Durham, North Carolina

Library of Congress Cataloging-in-Publication Data

Converging identities : Blackness in the modern African diaspora / Julius O. Adekunle, Hettie V. Williams.

 pages cm. -- (African world series)
 Includes bibliographical references and index.
 ISBN 978-1-61163-137-1 (alk. paper)
 1. African diaspora. 2. Blacks--Race identity. 3. Africa--Emigration and im-migration. 4. African diaspora in literature. I. Adekunle, Julius, editor of compilation. II. Williams, Hettie V., editor of compilation. III. Series: Carolina Academic Press African world series.

 DT16.5.C67 2013
 305.896--dc23

2013020254

Carolina Academic Press
700 Kent Street
Durham, North Carolina 27701
Telephone (919) 489-7486
Fax (919) 493-5668
www.cap-press.com

For the African Slaves:

They were Black Heroes,
The First African Diaspora, and
The Pioneers of Blackness Outside Africa

Contents

Part I · The Modern African Diaspora in Global Perspective

Part II · The Modern African Diaspora and Black Identity

Chapter 7 · Black Like Who? The Identity of an American President

Chapter 8 · Black First, But Not Only: Racial Identity Formation in a Changing Black 'Hood'

Chapter 9 · The African Diaspora in the U.S.: Cultural Clash and Identity Challenges

List of Tables and Figures

Series Editor's Preface

The *Carolina Academic Press African World Series,* inaugurated in 2010, offers significant new works in the field of African and Black World studies. The series provides scholarly and educational texts that can serve both as reference works and as readers in college classes.

Studies in the series are anchored in the existing humanistic and the social scientific traditions. Their goal, however, is the identification and elaboration of the strategic place of Africa and its Diaspora in a shifting global world. More specifically, the studies will address gaps and larger needs in the developing scholarship on Africa and the Black World.

The series intends to fill gaps in areas such as African politics, history, law, religion, culture, sociology, literature, philosophy, visual arts, art history, geography, language, health, and social welfare. Given the complex nature of Africa and its Diaspora, and the constantly shifting perspectives prompted by globalization, the series also meets a vital need for scholarship connecting knowledge with events and practices. Reflecting the fact that life in Africa continues to change, especially in the political arena, the series explores issues emanating from racial and ethnic identities, particularly those connected with the ongoing mobilization of ethnic minorities for inclusion and representation.

Toyin Falola
University of Texas at Austin

Acknowledgments

The editors of *Converging Identities* conceived the idea of a collaborative work with scholars in the field of African Diaspora and the response to our call for papers was impressive. The contributors to this volume showed tremendous interest not only in the subject, but also in the anthology. The editors appreciate the contributors whose efforts and insightful analyses have significantly strengthened the understanding of the various aspects of the African Diaspora. The book is interdisciplinary in approach and the ideas are well articulated. The names of the contributors appear atop the individual chapters and in the biography page. We thank the contributors also for their patience during the long period of editing and publishing this book.

We are thankful to Dr. Toyin Falola for his support, strong interest in the subject matter, and for facilitating the process of publication. We express our profound gratitude to our academic colleagues who reviewed the chapters and also to Kevin Young and Ms. Maria Geiger for their experience and patience in painstakingly editing and proofreading the manuscript. We appreciate the assistance we received from our colleagues in the Department of History and Anthropology, Monmouth University.

We express many thanks to Carolina Academic Press for accepting this project for publication. Last but not least, we appreciate our respective family members for their encouragement and support.

Julius O. Adekunle and Hettie V. Williams
Monmouth University, 2013

Introduction

Early civilizations have emerged and grown through the converging of people in areas that produced opportunities for development. Convergence promotes social interaction and increases the knowledge of and respect for other cultures. Multiculturalism is a product of convergence and brings flavor to human relations. No community, ancient or modern, has survived without relating with, borrowing from, and sharing with others. In modern history, the United States has become a country of diverse cultural groups and a nation of converging identities. Through historical connections, Africans have populated Europe and the Americas. Their presence in these places has given prominence to black identity and cultural studies. Thus African Diaspora constitutes a major part of the converging identities in contemporary history.

This anthology offers a unique approach and focus; it is interdisciplinary and concentrating mainly on the converging of identities of the African Diaspora in Europe and the Americas. Brazil and the Unites States have the highest numbers of the African Diaspora. This is the basis for the examination of the converging identities and blackness of the African Diaspora. The book is not about racial identity, but about how many ethnic backgrounds, especially people of African descent, have, for various reasons, populated the U.S. and other places. The African Diaspora is found all over the globe, but strong historical connection makes their presence and influence felt more in the U.S., whether in the past or in modern times. The major objective of the book is to examine, expose, and explain the power of converging identities, especially through the role of the African Diaspora, not only in the U.S., but also wherever they exist. The book seeks to examine how the African Diaspora either maintain or lose cultural and ethnic identity when they interact with other people. The book is also intended to discuss the role of the African Diaspora in the development of the communities in which they live.

The interplay of ethnic, cultural, national, and "racial" identities in the contemporary African Diaspora has almost reached the level of "identity" crisis. Many African-descended people in the Americas have begun to resist and challenge identities of color while others firmly embrace essentialist notions of race. Globalization has ensured the increased movement of people of African descent around the world coming from such places as Africa, Latin America, and the Caribbean; settling in places such as Canada and the United States. These sojourners of the contemporary African Diaspora are fighting to maintain control over the defining features of self and communal identities as they "clash" with American blacks over essentialist notions of blackness. Given that the most recent findings of geneticists, in regards to the meaning of race, sociohistorical relationships in terms of human identities (particularly, racial, ethnic, and cultural), are now in the process of a profound reconfiguration. The emergence of a new global discourse on ethno-racial and cultural identity is having a profound influence in shaping notions of blackness in the contemporary African Diaspora. The book focuses on questions such as: Who is black or *black enough*? What does it mean to be African American? What vestiges of an "African" culture survived the Middle Passage? What roles do gender and class play in this crisis and convergence of identities? Is there any identity crisis among Africans in diaspora when they naturalize in the U.S.? Why has the U.S. become a convergence point for immigrants? Why has *blackness* become an issue of academic discourse?

The book expands the debate on race, culture, ethnicity, and identity in discussions concerning the contemporary African Diaspora across global regions (with an emphasis on the Americas). The book informs both the academic and non-academic communities on questions related to the African Diaspora and their identities.

The essays in this book include topics related to race, gender, culture, ethnicity, and identity in relation to black Diaspora studies. The unique layout of this book is that it combines a cross disciplinary layout with a transnational scope. Most anthologies on the African Diaspora tend to be limited in scope or in terms of geographic focus. Realizing that Africans are scattered all over the world, therefore this anthology includes essays with global, regional, and cross regional concentrations while at the same time including essays on topics such as gender.

The target audiences for this book include undergraduate, upper level undergraduate, graduate students and scholars in the field. This is a text that can be used in courses on Africana studies, history, cultural studies, race studies, Diaspora studies, sociology, and ethnic studies.

The Structure of the Book

The book is divided into three parts.

Part I: The Modern African Diaspora in Global Perspective

In Chapter 1, Philip Kretsedemas presents the reader with a very different way of thinking about the meaning of blackness. The chapter explains that the U.S.-centered definition of blackness must be re-connected to an analysis of global structures of power and that this perspective can offer a more penetrating insight into the forms of socio-political marginality that are shared by native born and immigrant blacks. Philip draws correspondences between the situation of African Americans who have been "abandoned by the state" (notably, the victims of Hurricane Katrina), the situation of African asylum seekers in Western Europe, the experience of black immigrant populations that have been targeted for incarceration and deportation in the U.S. and the situation of the black poor in the Caribbean who have also been "abandoned" by their own national governments.

Gado Alzouma, in Chapter 2, argues that a black community is emerging in France, which the first manifestations date back to the riots of October and November 2005. In contrast with some authors, such as Pap Ndiaye, who contend that French Blacks are a minority, it is shown that Black identity in France is being reconstructed as a stable community identity based on new representations of blackness and africanity, which are being constantly nurtured and reconfigured in light of the events that unfold.

In Chapter 3, Barbara Streets delves into *Blackness*, as a social and cultural salve that serve as one tool in the defense against the internalization of oppression, and maintenance of psychological health. Delving or immersing into *Blackness* includes education about and the examination of resistance strategies employed by Africans to resist enslavement, for it is in the honoring of the past which gives strength to deal with the present. Using the framework of Afrocentricity, cultural immersion and Susan Folkman and Richard Lazarus coping model, Barbara explores the legitimacy of embracing *Blackness* as a buffer against the deleterious health effects of racism and as an emotional antioxidant for coping.

In Chapter 4, Cara Caddo points out that during the early and mid-twentieth century, a broad range of black individuals and organizations referred to cinema when attempting to make sense of abstract shared oppressions or claims to a common historical and cultural past. Debates abounded; but the conceptions of racial identity envisioned through cinema were also galvanized into actual cultural productions, political groups, and businesses with long-lasting consequences upon twentieth century black life.

In Chapter 5, Julie Iromuanya analyzes Dinaw Mengestu's *The Beautiful Things That Heaven Bears*, Ethiopian refugee Sepha Stephanos is racially black, yet ethnically distinct, economically visible, yet politically invisible. In occupying the interstice between the white hegemonic structure and the poor black underclass, the silent model/middleman minority becomes a speaker. This transformation is marked through Sepha's decision to take a side during the protests against the gentrification of his poor Washington, DC neighborhood. The chapter addresses the ways in which Mengestu tests the valuation of this intermediary space in *The Beautiful Things* convergence of contemporary race, citizenship, and economics as they relate to African sojourners in the metropolitan United States.

In Chapter 6, Okpeh Okpeh argues that given the reality of the interdisciplinarity of Diaspora Studies generally, and against the background of the revolution in information technology, and the implications of these on research in particular, African/Black Diaspora Studies hopes to be an important knowledge port if it transcends the methodology of simply narrating the global essence of the African as a response to the prejudices and stereotypes imposed on him by other races in the course of time. This, the chapter explains, can better be achieved if African/Black Diaspora Studies is rooted in history and evidence articulately interpreted.

Part II: The Modern African Diaspora and Black Identity

In Chapter 7, Hettie Williams examines the identity of the first self-identified African American president in U.S. history: Barack H. Obama. Obama's sense of racial self awareness is understood as "other black cosmopolitan." She argues that Obama's mixed race ancestry and transnational experiences have led him to develop a composite sense of ethno-racial self awareness that neither completely rejects nor accepts his multiracial identity as the only sense of self that informs his everyday awareness.

Barbara Combs, in Chapter 8, examines the role of race, class, and gender in the identity formation process utilized by the residents, business owners, and stakeholders in two historic, black gentrifying Atlanta neighborhoods under examination—the Old Fourth Ward and the West End. She discusses the areas that are undergoing black gentrification. Despite a deep sense of responsibility felt by some black gentrifiers, there is tension, which often develops in black gentrifying spaces as residents, new and old, struggle to find a sense of identity and group cohesion amidst disparate representations of blackness.

In Chapter 9, Julius Adekunle discusses the cultural clash and the challenges of identity that arise for the African Diaspora as a result of long term stay in the United States. Leaving Africa to live permanently in the United States is always considered a blessing. However, in their quest to pursue and enjoy sound and stable education, benefit from economic opportunities, and the prospect of living a secured life, African immigrants face major cultural and identity challenges. Julius examines the long term effect of living in the U.S. on the culture and identity of the African Diaspora, arguing that Africans often lose some of their cultural practices and face the challenge of identity, especially when they become American citizens, and their children are fully integrated into the American society.

Karen Bell based Chapter 10 upon wide ranging primary sources to reconstruct the history of Africans descendants and their identity in the low country during the nineteenth century. The letters of enslaved men and women preserved in plantation records and published primary sources tie together multiple discourses on the continuation of an African identity during the nineteenth century. This identity continued to inform the descendants of enslaved men and women during the twentieth century.

Andre Johnson in Chapter 11 offers a rhetorical analysis on several of Henry McNeal Turner's speeches and writings after the Civil War in the Reconstruction era. It is argued that Turner constructed a black identity that helped African Americans cope with the sufferings and frustrations that the post-bellum period brought. Further, the chapter argues that it was this focus on Black identity that helps establish the foundation of many of the identity studies of the twentieth century and beyond.

Part III: The Black Diaspora in Latin American Identity and Culture

Chapter 12 is a discussion of the black consciousness movement in contemporary Brazil. Reginald Daniel raises some questions about the changing racial paradigms in both Brazil and the U.S. He points out that some writers argued that U.S. society is becoming increasingly "Latinized" in that the ternary system of racial classification in Latin America, including in such places as Brazil, is on a converging path with racial systems in Latin America in which black consciousness has become more prevalent such as the case with Peru, Mexico, and Brazil thereby leading to the emergence of a binary system that divides whites from non-whites as has been the case in U.S. society historically.

Ashley Aaron discusses the issue of constructing identities in cyberspace among the Afro-Puerto Ricans and Afro-Dominicans in Chapter 13. Ashley argues that in the global age of the internet, many people use the World Wide Web to freely articulate how they choose to define and identify themselves. The internet has become a forum through which Afro-Latinos and Afro-Dominicans encourage cultural discourse and express their experiences in mixing with people of other cultural backgrounds.

The focus of Chapter 14 is about the similarities between Latinidad and the Louisiana Creoles, which Andrew Jolivette and Haruki Eda describe as very striking. While the Creole of Louisiana self-identify as multiracial, they directly connect their ancestry and culture to the people of France, West Africa, Spain, and to the Indigenous people of the Americas. They evolved a new culture even before the United States became independent.

Miguel Becerra discusses the plight of the Africans in Peru in Chapter 15. He focuses on the role of the media in the marginalization of the African diaspora, arguing that the blackface in the U.S. television and movies have heavily influenced the Peruvian media. He points out that the role of the blackface has had repercussions in the Peruvian society because it created a movement of opposition against blacks in Peru. The Peruvian media portrays racism against Afro-Peruvians through humor and comedy, thereby inherently reinforcing prejudice and discrimination.

The politics of the Afro-Mexican queen pageant is the focus of Chapter 16. Jorge Gonzalez examines the hidden agendas of NGOs behind Afro-Mexican queen pageants as well as how they are mirroring internal and external politics of representation. He explains the processes of how the ethnicization of blackness transforms the meaning and contours of blackness in Costa Chica.

Acronyms

AAA	Association for the Advancement of Africa
ACS	American Colonization Society
AME	African Methodist Episcopal
AMEA	Association of Multiethnic Americans
AMQP	Afro-Mexican Queen Pageant
ANPA	Association of Nigerian Physicians in the Americas
ASONEDH	Black Association in Defense and Promotion of Human Rights
AUC	Atlanta University Center
BFN	Biracial Family Network
CapD'iv	*Cercle d'Action pour la Promotion de la Diversité en France*
CEDET	Center of Ethnic Development
CONACULTA	National Council for Culture and the Arts
CONAPA	National Commission for Andean and Amazonian People
CRAN	Conseil Représentatif des Associations Noires de France
CRM	Civil Rights Movement
DEM	Democratas Party
DEMUS	Estudio para la Defensa de los Derechos de la Mujer
DGCP	General Direction of Popular Cultures
DIGEPOs	General Population Department of State
DST	Dialogical Self Theory
ECOSTA	Revista Fandango, Museo Regional de las Culturas Afromestizas, Barca-Costa, Ojo de Agua
FNB	*A Frente Negra*
GDP	Gross Domestic Product

GRADE	Grupo de Análisis para el Desarrollo
IBGE	Brazilian Institute of Geography and Statistics
IFA	Interracial Family Alliance
INEGI	National Institute of Statistics
INI	National Indigenous Institute
INSEE	Institut National de la Statistique et des Etudes Economiques
LUNDU	Center for Afro-Peruvian Studies and Empowerment
MASC	The Multiracial Americans of Southern California in Los Angeles
MNU	*O Movimento Negro Unificado*
MPPC	Motion Picture Patents Company
NAACP	National Association for the Advancement of Colored People
PNAD	*Pesquisa Nacional por Amostra de Domicílios*
PUMC	University of UNAM Multicultural Program
RACE	Reclassify All Children Equally
TEN	*Teatro Experimental do Negro*
UCN	*Union de la Communauté Noire de France*
UENF	Northern Fluminense State University
UERJ	University of Rio de Janeiro State University
UnB	University of Brasilia
UNESCO	United Nations Educational, Scientific and Cultural Organization
UNO	United Nations Organization
U.S.A.	United States of America
WWI	World War I
WWII	World War II

Part I

The Modern African Diaspora in Global Perspective

Chapter 1

Are You "Black" or "Ethnic"? The Dichotomous Framing of Immigrant Identity

Philip Kretsedemas

There has been a tendency in migration studies research to treat African, Afro-Caribbean, and Afro-Latino immigrant ethnicities as being in competition with the identities of native-born, black minorities. Immigrants who are racialized as black in the U.S. are perceived as being less prone to complain about racism than native-born blacks, and as being reluctant to identify as black. This leads to the following conundrum: a Nigerian immigrant who identifies with his inherited African culture can be seen as using this cultural identification to distance himself from U.S.-born blacks. If he makes a point of declaring himself to be Nigerian rather than African American or black, he can be read as implicitly saying, "I am not black" (or more specifically, "I am not like those *other* blacks"). Within the context of these identity choices, race and ethnicity seem to be two competing and mutually exclusive terrains of meaning. Black identifications presumably cancel out one's ethnicity (emphasizing a racial solidarity that renders the immigrant's cultural difference superfluous) and, conversely, ethnicity is viewed as a strategy that immigrants use to avoid being labeled as black. Apparently, it is not possible to both be "black" and "ethnic."

This chapter reviews some of the research that has shaped this dichotomous of framing black immigrant ethnicity. It bears emphasizing, from the start, that this will be a rather slippery process. For example, references are made to "black immigrants" and "black immigrant ethnicity" while also explaining that the meanings of these concepts have been contested by different bodies of research. For the purpose of this discussion, "black" refers to those national-origin populations that, according to phenotype, would be regarded as black in the U.S. This definition is consistent with the understanding of blackness as a

3

social fact that was introduced by Frantz Fanon.[1] From this perspective, blackness must be understood as a social condition—defined by others—that forces itself upon the individual.

This definition is just a starting point. The rest of the chapter will argue that the fact of blackness, especially as it concerns immigrant populations, is not defined by a stable and unitary social context, and that there are forms of migrant marginality that are not adequately captured by the concept of blackness. The discussion proceeds by reflexively applying and unpacking the concepts which are used to guide the discussion. Some new terminologies are deployed to help navigate these intersections of race, ethnicity, and migrant marginality. One such term is that of the "black/racialized immigrant." This term signals that immigrant racialization *can* be viewed through the lens of blackness, but that immigrants *can also* be racialized in different ways than black native-born populations. The term "black/racialized immigrant" makes it possible to acknowledge these points of intersection and tension that operate across the concepts of blackness and racialization.

This review will be approached with an attitude of respect toward the research that will be evaluated. Even though there will be a critique the dichotomous framing of race and ethnicity, it is acknowledged that this framework has been used, quite effectively, to document some important features of the black/racialized immigrant experience. The goal is not to question the empirical validity of this research, but to open up new ways of interpreting its findings. In the course of this discussion, attention will be drawn to the limitations of the nation-centered paradigm that is reinforced by the dichotomous framing of black/racialized immigrant and native-born identities. The chapter will also problematize the static conceptualization of race and ethnicity that underlies some of this research. Instead of attempting to make generalized statements about immigrant identity, it will be argued that it is more important for researchers to examine the social contexts and dynamics that are shaping the way these identities are being interpreted by immigrants.

The Dichotomous Framing of Black Immigrant Identity

Several studies have shown that African, Afro-Latino, and Afro-Caribbean immigrants emphasize their ethnic distinctiveness in order to avoid being perceived as black.[2] According to the conventions of race in the U.S, these immigrants are phenotypically black, but they have not developed a black self-concept. This observation about the disjuncture between racial self-concept and the social fact of blackness has been cited by many studies of black/racialized immigrant identity formation in the U.S.[3] This disjuncture also sets the stage for the competitive framing of racial and ethnic identity—in which ethnicity is treated as a phenomenon that (for better or worse) blocks the formation of a black, racial self-concept.

One of the best examples of this argument is provided by Tekle Woldemikael's research on Haitian migrants in the Midwest.[4] Woldemikael showed that first generation Haitian immigrants did not identify socially, culturally, or politically with native-born blacks. Although he observed that there were some exceptions to this rule (among Haitian freemasons), Woldemikael concludes that Haitian ethnicity functioned, primarily, to insulate Haitian immigrants from native-born blacks. This dynamic of ethnic-insulation led them to discount the salience of racial discrimination in the U.S., and to accept the racist stereotypes of native-born blacks that were being circulated through the white, mainstream society. Woldemikael also provided a number of suggestions for incorporating Haitian immigrants within the black, native-born population, which seem to be adapted from a straight-line assimilation model.[5] This included the adoption of English as the migrant's primary (and only) language, and a willingness to sever ties with Haitian ethnic networks. Woldemikael showed that second generation Haitian youth follow this pathway to incorporation and, as a result, they were "becoming black" (unlike their parents).

Woldemikael's research captured a dimension of the black immigrant experience that has been corroborated by the research that was referenced earlier.[6] However, it should not be regarded as the last word on the Haitian immigrant experience. For example, a study I conducted in Miami-Dade County shed light on a very different relationship between racial consciousness and immigrant ethnicity.[7] The goal of the study was to examine service barriers experienced by Haitian, African American, and Latina welfare recipients. Notably, Haitian welfare recipients were far more likely than African Americans or Latinas to believe that welfare care workers were treating them in a discriminatory manner. Haitian welfare recipients were also more likely than all other welfare recipients to see themselves as targets of racial discrimination in the wider society. Most important, they believed that they had become targets for discrimination, specifically because they were Haitian. These findings were consistent with perceptions of discrimination within the southern Florida Haitian population that were documented in my field interviews with Haitian service professionals.[8]

The identity politics of the southern Florida Haitian population confirm some of Woldemikael's observations. Haitian identity was understood to be an ethnicity that was distinct from a black, native-born identity. In contrast to

Woldemikael's findings, Haitians in southern Florida did not connect their ethnic identities to a discourse on "Haitian exceptionalism" (which insisted that racial discrimination was not a problem for Haitians). Instead, Haitians in South Florida used their ethnic identities to create narratives about racism and nativism that they encountered in the U.S.—and it was not unusual for Haitian migrants to claim that they suffered more discrimination than any other racial-ethnic population in South Florida.

Other studies have found that African and Afro-Caribbean ethnicity is often used in this way, to give voice to experiences of discrimination and marginality that are specific to the migrant population.[9] These grievances are couched in a discourse on ethnicity. When race factors into these narratives of discrimination, it is not strictly in terms of skin color, but through accounts of how other people have stigmatized or excluded the migrant on the basis of their cultural difference. The migrant is not just racialized as a darker skinned person, but as the bearer of an "alien" (nonwhite) cultural difference—which may be signaled by their accent, their name, or by the display of ethnic diacritica and so on.

Even though this kind of discrimination appears to target ethnic minorities, it is not just ethnic discrimination. It is a kind of exclusion that could affect all ethnicities regardless of race. It is more accurately described as cultural racism,[10] which is a kind of exclusion that translates white/nonwhite racial hierarchies through the language of culture. Cultural racism must be situated in light of a number of global, political, and economic transformations that have increased the flow of non-European migrants to the Western industrialized world. It is also informed by a racial commonsense that is much broader than acts of discrimination that target one, particular migrant group. Cultural racism can only take root once the very idea of immigration has become racialized. The migration flow becomes the "new racial threat" because it is, presumably, the conduit for the demographic transformation that is changing the racial complexion of the host society.[11]

On the one hand, this is a very diffuse kind of racial anxiety that produces forms of discrimination that are directed at many different, racialized migrant populations. On the other hand, black/racialized migrants tend to experience this discrimination in a way that renders them visible in their cultural particularity. Furthermore, the racialized cultural attributes that distinguish these migrants from the white, native-born population also distinguish them from native-born minorities. So it only "makes sense" for the migrant to translate their experiences of discrimination through the language of ethnicity.

In this case, ethnicity is not simply a denial of the reality of racism—as Woldemikael has argued. The language of ethnicity is also being used to respond to a type of racism that is specific to black/racialized immigrant populations. Having acknowledged this, my argument still does not invalidate Woldemikael's findings. The cultural racism that has been described, and the anti-black racism that Woldemikael documents in his research, are not mutually exclusive phenomena, but they must be situated historically. It can be argued that U.S. immigration flows (even when they were mostly "white") have always been racialized. The association of U.S. immigration with brown and black bodies is a phenomenal that only begins to take shape in the late twentieth century.[12] Furthermore, the latest immigration boom (triggering a new wave of anti-immigrant and anti-Latino xenophobia) in the U.S. began after Woldemikael completed his research in the late 1980s. It bears noting that I am describing a body of racial sentiments and anxieties that has intensified from the early 1990s onward, whereas Woldemikael is describing a racist commonsense that can be traced to the color caste system of the colonial era. Again, these two types of racism are not mutually exclusive phenomena. They co-exist in the present day and they can be used to mediate the same racial structures and inequalities, but their immanent form is different. There are racial distinctions and exclusionary dynamics that are rendered visible by a theory of cultural racism that cannot be adequately explained by a more conventional understanding of anti-black racism (and vise versa).

It is also important to note that native born racial minorities and foreign-born racial minorities interpret discrimination in different ways. Some studies have shown that perceptions of discrimination between these populations can vary significantly, depending on the type of discrimination being assessed.[13] Native-born blacks are more likely to view employment discrimination as a major problem. In contrast, black/racialized immigrants are more sensitized to the problem of housing discrimination.[14]

These findings shed some more light on the "contradictory" findings of my study, and that of Woldemikael. The participants in my study produced a Haitian-specific discourse on discrimination, and the participants in Woldemikael's study treated the problem of discrimination as something that was largely alien to Haitians. My research was focused on examining Haitian welfare recipients' quality of service delivery and service access (including access to public housing). Woldemikael, on the other hand, was studying a population that did not see employment discrimination as a problem because it had been successfully incorporated into the local labor market.

These differences draw attention to the fact that we were studying two very different Haitian migrant cohorts. The Midwest, for example, has never been a primary destination for Haitian immigrants. In contrast, Miami ranks among the top three hubs for Haitian immigration in North America, and it has also been the recipient of the poorest and most stigmatized Haitian migrant flows in U.S. history.[15] Although Miami has a much larger racial minority population than most Midwestern towns, this has not worked to the benefit of Haitian immigrants, who found themselves competing for scarce resources against an equally marginalized African American population, a much larger and very robust Cuban-Latino "enclave economy," and a powerful but defensive white population that had been reduced to a numerical minority by the late 1980s.[16]

In contrast, small Midwestern towns with large, white majority populations offer a very different climate of reception for black/racialized immigrants. In this environment, where the white majority does not perceive minorities as a fast-growing "demographic threat" and where Haitians are entering as economic migrants the (as opposed to unwanted refugees) they are more likely to be received as "model minorities." Once again, these differences do not invalidate Woldemikael's research. Instead, they draw attention to the fact that migrant identity can be used to navigate the intersections of race and ethnicity in many different ways. The arguments advanced by Woldemikael only become problematic when they are used as a general template for thinking about black/racialized immigrant identity, or about "race relations" between native-born and foreign-born black populations. The identities of these immigrants are not simply black or ethnic—and the presumption that these immigrants cannot adjust to U.S. society unless they "pick a side" misses some very important aspects of their experience.

Nevertheless, the dichotomous framing of race and ethnicity has been a durable feature of the academic research on black/racialized immigrants. It surfaces in other studies that, in comparison to Woldemikael, have made very different claims about the relationship between black immigrant and black native-born populations. In Mary Waters' research, for example, the valuation of black immigrant ethnicity is reversed.[17] Rather than treating immigrant ethnicity as an obstacle for black racial consciousness, the black identities of the native-born population are treated as an obstacle to immigrant mobility. Waters' research focused on immigrants from the Anglophone Caribbean in the New York City area, which has historically contained the largest concentration of Caribbean immigrants in the U.S. Waters found that most of the people she interviewed preferred to identify as West Indian. This identity choice illustrated how the national identities of her respondents were being converted into an "American ethnicity."[18] Consistent with the findings of other researchers, Waters explained how these identities were also constructed in opposition to ideas about Americanization.[19]

Americanization, in this case, was associated with the culture of the black urban poor, which was associated, in turn, with downward mobility and a combative stance toward the mainstream society. Hence, the assumption of many Caribbean immigrant parents was that the Americanization of their children was a gateway to juvenile delinquency. This interpretive framework echoes the segmented assimilation thesis, which has explained how integration can function as a mechanism for downward mobility, tracking immigrants into the lower tiers of the U.S. economy.[20] These arguments have also suggested that the fate of darker-skinned, second generation immigrant youth, may be very similar to that of the black, native-born, urban poor. If these immigrant youth integrate into U.S. society by modeling the culture and identities of native-born blacks, the presumption is that they will find themselves in the same socio-economic situation. As a result, immigrant ethnicity becomes a way of escaping the trap of segmented assimilation.

These arguments are reproduced in Waters' research, which uses the identity choices of second-generation migrant youth as an indicator of their patterns of association (with black American or immigrant/ethnic youth) and their orientation toward social mobility. Her findings demonstrate that Caribbean migrants in New York City use their ethnicity in very deliberate ways to avoid the stigma and forms of social exclusion that are associated with native-born blacks. Waters' research is generally sympathetic toward the practical concerns of the migrants she studied (though she does question the long term viability of their ethnic identity politics). She also presents the oppositional framing of immigrant ethnicity and black native-born identity as a social fact that emerges organically from her data. Debates over the "truth" of immigrant perceptions of native-born blacks do not obviate the fact that many immigrants actually hold these perceptions, and then use them to structure their ideas about ethnic identity and social mobility in the U.S. Waters' research provides an exhaustive and influential account of these ideational dynamics.

There are moments in her analysis where it appears that the oppositional framing of immigrant ethnicity and black native-born identity is being actively chosen as the preferred framework. Waters observes, for example, that Caribbean migrants interpreted their identities in ways that were not strictly "black" or "ethnic," but she consistently gives more weight to interpretations that operate within the boundaries of the dichotomous framework. For example, she observes that some Haitian youth used "cover up" identities (believing they will find more social acceptance from people in the U.S. if they pretend they are African American), but dismisses this as confusion on their part-not understanding the cultural capital of their own immigrant identities.[21] One reason why these cover up identities may have appeared to be a peripheral phenomenon is because this research was being conducted in New York. As noted earlier, Miami has played host to the poorest concentration of Haitian migrants on the eastern seaboard, and to the largest concentration of Haitian "boatpeople." This situation, which was most intense in the early 1980s, made it near impossible for Haitian identity to be constructed as an American ethnicity in the public sphere. Cover-up identities were a pervasive feature of the identity politics of Haitian youth (and many adults) throughout the 1980s.[22] Even though the cover up is largely regarded as a thing of the past by most Haitian community leaders in South Florida, it is still an important feature of the collective historical memory of this community.

In her dismissal of Haitian cover up identities, Waters makes an assumption that is similar to that of Woldemikael. Even though both researchers have produced important analyses of the way immigrant ethnicity was constructed in New York and the Midwest (and at different points in time), both researchers make general statements about immigrant ethnicity which, on closer inspection, should be attributed to the social conditions to which these identities are being adapted. There is nothing especially new about this observation that "social context matters." It is a basic premise of the social constructionist thesis that has been embraced by many ethnicity theorists. And, there is still a tendency, within many studies, to presume that there are some "essential" features of these ethnic identities that can be generalized across all social contexts. These sorts of assumptions enable the dichotomous framing of race and ethnicity, and the tendency to overlook other expressions of immigrant identity that do not seem to fit this framework.

Waters also observed that some Caribbean New Yorkers had "immigrant identities" that were not West Indian ethnic identities or black American identities.[23] These people were more likely to gravitate toward a pan-African identity politics that was not invested in making competitive distinctions between black immigrant and native-born identities. Studies show that this kind of pan-African consciousness can be interwoven with the ethnic identity politics of African migrant populations.[24] While these groups still distinguish themselves from U.S. blacks, pan-Africanist discourse can be used as groundwork for entering into dialogue with other kinds of black/African identities. In this case, there is no strict dichotomy. Cultural distinctions between U.S. blacks and black immigrants can co-exist with pan-ethnic discourses that embrace (or which are at least nominally tolerant of) these distinctions. In Waters' research, the assumption is that these sorts of identities will fade away over time, as the immigrant adjusts to life in the U.S. and makes a final decision on which side of the line they will stand, be it black or ethnic.

What Lies Beyond the Dichotomy?

The issue with the dichotomous framework is not problematic simply because it is dichotomous, but also because it tends to over-generalize the identities that it is describing. It assumes that racial and ethnic identities are not only inherently different, but that they carry a political charge (one being more radical and oppositional, and the other more adaptive and pragmatic) that remains fairly stable across all social contexts. However, the social context can play a more important role in defining this political charge than is often assumed.

When one accounts for these contextual factors, ethnicity begins to lose its coherence as a reliable indicator of immigrant attitudes and behaviors. Instead of using ethnic identity as a general template that explains how immigrants adapt to a given social context, it can be viewed as a highly variable phenomenon that must be explained in light of this social context. This argument dovetails with Tukufu Zuberi's critique of the use of race as an explanatory variable.[25] Zuberi's argument is focused on the legacy of scientific racism in social statistics which led race to be treated as a biological phenomenon. In contrast, immigrant identities are explicitly understood to be social constructs and they are typically treated as ethnicities, not racial categories. Nevertheless, there are features of Zuberi's argument that still apply.

Zuberi notes, for example, that race must be understood as an interpretive framework that over-determines the interpretation of concrete data. In deracializing social statistics, it is necessary to critically examine the assumptions about race that are used to organize our perception of the data. In other words, Zuberi's main point of contention does not concern the credibility of particular findings, but in the way these findings are framed. He also argues that race can be a legitimate object of study if it is understood to be a socially constructed classification that can shape the way that people are treated. In this case, race is not used to explain why people act the way they do (or why they have particular aptitudes and attributes), but the way they are being classified in particular social contexts.

Zuberi argues that there is much more to be learned from studies that attempt to explain race, as opposed to studies that use "race" as an explanatory vehicle. It is argued here that this same principle can be extended to the study of immigrant ethnicity—but with some qualifications. Zuberi observes that racial classifications are usually imposed on individuals by institutions and socio-structural dynamics. Immigrant identities can be influenced by these same social forces, but they are also actively constructed by the individuals they purportedly describe. In this regard, they are examples of self-classification; the way immigrants identify themselves *can* provide important insights into the behavior of immigrants, thereby indicating the priorities and preferences that are likely to guide their actions. Nevertheless, it is still important to guard against making broad generalizations about what these identities mean, and how they are used.

Instead of making conclusive statements about the identities themselves (which makes it possible to come to the conclusion that "African immigrants just do not get along with native-born blacks"), it becomes more important to understand the micro and macro socio-political context that is shaping the way these identities are being interpreted. The problem with the dichotomous framework is not that it is used to draw attention to actually existing differences and tensions, but that it often becomes the dominant interpretive framework for the research.

The problems that many black/racialized immigrants associate with African American culture can be more accurately described as conditions that stem from the marginal socio-economic and political situation of the poorest, black urban neighborhoods. This is the context that has informed the assumption that black identities correlate with downward mobility. Although immigrant parents may make these sorts of monolithic assumptions about black American identities, researchers should exercise some caution.

There are other variations of African American or black American identity that are positively associated with academic achievement and incorporation within the networks of black professional elites.[26] Afro-Caribbean migrants have historically relied on these professional networks to help them become integrated into the U.S. middle class. Research on the labor market incorporation of black immigrants (especially from the Anglophone Caribbean) has shown that these migrants are mostly concentrated in the same employment sectors as African Americans.[27] There is also evidence that Dominican immigrants who identify as black or Hispanic are more acculturated and have higher levels of occupational achievement than immigrants who identify with the mestizo racial categorizations of their homeland.[28] In contrast, the decision of Latino immigrants to identify as mestizo, or even as white, is not always an indicator of higher social status and upward mobility. In many cases, it is an indicator of their cultural isolation from the mainstream, which correlates with employment in low wage, ethnically segmented employment sectors. Moreover, occupational segmentation and residential segregation tend to diverge for these populations. Light skinned Latinos may be spatially segregated from darker skinned minorities (and may even find a niche in white non-Latino neighborhoods) but still have lower incomes than more acculturated black minorities. For example, Haitian and Jamaican female-headed households in New York City have higher incomes and occupational prestige than similar kinds of Puerto Rican households, despite being limited to "black neighbor-hoods."[29] This phenomenon illustrates that there are social dynamics that track black/racialized immigrants into the same employment sectors that have been historic gateways into white collar work for native-born blacks—and under these conditions, black identifications become positively associated with upward social mobility.

It is also important to note that many of the social problems that immigrant parents associate with Americanization (and with native-born blacks in particular) are relatively new developments. The rise of the underground drug industry, mass incarceration, and the hyper-segregation of poor, black urban populations—which compose the socio-political backdrop for the oppositional youth culture feared by immigrant parents—have all taken shape in the post-Jim Crow era. Prior to this time, most Caribbean immigrants were incorporated within U.S. black communities and often played a leadership role in the advocacy of the black American populations.[30] There were tensions between Caribbean immigrants and native-born blacks during this time, but it was also common for Caribbean immigrants to downplay the public expression of their ethnic identities in the interest of racial solidarity with native-born blacks.[31] These accounts of Caribbean migrant identity in the Jim Crow era offer an important point of contrast with the competitive framing of black/ethnic identities in the current era. They beg the question, "What happened?" How did Caribbean immigrants go from being a more or less integrated cultural minority within the black American population to being a distinct ethnic group whose identities are defined in opposition to the black American population?

This issue has not been explored in much depth by the academic literature on immigrant ethnicity and black immigrant populations. The current context is taken as given, but with little consideration of how it came to be. The reasons why so many Caribbean immigrants became (or appeared to be) "assimilated blacks" in the Jim Crow era, can be explained in light of the immigration and domestic policies of that era, the socio-political organization of black communities, the structure of opportunities that existed for Caribbean immigrants, and the public discourse on race.

From the end of the Jim Crow era to the present, the relationship between these factors has been transformed in some very important ways. This is due to the neoliberal restructuring of the U.S. economy, a new immigration boom era, and a complex public discourse on race and ethnicity that has conferred more visibility on cultural differences within racial minority populations. This could also be described as the emergence of a new politico-discursive regime, one that transformed the narratives and institutional practices that were used to manage racial minority populations.

While some of the limitations of the academic research on black/racialized immigrants have been discussed, this research has still provided a very rich account of the factors shaping immigrant ethnicity. The popular media, on the other hand, has a history of using these "tensions" between immigrant and native-born blacks to spin narratives that justify the marginalization of some minority populations, and affirm the meritocratic values of the mainstream society. Shortly after national-origin restrictions on immigrant recruitment were lifted in 1965, there was a new interest in contrasting the success of Asian "model minorities" to the marginality of black Americans.[32] The black/racialized immigrant experience has been subjected to a similar model minority treatment, which has been used to suggest that the primary cause of black marginality in the U.S. is not racism but a defeatist orientation toward the mainstream society.[33]

What is most important to consider is the reason why these sorts of comparisons have become more salient in the current era. The most obvious answer to this question is that there are more racialized immigrants entering the U.S. It is important, however, not to lose sight of the political subtext and policy implications of this field of debate. The idea that black/racialized immigrants are model minorities who have transcended the barriers that native-born blacks have failed to overcome is part of a broader field of discourse on colorblindness, which insists that race and racism are no longer a significant fact of life in the U.S.[34] It follows that the affirmative action policies, anti-discrimination laws, and other racial justice measures are not needed to correct the disparities that have lingered (and intensified) since the end of Jim Crow. Instead of seeing these racial disparities as products of institutional discrimination, they can be attributed to the inherent cultural and human capital deficiencies within minority populations that refuse to conform to the social contract that all the other minority populations that have succeeded in the U.S. have embraced.

In addition to these transformations—in the way that race and ethnicity is being framed in the current era—a number of structural transformations have altered the relationship between immigrants and the mainstream society. One of the most important features of these transformations is the erosion of migrant legal status and migrant rights. U.S. migration flows have steadily increased over the past several decades, but the number of migrants being admitted with the right to become permanent residents has grown markedly smaller. The vast majority of new immigrants enter with temporary visas. Only a minority of the temporary visa holders becomes legal permanent residents, and this process often takes a decade or more.

This shift toward a paradigm of temporary legality has been accompanied by massive spending increases on immigration enforcement (and rising deportation levels) and new restrictions on the social and legal rights of noncitizens.[35] Meanwhile, immigration enforcement practices have been extended further into the legal resident population, and other federal and local laws have restricted immigrant access to social rights. As several migration scholars have explained, this enforcement apparatus has been informed by racialized ideas about new migrant flows and national security.[36] It is also significant that U.S. naturalization rates have decreased (proportionate to the general increase in migration levels) during this period, whereas Canadian naturalization rates have increased. This situation has not been caused simply by a lack of interest in citizenship on the part of immigrants, but by an absence of investment on the part of the U.S. government in programs that facilitate the legal-political incorporation of immigrants.[37] The priorities guiding U.S. immigration policy seem to be oriented toward recruiting migrants as expendable "economic guests," reserving green card and citizenship status as a privilege to be granted to a select few.[38]

The signals sent by such policies discourage many noncitizens from thinking of themselves as permanent settlers. This situation also sheds new light on the transnational identities that have been attributed to recent immigrants. Rather than viewing these identities as innovative acts of cultural agency, they can also be seen as adaptations to an increasingly defensive and enforcement-oriented immigration regime. It becomes important to maintain ties with the politics, culture, and social networks of the homeland because one never knows how things will "work out" in North America. These reciprocal bonds with the homeland are further reinforced by the flow of remittances from migrants in the global North to families and friends in the global South, and also by the deliberate efforts of postcolonial governments to cultivate an "expatriate patriotism" among its nationals living abroad. Meanwhile, as Ogbu Kalu has observed, the global network of migration that delivers migrants to North America (both legally and illegally) is a structured social world in its own right.[39] It is not unusual for migrants—and African migrants in particular—to spend years traversing these networks, cultivating a very distinct kind of bond between "fellow travelers." After migrants find a way to North America (and even after securing permanent residence) they are often reliant on ethnic networks to find housing and jobs.

These trends paint a very different picture of the future of ethnicity than has been provided by some critics of ethnicity theory.[40] Although these critiques have provided some insights into the limitations of ethnicity theory, they define immigrant ethnicity as a "false ideology," which distorts the real nature of the race and class hierarchies that compose U.S. society. They do not give sufficient consideration to the real structural transformations that have taken shape alongside the new immigration, which are shaping the socio-economic policy and political climate to which immigrants are adapting. It becomes difficult to see that ethnic networks have become more salient for immigrants precisely because the avenues for integration and upward mobility that were available to earlier cohorts of mostly white European immigrants have deteriorated—or that immigrants may use their identities to cope with the unique ways they are racialized, and not simply to deny the reality of racism in U.S. society. It is presumed that immigrant ethnicity is used, opportunistically, to enhance the immigrant's standing with the pre-existing race and class hierarchies of the U.S. These arguments contribute, once more, toward the dichotomous framing of black/racialized immigrant identity.

Black Immigrant 'Racial Escapism' Revisited

Another feature of the broader context that is obscured by the dichotomous framing of immigrant identity is the postcolonial moorings of these identities. The mutually exclusive options that define this dichotomy are entirely oriented toward the U.S. national context. If immigrants adopt a black identity, they have clearly chosen to throw their lot in with racial minorities "here" in the U.S. (becoming Americanized). If they identify as an "ethnic," it is also presumed that this decision is determined entirely by their interest in improving their social standing "here" in the U.S.

Little consideration is given to the fact that, especially for black/racialized immigrants, this ethnicity is usually derived from a postcolonial national identity. Whereas the ethnicity is oriented toward the new land, the postcolonial national identity is still being shaped by the political culture and opportunity structures of the old country. For example, U.S.-born persons view many Dominican Latino migrants as black. In the Dominican Republic, the discourse on national identity has been historically defined in opposition to "Haitian blackness."[41] There is also a long history of Haitians being incorporated into the Dominican Republic as racialized "illegal" migrant labor, as well as a history of Dominican genocidal violence against Haitians.[42] While Haitians and (some) Dominicans are viewed as black immigrants in the U.S., the meaning of blackness for Haitian and Dominican immigrants is being filtered through the lens of two very different national cultures. In order to acknowledge these differences, it is necessary to examine the way that the political culture and racial discourse of their homelands shapes how they come to terms with the meaning of race in the U.S.

Again, this is not to deny that African, Afro-Caribbean, and Afro-Latino immigrants are often dismayed by the state of "race relations" in North America, or that they often insist that they have never experienced racism until they migrated to North America. A more careful consideration should be given to the utterances of black/racialized immigrants on the subject of race. While not assuming that the migrant is learning what it means to be black for the *first time*, it would be more helpful (and accurate) to consider that they are being exposed to a *new* kind of racial discourse and experience of blackness.

Most of the research on black/racialized immigrants has acknowledged that these immigrants enter the U.S. with *some* pre-existing ideas about race. The difference between a dichotomous and non-dichotomous treatment of this subject lies in the degree of emphasis that is placed on the postcolonial context. In the former case, the postcolonial context is presumed to have a fading influence on the identity that the immigrant adopts in the new land and, just as important, it is not explicitly identified as *postcolonial*. It is treated as the lingering effect of the culture of the sending nation—a standard feature of any immigrant experience. In the latter case, there is more emphasis on the way in which the cultural narrative of these postcolonial identities are continually evoked and reinforced by the migrant's situation in the new land, and by their connections to people back in the homeland.

The distinction between the "new" and "old" land begins to blur (a situation that is reinforced by the increasingly ambiguous legal distinction between the permanent settler and the temporary visitor). The immigrant does not unequivocally identify as a foreign national, or as a "new American," but as the member of a cultural Diaspora that is being simultaneously influenced by the postcolonial identities of the old land, and the ethnicities and racial politics of the new land.[43] It is also important to acknowledge what is distinct about postcolonial national cultures-especially the culture of former slave colonies-which are organized around narratives and identities that have been imprinted by a legacy of colonial era racial hierarchies and legacies of anti-colonial resistance. Immigrants from these societies do not enter the U.S. completely naïve to the reality of race and racism. It is more plausible to assert that they enter with a sophisticated understanding of race, but one that is not attuned to the history and meaning of race in the U.S.

This perspective comes across more clearly in the research and theory that some Caribbean and critical race scholars have produced.[44] In all of these accounts, the black/racialized immigrant is treated as an active interpreter who is always synthesizing the identities and discourses of the new land through a pre-existing political-cultural framework which, in turn, shapes the way they position themselves as a racial-ethnic subject. Roy Bryce-Laporte provides an excellent example when he challenges the presumption that Afro-Caribbean migrants have no experience with anti-black racism prior to entering the U.S. He writes:

> In many [Caribbean] countries, the white or lighter-skinned elite has capitalized on the myth of no racial problem and has disseminated a false ideology and image of racial egalitarianism to their advantage. Lower- and middle-class citizens of such countries come to accept this myth, which on one hand is ego-inflating and perhaps self-fulfilling, but, on the other, is the basis of a vicious, self-defeating trap which prevents them from responding to subtle racist abuses directly or publicly lest they be considered racist and unpatriotic .... Black immigrants from such countries often themselves subscribe to the myth once they reach America by denying the existence of color problems at home, often in the pathetic hope that they would escape the stigma and mistreatment directed at native black Americans by the larger society, as well as give the impression that they were not lower class and therefore not conceived as blacks or vice versa back home.[45]

Ironically, Bryce-Laporte's writing pre-dates most of the academic research on black/racialized immigrants and yet, his insights seem to have been overlooked by much of this research. He explains that, prior to entering the U.S., most Caribbean immigrants have already been exposed to framing and counter-framing strategies about race, color and ethnic prejudice. If these migrants appear to lack a black racial consciousness, it is not because they are wholly unfamiliar with discourses on black identity or racial injustice. It is also likely that they have been exposed to a postcolonial version of colorblind racism.

Like North American versions of colorblind racism, this is a discourse which insists that racial discrimination is a thing of the past, and that class and status inequalities are now the "big problem" in these societies (despite the fact that race and color hierarchies inherited from the colonial era are still an endemic feature of the popular culture and socio-economic strata of these nations). In the U.S., the dismantling of Jim Crow is the watershed moment that set the stage for these discourses on the end of racism. In postcolonial nations, it is the transition to national independence and the emergence of a new postcolonial black political leadership which commands the reigns of the state. This new political leadership converts the insurgent anti-colonial identity politics (unified by its oppositional to white/colonial rule) into a more consensual kind of identity politics that is amenable to the developmentalist objectives of the state. This process gives rise to a new kind of political formation, the black electoral majority.

Discourses on national identity are often crafted in ways that implicitly or explicitly reference this black majority identity, even if (as in the case of Jamaica) the official discourse on national identity gravitates in the direction of multiculturalism. As a result, constructions of blackness become incorporated into a majoritarian identity as opposed to a stigmatized minoritarian identity. The important point is that the socio-political context from which black immigrants are coming from matters. This, in turn, requires a shift in perspective from focusing on what the immigrant lacks, and toward a focus on what the immigrant is bringing with them. It is important to consider that the rejection of black identity in the U.S. (when this does occur) is also a rejection of a black *minority* identity. What is "new" to these migrants is not the simple fact of being recognized as black, but the political situation of black populations in the U.S.

Conclusion

As several theorists have observed, the explanatory frameworks being used by social researchers still seem to be mired in an analysis of national contexts.[46] It also follows that theories of immigration and immigrant identity must be further developed in order to offer more comprehensive accounts of the global nature of the phenomena they are trying to explain. This chapter has made a complementary argument that it cannot be assumed that immigrants are "here" in the same way as U.S.-born minorities. Although they may physically live in the same neighborhoods and work similar jobs as native blacks, the combination of social supports, disciplinary mechanisms, deprivations and political-cultural influences acting on them do not stem only from their immediate national context—and this carries implications for the way black/racialized immigrants view race. There is certainly some overlap between these forces and the ones acting on U.S.-born minorities, but they are not simply isomorphic to one another.

The challenge is to develop a critical analysis of race and ethnicity that resists the temptation of reducing race and racism to a single historical experience, or to assume that each national context has its own separate and distinct history of race. It is more important to explore variations in race and racism that cut across multiple contexts. The challenges discussed in this chapter cannot be sufficiently understood just by focusing more attention on the transnational dimensions of immigrant identity. The limitation of this valuable advice is its territoriality (even though, ironically, it seeks to transcend the limits of a nation-based territoriality). It reminds us that the things we are observing "here" (in whatever national or local context we are studying) are always being shaped by a panoply of factors that may be going on "over there," but which are also connected to what is happening "here." The main lesson is that is necessary to expand and complicate the geo-political framework that is guiding our analyses. The critique of the dichotomous framing of black immigrant identity addresses another, very distinct kind of problem, which had more to do with the way that racial and ethnic identities are being conceptualized.

This problem can be described as the lingering effects of a race relations model, which has been used to describe the tensions and misunderstandings between black immigrant and black native-born populations. This conceptual framework leads researchers to make statements about the causes and outcomes of these "tensions" which are generalized to both populations. For example, Caribbean immigrants who identify with native-born blacks experience downward mobility, or Haitian ethnicity (or black immigrant ethnicity more generally) obstructs the ability of these migrants to understand race and racism in the U.S., or African immigrants in general do not see themselves as black and do not really "get along" with African Americans. These statements may be accurate descriptions of the attitudes of particular populations at a given point in time, but they become conceptually problematic, as explanations, when they are presented as social facts that are taken to be generally true of the populations that they are purportedly describing. Instead of explaining the identities, the identities become explanatory vehicles. This makes it possible to insinuate that Haitian ethnicity is "causing" some immigrants to avoid identifying with blacks in the U.S.

The arguments presented in this chapter have paid more attention to the fluidity of immigrant identities-understanding that this fluidity is an integral feature of their socially constructed character. These identities are being used to interpret and adapt to different types of social contexts. It is important to understand the immediate (local) social context, and it also helps to account for the way this local context is being informed by global dynamics, but there are other kinds of contexts. For example, there are contexts that are specific to the history and politics of racial discourse-like the post Jim Crow politico-discursive regime that was discussed earlier. There is also a "deeper" racial context of anti-black racism that traverses these different epochs of racial discourse.

The discussion in this chapter has not made any presumptions about the "causal power" of any of these contexts. They all matter, for they all interact with and shape each other. The main concern has been to argue that the context matters, and that if we pay serious attention to these contexts, the research on black/racialized immigrants will have to move beyond the dichotomous framework that has been criticized throughout this chapter. There are many instances in which African, Afro-Caribbean, and Afro-Latino immigrants may feel compelled to "choose" between identifying as a black person or with their immigrant ethnicity. There are other ways in which immigrant ethnicity can be used to engage U.S. black identities (through a panAfricanist identity politics). There are also features of black immigrant identity that cannot be reduced to an "ethnicity" which are informed by postcolonial discourses on race and class—and these ideas can also play a role in shaping the way black immigrants view race in the U.S. There are experiences of racial marginality that are specific to immigrant populations which can give rise to a particular kind of critical consciousness that is integrated within the ethnic identity politics of the group and which, in some cases, may lay the groundwork for solidarities with other racialized immigrant populations. The point of all of these examples is that discourses on race and ethnicity do not always take the form of mutually exclusive interpretive frameworks. Discourses on race and ethnicity can also be synthesized within black/racialized immigrant identities. To explain these dynamics, migration researchers must ask new kinds of questions that are not derived from the polarizing statement: "Are you black or ethnic?"

Notes

1. Frantz Fanon, *Black Skin, White Masks* (New York: Grove Press [1952] 2008), 89-119.

2. For some examples see, Kristine Ajrouch and Abdi Kusow, "Racial and Religious Contexts: Situational Identities among Lebanese and Somali Muslim Immigrants," *Ethnic and Racial Studies.* 30: 1 (2007) 72-94; Katja Guenther, Sadie Pendaz and Fortunata Makene, "The Impact of Intersecting Dimensions of Inequality and Identity on the Racial Status of Eastern African Immigrants," *Sociological Forum,* 26: 1 (2011) 98-120; David Mittleberg and Mary Waters, "The Process of Ethnogenesis Among Haitian and Israeli Migrants in the United States," *Ethnic and Racial Studies,* 15:3 (1992) 412-435; Reuel Rogers, " 'Black Like Who?' Afro-Caribbean Immigrants, African Americans and the Politics of Group Identity," in *Islands in the City,* ed., Nancy Foner (Berkeley, CA: University of California Press, 2001), 163-192.

3. Kay Deaux, Nida Bikmen, Alwyn Gilkes, Ana Ventuneac, Yvanne Joseph, Yasser Payne, and Claude Steele, "Becoming American: Stereotype Threat Effects in Afro-Caribbean Immigrant Groups," *Social Psychology Quarterly,* 70: 4 (2007) 384-404; Cynthia Feliciano, "Education and Ethnic Identity Formation Among Children of Latin American and Caribbean Immigrants," *Sociological Perspectives*, 52: 2 (2009) 135-158; Xue Lan Rong and Paul Fitchett, "Socialization and Identity Transformation of Black Immigrant Youth in the United States," *Theory into Practice,* 47: 1 (2008) 35-42; David Sears and Victoria Savalei, "The Political Color Line: 'Peoples of Color' or Black Exceptionalism?" *Political Psychology, 27*: 6 (2006) 895-924.

4. Tekle Woldemikael, "A case study of race consciousness among Haitian immigrants." *Journal of Black Studies*, 20 (1989) 224-239; *Becoming Black American: Haitians and American Institutions in Evanston, Illinois* (New York: AMS Press, 1989).

5. Famously associated with the research of Lloyd Warner and Leo Srole, *The Social Systems of American Ethnic Groups* (New Haven, CT: Yale University Press, 1945), which posited the steady inter-generational erasure of ethnicity as migrants and their offspring integrated into the white mainstream society. For a contemporary review and critique of this model, see Ruben Rumbaut, "Paradoxes (And Orthodoxies) of Assimilation," *Sociological Perspectives*, 40: 3 (1997) 483-511.

6. See note 3.

7. Philip Kretsedemas, "Language Barriers and Perceptions of Bias: Ethnic Differences in Immigrant Encounters with the Welfare System," *Journal of Sociology and Social Welfare*, 32: 4 (2005) 109-123.

8. Some of the findings from the interviews were published in the following reports, Philip Kretsedemas, "Avoiding the State: Haitian Immigrants and Welfare Services in Miami-Dade County," *Immigrants, Welfare Reform, and the Poverty of Policy,* eds., Philip Kretsedemas and Ana Aparicio (Westport, Conn & London: Greenwood-Praeger, 2004), 107-136; Philip Kretsedemas, "Immigrant Households and Hardships after Welfare Reform: A Case Study of the Miami-Dade Haitian Community," *International Journal of Social Welfare,* 12: 4 (2003) 314-325.

9. Katja Guenther, Sadie Pendaz and Fortunata Makene, "The Impact of Intersecting Dimensions of Inequality and Identity on the Racial Status of Eastern African Immigrants," *Sociological Forum,* 26: 1 (2011) 98-120; Dianna Shandy and Katherine Fennelly, "A Comparison of the Integration Experiences of Two African Immigrant Populations in a Rural Community," *Journal of Religion and Spirituality in Social Work,* 25: 1 (2006) 23-45.

10. For a seminal discussion see, Etienne Balibar, "Is There a Neo-Racism?" in E. Balibar and I. Wallerstein, ed., *Race, Nation, Class: Ambiguous Identities* (New York: Verso, 1991).

11. For examples of this type of anti-immigrant discourse see, Patrick Buchanan, *State of Emergency: The Third World Invasion and Conquest of America* (New York: St. Martin's Griffin, 2007); Samuel Huntington, *Who Are We? The Challenges to America's National Identity*, (New York: Simon and Schuster, 2005).

12. A notable exception is the historic racialization of Mexican nationals and immigrants that stretches into the nineteenth century. During this time, however, Mexicans were not uniformly racialized as a nonwhite population, but as a population composed of white and nonwhite segments, that was still legally regarded as white, due to the strategic, geo-political interests of the U.S. state. See, Ian Haney-Lopez, *White by Law: The Legal Construction of Race* (New York: NYU Press, 2006). Even so, the popular conception of U.S. immigration flows being not just nonwhite, but non-European—in which brown and black bodies begin to dominate the popular image of the migration flow—does not begin to take shape until the 1970s, after Latino and Asian migrants become the "new majority" within the U.S. immigration flow.

13. Janel Benson, "Exploring the Racial Identities of Black Immigrants in the United States," *Sociological Forum*, 21: 2 (2006) 219-247.

14. This finding comes from Benson's research (Ibid) and is corroborated by Lance Freeman's research which shows that spatial/residential segregation between black immigrants and white populations is very durable—and is not substantially lessened by socio-economic mobility of black immigrant populations. See, Lance Freeman, "Does Spatial Assimilation Work for Black Immigrants in the U.S.?" *Urban Studies*, 39: 11 (2002) 1983-2003.

15. For more on this context for Haitian migration to South Florida see. Alex Stepick, *Pride Against Prejudice: Haitians in the United States* (Boston, MA: Allyn and Bacon, 1997).

16. Alejandro Portes and Alex Stepick, *City on the Edge: The Transformation of Miami* (Berkeley, CA: University of California Press, 1994).

17. Mary Waters, *Black Identities: West Indian Immigrant Dreams and American Realities* (Cambridge, MA: Harvard University Press, 1999); Mary Waters, "Ethnic and Racial Identities of Second-Generation Black Immigrants in New York City," *International Migration Review*, 28: 4 (1994) 795-820.

18. The general idea being that ethnicity is a strategic adaptation of the migrant's culture to the political culture and opportunity structures of the new land. As a result, the migrant remains conspicuously "ethnic" but this ethnicity is also a unique product of their engagement with U.S. society—it is no longer merely an extension of their inherited culture identity. This explanatory framework is a hallmark feature of strategic and social constructionist explanations of ethnicity. For examples see, John Higham, *Send These To Me: Jews and Other Immigrants in Urban America* (New York: Atheneum, 1975); Philip Kasinitz, *Caribbean New York: Black Immigrants and the Politics of Race* (Ithaca, NY: Cornell University Press, 1992).

19. The term "Americanization" initially had positive connotations, being associated with the process of cultural, civic, and structural assimilation into U.S. society. But, more recently, Americanization has become a euphemism for the negative effects of "integration" for many immigrants—in which becoming like other U.S. citizens equates with higher rates of mental and physical health problems, and a weaker and more diffuse family structure. See, for example, Nancy Landale R. Oropesa, Daniel Llanes and Bridget Gorman, "Does Americanization have Adverse Effects on Health?: Stress, Health Habits, and Infant Health Outcomes among Puerto Ricans," *Social Forces*, 78: 2 (1999), 613-641; Ruben Rumbaut, "Paradoxes (And Orthodoxies) of Assimilation," *Sociological Perspectives*, 40: 3 (1997) 483-511. This Americanization discourse echoes many of the same themes as the segmented assimilation

thesis, explaining how immigrants can be integrated, with negative effects, into an unequal social system. See, Alejandro Portes and Min Zhou, "The New Second Generation: Segmented Assimilation and Its Variants," *The Annals of the American Academy of Political and Social Science*, 530 (1993)74-97.

20. Portes and Zhou, Ibid; Herbert Gans, "Second Generation Decline: Scenarios for the Economic and Ethnic Futures of the Post-1965 American Immigrants," *Ethnic and Racial Studies*, 15: 2: (1992) 174-192.

21. Mary Waters, "Ethnic and Racial Identities of Second-Generation Black Immigrants in New York City," *International Migration Review,* 28: 4 (1994) 795-820 at 812.

22. Stepick, *Pride Against Prejudice.*

23. Waters, Ibid, 809-811.

24. E. Chacko, "Identity and Assimilation among Young Ethiopian Immigrants in Metropolitan Washington," *Geographical Review*, 93: 4 (2003) 491-506; Jennifer Jackson and Mary Cothran, "Black versus Black: The Relationships among African, African American, and African Caribbean Persons," *Journal of Black Studies*, 33: 5 (2003) 576-604.

25. Tukufu Zuberi, *Thicker Than Blood: How Racial Statistics Lie* (Minneapolis, MN: University of Minnesota Press, 2003).

26. Kathryn Neckerman, P. Carter and J. Lee, "Segmented Assimilation and Minority Cultures of Mobility," *Ethnic and Racial Studies*, 22 (1999) 945-965.

27. Kristin Butcher, "Black Immigrants in the United States: A Comparison with Native Blacks and Other Immigrants," *Industrial and Labor Relations Review*, 47: 2 (1994) 265-284; Matih Kalmijn, "The Socioeconomic Assimilation of Caribbean American Blacks," *Social Forces*, 74: 3 (1996) 911-930; Suzanne Model, "Caribbean Immigrants: A Black Success Story?" *International Migration Review*, 25: 2 (1991) 248-276.

28. Jose Itzigsohn and Carlos Dore-Cabral, "Competing Identities? Race, Ethnicity and Panethnicity Among Dominicans in the U.S.," *Sociological Forum,* 15: 2 (2000) 225-247.

29. See Sherri Grasmuck and Ramón Grosfoguel, "Geopolitics, Economic Niches, and Gendered Social Capital among Recent Caribbean Immigrants in New York City," *Sociological Perspectives,* 40: 3 (1997) 339-363. Although there is a kind of hyper-segregation that is specific to black populations (immigrant and native-born) it does not always correlate with limited occupational mobility. This is perhaps why black immigrants are more likely to raise complaints about residential segregation than employment discrimination (as noted by Janel Benson, "Exploring the Racial Identities of Black Immigrants in the United States," *Sociological Forum.* 21: 2 [2006] 219-2470.

30. Roy Bryce-Laporte, "Black Immigrants: The Experience of Invisibility and Inequality," *Journal of Black Studies,* 3: 1 (1972) 29-56; John Walter and James Rigali, "The Anglophone Caribbean Immigrant and Partisan Politics in New York, 1900-1972," *Afro-Americans in New York Life and History*, 30: 1 (2006) 19-75.

31. The earliest account of these tensions (and use of Caribbean ethnicity as a distancing strategy vis-à-vis native-born blacks) is Ira Reid's *The Negro Immigrant* (New York: Columbia University Press, 1939). For an account of Caribbean migrants "assimilation" into the African American population see Walter and Rigali (Ibid) and Nancy Foner, "West Indian Identity in the Diaspora: Comparative and Historical Perspectives," *Latin American Perspectives*, 25: 3 (1998) 173-188.

32. Rachel Rubin and Jeffrey Melnick, *Immigration and Popular Culture: An Introduction* (New York: New York University Press, 2006).

33. Vilna Bashi-Bobb and Averil Clarke, "Experiencing Success: Structuring the Per-

ception of Opportunities for West Indians," in Nancy Foner ed., *Islands in the City* (Berkeley, CA: University of California Press, 2001), 106-136.

34. See, Eduardo Bonilla Silva, *Racism Without Racists*, 3rd ed. (Lanham, MD: Rowman and Littlefield, 2003); Lani Guinier and Gerald Torres, *The Miners Canary* (Cambridge, MA: Harvard University Press, 2002).

35. For various accounts of these developments see, David Brotherton and Philip Kretsedemas, eds., *Keeping Out the Other: A Critical Introduction to Immigration Enforcement Today* (New York: Columbia University Press, 2008).

36. Payal Banerjee, "Transnational Subcontracting, Indian IT Workers, and the U.S. Visa System," *Women's Studies Quarterly*, 38: 1/2 (2010) 89-110; Bill Hing, *Defining America Through Immigration Policy* (Philadelphia, PA: Temple University Press, 2003); M. Ibrahim, "The Securitization of Migration: A Racial Discourse," *International Migration*, 43: 5 (2006) 163-187; Irum Sheikh, "Racializing, Criminalizing, and Silencing 9/11 Deportees," David Brotherton and Philip Kretsedemas, eds., *Keeping Out the Other: A Critical Introduction to Immigration Enforcement Today* (New York: Columbia University Press, 2008): 81-107.

37. Irene Bloemraad, "Becoming a Citizen in the United States and Canada: Structured Mobilization and Immigrant Political Incorporation," *Social Forces*, 85: 2 (2006) 667-695.

38. Philip Kretsedemas, "The Limits of Control: Neoliberal Priorities and the U.S. Nonimmigrant Flow," *International Migration*; 50: s1 (2012) e1-18.

39. Ogbu Kalu, "The Andrew Syndrome: Models in Understanding Nigerian Diaspora," in Jacob Olupona and Regina Gemignani, eds., *African Immigrant Religions in America* (New York: New York University Press, 2007), 61-88.

40. For a defining example of this argument see Stephen Steinberg, *Race Relations: A Critique* (Stanford, CA: Stanford University Press, 2007), 111-148.

41. Silvio Torres-Saillant, "The Tribulations of Blackness: Stages in Dominican Racial Identity," *Callaloo*, 23: 3 (2000): 1086-1111.

42. James Ferguson, *The Dominican Republic: Beyond the Lighthouse* (London: Latin America Bureau, 1992).

43. There are many accounts of these flexible migrant identities. For some examples see, Elazar Barkan and Marie-Denise Shelton, eds., *Borders, Exiles, Diasporas* (Stanford, CA: Stanford University Press, 1998); Aiwha Ong, *Flexible Citizenship: The Cultural Logics of Transnationality* (Durham, NC: Duke University Press, 1997); Nina Glick Schiller, Linda Basch and Cristina Szanton Blanc, "From Immigrant to Transmigrant: Theorizing Transnational Migration," *Anthropological Quarterly*, 68: 1 (1995) 48-63.

44. Charles Carnegie, "A Social Psychology of Caribbean Migrations: Strategic Flexibility in the West Indies," in *Caribbean Exodus*, ed., Barry Levine (New York: Praeger, 1987), 32-43; Vilna Bashi, *Survival of the Knitted: Immigrant Social Networks in a Stratified World* (Stanford, CA: Stanford University Press, 2007); Jemima Pierre, "Black Immigrants in the U.S. and the 'Cultural Narratives' of Ethnicity," *Identities*. 11:2 (2009) 141-170; Milton Vickerman, "Tweaking a Monolith: West Indian Immigrant Encounters With 'Blackness,'" in *Islands in the City*, ed., Nancy Foner (Berkeley, CA: University of California Press, 2001), 237-256. Notably, all of these accounts have been informed by the Afro-Caribbean experience (and the experience of Jamaicans in particular). Some caution should be exercised in extending this explanatory framework to the African or Afro-Latino migrant experience— even though it is not wholly irrelevant to this experience. It bears noting, however, this focus on the Jamaican experience is not unwarranted, since Jamaicans have historically

composed the largest national-origin group within U.S. black immigrant flow.

45. Roy Bryce-Laporte, "Black Immigrants: The Experience of Invisibility and Inequality," *Journal of Black Studies,* 3: 1 (1972), 29-56 at 39.

46. Linda Bosniak, "Citizenship, Noncitizenship and the Transnationalization of Domestic Work," in *Migration and Mobilities: Citizenship, Borders and Gender,* ed., Seyla Benhabib and Judith Resnick (New York: New York University Press, 2009), 127-156; Sandra Braman, "Interpenetrated Globalization: Scaling, Power and the Public Sphere," in *Globalization, Communication and Transnational Civil Society*, ed., Sandra Braman and Annabelle Sreberny-Mohammadi (Cresskill, NJ: Hampton Press, 1996), 21-36; Saskia Sassen, *A Sociology of Globalization* (New York: W. W. Norton, 2007); Yasmin Soysal, "Toward a Postnational Model of Membership" in *The Citizenship Debates: A Reader,* ed., Gershon Shafir (Minneapolis: University of Minnesota Press, 1998), 189-217.

Chapter 2

Blacks in France: A Minority or a Community?

Gado Alzouma

This chapter argues that a Black community is emerging in France, with the first manifestations dating back to the riots of October and November of 2005. In contrast with some authors who contend that French Blacks are a minority, this chapter demonstrates that Black identity in France is being reconstructed as a stable community identity. This identity is based on new representations of blackness and Africanity, which are constantly being nurtured and reconfigured in light of unfolding events. It is evident in the way in which various online groups of francophone Blacks, Black associations and organizations, and Black political agents and activists are redefining and reformulating—for themselves and others—what it means to be Black or African in France. The chapter falls within the framework of the structuralist-constructivist theory devised by Pierre Bourdieu, which approaches identity definition and expression as a "symbolic struggle over the power to produce and to impose a legitimate vision of the world."[1] Depending on the positions they occupy, agents endowed with specific dispositions have different "visions of social divisions,"[2] which are visions of themselves and others that they constantly strive to maintain, reinforce, and impose.

Until recently, Blacks in France have not been the subjects of social science research, apart from studies on the Antilles or on migration from sub-Saharan Africa. Blacks in France have never been recognized as either a subject worthy of research or as a distinct group—not, at least, if popular taxonomies and the categories of ordinary discourse are to be believed. For all intents and purposes, France's Blacks have remained what Joan Stavo-Debauge[3] terms "socially invisible," and have not been regarded as agents endowed with a shared consciousness, or as agents politically and socially engaged and capable of being mobilized. With the passage of the Taubira law in 2002,[4] followed by the suburban riots of 2005,[5] France's Blacks burst onto the media and political scene

27

as actors to which political and media discourse would henceforth refer as an actual social category. This evolution continued via a series of writings on France's Blacks by various academics, political luminaries, and opinion leaders such as François Durpaire,[6] Patrick Lozès,[7] Ramatoulaye Yade-Zimet,[8] and Pap N'diaye,[9] as well as in academic journal articles by Joan Stavo-Debauge,[10] Fred Constant,[11] Christian Poiret,[12] and Elikia Mbokolo.[13] All of these writings dealt with two main issues in one way or another: the so-called invisibility of France's Blacks, and the fundamental, epistemological question of whether France's Blacks are a minority or a community.

Are Blacks a Minority or a Community?

Among those who regard France's Blacks as a minority is notably Pap N'diaye, whose seminal book *La Condition Noire* ("The Black Condition") spurred a number of studies on them. N'diaye rejects the idea that France's Blacks are a distinct community based on the idea that, as a group, they are too culturally heterogeneous. N'diaye points out that French Blacks can be regarded as a minority by virtue of their shared social experience. He arrives at this conclusion by focusing on "the phenomenon by which specific groups, 'minorities,' are discriminated against, that is to say how they become objects of differential treatment based on illegitimate criteria."[14] N'diaye defines this minority group—the "black minority"—as a "group of people who share, willy-nilly, the social experience of being generally regarded as black."[15] For him, French Blacks are a group whose members have a shared historico-cultural experience based on the perception that to be Black is to have a distinct identity—one that is externally defined by others' perspective, or what he terms, "a social process of *minority-ization*."[16] N'diaye refers to the "concrete social experience" among Blacks in France (e.g., interrelations between Blacks, creation of diverse organizations, engagements in social movements, definition of self and others, inter alia)[17] as the expression of a "minority logic," as opposed to a "community logic."[18] N'diaye distinguishes between an identity that is based on common experiences and common interests (which he characterizes as "fine"), and one based on common origins and common cultures (which he characterizes as "dense"). The former is related to the notion of minority, while the latter is related to the notion of community.

Before N'diaye's book was published, several anthropologists, including Didier Fassin[19] and Joan Stavo-Debauge,[20] published a series of studies focusing on France's Blacks. Of particular importance are Stavo-Debauge's writings on the reasons for the invisibility of France's Blacks in the social sciences, which he attributes to "the dynamics of writing and problematizing in the social sciences—a dynamic rife with anxiety and 'dread' that bogs authors down in a morass of intellectual, practical, and political paradoxes and inconsistencies."[21] It is the social sciences authors' preconceived ideas regarding what they deem to be in Blacks' interest that drive this reluctance and refusal to engage in an activity they associate with a kind of "labeling" of Black people. However, Stavo-Debauge appears to lean toward the view that France's Blacks, do in fact, constitute a bona fide community. According to Stavo-Debauge:

> The recognition, by those concerned, of collective responsibility for a specific 'racial' wrong may—and I would add, must—be enough to nurture in them solidarity and a shared consciousness, both of which are necessary for the birth of collective action and engaging in a struggle against 'racial' discrimination. Moreover, it would appear that this minimal form of community, one based on mutual recognition of a shared exposure to wrongs and misdeeds, nonetheless exists, as is evidenced by numerous events and organizations—and now even the French press acknowledges that there are Blacks in France.[22]

The preference for the term *minority* as opposed to *community* stems, in the minds of N'diaye and others, from the fact that the notion of community is inescapably associated with social cohesion and common values (i.e., sameness) whereas minority is primarily associated with victimization and a togetherness built on a common experience and even social movements—namely, groups with the capacity to mobilize and demonstrate. This same theme is taken up by Constant,[23] who, like N'diaye, regards France's Blacks, as a "minority of color," which he defines as follows:

> The term black minority means a specific population whose nature is determined by geographic, historic, and social factors, and which, objectively speaking, is extraordinarily fragmented and possesses no 'community of consciousness'—but instead has the oftentimes passive feeling of shared racial 'belonging'; a perception that is reflected back at Blacks by the mirror of French society, but that has no impact on the hierarchies of status and prestige (such as in the national and foreign spheres) that characterize this society.[24]

Constant draws a very sharp distinction between the concept of minority, and that of community. In doing so, he emphasizes that France's Blacks do not constitute a community because "this population is not a 'community' that is organized around specific institutions, norms, practices and constraints."[25]

The current discussion explores how France has recently witnessed the emergence of a Black community consciousness, as evidenced and embodied by the multiple debates following the events of October 2005; the recent changes in the discourse of the media about Blacks in France; some institutional changes (for example, the Taubira law); the creation of multiple online discussions forums and websites devoted to all aspects of Blacks' life in France; and many organizational initiatives. A series of events, including Barack Obama's election as president of the United States in 2008,[26] have helped cement this nascent feeling of community. Furthermore, the awareness of being Black plays a major role in the emergence of community consciousness. However, this chapter differs on this topic from Constant, who says: "It would appear that having the same skin color does not necessarily translate into either a convergence of interests or a similarity of viewpoints or spontaneous tacit agreement within the various segments of France's black population or this population as a whole."[27]

The discussion in this chapter approaches "color consciousness" as an important dimension of the community's existence as a distinct group endowed with some level of self-awareness. From this perspective, the community is not distinct from the ethnic group, in particular if account is taken of the multi-cultural, multi-ethnic, or multi-racial context of contemporary France. The community is formed as a result of the interactions among the different groups living in France, and the interactions between a particular group, the global society, and the state. As such, it is important to adopt a relational and dynamic approach when defining community rather than a fixist approach. This is because, as Barth theorized,[28] the "boundaries" of the community, as well as its identity, may be created or may change as a result of the previously mentioned interactions.

The literature on France's Blacks does contain clear signs of a feeling of community affiliation emerging at a particular time, under particular circumstances, among Black people in France when those involved found themselves confronted with particular problems. Christian Poiret alludes to this feeling when interviewing Black people:

> First and foremost, the persons interviewed often indicated that there was a decisive moment when everything changed and they began to think of themselves as Black, and then actively lay claim to this identity. This decisive moment appears to consist in a dawning awareness of the systemic nature of discrimination, an awareness that is generally prompted by repeated unsuccessful efforts to find a job.[29]

Another example of such a pivotal moment is Obama's election as President of the United States. Following Obama's victory in the Presidential Election, the French Press repeatedly posed the same question on French website message boards, and in political debates: "Is a Barack Obama possible in France?" To put it more bluntly, could a Black man be elected president of France? For the most part, the answer was a resounding "No." At best, people believed that a Black could not aspire to France's highest office in the status quo. Yet, these debates brought into sharp focus the whole gamut of the experience of French Blacks; as a result, many Blacks have gradually come to see themselves as part of a distinct "Black" community—a community with a shared consciousness.

This chapter will demonstrate how the interactions between Blacks and the state, Blacks and wider society, and Blacks and the media have incited the Black people of France to mark their difference, and build the frontiers of the group through a number of associative engagements, new forms of sociability (e.g., the creation of Black cybercommunities), and social and political practices that all contribute to manifest the existence of a community. To understand this, it is important to first examine the status of Black people in France.

Is Racial Diversity Taboo in France?

A close examination of the current social and political status of France's Black population clearly shows why the question of the possibility of a "French Obama" has elicited such an overwhelmingly negative response. In the first place, French Blacks—even Antilleans, whose ancestors were brought to France more than four centuries ago—are regarded by most French people as foreigners or immigrants. Thus, it is not surprising that website message boards, radio, and television talk shows, and the press often contain comments to the effect that, if Blacks are not happy in France, they should "go back where they came from." It apparently never crosses the minds of such commentators that the Blacks they are addressing may well come from the Antilles, and have therefore been French for many centuries, knowing no other homeland than France. The official discourse notwithstanding, this perspective indicates that, for many French people, France is an ethnically homogeneous nation—namely, a white nation in which Blacks are regarded as foreigners, and whose status as French citizens is questionable.

Indeed, a significant portion of the French population appears to believe that French identity is exclusive, and that there is, as Herman Lebovics put it, a "real France." Rosemarie Scullion, citing Lebovics, defines this "real France" as "a monolithic model of national identity formation, holding that there is only one way to participate in the culture of a country, and only one natural organization that fits the society."[30] This concept is a near neighbor to the notion of *jus sanguinis* ("right of blood"), which argues that citizenship derives from parentage and—along with *jus soli* ("law of ground or birthright citizenship")—determines the manner in which French nationality is acquired. It is therefore not in the least surprising that large swathes of the French population base their understanding of what it means to be French on the principle of *jus sanguinis* which, according to Christophe Vimbert[31] was in effect in French laws between 1804 and 1889. Indeed, France's extreme right often speaks in terms of "intrinsically French people" as opposed to the remainder of the French population; in so doing, it intimates that only the former group is genuinely "French" as defined by criteria that are bio-psychological (namely, skin color and perceived loyalty to France), cultural (i.e., speaking French fluently as their native language), and historical (i.e., the French nation's long history stemming from a mixture of Gallic tribes).

This vision of France as a nation in which Blacks are excluded is deeply rooted in French history. As Elikia Mbokolo points out, "apparently at a very early stage, Blacks were a burdensome peculiarity whose implications are with us to this day."[32] Mbokolo adds that the need to preserve the "purity of blood" combined with the "foreign origins" of Blacks and their "alleged inability to meld with French society without shaking it to its roots" has always provided a pretext for a certain amount of segregation between French "Whites" and "Blacks," as well as the unequal treatment inflicted upon Blacks—despite a royal edict issued in 1315 that granted "natural rights" to any person who treads on French soil. This right was never granted to French Blacks. In fact, according to Mbokolo, an edict issued in 1716 stated that this right was to be denied to any Black person who happened to be residing in France, for any reason whatsoever.

This edict was reinforced throughout the eighteenth century by new laws that "promulgated more stringent conditions for Blacks to enter France and take up residence there; required Black slave owners to declare their slaves to the authorities; set limits on how long Blacks could remain in France; and prohibited marriage, even with the master's consent."[33] These evolutions culminated in 1777 with the "royal edict on the policing of Blacks," which governed the conditions under which Blacks could remain on French territory and resulted in "black repositories,"[34] internments, expulsions, and prohibitions against living in France—all of which are still very topical in France. Thus, the resulting discrimination against Blacks in France today, even those who were born and have made their homes in France, is merely a way of continuing to enforce the policies that prevailed during the slavery and colonial periods. The continuity of these policies is also reflected by the general perception that Blacks are only tolerated in France as a kind of foreign body, but never as full-fledged members of the body politic.

The second reason why Blacks are not accepted or viewed as full-fledged citizens has to do with the ideal of French universalist republicanism and the rejection of what the French call *communautarisme* (group-based identity politics and multiculturalism). The French Republic is regarded as a single and indivisible entity that makes no distinction between its citizens in terms of their gender, religion, or ethnic origin; thus, by extension, all French citizens are supposed to be absolutely equal before the law. In France, ethnic or racial communities or minorities are simply not recognized. Consequently, they cannot be granted special rights. This is the very essence of the French universalist republican ideal—an essence that strictly prohibits *communautarisme*. *Communautarisme* is perceived as a threat to social harmony, which is in turn achieved primarily through integration and assimilation—in short, through a homogeneous melting pot of cultures and nationalities fostered by assimilationist policies during the colonial period and a policy of integrating immigrants into French society after the various French colonies gained their independence. From the standpoint of social research, political ideology and culture, and social phenomena, the main effect of France's universalist republicanism and the banning of *communautarisme* or group-based identity politics has been to consign France's Blacks to a state of invisibility, which at the institutional level and in the social sciences has resulted in a total lack of any sociological or anthropological category known as "French Blacks."[35]

A group identified as "French Blacks" that is amenable to identification or mobilization is wholly absent from the social-research radar in France. Unfortunately, this does not prevent Black people from existing as a category of common parlance, or a fragmented category that goes by a multitude of names used by both the general population and social scientists. For example, young French people tend to use the English term "Blacks" or the French term *Africains* ("Africans") to refer to Franco-Africans. However, as Stavo-Debauge[36] points out, terms such as *Domiens* ("Domiens") for persons of Antillean descent or "immigrants of sub-Saharan origin" for people of African descent are also very common. By the same token, in the cultural domain, the existence of Black American music or "negro-African literature"[37] is widely recognized, and such terms are common. Nonetheless, the notion that there are different races—at least from a perceptual standpoint and in the popular mind—has persisted in France to this day. According to a 1999 Louis Harris poll on the attitude of French people toward racism, "more than seven respondents out of ten expressed the view that they are more or less racist."[38] The poll was based on a representative sample of 1,012 persons, aged 18 and older.

If the notion of race is so vehemently rejected in France, it is not so much due to anti-racist reasons, but rather political and social attitudes that—by denying the Blacks of France a legal and social existence—consign them to a state of limbo as a social group that is denied civil rights and toward whom the government has no obligations. Here also lies the reluctance to designate French Blacks as a community, as this implies cultural and political rights, as well as a distinct cultural identity for people living in a multicultural society. To designate French Blacks as a minority helps fragment them. Also, the notion of "minority" is compatible with the French-style republican ideal, while the concept of "community" will necessarily connote multiculturalism and *communautarisme*, all strongly opposed by the French political elite, and many social science researchers, journalists, intellectuals and common citizens.

One of the main consequences of Blacks' invisibility is the absence of any social policy on their behalf, inasmuch as Blacks do not have the status of a social group on a par with that of women, the elderly, the unemployed, or even immigrants, according to the taxonomy used by the French statistics office Institut National de la Statistique et des Etudes Economiques (INSEE), whose studies have a major influence on French social and economic policy. The lack of statistics on French Blacks makes it impossible to determine the extent to which they are the victims of discrimination, or even to measure parameters such as their demographic and electoral clout. Consequently, France's purported republican equality has long concealed a less savory reality—namely: unequal representation of the country's various ethnic groups in its political and managerial class, in the National Assembly, in large French corporations, and in well-paying jobs. This has always been concealed or justified on the grounds that French society is "color blind," or that the country should not gather statistics on the ethnicity of its elites.

Ethnic Statistics and Black Diversity

French Black organizations, including *Conseil Représentatif des Associations Noires de France* (CRAN),[39] have engaged in such quantifications in order to draw attention to the monolithic nature of France's power elite. CRAN commissioned a study in 2006[40] on the demographic weight of French Blacks and inequality in terms of employment and decision-making positions. This study found that 61 percent of French Blacks were the victims of a racist incident in the previous year, and at least 10 percent of the respondents stated that they had been the victim of a racially motivated attack or had been denied housing on account of their skin color. Worse still, although Blacks account for 5 million of France's population of 60 million, France's 577-member National Assembly includes only two black representatives. The revelation of these facts placed the issue of ethnic statistics on the national agenda, where it has since become a central feature of popular and political debate. The CRAN study also discredited the dogma of the universalist republican ideal, which—as previously discussed—is based on the rejection of *communautarisme* (i.e., group-based identity politics). The study revealed the existence of *banlieues* ("suburbs")—in effect, ghettos housing most of France's Black and North African population—as highly ethnicized communities that, in large cities, are nothing more than racially segregated housing, although not referred to in such terms.

Blacks in France: A Fragmented Community

Other characteristics of French Blacks shed light on their situation in France. First, French Blacks do not have a common culture, like that of African Americans. This is one of the main reasons why most authors refuse to regard France's Black population as a community, as this putative Black French community is a very mixed bag. On the one hand, France's Black population only shares a common history as an imagined community that originated on one continent. On the other hand, the experience of slavery—among other evolutions—appears to be a differentiating criterion. Hence, a distinct difference exists between second and third-generation French Blacks, Antilleans, and Africans in terms of their attitude toward their "Blackness." France's African immigrants identify more strongly with their countries of origin nowadays than was the case when modern African nations first gained independence half a century ago. Being a Francophone also does not create a sense of shared identity among such immigrants, as hundreds of African languages are still spoken in the various Francophone African nations. Another factor is that Africa is a patchwork of religions comprising Christians, Muslims, and practitioners of traditional religions. One could, in fact, argue that Africanness is a stronger feeling among European members of the African Diaspora, who are suddenly confronted with racism and their *négritude,* and who are forced to recast their identity in such a way that their nationality takes a back seat.

Many Antilleans refuse to identify in any way with Africa, or even to be defined as "Blacks."[41] For Claude Ribbe and some other Antillean intellectuals, this refusal takes a number of forms, with the first and foremost being a universalism that rejects all forms of "Black *communautarisme*" (i.e., a universalism whose highest aim is for all citizens to be devoid of any "particularistic" ties). A second form of this refusal to be identified as African is *Créolité,* which apart from being a literary movement, is also an identity movement developed in response and opposition to négritude and of which Confiant,[42] along with Chamoiseau and Barnabé,[43] was a founder. The third form of refusal is domism,[44] which classifies Blacks according to the geographical region in which they happen to live, regardless of whether or not they are descended from slaves or live in one of France's overseas departments. In reality, although domism has never explicitly advocated such a classification system, it nonetheless acknowledges the existence of an identity that is forged overseas, on the islands, and that is different in terms of both its historical experience and the "biophysical heritage borne of mixed-race ancestry"[45] that is part and parcel of the African experience of négritude.

The universalist mindset disallows distinguishing between French citizens on the basis of class or race. This attitude is rooted in the vision of a "universalist and abstract France, the France of the community of citizens; a France that is catastrophically disembodied."[46] According to Constant, this France is based on the myth of the "republic one and indivisible." Meanwhile, *Créolité* seeks to forge a new identity that draws upon European and African elements while setting itself apart from them by refusing any racial affiliation. As Beverly Ormerod[47] explains, *Créolité* "sets aside Négritude as an 'African illusion' that encouraged, no less than did French colonialism, the West Indian's mistaken tendency to seek his identity outside his island and through a foreign culture … *Créolité* focuses sharply on Martinique and small countries resembling it, describing itself as 'the interactional or transactional aggregate of Caribbean, European, African, Asian, and Levantine cultural elements, united on the same soil by the yoke of history.'" Hence, *Créolité* is a new identity, one that encapsulates the experience of the descendants of slaves—an experience that is distinctive in the sense that it springs from multiple and multiform sources and that Blacks who remained in Africa never confronted it. *Créolité* is also a shared culture whose primary manifestation is the existence of a shared language:

> Creole culture is seen as the result of a process of adaptation that started with the plantation days: a mixed culture that arose from the forced, non-harmonious confrontation of different languages, customs and world-views. Its manifestations are perceived beyond the Caribbean and American regions: (Creole) authors claim to have Creole affinities with the Seychelles, Mauritius, Reunion, and other African, Asian and Polynesian peoples. On the other hand (and unlike Glissant), they recognize only a limited, geopolitical solidarity with the Caribbean archipelago as a whole, since they consider the process of creolization not to have taken place in certain regions like Andalusian-influenced northern Cuba or the Hindu-dominated cane cutting areas of Trinidad.[48]

Creolist theories are primarily opposed to theories on the other side of the Atlantic that identify with a global Black community, whose roots are to be found in Africa and whose identity resides on the affirmation of "Blackness." This view is similar to a stance that Tunde Adeleke terms *gloracialization*:

> [A] unifying racialized paradigm designed to defend Blacks against the perceived threat of a global Eurocentric order. Gloracialization essentializes race as a unifying umbrella for all Blacks, regardless of geographical location. It advances a monolithic construction of Africans and Blacks in diaspora as one people united by negative experiences emanating from historic encounters with Europeans.[49]

Whereas *Créolité* emphasizes the particularisms and diversity of populations that stem from the slave trade, pan-Africanism (or what Adeleke termed gloracialization) seeks to create a worldwide Black consciousness whose muse, so to speak, is Africa, in its capacity as a guiding light for identity from a historical, geographical, and psychological standpoint. Pan-Africanism forges a link between disparate Black communities by opposing the dominant white hegemony via a global racial consciousness that is embodied by the emergence of charismatic world-class Black figures such as Barack Obama on the one hand, and by Blacks the world over identifying with this shared paradigm on the other.

The fourth form of some Antillean intellectuals' refusal to identify with Africa is a paradigm embodied by the writings of the Antillean philosopher Ribbe.[50] It is a Universalist mindset characterized by a peculiar refusal, on the part of Ribbe, to be classified or identified as a "Black person." For Ribbe, there is no such thing as a Black person or white person—terms he feels merely attest to the dominance of racist ideology in France. Ribbe refuses to accept any ethnic assignation or categorization based on skin color. He manifests a hostile or antagonistic attitude toward any idea of "Black consciousness." Indeed, Ribbe has repeatedly exhibited this hostility to Black consciousness by, for example, advocating that racism charges be brought against CRAN for having demanded that the French government collect statistics on the country's ethnic groups.[51] In keeping with this stance, in order to avoid any reference to racial community, Ribbe only recognizes the existence of individuals and analyzes their relations, successes, and failures from a meritocratic standpoint and as a manifestation of individual qualities. However, Ribbe does emphasize the fact that there are individuals in France with just as much merit as Obama, although their ambitions are blighted by France's racist policies.[52] Ribbe's solution for abolishing this discrimination is not affirmative action, but rather social policies and legal reforms that would promote social justice without regard for skin color.

Ribbe's position differs from that of most French black organizations such as CRAN that are pushing for more racial and ethnic diversity in public sector employment in terms of access to France's elite graduate schools known as *grandes écoles* and in the policymaking sphere. Such demands on the part of CRAN and a host of other Black organizations that have emerged since the 2005 riots appear to be the manifestation of the advent and progressive strengthening of a Black consciousness in France and a proactive, mobilized community. As will be discussed in the next section, this evolution—in effect, an American-style Black movement—is increasingly being recognized by the French government, the social science community, and France's Blacks themselves.

A Shared Consciousness

The French suburb riots in October and November 2005 have been instrumental in creating a shared Black consciousness and initiating the process of building a Black community in France. Prior to the riots, France's Black population had no real sense of shared Blackness. This awareness was spurred above all by passage of the Taubira law and the creation of community organizations such as CRAN, which fight discrimination by applying the lessons learned from American affirmative action policies and practices. In this regard, Obama (as a shining example of Black identity) took on some importance, as the Obama phenomenon is regarded as the culmination of affirmative action—a policy that many French Blacks feel could be profitably applied in France. Thus, for the first time ever, the existence of a Black community was affirmed in political and social discourses and through political demonstrations.

The Black community's existence was first validated by a move toward diversity at the highest levels of the French government; Rama Yade, representing the Black community was named human rights and foreign state secretary. For many, Yade is France's answer to Condoleezza Rice, and her appointment reflects a certain "Americanization" of French politics, if not the beginnings of at least a modicum of affirmative action. French President Nicolas Sarkozy also took steps to institute diversity by appointing Yazid Sebag as Minister of Diversity. Sebag introduced a bill calling for a new policy of diversity that focused on reforming the elite schools where France's future political and business leaders are trained.[53] Thus, France's power elite has been forced to call into question the foundations of France's republican and universalist ideals as well as the absence of racial and ethnic diversity among France's ruling class.

The recognition of diversity translates into the existence of a new vision of social divisions, for such recognition spawns—albeit willy-nilly—a new social category (i.e., the Black community) that heretofore was never even so much as mentioned. This social group has in turn begun to manifest its existence by means of organizations, petitions, literature, and demonstrations. In so doing, a segment of the French population that was once shapeless, heterogeneous, composed of individuals, and perceived solely in a negative light has now become an identifiable group with a bona fide name and bona fide representatives.

Identity Markers of the Black Community

Communities are created and also shaped through symbolic representations, images, and the opposition to others, which is why it is not possible to understand the formation of the Black community in France if we do not understand the way in which Blacks position themselves in the struggle for the imposition of "a legitimate vision of the world"[54]—in other words, the way they see themselves and the way others see them. Because of their cultural heterogeneity, N'diaye[55] and others refuse to characterize Blacks in France as a community. However, we also know that despite their cultural heterogeneity, Blacks are mainly perceived in an indistinct, uniform manner—even culturally—by the rest of the French population.

In France, Blacks are expected to have a set of dispositions, ways of being in the world, and ways of thinking—in short, a set of *habitus*—that are perceived as proper, or culturally normative, by the French nation at large (or as a whole). These dispositions and ways of being are understood as being cultural, psychological, or natural. Although they are composed of a set of clichés, stereotypes, and prejudices that qualify as racist, they form the basis of what most French people believe about Black or African cultures, as a perceptual template to generate and explain the way in which Black people behave in everyday life. These behaviors are coupled with psychological or natural dispositions. For many French people, it is because Blacks are supposed to possess these so-called cultures that they fail to integrate and become fully French.

The problems Black people in France face (ghettoization in the suburbs, poverty, marginalization, delinquency, etc.) have long been perceived as the result of lack of integration or cultural assimilation. They were understood as the result of a communautarizme and an inward looking "retreatism" in the Mertonian sense of the term.[56] In the French psyche, there was a correspondence between the color of the skin and the culture of the different communities living in France. Some of those cultures, such as North African Islamic and West African cultures, were often judged to be incompatible with French values or the values of republicanism. They were therefore deemed "impossible to incorporate to the standards of a vague Frenchness supported by the authorities and the media."[57] That imagined Frenchness dictated that people of different cultures or colors abandon their "particularities," or the community to which they belonged in order to become citizens or individuals without any particular ties.

Does French Policy of Assimilation Continue?

What does this Black culture consist of for Black people themselves? What does being Black mean in France? What does Black community consist of? As this discussion will demonstrate, the Black community exists through a shared set of cultural traits, associations, organizations, symbols, shared material and immaterial patrimonies, and affective relations. The notion of community in this perspective is understood in the way Barry Wellam defines it: "as networks of interpersonal ties that provide sociability, support, information, a sense of belonging, and social identity."[58] Provided that we do not hypostasiate this notion, that it is a relational and dynamic path as indicated in the introduction of this article, the Black community in France has all of these traits.

The first trait and the most important one is the feeling of belonging to a group identified as "the Blacks." Because of its stigmatizing nature, that feeling of belonging may sometimes not be acknowledged, or may be denied by the individuals concerned. What is important is the place assigned to individuals by the wider society. This situation can be summarized using Fanon's[59] quip alluding to the fully assimilated Black who, by virtue of his education, aspires to be distinguished from other Blacks and identified with Whites who reject his pretensions by saying: "He may be a doctor, he is nonetheless Negro!" Thus, objectively speaking, if an individual is identified as Black by society, he or she may protest, but it will not change much. It can be added that the vast majority of people defined as Black have nothing to say on the matter; they either accept the fact with resignation or try to redefine the label as a positive identity value that is claimed and exhibited.

It is not difficult to demonstrate that the vast majority of Blacks in France accept as obvious the fact that they belong to a larger group popularly called "Blacks" in France. This is evident in the way that they speak about themselves and their experience of living in France, particularly in discussion forums about the Black or African Diaspora. It is obvious that those who visit these forums belong to the Black community even if they do not all have the same definition or common understanding of this notion. This community, can in turn, be identified by its members' shared interests, such as what they go online for in terms of group membership and support.

This is evident on the *AfriqueIndex* website[60] when consulting the index of websites known as community websites (i.e., African or Black Diaspora websites). According to the website, *AfriqueIndex* is presented as "a guide to the Internet directory of websites related to black Africa. Its purpose is to enable Internet users to find information and websites related to black Africa, whatever the theme (African politics; education and teaching in Africa; African art; African culture; economics; sport; tourism in Africa; etc.) and to find them easily. The team that maintains the directory of *AfriqueIndex* is located in France, near Paris."[61]

AfriqueIndex's community websites page (websites devoted to the Black Diaspora in France) includes fifty entries: eight dating sites; nine sites dedicated to news of Africa and the Black diaspora; ten association websites; three online forums; seven entertainment and art websites; five websites for Black women; and eight "various" websites. This number is not limited to one website: hundreds of websites have been set up by Black people and the Black Diaspora in France. *AfriqueIndex* does not list some of the most important of these websites, including Africamaat.com, Afrikara.com, or numerous blogs of influential activists, politicians, writers, and leaders. What the *AfriqueIndex* short list can help us do is gain an overview of the online Black community in France, or what Black people in France are interested in when they go online. These websites reflect the existence of a Black community in that they target an audience that defines itself as Black and that goes online to meet other Blacks and discuss things of common interest, such as news, leisure, or sociability. For example, Black women's websites are of interest to Black women who have a particular understanding of what being a Black woman means. In his book *Internet World: Hosting Web Communities*, Cliff Figalo defines this as "feeling part of a larger social whole," a "web of relationships," "an exchange … of commonly valued things," and "relationships … that last through time creating shared histories."[62]

The Internet has made possible the creation of virtual groups that share the fact of being Black, and which develop through online relationships and networks based on that reality. Although virtual, these relationships and networks primarily reflect what is happening in the real world. They would not have been possible and would not have acquired any meaning without the existence in the real world of corresponding groups with well-defined characteristics. These groups are communities because they express common interests, durable interactions among their members, and a common identification. Moreover, in the real world, a number of associations, organizations, places for sociability, etc., exist that reflect the existence of that community. For example, numerous Black associations and organizations exist that focus on Black people and Black interests, including *Union de la Communauté Noire de France* (UCN),[63] CRAN, *Cercle d'Action pour la Promotion de la Diversité en France* (CapD'iv),[64] and Africagora.[65] Charismatic Black political figures (Christiane Taubira or Rama Yade) also exist in France; their activities and engagements are centered on the Black community and they are viewed as representatives of people of Black descent. French-speaking Black literature reflects the concerns of the Black community.

Widely recognized African art and African artists, particularly Black musicians, Black sculptors, Black painters, and others exist. Numerous Black community-meeting places (bars, restaurants, and dances) are recognized as African or Black; their customers are overwhelmingly made up of Black people and their restaurants where they serve a "Black cuisine." Hair salons and African fashion boutiques cater to Black women. Numerous examples of Black media are evident and are composed of magazines, newspapers, and scientific journals (*Brune, Jeune Afrique*, and others). There are also Black actors, producers, and comedians, such as Dieudonné M'bala M'bala. Although people who participate in such community activities are obviously heterogeneous, they are nevertheless a community because they form a recognizable "whole." Members have relationships among themselves, and interact regularly based on their common interests and experiences. This community has recognizable boundaries because of the limited character of overlaps and "mixtures" with other groups. The community members are also held together by the way they are recognized and characterized by other groups of the wider society as belonging to a common whole.

Conclusion

In recent years, the problems facing the Black population in France have been associated with the emergence of a new French academic discipline: Black studies *a la française*. The advent of this discipline attests to the growing importance of France's Black community in the country's intellectual debates and the political and social awareness of the French citizenry. The fact that a fringe group of French academics has termed this movement a "minority" is reflective of two evolutions: first, the abiding influence of fundamentalist and universalist ideology on the social sciences in France and, second, the taboos, avoidance reactions, and received wisdom that structure academic discourse in

France. As Bourdieu[66] pointed out, science—like any other field—structures the discourse of its actors—or more accurately, stakeholders. Thus the fragmentation of the Black community has classically been used as an excuse for denying the existence of a Black community. However, this is barely justifiable.

Like any social group, the Black community is far from being homogenous; therefore, its consciousness has yet to be definitively stabilized. It is nevertheless constructing itself by drawing upon the available symbolic resources, which is in turn shaking the central dogma of the French republican and universalist ideal as well as the taboo against *communautarisme*. Consequently, France's Black community is forging an identity within the French nation. Although this community is a group in the making, it nonetheless has a real existence that is becoming more readily apparent with each passing day thanks to the following evolutions: the various Black organizations that have emerged; current trends of Black sociability such as online forums and meeting places; specific forms of entertainment; the existence of Black charismatic figures, artists, and musicians; the discourse of ethnic diversity, which is no longer taboo in France; the emergence of an academic discipline that is akin to Black studies in America; and debates provoked by the discourse of de-negation or affirmation of the historical culture of slavery. All of these are contributing, whether intentionally or not, to the construction of a Black consciousness and identity in France.

Notes

1. Pierre Bourdieu, "Social Space and Symbolic Power," *Sociological Theory* 7, No 1 (1989): 20.

2. Ibid.

3. Joan Stavo-Debauge, "L'invisibilité du tort et le tort de l'invisibilité." EspacesTemps.net, April19, 2007, http://espacestemps.net/document2233.html (Accessed March 25, 2011).

4. Christiane Taubira is a French female politician and activist born February 2, 1952, in Cayenne, French Guyana. She is a militant of the *Parti Radical de Gauche* (PRG) and "*deputee*" (a member of the French National Parliament). She is best known for the law that she devised and proposed that bears her name, the Taubira Law. Voted in on May 21, 2001, it recognizes the slave trades and slavery as a crime against humanity.

5. The riots started on October 27, 2005, in the Parisian suburb of Clichy-Sous-Bois and were declared "curbed" on November 19 by the police. Between these two dates, the riots extended into many French cities and involved French youth of immigrant origin as well as some youth traditionally identified as Whites. A report commissioned by the French government (Centre d'Analyses Strategiques, 2007) described the riots as "urban violence" that erupted in the fall of 2005 in France and were unprecedented in both their timeline and territorial expansion, economic cost, and their political, national, and international impact. They contrast sharply with the fighting reduced to a municipality for three or four days, such as those Venissieux experienced in 1981. Hundreds of affected communes contaminated each other for three weeks between October 27 and November 19 without interruption. This nationwide wave involved thousands of rioters and police, hundreds of locally elected officials, and associations, prefectures, and individuals caught in this tornado. Such riots are unique to France as no other country in Europe, not even Great Britain, has experienced similar events in their duration and in the number of municipalities affected.

6. François Durpaire, *France blanche, colère noire* (Paris: Odile Jacob, 2006).

7. Patrick Lozès, *Nous, les Noirs de France* (Paris: Editions Danger Public, 2006).

8. Ramatoulaye Yade-Zimet, *Noirs de France* (Paris: Calmann-Lévy, 2007).

9. Pap N'diaye, *La Condition noire: Essai sur une minorité française* (Paris: Calmann-Lévy, 2008).

10. Joan Stavo-Debauge, "L'invisibilité du tort et le tort de l'invisibilité," 2007.

11. Fred Constant, "Les Noirs en France: Anatomie d'un groupe invisible," http://www.udmn.fr/article.php?article_id=12 (Accessed December 25, 2010).

12. Christian Poiret, "Identification individuelle et identification collective des Noirs de France," 2006. http://www.capdiv.org/v2/articles/index.php?2005/05/26/24-conference-debat-les-noirs-en-france-anatomie-dun-groupe-invisible-3 (Accessed June 6, 2010).

13. Elikia Mbokolo, (n.d.), "Visibilité et invisibilité des élites noires sur la scène politique française." http://www.udmn.fr/article.php?article_id=16 (Accessed March 11, 2011).

14. Pap N'diaye, *La Condition noire: Essai sur une minorité française,* 21.

15. Ibid., 24.

16. Ibid., 58.

17. Ibid., 369.

18. Ibid., 368.

19. Didier Fassin, "Compassion and repression. The moral economy of immigration

policies in France." *Cultural Anthropology* 20, No 3 (2005): 362–87; Didier Fassin, and Fassin E, De la question sociale à la question raciale? Représenter la société française (Paris: La Découverte, 2006); Didier Fassin, "Riots in France and silent anthropologists (éditorial invité)." *Anthropology Today: Journal of the Royal Anthropological Institute* 22, No 1 (2006): 1–3.

20. Joan Stavo-Debauge, *La double invisibilité: à propos de l'absence d'un objet sociologique et de l'atonie d'un sujet politique. Réflexions sur la situation des Noirs dans les sciences sociales et dans la France contemporaine* (Paris: Cercle d'action pour la promotion de la diversité en France, CAPDIV, 2005).

21. Ibid., 150.

22. Ibid., 7.

23. Constant, "Les Noirs en France: Anatomie d'un groupe invisible," 2005.

24. Ibid. 1.

25. Ibid. 1.

26. The significance of Obama's nomination and election for French Blacks is reflected in the sentiments expressed by one of France's largest Black online communities, Grioo.com, in the wake of these events. From among the 117 threads containing the name "Obama," one entitled "Obama a-t-il une chance?" (Does Obama stand a chance?; http://grioo.com/forum/viewtopic.php?t=8750) seemed most appropriate for an understanding of the Obama phenomenon. It began on January 24, 2007, and its final message is dated February 13, 2009. During this period, 461 messages were posted, and the thread was looked up 82,355 times. The initial responses to the question expressed serious doubts about Obama's chances of winning. Another important aspect of the discussions was the fact that most participants expressed doubts about the possibility of a Black president in France. This theme was a leitmotif for the remaining 11 months of the discussion.

27. Fred Constant, "Les Noirs en France: Anatomie d'un groupe invisible," 2005. http://www.udmn.fr/article.php?article_id=12 (Accessed December 12, 2011).

28. Fredrick Barth, *Ethnic Groups and Boundaries* (Boston: Little, Brown and Company, 1969).

29. Christian Poiret, "Identification individuelle et identification collective des Noirs de France," 2006. http://www.udmn.fr/article.php?article_id=4 (Accessed December 12, 2011).

30. Rose-Marie Scullion, "Vicious Circles: Immigration and National Identity in Twentieth Century France," *Substance* 24 no ½ (2003): 35.

31. Christophe Vimbert, *La tradition républicaine en droit public français* (Havre: Université de Rouen, 1992).

32. Elikia Mbokolo, (n.d.), "Visibilité et invisibilité des élites noires sur la scène politique française." http://www.udmn.fr/article.php?article_id=16 (Accessed March 11, 2011).

33. Ibid.

34. Ibid.

35. Stavo-Debauge, 2005.

36. Ibid.

37. Lilyan Kesteloot, *Anthologie négro-africaine. Panorama critique des prosateurs, poètes et dramaturges* (Paris: EDICEF-Hachette, 1993).

38. Institut Louis Harris, "Les attitudes des Français face au racisme: Commentaires de l'Institut Louis Harris," mumianow.free.fr/acceuil/racisme.doc (Accessed January 25, 2010).

39. CRAN or *Conseil Représentatif des Associations Noires de France* ("Representative

Council of Black Associations in France") was founded in 2005 by a group of Black intellectuals, among them Patrick Lozès and Louis George Tin. From its inception, CRAN has aimed to fight racial discrimination in France, particularly against Blacks.

40. CRAN-Capdiv, "Résultats de l'enquête exclusive CRAN-Capdiv effectuée sur le site Grioo du 19 au 25 avril 2006" (Results of the CRAN-Capdiv Survey April 19–25, 2006), http://www.cran.ch/03_MenuVertical/2_Statistiques/Resultats-Enquete_CRAN-France.pdf (Accessed April 13, 2009).

41. This is particularly the case of the influential writer Claude Ribbe, whose views are mostly expressed on his blog (http://www.claude-ribbe.com/).

42. Raphael Confiant, *Aimé Césaire: Une traversée paradoxale du siècle* (Paris: Stock, 1993).

43. Patrick Chamoiseau, Jean Barnabé, and Raphael Confiant, *Éloge de la créolité* (Paris: Gallimard, 1989).

44. The word *domisme* (domism*) is derived from the French acronym *DOM* for *Départements d'Outre-mer* (overseas *départments* or districts, the main French administrative and territorial units) and is applied for the Antilles.

45. Beverly Ormerod, "The Martinican Concept of 'Creoleness': A Multiracial Redefinition of Culture," *Mots Pluriels* 7, 1998, http://motspluriels.arts.uwa.edu.au/MP798bo.html (Accessed March 11, 2011).

46. Fred Constant, "Les Noirs en France: Anatomie d'un groupe invisible," http://www.udmn.fr/article.php?article_id=12 (Accessed December 25, 2010).

47. Ormerod, "The Martinican Concept."

48. Ibid.

49. Tunde Adeleke, T., "Gloracialisation: The Response of Pan-blackists to Globalisation." *Globalisation* 5(1): 2005, http://globalization.icaap.org/content/v5.1/adeleke.html (Accessed March 11, 2011).

50. Claude Ribbe, "Anes noirs, ânes blancs," July 12, 2007, http://www.claude-ribbe.com/dotclear/index.php?2008/12/07/101-anes-blancs-anes-noirs (Accessed May 13, 2010).

51. Ibid.

52. Claude Ribbe, "Allocution prononcée le 10 mai 2010 à Paris, place du général-Catroux, pour l'abolition de l'esclavage," 2010, (Accessed May 13, 2010).

53. Laetitia van Eeckhout, "Yazid Sabeg ouvre la voie aux statistiques ethniques," *Le Monde* (March 6, 2009).

54. Pierre Bourdieu, "Social Space and Symbolic Power," *Sociological Theory* 7, No 1 (1989): 20.

55. Pap Ndiaye, *La Condition Noire*, 2008.

56. Robert K. Merton, "Social Structure and Anomie." *American Sociological Review* 3, No 6 (1938): 672–82.

57. Dominic Thomas, "Pap Ndiaye, La Condition Noire. Essai sur une minorité française," Gradhiva 10, February 3, 2009. http://gradhiva.revues.org/1594 (Accessed March 25, 2011).

58. Wellman, Barry. 2001. "Physical Place and CyberPlace: The rise of personalized networking." *International Journal of Urban and Regional Research* 25 (2): 227–252.

59. Frantz Fanon, *Black Skin, White Masks,* trans. by Charles Lam Markmann (New York: Grove Press, 1967).

60. http://www.afriqueindex.com/Afrique/afrique-index.htm.

61. http://www.afriqueindex.com, L'Afrique est ici. Accessed March 11, 2011.

62. Cliff Figalo, *Internet World: Hosting Web Communities* (New York: Wiley, 1998): 15.

63. The UCN (*Union de la Communauté Noire de France*; "Union of the Black Community of France") was founded in 2006 by the radio host Claudy Siar.

64. Capdiv or *Cercle d'Action pour la Promotion de la Diversité en France* "is a registered association ... composed of researchers, association leaders, people from civil society or the political world who want to reflect and make proposals to promote diversity in France" (Capdiv website).

65. Africagora, created in 1999, is a grouping of decision-makers, executives, and entrepreneurs from the Black Diaspora. It is chaired by Dogad Dogui. It advocates diversity and campaigns against ethno-racial discrimination.

66. Pierre Bourdieu, "Social Space and Symbolic Power," *Sociological Theory* 7, No. 1, (1989).

Chapter 3

The Comfort of *Blackness*: Using Cultural Immersion to Promote Mental Health

Barbara Streets

Race is a powerful social construct that impacts mood, volition, and health. This chapter details one of the numerous reasons why visiting West Africa is therapeutic for people of African descent: the use of cultural immersion as a defense to soothe the insults of racism and to maintain psychological health. This chapter argues that delving into *Blackness* can be a social and cultural salve, one that serves as a tool in the defense against the internalization of oppression, serving as emotional blocks against racism, and the maintenance of psychological health. Immersing into *Blackness* includes the education and examination of resistance strategies employed by Africans to resist enslavement. This chapter explores the legitimacy of embracing *Blackness* as a buffer against the deleterious health effects of racism and as an emotional antioxidant for coping.

Racism Exists

Racism exists in every facet of life,[1] but it is often denied. Teun A. van Dijk[2] outlines several ways in which individuals deny the existence of racism. He argues that this denial occurs on many levels. One type of denial is called *reversal*, which means, "We are not guilty of negative action, they are" and "We are not the racists, they are the real racists."[3] This can be seen in a recent case involving the edited video of Shirley Sherrod's address at a National Association for the Advancement of Colored People (NAACP) banquet in Georgia. In comparing the original footage with the edited version, as well as listening

to both Ms. Sherrod and statements from the family she assisted, one can as-
certain that even the well-meaning intentions and behaviors of historically
oppressed individuals can be construed and twisted by conservatives as evidence of racism.[4]

A recent online article entitled " 'Whites Suffer More Racism Than Blacks':
Study shows white American people believe they are more discriminated
against" further demonstrates a continued dismissal of the ways in which
racism continues to be experienced in the lives of visible ethnic and racial minority groups.[5] Disparities existing in education, employment, and housing
are intimately connected and related to a system of formal and informal practices that have privileged some groups and disadvantaged others.[6] For example, the median wealth of white households is twenty times that of black
households, and eighteen times that of Hispanic households.[7] Additionally,
"Blacks and Hispanics have borne a disproportionate share of both job losses
and the housing foreclosures."[8] In education, for individuals over age 25,
Whites are more than one and a half times as likely as Blacks to hold a bach-
elor's degree.[9] These disparities, which are often not critically examined by
privileged groups, create a worldview and life experience that is unknown
and often underappreciated.

Reversal of racism strategies obscures the systemic and institutional ways
racism continues to be experienced in the lives of visible ethnic and racial minority groups. In her classic work titled, *Understanding an Afrocentric Worldview*, psychologist Linda James Myers[10] notes that "European-Americans would
distort, deny, change, and repress their awareness of past behaviors and the
knowledge of the behaviors of their forbears to the extent that they would accept no responsibility for past actions and refuse to recognize any connection
of the past to their current functioning."[11] Denials of institutional racism often
occur in the twenty-first century U.S. because overt racist and discriminatory
practices are banned. North America proudly touts a visibly darker-skinned
president. However, racism exists and dominant groups are often oblivious to
this fact.

Racism Impacts Mental Health

Racism impacts mood, volition, and health.[12] This intolerance is a patho-
logical illness that impacts the sender and receiver not just "under the skin,"[13]
but also inside the mind. Studies have examined the impact of racism on
health,[14] and how racial inequality impacts biological well-being.[15] Experiences
of discrimination[16] and racism[17] can negatively impact mental health. Expe-

riences with discrimination may negatively impact cognitive engagement, self-esteem, and bonding.[18] One danger, in the medical field, for continuing to assign race groupings to people, in spite of prevailing evidence that race is biological fiction, is inaccurate genetic inferences for populations.[19] Instead, Ritchie Witzing[20] advocates for the use of the term ethnicity, which possibly provides more useful cultural information that can be used in clinical treatment and diagnosis.

The notion that race is a social construct and not a biological fact is accepted in many branches of the scientific community,[21] and has been demonstrated in legal scholarship.[22] In fact, 'racial' groups share a significant proportion (99.9%) of genes.[23] Though "races are still only human inventions,"[24] the emotional, psychological and biological impact of this social construct, racism, continues to unfold. According to Omi and Winant, race is "a matter of both social structure and cultural representation."[25] Race signifies difference and structures inequality. Racism is destructive psychologically, mentally, physically, culturally, and socially. Racism in housing, employment, the health, and legal systems, and in education yields consequences not only for the current recipient of racist practices, but also for generations to come. As a public health issue, racism has been responsible for the deaths of millions as often noted in two historical markers: the transatlantic slave trade and the Holocaust. Racist practices, such as the capture and transportation of Africans to the Americas, are a type of trauma that has had many implications. These include the financial, emotional, political, and social repercussions on subsequent generations of Americans of African descent.[26]

Buffers against Racism Are Essential

The perennial nature of racism requires the need for buffers in multiple institutional areas. These include social, legal, physical, and educational arenas. Practices such as racial socialization, which help buffer the deleterious impact of racism, promote resiliency in adults and children. Racial socialization pertains to the teaching of tasks, skills, dispositions, and abilities that help ethnically diverse children to thrive in an oppressive, hostile, or dismissive environment. Sometimes, such teaching is educational. Margaret Shih, Courtney Bonam, Diana Sanchez, and Courtney Peck found that helping participants understand the social construction of race served as a buffer against stereotype threat effects.[27] Essentially, educating students to resist the internalization of negative stereotypes was empowering. Racial socialization was found to relate to school engagement in a positive manner.[28] Lionel Scott found that racial socialization helped promote resilience and psychological adjustment in African Americans.[29]

Racial socialization in the form of an Afrocentric curriculum such as that discussed in the 1990s in African American immersion schools is another way to buffer African Americans against an emotionally hostile environment.[30] Researchers continue to identify the impact that culture can have on mental health recovery. For example, David Miller and Randall MacIntosh found that culturally relevant protective factors (a positive racial identity) can influence resiliency among minority adolescents.[31]

Cultural immersion as a socializing buffer can positively impact mental health. Intentional efforts to immerse oneself into study related to one's cultural history can promote a renewed sense of self, connectedness to others, and a desire to accept responsibility to uplift one's cultural group. Rose Morgan, Desideria Mwegelo and Laura Turner propose cultural immersion via study abroad as one way to increase understanding of their African sisters and the linkages between both cultures.[32] The benefits of this type of travel reported by the authors' compliments the tenets of racial socialization. Cultural immersion (via study abroad) to targeted spaces in Africa can be viewed as an intentional mental health effort to promote a racial socialization process that empowers, enlightens, and uplifts the Black spirit.

Cultural Immersion: Going Abroad to Maintain Psychological Health

According to Peter Crampton and his colleagues, cultural immersion is "an approach based on the principle that immersion in culture and language is an effective means of learning about oneself and about another culture [; it] provides opportunities for students to learn some of the principles associated with cultural safety."[33] Cultural immersion supports individuals interested in deepening the knowledge about their cultural heritage and using that information to buttress strength toward self-development and resistance to oppression.

Immersion into culture is one way to maintain psychological health. The term *immersion* is frequently associated with the laudable work of pioneers in the field of Black racial identity development and nigrescence theory.[34] As Janet Helms first used it, racial identity theory for people of color pertains to the developmental challenges and struggles related to "surmounting internalized racism in its various manifestations."[35] In her theory, the term *Immersion/ Emersion* pertains to an idealization of one's racial group, use of one's own racial group to self-evaluate, use of one's own racial group to self-define, and a denigration of that which is perceived as White. Frank Worrell and others suggest the need for two independent subscales to adequately demonstrate movement through Immersion/Emersion.[36]

To avoid confusion in the ongoing dialogue and research in nigrescence scholarship, I define how the term *Immersion* is used in this chapter. Immersion, specifically cultural immersion, pertains to the embracing and absorption of one's culture as a way to affirm, preserve, and surmount racism. It pertains to a process of actively researching, exploring, and examining one's cultural heritage and using lessons from that study to navigate and surmount racist experiences and lessen the consequences of debilitating emotional aggressions suffered in the present. Cultural immersion, as defined here, pertains to a willingness to be open to the power of one's spiritual ancestors to guide and support them.

Well aware of the vast diversity of experiences present in the Diaspora, my focus is on the one perspective of Blackness as I have experienced it as an African American in the USA. 'Black' is a self-proclaimed identity, where one is also identified in work and social community as Black or African American. As used here, Black equates to a US census racial designation, and an ethnic identity. As an ethnic identity, Black equates to a shared history in the United States with origins emanating from Africa, and the perception of a collective identity with other Blacks. As used here, Black has absolutely no connection with skin color or hair texture. Thus when the term *Blackness* is used, it refers to a shared history of African Americans with origins emanating from Africa, and a sense of collective identity with other Blacks in the African Diaspora.

Cultural Immersion into *Blackness*

From 2006–2010, I immersed in West African culture several times, four times to study dance, and one instance in a professional cultural exchange. On two occasions, this author visited Ghana and Guinea, and on one occasion, visited Benin. Though this first trip was initiated for multiple reasons, one clear reason had to do with needing a reprieve from personal experiences of racism in my professional work environment.[37] Racism experienced on the job has been my most taxing, damaging, and challenging professional experience to date. Visiting West Africa was a way to employ cultural immersion; it served as a defense to soothe the insults of racism, and helped maintain my psychological health. In the very first trip, prior to departure, I asked a mentor with whom I shared many experiences of racism what suggestions he could offer as I began the study abroad experience. He responded first by suggesting that I enjoy myself. Later, after submitting to continual requests, he asked me to reflect on the following statement:

> *How can I be me and deal with an imperfect world that is never going*
> *to be what I would hope and still maintain my integrity?*[38]

The statement, 'How can I be me?' recognizes that authenticity is vital for emotional health. Recognizing that identity is multifaceted, dynamic, and evolving, one part of 'me' was a dancer and felt most free in that medium; another part was one who wanted to *thrive,* not just survive in a racist environment; another part was one who felt connected to spirit when surrounded by dance and drum.

Going to West Africa meant going to a place where the majority of the time, and in most circles, at least phenotypically, the vast majority of people looked like me. The invisibility of my blackness in a sea of black beauty provided a flotation device; I could relax. If I dressed like the women in this new environment, if I assumed some culture specific feminine mannerisms, and if I adhered to behavioral expectations, at times, I could pass as a country national. The mere experience of being one among many was comforting. I was me, and I was home.

A pre-judgment based on race was not the most salient part of "me" in a world where most looked like me. For a brief time period, my phenotypically being was 'normal.' I could breathe. No doubt, other definers like language, gender, civil status, age, perceived wealth, and other categories of difference that carry meaning became salient depending on circumstance and location. For brief periods, there were moments akin to the comfort obtained from coming up from a watery depth to the surface and inhaling deeply, feeling renewed, free, and alive. Whereas the water might represent the stifling, pressured constraints of racism (in the U.S.), being in *this space* (West Africa), this oxygenated surface, offered equilibrium, albeit briefly. In these brief breaths, I remained delusion free of the politics of capitalism and the neo-imperialistic and oppressive practices that maintain power in the hands of foreigners, of religious colonization, 'unintended consequences' of monetary aid,[39] governmental waste of human potential, and multiple instances of inequality because the breath, though ephemeral, was real. I could be me, and still manage an imperfect world.

The Comfort of *Blackness*

The comfort is in knowing that in spite of it all, the resilience of a people cannot be crushed, and that I am a part of these people, and they are a part

Figure 1. Ganvie, Benin, 2009

of me. It is this knowing that strengthens the reserves for the struggles that await back home in the U.S., and fosters the respect I have for my brothers and sisters in West Africa. Delving into *Blackness* (as a social and cultural salve), served as one tool in the defense against the internalization of oppression, and maintenance of psychological health.

In delving or immersing into *Blackness,* I learned of the strength of our ancestors in a recent visit to Ganvié, a lake village near Cotonou, Benin, and home to 27,000 Tofinu people. These villagers live in homes constructed of bamboo situated on stilts on Lake Nokoué. Two of my colleagues and I rented a boat to glide us through one village. Our guide listed fourteen other stilt villages nearby. It was amazing to see homes, restaurants, places of worship, and the post office—all on stilts above water level (Figure 1). The Tofinu people fled from persecution to this swampy region in an effort to escape enslavement from the Dahomey slave-hunters in the seventeenth century. Knowing that the Dahomey would not venture into the water due to adherence to religious customs, they created a home and culture. The Tofinu sustain their livelihood from several forms of fishing. According to the guide, fishing from this area supports 15–20% of the Benin population. I respect the creative mastery to avoid capture, coupled with sustainable living in harmony with the environment as reflected in these villages.

On several occasions, I visited "slave castles" in Ghana (both Elmina Castle and Cape Coast Castle). Aware that the history of Africans in America does not begin with slavery in West Africa, these monuments are a frequented "first stop" for many people of African descent exploring their heritage and world history outside of the U.S. Insightful criticisms of the politics behind the naming of the fortresses as "slave castles" as well as the politics of the commodification of the sites are well noted by Brempong Osei-Tutu.[40] Notwithstanding, being inside the same dungeons where hundreds of enslaved men and women once treaded was a powerful experience. Learning about the exploitative conditions endured by the African captives before crossing the Atlantic was remarkable. Placing my hand atop the same structure where an enslaved and chained African carved his fingernails into the ground was unforgettable. Looking up from inside the dungeons at the ceiling that marked the bottom floor of a church (directly on top of the slave dungeons) where Christians sang and preached the gospel while ignoring the humanity of their brothers and sisters below was de-centering. Being in the same courtyard where African women were selected by European soldiers for sexual assault was horrifying. Though emotionally flooded by the torturous conditions, I am in awe of the strength and defiance toward the captors that the enslaved Africans exhibited.

On a fifth trip to West Africa, I walked the *Route des Esclaves* in Ouidah, Benin. I walked the four-kilometer route that marks the path that enslaved Africans took from the coast to waiting ships. This path led to the beach in front of the Door of No Return, the United Nations Educational, Scientific and Cultural Organization (UNESCO) Memorial to the transatlantic slave trade and one of the monuments associated with the Slave Route Project. Despite the numerous plural interpretations of slavery espoused by different monuments constructed in the area, my interest did not deviate from the viewpoint of the enslaved Africans and his/her narrative. This monument connects us to other revolutionary Diaspora fighters for liberation: Toussaint L'Ouverture, the liberator of Haiti, and Marcus Garvey, cultural revolutionary among African Americans. I paused before the marker, noting a 1990 archeological excavation that revealed the remains of hundreds of African bodies that resisted enslavement. A prayer made before the memorial gravesite included the wish that *I live a life that honors the sacrifice, history and integrity of my ancestors.* This prayer held the power and the comfort of *Blackness.*

Conclusion

As I reflected on the imperfect world of my ancestors, walked down the path taken by thousands, touched the spaces where their imprisoned bodies roamed, I felt I was left with few other alternatives for dealing with the racist environment back in the U.S. The zeitgeist present whispered: *You must thrive forward.* The comfort of *Blackness* comes from the recognition that the shared struggle is the link between now, then, and the future. The power that is gleaned from remembrance and mourning of the *Maafa* is that the resilience witnessed in the struggle is also the viewer's heritage, and that struggle continues. Other reflections included thinking that the source is always and will always be available to you, and the notion that if you align your consciousness and behavior with your passion, then you will find yourself right where you need to be. This framework reflects the works of scholars of an Afrocentric perspective on Black health and wellness.[41] The comfort of *Blackness* reflects a budding of mental consciousness into the values, responsibilities, and ethics of our African ancestors. It is an acknowledgement of one's historical place in the human story, and an awareness of resistance strategies utilized by our ancestors—and that this strength is available to me.

Intentional cultural immersion experiences complement culturally relevant education, promote self-reflection, and increase cultural self-esteem as well. Cultural immersion to specific locales in West Africa that educate or share historical or cultural information (such as museums, monuments, dance and drum centers/villages) can deepen a sense of connectedness to others. While cultural immersion experiences can and do occur in the home country, getting away to a new culture helps to widen one's perspective. Cultural immersion supports the embracing of *Blackness* as a buffer against the deleterious health effects of racism—it is an emotional antioxidant for coping.

As I revisit the impact of colonialism through cultural immersion, I am able to compare and contrast modern day colonial practices in a narrower sphere, which is the world of work, and reflect on strategies for enhanced coping. More importantly, via cultural immersion, as I align my spirit with my consciousness, I am immediately uplifted. This upliftedness is not ripe with a deluded, Pollyannaish perspective, but one of knowing that the world is, has been, and remains imperfect. It is a knowing that makes no apologies. Racism is a real experience in the lives of many, and is connected to negative health outcomes. We owe it to ourselves to do what we must to remain healthy. Cultural immersion into *Blackness* is one legitimate option.

Notes

1. Beverly Greene, "Institutional Racism in the Mental Health Professions," in *Racism in the Lives of Women: Testimony, Theory and Guides to Antiracist Practice*, eds. Jeanne Adleman and Gloria Enguídanos (New York: Harrington Park Press, 1995), 113–125. Jennifer L. Eberhardt and Susan T. Fiske, eds. *Confronting Racism: The Problem and the Response* (Thousand Oaks, CA: Sage Publications, 1998), ix–xiii. Suzy Fox and Lamont Stallworth, *Racial/ethnic Bullying: Exploring Links between Bullying and Racism in the US Workplace, Journal of Vocational Behavior* 66 (2005), 438–456. Elizabeth Higginbotham, *Too Much To Ask: Black Women in the Era of Integration* (Chapel Hill, NC: The University of North Carolina Press, 2001), 204–232.

2. Teun A van Dijk, "Discourse and the Denial of Racism," *Discourse and Society* 3, No. 1 (1992), 94.

3. Ibid.

4. Johnathan Gurwitz, "Racism, Bigotry of Every Stripe Still Exists," *San Antonio Express News,* (July 31, 2010), available in http://www.deseretnews.com/article/700052437/Racism-bigotry-of-every-stripe-still-exist.html.

5. *Daily Mail Reporter*, "Whites suffer more racism than blacks': Study shows white American people believe they are more discriminated against" (May, 2011). Available in http://www.dailymail.co.uk/news/article-1390205/Whites-suffer-racism-blacks-Study-shows-white-people-believe-discriminated-against.html.

6. Joshua Miller and Ann M. Garran, *Racism in the United States: Implications for the Helping Professions* (Belmont, CA: Brooks Cole 2008), 86.

7. Pew Research Center, "Wealth Gaps Rise to Record Highs between Whites, Blacks, Hispanics Twenty-to-One," *Pew Social & Demographic Trends* (July 2011). Available at http://www.pewsocialtrends.org/2011/07/26/wealth-gaps-rise-to-record-highs-between-whites-blacks-hispanics/?src=prc-headline.

8. Pew Research Center, "Adding Context to the Census Bureau's Income and Poverty Report," *Pew Social & Demographic Trends* (September 2011). Available at, http://www.pewsocialtrends.org/2011/09/12/adding-context-to-the-census-bureaus-income-and-poverty-report/.

9. National Urban League, "The State of Black America, Executive Summary," (2011). Available at, http://www.nul.org/content/state-black-america-executive-summary.

10. Linda J. Myers, *Understanding an Afrocentric Worldview: Introduction to an Optimal Psychology*, 2nd Edition (Dubuque, Iowa: Kendal/Hunt Publishing Company, 1993), 9.

11. Ibid, 9.

12. Nacey Dess, "The Race for Good Health," *Psychology Today* Vol. 32 No.2 (2001), 26.

13. Alan Goodman, "Why Genes don't Count For Racial Differences in Health," *American Journal of Public Health* Vol. 90, No.11 (2000), 1699–1702.

14. Rosalind M. Peters, "The Relationship of Racism, Chronic Stress Emotions, and Blood Pressure," *Journal of Nursing Scholarship* Vol. 38, No. 3 (2006), 234–240.

15. Clarence C. Gravlee, "How Race Becomes Biology: Embodiment of Social Inequality," *American Journal of Physical Anthropology*, Vol. 139, No. 1(2009), 47–57.

16. David R. Williams and Ruth Williams-Morris, "Racism and Mental Health: The African American Experience," *Ethnicity & Health*, Vol. 5, No.3/4 (2000), 243–268.

17. James H. Carter, "Racism's Impact on Mental Health," *Journal of the National Med-*

ical Association, Vol. 86, No. 7 (1994), 543–547.

18. Aryn Dotterer, Susan M. McHale and Ann C. Crouter, "Sociocultural Factors and School Engagement Among African American Youth: Roles of Racial Discrimination, Racial Socialization and Ethnic Identity," *Applied Developmental Science*, Vol. 13, No. 2 (2009), 61–73.

19. Richie Witzig, "The Medicalization of Race: Scientific Legitimization of a Flawed Social Construct," *Annals of Internal Medicine*, Vol.125, No. 8 (1996), 675–679.

20. Ibid, 675–679.

21. Alan Goodman, "Why Genes don't Count (For Racial Differences in Health)," *American Journal of Public Health*, Vol. 90, No.11 (2000), 1699–1702. Audrey Smedley and Brian D. Smedley, "Race as Biology is Fiction, Racism as a Social Problem is Real: Anthropological and Historical Perspectives on the Social Construction of Race," *American Psychology*, Vol. 60, No.1 (2005), 16–26.

22. Ian Haney-López, *White by Law, the Legal Constitution of Race* (New York: New York University Press, 1996), 1–40. Bill O. Hing, "Vigilante Racism: The De Americanization of Immigrant America," *Michigan Journal of Race and Law*, Vol. 7 (2002), 1–16.

23. Pounder, C.C. H., Larry Adelman, Jean Cheng, Christine Herbes-Sommers, Tracy Heather Strain, Llewellyn Smith, and Claudio Ragazzi. *Race: The Power of an Illusion* (San Francisco, Calif: California Newsreel, 2003). James Shreeve, "The Greatest Journey," *National Geographic Magazine*, (2006). Available, http://ngm.nationalgeographic.com/2006/03/human-journey/sheeve-text.html.

24. Ian Haney-López, *White by Law, the Legal Constitution of Race* (New York: New York University Press, 1996), 1–40.

25. Michael Omi and Howard Winant, *Racial Formation in the United States: From the 1960s to the 1980s* (New York: Routledge & Kegan Paul, 1986), 56.

26. Joy DeGruy, "Post Slavery Syndrome: A Multigenerational look at African American Injury, Healing and Resilience," in *Mass Trauma and Emotional Healing around the World: Rituals and Practices for Resilience and Meaning Making, Volume 2: Human Made Disasters,* eds. Ani Kalayjian and Dominique Eugene (Santa Barbara, CA: Praeger, 2010), 227–250.

27. Margaret Shih, Courtney Bonam, Diana Sanchez and Courtney Peck, "The Social Construction of Race: Biracial Identity and Vulnerability to Stereotypes," *Cultural Diversity and Ethnic Minority Psychology*, Vol. 13, No. 2 (2007), 125–133.

28. Aryn Dotterer, Susan M. McHale and Ann C. Crouter, "Sociocultural Factors and School Engagement Among African American Youth: Roles of Racial Discrimination, Racial Socialization and Ethnic Identity," *Applied Developmental Science*, Vol. 13, No. 2 (2009), 61–72.

29. Lionel D. Scott, "The Relation of Racial Identity and Racial Socialization to Coping with Discrimination Among African American Adolescents," *Journal of Black Studies*, Vol. 33, No. 4 (2003), 520–538.

30. Lani V. Jones, Eric R. Hardiman and Jenneth Carpenter, "Mental Health Recovery: A Strengths Based Approach to Culturally Relevant Behavior in the Social Environment," *Journal of Human Behavior in the Social Environment*, Vol. 15, No. 2/3 (2007), 251–269.

31. David Miller and Randall MacIntosh, "Promoting Resilience in urban African American Adolescents: Racial Socialization and Identity as Protective Factors," *Social Work Research*, Vol. 23, No. 3 (September 1999), 159–169.

32. Rose Morgan, Desideria Mwegelo and Laura Turner, "Black Women in the African Diaspora Seeking Their Cultural Heritage Through Studying Abroad," *NASPA Journal (National Association of Student Personnel Administrators)*, Vol. 39, No. 4 (2002), 333–353.

33. Peter Crampton, Anthony Dowell, Chris Parkin and Caroline Thompson, "Combating effects of racism through a cultural immersion medical education program," *Academic Medicine: Journal Of The Association Of American Medical Colleges*, Vol. 78, No. 6 (June 2003), 596.

34. Janet E. Helms, "An Update of Helm's White and People of Color Racial Identity Models." In *Handbook of Multicultural Counseling*, eds., J. G. Ponterotto, J. M Casas, L. A. Suzuki, and C. M. Alexander (Thousand Oaks, California: Sage, 1995), 181–198. William E. Cross Jr., "The Negro to Black Conversion Experience," *Black World*, Vol. 20 (1971), 13–27. Frank C. Worrell, William E. Cross and Beverly J. Vandiver, "Nigrescence Theory: Current Status and Challenges for the Future," *Multicultural Counseling and Development*, Vol. 29 (2001), 201–213.

35. Janet E. Helms, "An Update of Helm's White and People of Color Racial Identity Models," in *Handbook of Multicultural Counseling*, eds., J. G. Ponterotto, J. M Casas, L. A. Suzuki, and C. M. Alexander (Thousand Oaks, California: Sage, 1995), 184.

36. Frank C. Worrell, William E. Cross and Beverly J. Vandiver, *Nigrescence Theory: Current Status and Challenges for the Future, Multicultural Counseling and Development*, Vol. 29 (2001), 201–213.

37. Barbara F. Streets, "Deepening Multicultural Competencies through Immersion in West African Dance Camps," *Journal of Dance Education*, Vol. 11, No. 3 (2011), 83.

38. Gerald Porter, personal communication, 2006.

39. Danbisa Moyo, *Dead Aid: Why Aid is not Working and how there is a better way for Africa* (New York: Farrar, Straus and Giroux, 2009).

40. Brempong Osei-Tutu, "The African American Factor in the Commodification of Ghana's Slave Castles," *Transactions of the Historic Society of Ghana* (2002), 115–133. Brempong Osei-Tutu, "African American Reactions to the Restoration of Ghana's Slave Castles," *Public Archaeology* (2004), 195–204.

41. Linda J. Myers, *Understanding an Afrocentric Worldview: Introduction to an Optimal Psychology*, 2nd Edition (Dubuque Iowa: Kendal/Hunt Publishing Company 1993), 7–29. Wade W. Nobles, "African Philosophy: Foundations for Black Psychology," in *Black Psychology*, ed., R. L. Jones (New York: Harper & Row, 1972), 18–32. Thomas A. Parham, Joseph L. White and Adisa Ajamu, *The Psychology of Blacks: An African American Centered Perspective* (Upper Saddle River, New Jersey: Prentice Hall, 2000).

Chapter 4

Envisioned Communities: The African Diaspora and Interwar Race Films

Cara Caddoo

On the morning of August 19, 1923, French police rushed into the Salle Marivaux Theater in Paris and shut its doors to the stunned public.[1] The theater manager pleaded with the police; he could see no reason why the venue should be closed. He had followed all necessary regulations, and had obtained approval for the film, *La Naissance d'une nation,* from the board of censors. The Prefecture of the Police simply responded that their actions were necessary "for the good of the public."[2] A more detailed explanation emerged the following day. The order had been issued directly by Premier Raymond Poincaré; he objected to *La Naissance d'une nation*'s depiction of black and white relations, and argued the ban was necessary to "avoid race troubles between foreign visitors and French negroes."[3] Reporters stationed in the city were taken aback by the Poincaré's sudden decision. The film, known in the United States as *Birth of a Nation,* was certainly controversial; but it had screened in France during the war, and the government had already passed it for re-release.[4]

Poincaré's turnabout followed on the heels of a well-publicized incident in the French capital. Two weeks earlier, a group of white American tourists had complained about the presence of black clientele at the El Garòn nightclub in Montmartre. Management escorted two black men out of the club, one of whom turned out to be the well-connected "Dahomean Prince," Kojo Touvalou Houénou.[5] Outraged black residents of Paris, including a contingency of Senegalese deputies, immediately drew a connection between the event and the influence of American racial propaganda upon France—especially the all-pervasive moving image. Across the Atlantic, *The Chicago Defender* watched the drama unfold. The paper reported that Americans, "greedy for gold and warped

61

with racial and color prejudice," were using their "detestable films" to transplant Jim Crow segregation overseas.[6] The *Baltimore Afro-American* similarly believed white Americans were attempting "to institute the 'color line' in Paris as they have instituted it in Cuba and one or two South American countries ...."[7] Black American newspapers resoundingly approved of the French government's orders to block the film and remove its advertisements from Parisian theaters. Reporters depicted the event as an exercise in democratic justice—and as a political necessity for the French Republic. The *Pittsburgh Courier* wrote: "[Poincaré] is being pressed on his present course by Negro deputies and by fear of losing their support in the Algerian elections." Nodding to the black American veterans of World War I, the paper explained France could not militarily afford to "affront her North African citizens."[8]

The responses to *La Naissance d'une nation* bore the footprints of an older history. The significance of the ban resonated widely because of the prominence and ubiquity of cinema in early twentieth century Black life. Of course, conceptions of "the race" developed prior to and alongside those formed in conversation with cinema—ideas of what it meant to be Black took countless routes, many of which bypassed the moving image altogether.[9] However, a surprisingly broad range of individuals and organizations talked about, organized around, or produced cinema when attempting to make sense of abstract shared oppressions or claims to a common historical and cultural past. From London, England to Louisville, Kentucky, the Black press reported on the latest happenings in the motion picture world. Artists and intellectuals of the Harlem Renaissance and the Negritude Movement reflected on film's significance and role in shaping black identity. A spectrum of ideologies, from Garveyites to black Marxists, linked racism to the influence of motion pictures. Little consensus existed on how to represent the race, but a mutual desire to re-appropriate depictions of blackness in moving pictures was distinctive of interwar black politics. In essence, the diaspora envisioned itself through a shared interest in cinema as a global industry and as a medium of representation.[10]

Cinema and interwar diasporic thought swept into the twentieth century on the same coattails of change. Industrialization and urbanization, in particular, brought together the social practices and technologies that converged into modern cinema. Similarly, the migration of African, American, and European black populations into urban industrial centers produced new demands for commercial amusements. Black workers sought leisure activities that enabled them to reclaim their bodies and a sense of autonomy after grueling hours of industrial and domestic labor.[11] Cinema emerged to meet their demands; its emphasis on visual and cognitive stimulation and its ability to fit into the burgeoning culture of consumption produced a form of media with an exceptional ability to express and mediate modern life.[12] Additionally, the global film industry facilitated the development of transnational thought. Systems of international distribution created powerful tools for disseminating ideas to large numbers of people across vast geographical spaces.[13] And compared to most books or newspapers, cinema was less reliant upon text; its visual vernacular required relatively little translation as it traveled across the linguistic borders of the African diaspora.[14]

This chapter examines the transnational black identity envisioned and promoted by the early race film industry.[15] Scholars have focused on the conspicuously national themes of loyalty, patriotism, and the American West in interwar race films. Jacqueline Stewart, J. Ronald Green, Pearl Bowser and Louise Spence, and Dan Moos have explored how black Americans claimed their rights as citizens through cinema and spectatorship.[16] However, examining the content of these films in relation to the race film industry's business strategies brings to relief the interconnected development of black national and international identities. The Foster Photoplay Company, The Lincoln Motion Picture Company, Oscar Micheaux, and other race film producers marketed themselves and their films as tools for black progress. They believed self-sufficient Black industries were essential to the collective advancement of the race. A profitable Black film industry, race producers argued, could effectively blunt the pernicious propaganda of white Hollywood. This vision of cooperative Black progress was not unique. But because the moving picture industry was global from its inception, race film companies were especially aware of their place within the international economy.[17] In particular, the desire for overseas markets produced an often-overlooked articulation of diasporic consciousness.

An Image Spans the Globe

On July 4, 1910, a resounding left hook catapulted the race question to the center of international debates over film censorship. Black pugilist Jack Johnson had knocked "The Great White Hope," Jim Jefferies, nearly unconscious in the most anticipated boxing match of the new century. A dozen Motion Picture Patents Company cameras captured the action.[18] For the first time in the history of professional boxing, a black man held the sport's most coveted title—Johnson was the undisputed heavyweight champion of the world. The news sparked off waves of riots and anti-black violence. As a test of mental acuity and physical stamina, boxing had become a cherished symbol of white masculine power. Johnson's victory threatened these beliefs and the tenants of scientific racism that supported them.[19] Authorities immediately instituted bans on the Johnson-Jeffries fight pictures across the colonial world. The Walsall Watch Committee and The London Country Council passed a resolution to outlaw films of Johnson's victory in late July.[20] Politicians in the United States responded likewise. Within days of the fight, state and local governments had announced plans to block exhibition of the films in North Carolina, Tennessee, and Connecticut.[21] In 1912, the U.S. Congress passed the Sims Act, which prohibited the transportation of fight films across state borders.[22] The act initiated the federal government's involvement in film censorship and tied it explicitly to the maintenance of the existing racial order.

On both sides of the Atlantic, black newspapers argued that censorship of the films indicated a shared global oppression of "the darker races." Tswana newspaper editor Sol Plaatje described the British Empire's response to the pictures as a form of colonial control. Permitting exhibition of the films in South Africa "will mean that the Natives will secure pictures of whites being chased by coloured men," he wrote, "and who knows what harm such pictures may do?"[23] In the United States, the *Baltimore Afro-American* criticized the hypocrisy of the "constant agitation against the moving pictures."[24] The *New York Age* agreed: "If a white man had won the battle there would have been no such outcry."[25] The paper then linked the control of the U.S. over the visual representation of blackness to the social and economic control of colonized Africans and Asians:

> The fight pictures were shut out of everywhere that the law and public opinion could accomplish it: especially was this done in European Africa. Johnson's single victory had the same shocking, awful influence on the English speaking peoples towards Africa and the black peoples that the Japanese victory over the savage Russian hordes had on the rest of Europe and America towards the red, the yellow and the black people of Asia.[26]

The black press noted that films depicting black achievements were censored, but those negatively depicting the race were freely exported across the world. Film critic Lester Walton wrote a scathing review of a French Pathé Company picture that showed well-behaved German children marching to church in their Sunday best, while black children were depicted as dirty "pickaninnies." Another scene, supposedly comic, showed a black woman being disinfected by health officials. "To every section of the globe are these motion pictures sent ..." Walton lamented, "... in England, Germany, France, and Russia the natives see only pictures of the worst of us ...."[27]

Walton and other critics called for black-produced moving pictures that could disseminate positive images of the race. But generating investments or demand for race films still proved a challenge. Would-be Black filmmakers struggled, and often failed, to raise funds for their projects. The first black-produced films were usually small-scale projects commissioned by an individual or organization for itinerant exhibition rather than for commercial distribution.[28] For example, traveling showman W.G. Haynes filmed the National Baptist Convention and Women's Auxiliary in 1905, and in 1910, the Tuskegee Institute produced a moving picture to promote the school and its vision of black economic development.[29] William Foster was one of the few pre-WWI producers to follow a business model centered on distribution. The experienced showman and relentless entrepreneur had once profited by selling buttons of Jack Johnson by mail order. In 1913, he announced plans for a new venture: the Foster Photoplay Company.[30] With dazzling language, Foster boasted his all-black crew would show the world the "best of the race."[31] The Foster Photoplay Company launched an impressive publicity campaign and produced *The Railroad Porter* in July. Foster enjoyed some short-lived success, but his company was an exception; the race film industry had yet to come to fruition.[32]

Conditions for independent film companies changed in 1915. That year, several factors converged to fuel the emergence of the race film industry. Black commercial theaters developed more stable networks through which film producers could distribute moving pictures.[33] In the spring, D.W. Griffith released *Birth of a Nation* to worldwide audiences. The economic success of his film, and its perceived effects upon race relations provided fresh impetus for the creation of Black independent film companies. Critics compared the censorship of Johnson's prizefight films to the unregulated depictions of black Americans in *Birth of a Nation*:

> American moneyed interests and their allies are trying hard to enslave the Negroes who fought and died to save the Union .... With this new slavery our fellow citizens are fighting [to] place the shackles on us again. WE, the American Negroes, prefer death rather than submit. Why were they so anxious to keep the Jeffries-Johnson fight off the screen? We, then, demand The Dirt of a Nation canned.[34]

Protests against Griffith's film introduced thousands of black Americans to formal politics and protest and greatly expanded the ranks of organizations such as the NAACP. The NAACP's national secretary, Mary Childs Nerney, explained that *Birth of a Nation* had "creat[ed] a powerful opinion against this idea of the Negro ...." Despite large-scale coordinated efforts, protests had "gotten nowhere." Nerney suggested the race produce its own films, explaining, "we cannot create [public opinion] except in some such spectacular way."[35] Her words resonated with a population disillusioned by scores of failed lawsuits, petitions, and pickets.

Arguing that "[m]oving picture producers and distributors have the biggest political influence of any industry in the world," black producers moved in to claim their piece of the pie.[36] Two critical changes in the American film industry enabled these companies to gain a foothold in the business. First, the move to incorporate race film companies occurred at a particularly opportune moment for independent producers. For years, Thomas Edison's Motion Picture Patents Company (MPPC) had monopolized film production and distribution in the United States through standardized run times, licensing fees, and rental prices. In 1911, the tides began to change as William Fox and other independent white producers launched a series of lawsuits and campaigns against the Edison Trust. In 1912, the Department of Justice joined the fray and sued the MPPC for engaging in unfair business practices.[37] By the time the Supreme Court declared the Trust illegal in 1915, independent companies had taken control of the industry.[38] Second, WWI transformed the international film market, pushing American film exports to unprecedented heights in the post war years as European film companies struggled to recover their markets. As Gerben Bakker has shown, European companies produced at least half of the films exhibited in the U.S. in the first decade of the century. During WWI, the European share of the American and international film markets virtually disappeared.

Investing in the Race

The desire to resist negative images was not the only—or even the primary impetus for the emergence of the new race film industry. Most companies explicitly linked racial progress to profits. Race film companies embraced the philosophy of self-help through black business ownership, an idea that was also promoted by the racial uplift ideologies of C.J. Walker and the black nationalism of Marcus Garvey.[39] The enormous profits earned by *Birth of a Nation* had also exposed the economic potential of the global film industry. Previously underfunded companies received startup capital, and scores of new organizations filed for business licenses. Booker T. Washington proposed making a moving picture based on his autobiography.[40] Several companies directly challenged *Birth of a Nation* with their film narratives and promotional materials. The Photoplay Corporation's *Birth of a Race* solicited nearly half a million dollars in investments.[41] From 1915 through the interwar years, black newspapers were filled with advertisements seeking investors for their projects. The black press heralded the organization of race film companies and the production of new films as an indication of racial progress.[42] Additionally, by incorporating themselves under names such as the Crispus Attucks News Review, the Eagle Film Company, Harlemwood Productions, the Progress Film Production Company, and The Democracy Photoplay Corporation, producers encouraged the public to associate social and political progress with race pictures.[43]

Many of these newly formed companies emphasized the patriotism and loyalty of African Americans. Frequently, fictional storylines and documentary footage underscored black contributions to the nation's war efforts. Films such as *The Colored American Winning His Suit, The Heroic Black Soldiers of the War*, and *Loyal Hearts* featured black soldiers and Red Cross nurses in France. Meanwhile, the distribution plans for race films indicated a nascent black diasporic consciousness. The names of many of these companies expressed transnational interests even as they produced films emphasizing black patriotism. These included the Congo Film Service, International Stage Players Pictures, Globe Pictures Corp, and the Pyramid Picture Corporation. The Lincoln Motion Picture Company's successful debut film, *The Trooper of Troop K*, highlighted the sacrifices black soldiers made for American interests in Mexico. George P. Johnson's plans to market the film included not only the southern United States, but also other countries such as Cuba.[44] Lincoln also claimed to have hosted a private screening in New York City for companies wishing to export Lincoln films to "Spain, Europe, Africa, Cuba, Hayti, Hawaii, Australia, South America and Australia (sic)."[45] The race film industry's emphasis on black contributions to America's war efforts paralleled similar claims to martial citizenship by black French colonial subjects. As responses to *La Naissance d'une nation* in 1923 illustrate, shared claims to national citizenship could foster transnational articulations of black identity.

Similarly, William Foster organized his Foster Photoplay Company with a global market in mind. The black press reported "that the great demand for colored comedies in Europe brought about the deal [for Foster's movie studio]."[46] Foster connected the promise of these markets to the social and economic advancement of the race. He explained that moving pictures were " … the first big opportunity ever presented to race business men to make money."[47] It was time, he announced, for black film companies to capture the international market for motion pictures depicting the race. Foster told the *Chicago Defender* that white-owned companies were already capitalizing on this demand. "Strange as it may seem," he explained, "Afro-American moving pictures are a big hit throughout Europe. Every big manufacturer in the country has made photoplays of the race and sent them to the old country."[48] Race pictures would show blacks in a different light, unlike "pictures [which appealed] only to the ignorant class and race-hating whites."[49] In other words, it would be foolish to let whites profit off of the global demand for products that black Americans were better equipped to produce.

Most explicitly, race film companies declared that a commitment to racial progress and international recognition required black individuals to invest in their stocks. The Democracy Film Corporation's ads boldly asserted that it was "[your] duty to your race to buy stock in the Democracy Film Corporation." Its planned production, *Injustice*, would "bring sympathy for the race throughout the world" and "show the world the beauty and virtue of the colored woman …." For those with limited liquid assets, "loyalty to your race" could be purchased with liberty bonds in lieu of cash.[50] The Lincoln Motion Picture Company ran similar half page advertisements in papers such as the *Chicago Defender* and the *Advocate*. Ads claimed to offer "*The Secret of Getting Rich!*" and explained that African Americans were "… disgusted in seeing themselves being burlesqued and made the 'goat.' "[51] Lincoln's advertisements explained that it would not only elevate the reputation of the race in America, but also across the entire world. The Foster Photoplay Company told potential shareholders that cinema was the "world's greatest educator." Moving pictures had long misrepresented the race to the outside world. It was now time to "have a spark of race pride" and "let the world see the best of the race," by investing in the company.[52]

Black Race Films and International Markets

Race film producers devised a range of strategies to tap into the international market. They connected their businesses to racial unity by producing projects with diasporic themes. In 1920, the Delsarte Film Corporation offered stocks to "careful investors" interested in a film about "The Abraham Lincoln of Haiti"—Toussaint L'Ouverture. The marketing campaign implied a common transnational history; black Americans were invited to celebrate L'Ouverture and emancipation in Haiti as a shared victory for the race. According to the Associated Negro Press, the picture was to screen simultaneously in Broadway theaters and in Paris, France for ten weeks in 1921. Afterwards, the film would be exhibited throughout the world.[53] Producers also sought performers whose names could draw audiences both at home and abroad. Jack Johnson, by then an international celebrity, fit the bill. Race producers scrambled to sign Johnson to their pictures. *The Chicago Defender* reported, "Jack Johnson's popularity through Mexico is the principal reason" that the Douglas Photoplay syndicate was "eager to secure him for a part at any cost."[54]

Even themes of American exceptionalism gestured to a greater transnational sense of identity as American-produced race films sought to create a specific niche in the global moving picture market. Following WWI, the growing dominance of Hollywood compelled various national cinemas to develop distinguishing characteristics in order to remain competitive. German Expressionism, for example, enabled Weimar Republic filmmakers to compete with higher-budget imported moving pictures.[55] Race film producers responded to the popularity of Hollywood-style cinema by building upon the industry's conventions and by highlighting the unique qualities of black-produced film. For instance, the genre of the American Western was not only popular in America, but also among black filmgoers across the diaspora. The widespread appeal of the genre indicated that spectators read these films as more than stories of the literal promises of the American West.[56] From the 1920s to the post World War II era, the demand for Westerns outpaced that of all other genres in places such as Kenya, the Rhodesias, and South Africa.[57] It is no surprise then, that race film companies (which longed for foreign distribution to global black and white audiences) produced so many pictures about black cowboys and the frontier.[58] Films such as *The Homesteader*, *The Bull Dogger*, and *Black Gold* featured black protagonists who overcame obstacles and fought to achieve their dreams.[59] The Black Western emphasized desires that were hardly unique to the United States; narratives of democracy, independence, and economic mobility could therefore bridge national and international aspirations.

Another challenge for many race film producers was distribution. Developing international networks of distribution required extensive marketing channels. During the 1910s and 1920s, a symbiotic relationship developed between the black press and race film producers. George P. Johnson, like many of those involved in the business—including Foster and Micheaux—had long been connected with the black newspaper industry. Johnson had run a black paper in Tulsa, Oklahoma before joining Lincoln as the company's booking manager. Johnson utilized his connections and knowledge of the black press to disseminate information about the Lincoln Company's newest releases and to attract investments. Lincoln advertisements, like most successful race film companies, appeared in papers across the country. By the 1920s, motion picture industry advertisements constituted an important percentage of newspaper revenue.[60] In order to attract advertisements, papers claimed wide distribution domestically and abroad. Even small Midwest papers such as *The Bystander* of Des Moines, Iowa promised Lincoln that its advertisements would reach "thirty-eight states and two foreign countries."[61] Other newspapers provided advice on how to expand their shared markets. For example, Romeo Dougherty of the *New York Amsterdam News* suggested the Lincoln Company distribute its films in the Caribbean:

By the way (again), our papers are being circulated to a great extent in the new Virgin Islands and as they have at least one moving picture house, I was wondering if you could not get in touch with the people there and try to do some business … they have never seen a colored motion picture acted by colored people I figure it would be a knock-out as the bulk of the population is colored. If you so desire you can write to Mr. E. Sebastian ….[62]

By coordinating business practices, race film companies and black newspapers worked together for their mutual benefit. In fact, some race film producers even worked concurrently within the black press. In 1923, George P. Johnson organized The Pacific Coast News Bureau, a Los Angeles based business dedicated to "disseminating Racial News of National and Inter-national Importance."[63] Johnson selected news he deemed "of interest" to the race, but also received requests for coverage on topics such as black business opportunities in Mexico.[64] Writing under the pseudonym, "George Perry," Johnson sometimes reported directly for papers such as *The Chicago Defender*. Not surprisingly, both Pacific News Bureau and "George Perry" specialized in entertainment news. Dispatches on German censorship of Famous Players—Lasky Productions' "off color" depictions of Africans, as well as news of the foreign government's efforts to rule out films offensive to Latinos were interspersed with stories encouraging readers to support race films.[65]

Many companies solicited funds by boasting of foreign markets, but ultimately failed to produce any films to export. A few individuals attempted to unscrupulously capitalize on the race film "craze." The white-owned Delight Film Corporation of Chicago, Illinois, run by Stephen Von Lorthy, claimed to have connections to the industry "both in this country and abroad."[66] Delight "flooded the United States with circulars, mail and half page advertisements" with plans to film an all-black version of Othello.[67] Investigations later revealed that the company was "swindling" funds without any real plans to produce moving pictures.[68] Other companies were more sincere in their claims, but equally flawed in their execution. The Constellation Film Corporation advertised its "Class A stock" in the *Crisis*. Describing itself as an enterprise devoted to the "elevation and the picturization of [the race's] brightest side," the company estimated its foreign business in the West Indies and South America would substantially increase its profits.[69] Relying too heavily on undeveloped markets contributed to Constellation's failure to produce any films.[70] But even organizations with impressive backing such as the Monumental Film Company had difficulties. Listing W.E.B. Du Bois, Leila Walker Wilson (heir to the Walker hair fortune), and Alice Dunbar Nelson on its glamorous advisory board, Monumental claimed its productions would "attract national and international attention."[71] Nevertheless, the company only produced one or two films during its short existence.[72]

Oscar Micheaux and the Open Frontier

Perhaps more than any other race filmmaker, Oscar Micheaux was acutely aware of the need to generate widespread publicity for his films. Micheaux's enterprising tactics exemplify how race film companies' desires for broader markets ushered in diasporic connections. Scholars of Micheaux's books and films have examined his rugged American individualism and his eschewal of particular internationalist politics. Moos dubbed Micheaux a "black Turnerian," and Green has written: "... Micheaux might have considered aspects of PanAfricanism and Negritude to be unprogressive."[73] According to Joseph Young, "Micheaux would not or could not understand the Pan African movement ... [n]or would he comprehend the importance of Negritude."[74] Additionally, Pearl Bowser and Louise Spence have written that Micheaux may have made claims to international markets because he considered Europe "glamorous." Though the Americanism of Micheaux's films have been well documented, it is also important to consider the deeper motivations—such as the quest for profits—that drove Micheaux's internationalism. Certainly, Micheaux did not directly associate himself with any formal Pan Africanist movement.[75] But during the interwar years, he attempted to attract an international market by featuring broadly appealing storylines and characters, and by employing the international celebrity, Paul Robeson.

As Bowser and Spence have pointed out, Micheaux connected black economic autonomy to racial uplift.[76] In 1905, he acquired a tract of land in South Dakota through the Homestead Act. Through the black press, he encouraged fellow African Americans to take advantage of the government's land grants. Micheaux believed the West offered the race boundless opportunities. In an article for the *Chicago Defender*, he argued, "the Negro must become more self-supporting. Farm lands are the bosses of wealth."[77] Micheaux emphasized similar themes of self-determination as a race filmmaker. He frequently implored fellow members of the race to support black businesses, thereby limiting the power white industry had over their lives. As an avid businessman, his enthusiasm for enterprise fueled his interest in the race film industry. As a filmmaker, Micheaux envisioned a frontier with even greater potential for freedom and prosperity than the mythical American West. His frontier spanned the globe beginning with the vast black populations whose full commercial potential and desire for self-representation were still yet unfulfilled.

While Micheaux was in production for *Within Our Gates*, he sent a letter to George P. Johnson describing his plans to distribute his moving pictures internationally. After finishing the film, he intended to shoot one more—probably *The Brute*—and then find "somebody to go abroad in the interest of our pictures for world distribution" so he could dedicate his time to production.[78] Micheaux probably expected to find an international market for his older films, *Symbol of the Unconquered* and possibly *The Homesteader,* in addition to his latest features.[79] Micheaux eventually decided against sending a representative abroad, or he may have been unable to find a suitable candidate to travel overseas for his company. In January of 1920, he announced that he was planning to take the trip himself. Micheaux remarked: "The appreciation my people have shown my maiden efforts convince me that they want Racial photoplays, depicting Racial life, and to that task I have consecrated my mind and efforts."[80] By "my people," Micheaux was referring simultaneously to his fellow black Americans as well as the global black audiences he hoped to encounter during his journey.

It is unlikely that Micheaux made his way to Europe. His name does not seem to appear on the Entry/Exit records of major American and Western European ports that year.[81] Instead, his ambitions were probably placed in the hands of another enterprising individual. In 1913, Joseph Pierre Lamy had immigrated to New York from France. His skills were well matched for film export. He could read and write in French and English, and possibly Spanish since he lived with his Spanish-speaking mother-in-law.[82] Lamy worked in some capacity with Fox Pictures' export business during WWI, but a few years later, it appears he was acquiring new clients.[83] Lamy and Micheaux probably met in New York after Oscar moved his company to Harlem from Chicago in 1920. It is unclear whether Micheaux sought out Lamy, perhaps through mutual acquaintances or by finding his name in a professional directory, or if Lamy recruited Micheaux, knowing the demand for "colored films" in Europe. Micheaux probably entrusted his films in Europe to Lamy, who traveled between New York, France, and England in 1920–1921.[84]

In the Fall of 1921, Swan Micheaux, Oscar's brother and business partner, informed George P. Johnson that the company had just completed a deal to sell "all of our Foreign Rights on *Within Our Gates* and *The Brute*," and was "shipping a bunch of prints this week."[85] The Micheaux Film Company's letterhead was also updated to include: "Foreign Distributions by Joseph P. Lamy NEW YORK LONDON PARIS."[86] In the January-February 1921 issue of *Competitor Magazine*, Oscar Micheaux announced that his films were "being shown in all the leading countries of Europe, including England, France, Italy, Spain, and in Africa and in the leading South American Republics."[87] Whether Micheaux was exaggerating his claims or to what extent he was able to profit from his film distribution overseas is uncertain. Yet evidence of his efforts emerged when *Within Our Gates,* a film previously considered lost, was discovered in Spain with Spanish subtitles. It was renamed *La Negra,* and the Spanish version of the film is the only extant reproduction of Micheaux's original work.[88] Another Micheaux film, *The Symbol of the Unconquered,* was uncovered in Belgium with French and Flemish subtitles. Since Lamy specialized in exports to Belgium, France, and Switzerland, it is possible he played a part in the deal.[89]

Micheaux worked to improve his marketability abroad once his appetite for an international market was ignited. He was able to get a major company, Pathé Exchange, to distribute his films in 1923.[90] But Micheaux still needed to act as the primary salesperson for his work.[91] In 1924, he told the *Chicago Defender* that *Birthright* was breaking records from Atlanta, Georgia to the Caribbean island of Nassau.[92] During these years, Micheaux produced several films that grappled with diasporic themes, including *Marcus Garland* (1927) and *A Daughter of the Congo* (1930). Most significantly, Micheaux sought to exploit Paul Robeson's fame in England in order to boost his domestic and international sales. In 1924, Robeson's performance in Eugene O'Neill's *All God's Chillun Got Wings* garnered international attention. The black press in the United States proudly described Robeson's accomplishments overseas, boasting that he had become "an actor of note" for his work on the London stage.[93] Micheaux was cognizant of Robeson's fame abroad when he hired Robeson to play the dual role of Isaiah T. Jenkins and his twin brother, Sylvester in *Body and Soul.* Advertisements for the film prominently featured Robeson as the star "who electrified London audiences with his masterly acting."[94]

When *Body and Soul* was in post-production, Micheaux again made plans for a trip across the Atlantic.[95] The limited profits from the American market were making it difficult for him to compete with Hollywood, even at home. As film critic D. Ireland Thomas reported, "the producer of Race pictures is forced to get his profit out of a few Race theaters, while the white productions encircle the globe. Mary Pickford is just as popular in China as she is in America, etc."[96] Micheaux believed race filmmakers were "pathfinders," but without "active encouragement and financial backing" it was unfair to hold them to the same standards as Hollywood pictures. "[I]f the race has any pride," he explained, "it is well to interest itself in and morally to encourage such efforts."[97] Micheaux planned to depart the country in April, only one month after he finished shooting *Body and Soul.* The purpose of his trip, he explained, was to "obtain world distribution of Micheaux films."[98] His itinerary included "all the larger cities on the continent" and several stops in Russia. Micheaux also hoped to obtain distribution in Egypt, explaining that he would probably visit Cairo during his journey. Little is known about the ultimate success of Micheaux's plan. Again, his name does not seem to appear in the records of major ports. However, during this time, *Body and Soul* was submitted to the British Board of Film Censorship. The film was classified and approved for exhibition in England in 1927.[99]

By the winter of 1925, Micheaux still had his eyes on international distribution, but some of his goals had changed. This time, he described plans to embark on a journey to South America, explaining he intended to "place the Micheaux Products" in the West Indies and South America.[100] For the first time, his itinerary focused primarily on regions with large black populations. He explained that a "publicity campaign will also be launched to acquaint the citizens with colored productions."[101] In the same year, Micheaux filed for a New York State license for a film entitled *Marcus Garland*.[102] Although copies of the film are no longer in existence, the black press reported that it was loosely based upon Marcus Garvey. Thomas Cripps wrote that the film, "parodied Garvey as a mountebank who exploited the weakness of the black lower class."[103] Micheaux's plans to visit the West Indies and his desire to produce topical films may have motivated him to direct a film about the well-known Jamaican Pan Africanist. According to the Pittsburgh *Courier*, the "exciting story of love, intrigue, and the gamble for the control of a continent," began production in 1928.[104]

Despite their efforts, race producers such as Micheaux only managed to move into a tiny percentage of the total international film market. The industry was ruled by the "great film companies who seem[ed] to have a monopoly of the business."[105] The ability of black film companies to compete globally became even more difficult with the widespread implementation of expensive sync sound technology in 1927. Meanwhile, Hollywood's influence overseas continued to concern the diaspora. Carter G. Woodson wrote that American racism was creeping into France through the moving pictures. It was for this reason, "[t]he influence of the United States commerce on internal matters in France and elsewhere in Europe, then must not be considered insignificant."[106] Jamaican born historian and journalist, J.A. Rogers found the "Race Grossly Misrepresented By American Motion Pictures in Europe." Rogers pointed out that although the race had a rich history in Provence of Ethiopian Phoenicians and Moors, the prevailing assumption there was that all blacks were like the "servants" and "jazz players" from American movies. From Avignon, France, he wrote: "… I have discovered these days it is absolutely impossible to escape the color question. I went to a moving picture theater and there was an American picture with Negroes in it doing the usual niggerisms, just as in Milan there was the odious *Birth of a Nation*."[107] The future looked increasingly bleak for independent black film producers.

The Twilight of an Era

By the late 1930s, the potential for race films to compete in the international market was clearly waning. The Depression, an inability to compete with the increasingly expensive technologies of standard Hollywood films, and the impenetrable networks of international distribution, all brought about the end of an era. In 1936, Ralph Mathews of the *Baltimore Afro-American* mourned the dispersal and death of the leaders of the race film industry.[108] Even Oscar Micheaux, whose career had endured far longer and had been more prolific than other filmmakers had fallen "on evil days and ha[d] produced no films in the past year."[109] By 1937, Micheaux no longer boasted of international distribution for his films. His market was now "circumscribed to the few houses which cater to colored patronage exclusively and a few white houses on a midnight bill."[110] He implored black audiences to understand the limitations set upon race films: "The theatregoer often expects a colored picture to reach the same standard set by Hollywood productions which have millions to spend and a world-wide market from which to extract a return on their investment."[111]

When the international markets closed to Hollywood during WWII, some proponents of black independent cinema thought a new opportunity had opened to regain the market. African American actor Clarence Muse attempted to rally the race film industry:

> I can't UNDERSTAND why the PRODUCERS of COLORED PICTURES are so SLOW in nailing the SUCCESS sign, now WHEN all the world is at WAR ... Rise up, thinking men and women, POOL your DOLLARS, make money for YOURSELVES, but above ALL give YOUNG AMERICAN NEGROES a chance ... DEMAND MORE colored pictures, and DO YOUR bit in HELPING to MAKE A MAJOR COMPANY. MOBILIZE for JOBS while the WORLD screams WAR.[112]

The war, however, dealt another blow to the race film industry, not because of the loss of what was then an almost nonexistent foreign market, but because Hollywood turned inward in its search for new audiences. White production companies produced a growing number of films for black audiences. Lillian Johnson of the *Afro-American* noted that Hollywood, "with many of its foreign markets closed because of the war, has cast down its bucket where it is, so to speak, and has looked around for the small fellows who might have something to spend for entertainment."[113] Additionally, Hollywood began casting black actors in higher profile roles. In 1940, for example, Hattie McDaniel won an Oscar for her role as Scarlett O'Hara's loyal servant, Mammy, in *Gone With the Wind*.

Conclusion

Although the race film industry languished for decades, the desire to produce black independent cinema was never abandoned. Some early race films survived, and were exhibited long after the industry had disappeared. According to Patrick McGilligan, at the time of Micheaux's death, his film *Harlem After Midnight*, was playing at the Ambassador Theater in Jamaica.[114] Film historians continue to discover evidence of Micheaux's work in Belgium, Spain, England, and even in Sweden.[115] It would not be until the 1960s that another generation of black independent filmmakers began to garner international attention. They have been credited with inaugurating diasporic cinema, but the transnational connections and ideas generated through black moving pictures had emerged much earlier.[116] Almost half a century before Ethiopian filmmaker Haile Gerima reawakened the world to diasporic cinema, William Foster wrote that motion pictures, more than anything else, awakened blacks to "race consciousness."[117] Like the earliest race companies, the independent black filmmakers of the 1960s transformed emotional and intellectual notions of interconnectivity into actual cultural productions, political movements, and industries. Both generations of filmmakers illustrate the critical role cinema has played in envisioning and articulating black identity in the twentieth century.

Notes

1. *Chicago Defender*, September 15, 1923, 7.
2. Ibid.
3. *New York Times*, August 20, 1923, 14.
4. *Chicago Defender*, September 1, 1923, 12; *The Pittsburg Courier*, September 1, 1923, 13.
5. Melvyn Stokes, "Kojo Touvalou Houénou: An Assessment," *Transatlantica* 1 (2009).
6. *Chicago Defender*, September 1, 1923, 12.
7. *Baltimore Afro-American*, June 27, 1923.
8. *Pittsburgh Courier*, September 15, 1923. The film was later approved for exhibition; *The Chicago Defender*, Nov. 17, 1923, 2.
9. I borrow the term "the race" from the black press race film companies and use it throughout to avoid anachronisms whenever possible. The term was employed by the individuals and organizations during the interwar years to refer to black persons of the United States, and often, of the greater African diaspora—depending on the context.
10. Benedict Anderson, *Imagined Communities: Reflections on the Origin and Spread of Nationalism* (New York: Verso, 1983).
11. Tera W. Hunter, *To Joy My Freedom* (Cambridge, MA: Harvard University Press, 1997); Robin D.G. Kelley, *Race Rebels: Culture, Politics, and the Black Working Class* (New York: The Free Press, 1994). Kathy Peiss, *Cheap Amusements: Working Women and Leisure in Turn-of-the-Century New York* (Philadelphia: Temple University Press, 1986); Roy Rosenzweig, *Eight Hours for What We Will: Workers and Leisure in an Industrial City, 1870–1921* (New York: Cambridge University Press, 1983).
12. Leo Charney and Vanessa Schwartz, *Cinema and the Invention of Modern Life* (Berkeley: University of California Press, 1995), 10.
13. *The Clansman*, Dixon's play which inspired the moving picture, *Birth of a Nation*, spurred protests across the nation. However, theatrical performances reached relatively smaller audiences and geographical areas. This limited the ability and motivation to organize large-scale campaigns around them.
14. Brent Hayes Edwards, *The Practice of Diaspora* (Cambridge: Harvard University Press, 2003). Walter Benjamin, "The Work of Art in the Age of Mechanical Reproduction," *Illuminations*, trans. Harry Zohn, ed. Hannah Arendt (New York: Schocken Books, 1968).
15. The race film industry, which spanned from roughly 1909 to World War II, usually employed primarily black casts and was produced largely for black audiences. However, as Jane Gaines has explained, the race film industry, with its many contributors, had had mixed race origins. Jane Gaines, *Fire and Desire* (Chicago: University of Chicago Press, 2001).
16. Jacqueline Stewart, "Negroes Laughing at Themselves? Black Spectatorship and the Performance of Urban Modernity," *Critical Inquiry*, Vol. 29 (Summer 2003); Jacqueline Stewart, *Migrating to the Movies: Cinema and Black Urban Modernity* (Berkeley and Los Angeles: University of California Press, 2005); J. Ronald Green, *Straight Lick: The Cinema of Oscar Micheaux* (Indiana: Indiana University Press, 2000); Pearl Bowser and Louise Spence, *Writing Himself Into History: Oscar Micheaux, His Silent Films, and His Audience* (New Brunswick: Rutgers University Press, 2000); Dan Moos, "Reclaiming the Frontier: Oscar Micheaux as Black Turnerian," *African American Review*, Vol. 36 (2002).

17. Cinema was increasingly recognized as a tool for governments to disseminate or control ideas to the masses. Governmental regulation policies reflected the belief that cinema shaped popular ideas and attitudes and an increasing consensus that the moving image could reach the masses unlike any other form of media. George Creel had utilized films in his campaigns for the Committee on Public Information and in 1922, the Soviet Union officially adopted film as the tool for state propaganda. England had carefully monitored the production and import of films, particularly in regard to its colonies as reflected in the Cinematograph Films Act of 1927 and the formation of the Indian Cinematograph Committee.

18. Dan Streible, "Race and the Reception of Jack Johnson Fight Films," in Daniel Bernardi, ed., *The Birth of Whiteness* (New Brunswick: Rutgers University Press, 1996), 181.

19. Gail Bederman, *Manliness and Civilization* (Chicago: University of Chicago Press, 1995).

20. Quoted in Stephen Bourne, *Black in the British Frame* (New York: Cassell, 1998), 6.

21. *New York Daily Tribune*, July 5, 1910, 2.

22. Lee Grieveson, "Fighting Films: Race, Mortality, and the Governing of Cinema, 1912–1915," *Cinema Journal* Vol. 38. No. 1 (Autumn, 1998), 43.

23. Sol T. Plaatje, *Native Life in South Africa, Before and Since the European War and the Boer Rebellion* (1914; Project Gutenberg, 1998), Chap. xxi, http://www.gutenberg.org/cache/epub/1452/pg1452.html.

24. *Baltimore Afro-American*, Aug. 6, 1910, 4.

25. *New York Age*, October 5, 1911, 6.

26. *New York Age*, July 18, 1912, 6.

27. *New York Age*, June 5, 1913, 6.

28. Also see: H.C. Conley and his company traveled to Canada and Mexico with moving pictures featuring "scenes of their travels [and] the progress of the successful Afro-Americans," reported in the *Washington Bee*, August 31, 1907, 5. and "Johns Henry's Four Years At Hampton" "prepared by" Leigh-Richmond Minor, an instructor at the Hampton Institute, reported in the *Baltimore Afro-American*, February 7, 1914, 3.

29. *Freeman*, November 4, 1905, 7. *New York Age*, 10 January 1910, 6.

30. Foster's entrepreneurial spirit was well known, if not infamous. After his motion picture company folded the *Chicago Tribune* referred to him as Los Angeles' unofficial "Bureau of Information on all affairs.... Foster has been a complete failure in business. His first flop was in the racehorse business. His next was in the moving picture business and his next flop was in the newspaper business, but Foster is well known and keeps trying and refuses to give up." *Chicago Defender*, Feb 1, 1936, p. 14. Foster's ads for the Jack Johnson buttons ran in papers such as the *New York Age*; for example, see *New York Age*, February 17, 1909, 6.

31. *New York Age*, 31 July 1913, 6. *The George P. Johnson Negro Film Collection*, reel 4.

32. Henry T. Sampson, *Blacks in Black and White: A Source Book on Films* (Metuchen, NJ: Scarecrow Press, 1995).

33. Ibid.

34. "The Dirt of a Nation," *The Chicago Defender*, June 5, 1915, 8.

35. Quoted from Thomas Cripps, "The Making of a Birth of a Race," in Daniel Bernardi, ed. *Birth of Whiteness: Race and the Emergence of U.S. Cinema* (New Brunswick, NJ: Rutgers University Press, 1996), 43.

36. "President Wilson Killed the Bill," *Chicago Defender*, June 19, 1920, 20.

37. Eileen Bowser, *The Transformation of Cinema: 1907–1915* (Berkeley and Los Angeles: University of California Press, 1990). Gerben Bakker, "The Economic History of the International Film Industry," EH.Net Encyclopedia, ed., Robert Whaples, http://eh.net/encyclopedia/article/bakker.film, February 10, 2008.

38. Bakker, 2008.

39. A few films were produced for non-commercial use. Sol Plaatje, exhibited self-produced films alongside those he procured from Tuskegee University's Robert Russa Moton throughout South Africa. Glenn Whiley Reynolds, "Image and Empire: Cinema, Race, and Mass Black Spectatorship in Southern Africa, 1920–1940," Ph.D. Dissertation, Stonybrook, SUNY, Department of History, 2005.

40. Quoted from Cripps, "The Making of a Birth of a Race," 43.

41. Cripps, "The Making of a Birth of a Race."

42. For example, see *New York Age*, November 11, 1915, 1.

43. *The George P. Johnson Negro Film Collection* (Los Angeles, CA: University of California, Library Photographic Department). Also see Henry T. Sampson, *Blacks in Black and White: A Source Book on Films* (Metuchen, NJ: Scarecrow Press, 1995).

44. "Telegram of George P. Johnson to D. Ireland Thomas," 12/2/1921, *The George P. Johnson Negro Film Collection*, reel 7.

45. *Advocate*, May 18, 1917, 4. Also ran May 25, June 1 and June 8, 1917.

46. *New York Age*, April 9, 1914, 6.

47. *Chicago Defender*, June 20, 1914, 4.

48. Ibid.

49. Ibid.

50. *The George P. Johnson Negro Film Collection*, reel 4.

51. *Advocate*, May 18, 1917, 4. Also ran June 8, June 1 and May 25.

52. *The George P. Johnson Negro Film Collection*, reel 4.

53. Clarence Muse, a celebrated black actor and writer, organized Delsarte in 1920. Muse wrote the screenplay and played the title role in what was reported as a $90,000 production. *The George P. Johnson Negro Film Collection*, reel 4.

54. "Jack Johnson a Movie Star," *Chicago Defender*, November 1, 1919, 1.

55. Thomas Elsaesser, "Social Mobility and the Fantastic: German Silent Cinema," in Mike Budd, ed., *The Cabinet of Dr. Caligari: Texts, Contexts, Histories* (New Brunswick, NJ: Rutgers University Press, 1990).

56. For example, a woman from the Copperbelt in Zambia explained why she liked "cowboy films best" to Hortense Powdermaker in 1951: "I like to see how to throw good blows so that I can kick anybody who interferes with my business, for example, if my husband interferes." Hortense Powdermaker, *Copper Town* (New York: Harper and Row, 1962), 256 quoted in Glenn Whiley Reynolds, "Image and Empire: Cinema, Race, and Mass Black Spectatorship in Southern Africa, 1920–1940," Ph.D. Dissertation, Stonybrook, SUNY, 2005.

57. Julia Leyda, "Black-Audience Westerns and the Politics of Cultural Identification in the 1930s," *Cinema Journal*, Vol. 42. No. 1 (Autumn, 2001) and Glenn Whiley Reynolds, "Image and Empire: Cinema, Race, and Mass Black Spectatorship in Southern Africa, 1920–1940," PhD Diss., Stonybrook, SUNY, 2005.

58. Also, genres such as Italian "Spaghetti Westerns" exemplify the versatility of genres

and their expropriation onto different cultural contexts.

59. Sampson, 1995.

60. See, for example, marketing materials and letters addressed to George P. Johnson, *The George P. Johnson Negro Film Collection*, reel 7.

61. "Letter from *The Bystander* to George P. Johnson," *The George P. Johnson Negro Film Collection*, reel 7.

62. "Letter from Romeo Doguherty to George P. Johnson," August 7, 1917, *The George P. Johnson Negro Film Collection*, reel 7.

63. The agency's reports were published by black newspapers across the country. Its international coverage was varied, reporting on Haitian airline services, the French treatment of black American soldiers, and curious reports such as the story of black South African who'd been hired as a valet for a pig in Johannesburg. *The George P. Johnson Negro Film Collection*, reel 10 (Pacific Coast News Bureau folder).

64. Johnson's coverage included topics such as "Porto Rican" cotton laborers, Liberian Trading Companies, and the scientific history of Ethiopia.

65. *Pittsburgh Courier*, September 3, 1927, SM2.

66. *The George P. Johnson Negro Film Collection*, reel 4.

67. Ibid.

68. Ibid.

69. *The George P. Johnson Negro Film Collection*, reel 3.

70. "Constellation," 2, *The George P. Johnson Negro Film Collection*, reel 3.

71. *The George P. Johnson Negro Film Collection*, reel 7.

72. Ibid, reel 8.

73. Moos, "Reclaiming the Frontier"; Green, 222.

74. Joseph. A. Young, *Black Novelist as White Racist: The Myth of Black Inferiority in the Novels Of Oscar Micheaux* (Westport, CT: Greenwood Press, 1989).

75. See Brent Edwards, "The Uses of Diaspora," and George Shepperson, "Pan-Africanism and 'pan-Africanism': Some Historical Notes," *Phylon* 23 (Winter 1962): 346–58.

76. Pearl Bowser and Louise Spence, *Writing Himself Into History: Oscar Micheaux, His Silent Films, and His Audience* (New Brunswick: Rutgers University Press, 2000).

77. Oscar Micheaux, *The Chicago Defender*, March 19, 1910, 1. Micheaux's novels also painted the kind of nostalgic images of the American West associated with Frederick Jackson Turner.

78. "Extracts from letter from Oscar Micheaux," in *The George P. Johnson Negro Film Collection*, reel 8.

79. The journey may have been exhausting for Micheaux offered a job to Johnson when he returned in March. *The George P. Johnson Negro Film Collection*, reel 8. Also see George P. Johnson interview by Elizabeth I. Dixon and Adelaide G. Tusler, 1970, transcript, *George P. Johnson Collector of Negro Film History*, University of California, Los Angeles Oral History Program (Los Angeles: The Bancroft Library).

80. *Chicago Defender*, January 31, 1920, 8.

81. My own research and that of other film historians have not produced evidence of Micheaux's travels to Europe during this period. However, due to the unreliability of many import/export records and vast alternative routes he might have traveled through, this cannot serve as conclusive evidence of his international travel.

82. Fourteenth Census of the United States Federal Census Record—1920, Census Place:

Manhattan Assembly District 7, New York.

83. World War I Draft Registration Cards, 1917–1918 for Joseph Pierre Lamy. New York County, New York, Roll: 1766147; Draft Board: 124.

84. 15 Dec. 1920. Port of Arrival: Key West, Florida (Departure: Havana, Cuba), *Florida Passenger Lists, 1898–1951*; 2 Feb 1921 Port of Arrival: Plymouth England, *UK Incoming Passenger Lists*, 1878–1960, original data: Board of Trade: Commercial and Statistical Department and successors: Inwards Passenger Lists. Kew, Surrey, England: The National Archives of the UK (TNA). Series BT26, 1, 472 pieces. July 21, 1921. Port of Arrival: New York, New York (Departure: Boulogne-Sur-Mer), *New York Passenger Lists, 1820–1957*.

85. "Swan Micheaux to George P. Johnson," September 7, 1921, *The George P. Johnson Negro Film Collection*, reel 8.

86. *The George P. Johnson Negro Film Collection*, reel 8.

87. Quoted in Bowser and Spence, 30.

88. Pearl Bower, Jane Gaines, and Charles Musser, eds., *Oscar Micheaux and His Circle* (Bloomington: Indiana University Press, 2001).

89. Wid's Year Book, 1921.

90. Patrick MgGilligan, *Oscar Micheaux: The Great and Only: The Life of America's First Black Filmmaker* (New York: Harper Collins Publishers, 2007).

91. Ibid.

92. D. Ireland Thomas, *Chicago Defender*, August 16, 1924, 7a.

93. *Broad Axe*, December 2, 1922, 2.

94. *Pittsburgh Courier*, December 12, 1925, 11.

95. *Pittsburgh Courier*, February 14, 1925, 3. This trip may have been planned in place of his delayed 1924 journey.

96. *Chicago Defender*, January 10, 1925, 6.

97. *Baltimore Afro-American*, December 27, 1924, 7.

98. *Pittsburgh Courier*, February 14, 1925, 3.

99. According to the BBFC, two minutes and forty seconds of footage were cut from the film. The "A" rating suggested some councils had ruled that minors must be accompanied by adults in order to see the film. British Board of Film Classification, "Body and Soul Classified 26 July, 1927," http://www.bbfc.co.uk.

100. *Baltimore Afro-American*, December 12, 1925, 4.

101. Ibid.

102. Bernard L. Peterson, Jr., "The Films of Oscar Micheaux: America's First Fabulous Black Filmmaker," *Crisis* 86 (April 1979): 138. Also see Pearl Bower, Jane Gaines, and Charles Musser, eds., *Oscar Micheaux and His Circle* (Bloomington: Indiana University Press, 2001), 276.

103. Cripp's description was based on an excerpt from an American Film Institute Catalogue. Cripps in *Representing Blackness: Issues in Film and Video* by Valerie Smith (New Brunswick, NJ: Rutgers University Press, 1997). The assumptions about Micheaux's films have been reproduced in much of the scholarship including Jesse Algeron Rhines' *Black Film, White Money* (New Brunswick: Rutgers University Press, 1996). The articles appear to be based on Kenneth White Munden, *American Film Institute Catalogue* (Berkeley: University of California Press, 1976), 492, which lists the film date as 1925. According to Bernard Peterson, Micheaux filed for a New York State license for the film in 1925.

104. *Pittsburgh Courier*, August 25, 1928, 2.

105. *Baltimore Afro-American*, January 8, 1927, 11.

106. Carter G. Woodson, *The Chicago Defender*, September 24, 1932, 14; *Chicago Defender,* October 1, 1932, 14 *Chicago Defender,* October 8, 1932, 14; and *The Chicago Defender* December 31, 1932, 14.

107. J.A. Rodgers, "Rogers Finds Interesting Race History in France," *Pittsburgh Courier*, July 9, 1927, A1.

108. Ralph Mathews, "The Villain of 'The Wages of Sin,'" *Baltimore Afro American*, January 18, 1936.

109. Ibid.

110. *Baltimore Afro-American*, February 27, 1937, 11.

111. Ibid.

112. Clarence Muse, "What's Going On in Hollywood," *Chicago Defender*, June 1, 1940, 21.

113. Lillian Johnson, "Light and Shadow," *Baltimore Afro-American* (1893–1988); Jan 13, 1940, 13.

114. MgGilligan, *Oscar Micheaux.*

115. Gustafsson writes that *The Brute* (renamed *The King of Boxing*), *The Symbol of the Unconquered*, and *Within our Gates*, which was renamed *Chocolate Kiddies were exhibited in Sweden, Gustafsson*, 30–49.

116. Earlier scholars who have pioneered the study of race films include: Donald Bogle, *Toms, Coons, Mulattoes, Mammies & Bucks: An Interpretive History of Blacks in American Films* (New York: Continuum, 2003); Henry T. Sampson, *Blacks in Black and White: A Source Book on Films (*Metuchen, NJ: Scarecrow Press, 1995); Jane Gaines, *Fire and Desire* (Chicago: University of Chicago Press, 2001); and Thomas Cripps, *Slow Fade to Black: The Negro in American Film, 1900–1942* (New York: Oxford University Press, 1993).

Outside of the United States, Tommy Gustafsson has investigated the reception of Micheaux's films in Sweden. Tommy Gustafsson, "The Visual Re-creation of Black People in a 'White' Country: Oscar Micheaux and Swedish Film Culture in the 1920s," *Cinema Journal* 47, No. 4 (Summer 2008): 30–49. Steven Bourne has briefly considered the reception of black American cinema in Britain and the acting career of Paul Robeson. Stephen Bourne, *Black in the British Frame* (New York: Cassell, 1998).

117. *Indianapolis Freeman*, December 20, 1913, quoted in Gaines, 2001.

Chapter 5

The Middleman Speaks: Race, Citizenship, and Labor in *The Beautiful Things That Heaven Bears*

Julie Iromuanya

On February 10, 2007, the then Illinois senator, Barack Hussein Obama, announced his candidacy for President of the United States of America (U.S.A). Less than a month later, Ethiopian-born writer Dinaw Mengestu published *The Beautiful Things That Heaven Bears*, a novel about Sepha Stephanos, an Ethiopian immigrant who owns a grocery store in inner-city Washington, D.C. Stephanos is caught between the white gentrifying power structure and the indigent African American residents of the neighborhood. Mengestu's novel literarily re-imagines the era that elected our nation's first African American president. A key concern at the heart of Obama's election and Mengestu's narrative is the connection between race, citizenship, and economic and political power.

The positionality of Mengestu's Ethiopian immigrant protagonist—between his African American neighbors and his white neighbor and love interest, Judith—reflects a shifting discourse on the connection between citizenship and race in the United States. More than essentialized racial signifiers of "blackness," cultural and historical signifiers enable Sepha to attain economic mobility. His foreignness positions him in a liminal racial status, making him not quite "black." This enables him, as a grocery owner in the poor African American community, to supplant the traditional "middleman minority" in the intermediary position between producer—the white hegemonic establishment—and consumer—the African American residents of the inner-city neighborhood. Mengestu imagines this intermediary position created by the axis of race, nation, citizenship, and labor as a transformative space, further articulating the need to examine the ways in which new African Americans destabilize their accepted conceptions of race and ethnicity in the U.S.

Middleman Minorities

Historically, in ethnic enclaves and ghettos, the traditional contact zone for the elite and underclass has been the "middleman minority" as noted in *The Beautiful Things That Heaven Bears*. According to Irwin Rinder, the interstice between the elite and the masses is characterized as a "status gap."[1] In treating the larger framework of middleman minorities, Edna Bonacich adds that middlemen minority groups "plug the gap between elites and masses"[2] and "tend to occupy such a place between producer and consumer, employer and employee, owner and renter, elite and masses."[3] Pyong Gap Min further contends that:

> those minority groups that specialize in small business but lack political power often play a middleman minority role. Middleman minorities are usually found in societies rigidly stratified between two racial groups and are usually brought to the host society by the ruling group to distribute its products to minority members.[4]

In such a place, middleman minorities have historically borne the brunt of racial-economic tension in riots, pogroms, violent attacks, and civil acts of resistance. Mengestu's narrator Sepha Stephanos occupies such a role comparable to that of traditional middleman minorities like Koreans, Jews, and the Chinese in the U.S.—and the immigrants, largely African, who have recently begun to occupy this intermediary position in urban centers throughout the United States in the role of street vendors, small business owners, and black hair salon proprietors.

This chapter outlines the ways that Mengestu uses the recent African immigration to the U.S. in order to destabilize and further reimagine three specific aspects of the traditional "middleman minority" position: racial-ethnic indeterminance and its connection to citizenship, economic power, and political (in)visibility.

Citizenship and Race

That the racial anxieties of *The Beautiful Things* are inextricably tied to notions of citizenship is apparent early on. Appropriately, our nation's capitol serves as the backdrop of the novel with the iconic image of the White House looming in the periphery. Washington, D.C. and all of its signifying attributes are coded in the language and currency of the city—in Sepha's former employer, the Capitol Hotel, and his current place of abode, Logan Circle. His neighborhood is home to a tributary statue of General John Alexander Logan, the American Civil War Union soldier "perched high on his horse in the center of the circle."[5] Although the landmark is a reprieve that reminds Sepha of late-afternoon walks with his father in Ethiopia before the start of the Red Terror, the site also recalls the "seven bodies neatly lined up in the center of the grass" on January 23, 1977, on the last of his walks with his father.[6] Likewise, General Logan, in his heroic stance, gestures toward a bloody past that decided the liberty and citizenship of African Americans.

Blackness is connected to the notion of citizenship. Beginning with the three-fifths compromise and the thirteenth and fourteenth amendments, the racially coded black body has been constructed as a politically and legally contested space. In the earliest conception of critical race theory, W.E.B. Du Bois articulates this notion most poignantly when he states, "one ever feels his two-ness,—an American, a Negro ... he simply wishes to make it possible for a man to be both a Negro and an American."[7] Whiteness is unquestionably American, while blackness—more specifically the "colored" body—is fundamentally suspect.[8]

For European immigrants, the category of racial whiteness became the veritable blanket that cloaked the "alienness" that had initially been viewed as racial difference with each successive immigrant population. In spite of their distinctions Irish, Polish, Italian, and Greek immigrants became "white" and their diversity was explained in terms of "ethnic" rather than racial difference. According to Yoku Shaw Taylor, recent post-1965 immigration law reform, like the Hart-Cellar Act (which privileges family reunification and refugee status, as opposed to the previous national-origins quota system), ultimately attempts to reverse de facto discriminatory practices supported by de jure institutions governing citizenship—policy intending to favor European immigration.[9]

It is not merely that citizenship is an unquestioned privilege of whiteness; it is the inestimable connection to legality, hegemony, and protection that is central to the text of the white body. Conversely, the black body is viewed as unprotected, suspicious, and illegal. At first, whites exist as an abstract presence in the novel's realm, related to only in terms of peripheral artifacts like General Logan's statue and the White House; however, whiteness is ultimately embodied in Judith when she moves into the neighborhood. Sepha, like all of his neighbors remarks upon her presence:

> At first I had assumed that she was an agent of some city bureaucracy, assigned to the neighborhood to report on the condition of its aging buildings, to determine whether they were in need of repair or demolishment. Before Judith, these were the only reasons white people had ever come into the neighborhood: to deliver official notices, investigate crimes, and check on the children of negligent parents.[10]

Judith's whiteness is the clearest signifier of hegemony in the text. Most importantly, the relationship is paternalistic, intrusive, and institutional. While enforcing a separate set of codes, white institutional power structures ultimately strip the residents of the codes that govern their own community.

Versed in the language of hegemony, intra-racially the notion of American citizenship is also a fundamental determinant for blackness within the native African American community. For the broader interracial nation, the concept of the black ethnic self is fairly new, if not entirely absent. Although black immigrants from the Caribbean and Africa and their descendents have remained an invisible political body, scholars like Yoku Shaw-Taylor and Stanley Tuch have begun exploration into the intraracial diversity hidden beneath the cloak of "blackness."[11] Principally, they speak to the charges from politically visible African Americans such as Alan Keyes and Henry Louis Gates, Jr., and historically black institutions including the churches, colleges, and universities that have privileged the national memory of slavery and the Jim Crow Era caste system over the global scale memory of colonization and racism. Again, *their* conception of blackness is fundamentally connected to the notion of American citizenship, rather than phenotypic expression, or the shared global experience of black subjugation.

In such a position, Mengestu articulates the response of an Ethiopian immigrant who unwillingly occupies the neither here/neither there space, tied explicitly to essentialized views of citizenship. Early in the novel, Sepha reflects that "[h]ere in Logan Circle … I didn't have to be greater than what I already was. I was poor, black, and wore the anonymity that came with that as a shield against all of the early ambitions of the immigrant."[12] The trouble with Sepha's attempts to assimilate into the African American community is that his black face does not guarantee immediate, unchallenged membership, nor does his naturalization. Instead, his encounters with neighborhood residents like Mrs. Davis reaffirm this intraracial essential difference.

In one scene, when Sepha declares, "'It's a free country,'" Mrs. Davis replies, "'What do you know about free countries? You didn't even know what that was till you came here last week, and now you're telling me people can live where they like. This isn't like living in a hut, you know. People around here can't just put their houses on their backs and move on.'"[13] This is the first conversation that Sepha has with his neighbor about Judith moving into the neighborhood, and while Judith's citizenship is never challenged, Sepha's is. The humor illustrates the underlying intra-racial divisions at the heart of the novel. Sepha's foreignness/alienness defamiliarizes the "black face" that he hopes will grant him admission to the community. Furthermore, despite living in the U.S. for seventeen years, Mrs. Davis views him as a transient with no real, long term stake (both material and social) in his surroundings. Sepha has made the mistake of assuming that legal naturalization makes him American, and thereby African American.

Sepha occupies the "status gap" between the hegemonic whites and the subjugated black underclass, like traditional middleman minority groups. Middleman minorities are racially indeterminate in binary racial classification systems. While the American "one drop rule" created a racial classification system that attempted to simplify racial representation into two distinct and opposing groups—white and black—ethnic and racial "others" have historically troubled this system. During the Jim Crow era, the racial status and rights of traditional middleman minority groups such as Koreans, Jews, and the Chinese were continually in flux, determined by political or economic factors that often shifted depending on geographic region. The traditional middleman minorities, once members of immigrating groups themselves, occupied this role due in large part to their ambiguous positionality in the highly stratified American racial schema and its ties to their contested citizenship.

Like the middleman minorities before him, Sepha is perceived of as a transient sojourner, and as such, his loyalties—both intra- and international—are in question. On the one hand, Sepha initially resists assimilation and self-identifies as a sojourner, because he considers the U.S. to be a temporary domicile. "In those days," he recalls, "I believed it was only a matter of weeks or months before I returned home to Ethiopia. I spent all of my energy and free time planning for that. How was I supposed to live in America when I had never really left Ethiopia? I wasn't, I decided. I wasn't supposed to live here at all."[14] Sepha's troubled relationship with Ethiopia, as a child of revolution, is at the root of his identity. However, after living with his uncle in an Ethiopian apartment building, literally, "as close to living back home as one can get,"[15] he leaves his uncle's suburban abode and migrates to the inner-city. There, with the support of his friends, Ken the Kenyan and Joe from Congo, he attempts to embody the American mythos of classic independence, wealth, and power through entrepreneurship: "the opening of my store—'our store,' as we referred to it that night—was supposed to signal a departure from frustrating, underpaying jobs and unrealized ambitions."[16] Like many immigrants, particularly those of developing nations, Sepha's ambitions are connected directly to his purpose to embody "the consolation prize for not being home."[17]

Even after Sepha realizes the U.S. as a permanent residence through his ownership of the store, many, like Mrs. Davis, still question his loyalties. When Mrs. Davis says, "'You didn't even know [about life in America] until you came here last week .... This isn't like living in a hut, you know. People around here can't just put their houses on their backs and move on,'"[18] she is intuitively conflating the distanced abstractions of historical memory that are imbued by the intersectional precepts of time and space, with racial membership. Like the black underclass and middleman minorities, no matter how long Sepha remains in the U.S., he will be inassimilable in the larger American society. As an immigrant, one's very nature is connected to mobility, and as a foreigner or "stranger," it is his perceived mobility—and ultimate transience—that makes him suspect.

Labor and the Economic Positionality of Middleman Minorities

In occupying the fissure between the dichotomous absolute bodies of race, Sepha's value is in his role as a conduit for commodities. Indeed, perceptions of immigrants as thrifty, hard workers trump racial status, and in some cases, create economic opportunities for black immigrants such as Mengestu.[19] Historically, sojourning immigrant groups occupy lucrative trades that are quickly liquefiable with an immediate return.[20] As an intermediary, Sepha has economic power, and for the majority of the novel, as Dayo Olopade suggests, he constructs his identity through "commercial self-positioning."[21] Although Olopade observes Sepha's assertion of transnationality, this chapter looks specifically at the ways he constructs his identity as a laborer in response to his perceived racial identity and status as a sojourner.

Throughout the novel, as his stockholdings improve, the condition of the store improves.[22] Of the construction workers who consume on the part of the new white residents, he thinks, "It was partly because of them [the workers] and what they did to the house and the others in the neighborhood that I added the deli counter to my store in January, hoping that perhaps I, too, could profit from the houses that gleamed with their newly restored glory."[23] When a building is torn down by a renovator, he muses, "At least half the people who lived in it had been regulars at my store, and when the building went, they and their small daily purchases went with it."[24] Even in the middle of the violence that wreaks havoc on the neighborhood, Sepha can only think of it in relation to the immediate surplus value at stake: "Those three days were a boon for my little store. It was almost like old times, with my register ringing and a buzz of numbers and voices constantly floating around in my head. I made enough each of those days to walk home at the end of the night grateful and relieved. America was a beautiful place once again."[25] The beauty of America, and ultimately his perception of freedom, is explicitly coded through the currency of the dollar.

Commercialization and individual enterprise are as deeply rooted in capitalist philosophy as they are in notions of American national identity, but it is one that is perplexed by the presence of sojourning immigrant groups who are assumed to have no long-term stake in the land. Silvia Pedraza categorizes the types of economic societies each historical immigrant population encountered in this way: first wave, colonial and agrarian; second and third wave, urban and industrial; and fourth wave, postindustrial service-oriented.[26] Unlike the previous immigration periods that relied on agrarian or manufacturing economies, the postindustrial society in which the novel takes place relies almost exclusively on specialized training and skilled labor, privileging the immigrants who possess information and technology in the areas that the U.S. is lacking, and segmenting those that do not into the lower rungs of service-oriented labor. Mengestu illustrates this stratification through the friendship between Sepha and his friends Ken the Kenyan and Joe from Congo, who, with him, begin as restaurant employees at the Capitol Hotel and respectively ascend to the roles of engineer and waiter. Sepha constitutes an often overlooked economic axis of the post-industrial society, on which I focus in this paper.

Postindustrial growth is realized not only through specialized occupations, but also through the freedom, wealth, leisure and most importantly, the technologies that make it possible for consumers to adapt their surroundings to their insatiable consumptive desires. In *The Beautiful Things*, this is most visible through the national capitalist project of homeownership, where the investment promotes a citizenry with a long-term stake and interest in their immediate physical and ultimately psychic location. Moreover, this is systematically tied to whiteness. Preceding the crisis moment of the text, Sepha realizes that he has unwittingly observed Logan Circle's gentrification over a period of time: "Two years ago I would spot the occasional odd face walking past my storefront windows—a white woman carrying groceries home early in the evening, a man jogging with his dog shortly after dusk—and think little of it,"[27] he observes. "It wasn't until the summer before Judith moved into the neighborhood that the change began in earnest, which is to say it became inevitable.... The entire time we stood out there I heard only one person say anything at all, nothing more than a simple phrase, 'white people.'"[28] The singular phrase "white people" becomes the language with which residents interpret hegemony. This is, in turn, connected to home ownership.

The sojourner's identity is inextricably tied to small, individual commercial short-term investment and racial indeterminance. Alongside one another, the competing nationalist ideologies of the home and the small business represent dualistic constructions of citizenship and residency in the novel. As such, Sepha's store and Judith's house become the chief signifiers of two types of economic power, and furthermore, the ultimate pivot for the novel's climactic violence. At first, Judith's house is considered a "tragic wreck of a building."[29] However, when the renovations are complete, Judith moves into a home that is a spectacle and is ultimately demolished at the close of the novel by the African American residents. While observing Judith's home, Sepha muses, "It was the same thing with all of the other newly refurbished houses in the neighborhood.… There was something about affluence that needed exposure, that resisted closed windows and poor lighting and made a willing spectacle of everything. The houses invited, practically begged and demanded, to be watched."[30] Gentrification is an outgrowth of postindustrial economies that consider products only in terms of their consumptive value and Judith's house becomes a commodity emblematic of hegemonic power.

The native African American residents of Logan Circle, with their own precarious citizenship, do not stand to benefit from the renovations to the land they occupy, and by all accounts, do not own. Instead, as their neighborhood gains market value, the exchange rate devalues the African American consumer's dollar. This mirrors superexploitation models at the micro-economic level that place African Americans and other minorities in expendable service roles. As a result, according to Iris Young, "these jobs entail a transfer of energies whereby the servers enhance the status of the served" and "where those others receive primary recognition for doing the job."[31] In essence, the process of transfer results in an unequal exchange. As labor theorists such as Marx have contended, the labor theory of value in a capitalist economy posits that "[p]rofit is possible only because the owner of capital appropriates any realized surplus value."[32] In the superexploitation model, "oppression occurs through a steady process of the transfer of the results of this labor of one social group to benefit another.…" These relations are produced and reproduced through a systematic process in which the energies of the have-nots are continuously expended to maintain and augment the power, status, and wealth of the haves.[33]

Furthermore, the current central banking system enables an omnipresent hegemonic institutional force to mandate the unequal exchange. Indeed, after observing the "excesses"[34] of Judith's home, Sepha views his own home as "shabbier, smaller, and more desolate than [he] remembered, as if while [he] was eating dinner someone had entered [his] apartment and stolen a few years off the furniture."[35] Like the other gentrified properties, Judith's home is legitimized by hegemonic institutions and increases in value, while the native African American residents are evicted from their homes. As such, her home becomes the first target of their violence, while Sepha's store becomes the last.

Political Voicelessness to Voice

In spite of Sepha's economic power, like traditional middleman minorities and intermediaries, they have little control over the conditions that beget surplus income: surplus value is controlled by elites. Middleman minorities are politically voiceless. Like Min, Bonacich observes that middleman minorities tend to "avoid involvement in local political affairs except those that directly affect their group."[36] Furthermore, John Arthur calls Africans "invisible sojourners" because of their inability or unwillingness to participate politically, as they privilege immediate economic capital over civil and social capital in a Booker T. Washington vein. Because of this, Sepha is initially relegated to a voiceless role in the text. During an exchange with Mrs. Davis, he muses, "I was in no position … to say what was right or wrong. I was not one of 'these people,' as Mrs. Davis had just made clear to me. I hadn't forced anyone out, but I had never really been a large part of Logan Circle either, at least not in the way Mrs. Davis and most of my customers were. I had snuck in the neighborhood as well. I had used it for its cheap rent, and if others were now doing the same, then what right did I have to deny them?"[37] Later, he recalls, "I stepped outside of my store once to see what was happening, but I knew my place. It was behind the counter, not in the middle of a dispute in which I had no part to play."[38] "Behind the counter," as a conduit for material capital, Sepha has immediate relevance, but outside of that role, he has no value.

In reimagining the African as the new middleman minority in the contemporary postindustrial landscape, Mengestu uses the literary imagination to centralize this position and destabilize racial, ethnic, and economic boundaries. At the height of the crisis moment of the text, Sepha is forced to make a decision and form an alliance with the white elite, or the black underclass. Led by Mrs. Davis, the African American residents organize a town hall meeting to confront "them," the whites whom the residents perceive of as "responsible not only for the evictions in the neighborhood, but for every single slight and injury each person in that room had suffered, from the children who never made it past junior high, to the unpaid heating bill waiting in a dresser drawer."[39]

When Sepha enters the room, he unwittingly enters a combat zone, with Judith acting as representative of the white governing body, and Mrs. Davis representative of the subjugated underclass. At first, he attempts to remain invisible at the back of the church, but Mrs. Davis admonishes him to move to a visible, moreover central position in the room. Sepha remarks, "Judith moved her coat off the seat next to her. Mrs. Davis caught the gesture and followed me with her eyes to see where I was going to sit…. There were definite sides, and the people in that room were all waiting to see which one I was going to choose."[40] In spite of the fact that Judith makes space for him, Sepha does not sit next to her. In doing so, the internal crisis moment of the book is enacted through the crisis action of Sepha performing his chosen identity. Judith is figuratively tried and convicted by the church tribunal, and Sepha's action is ultimately a political oration. As a common enemy, Judith is sacrificed so that he may have membership in the African American body politic.

The ultimate sacrifice is Sepha's grocery, the greatest signifier of Sepha's status as a "stranger" both within, and beyond, the African American community. In order to assimilate into the community, and in order to have a political voice, he can no longer play the role of the middleman minority. Sepha abandons the store, and, in a street riot, residents vandalize it.

Conclusion

At the novel's conclusion, Sepha remarks on his father's saying, "A bird stuck between two branches gets bitten on both wings," and fittingly adds, "a man stuck between two worlds lives and dies alone. I have dangled and been suspended long enough."[41] It is worth acknowledging the implications of such a closing: Will Sepha, and other middleman minorities like him, remain in this abject liminal state, caught between a racially and economically divided world, and forced to choose in order to have political viability? Or will the complexities of this space offer a fruitful site where the realities of a flux and changing world can be realized?

Perhaps, most importantly, the conclusion only seeks to affirm the need to recognize the evolving definitions of what it means to be African and American in the modern and globalized America of today. Like President Barack Obama's election, *The Beautiful Things That Heaven Bears* reveals that the racial-ethnic perception of African immigrants, by themselves and others, destabilizes the historical binary racial classification system and ultimately evinces a new narrative about the currency of racialized bodies in a postindustrial service-oriented society that is fast becoming transnational. In such a world, the son of a white American mother and a black Kenyan father can be elected to the highest office in the nation. In such a world, the traditional categories of race, economy, nation, and citizenship—and their relation to political viability—are frequently tested and continue to renew how we define what it means to be American.

Notes

1. Irwin Rinder, "Strangers in a Land: Social Relations in the Status Gap," *Social Problems* 6 (Winter 1958–1959), 253.

2. Edna Bonacich, "A Theory of Middleman Minorities," *American Sociological Review* 38 (October 1973), 584.

3. Ibid., 583.

4. Pyong Gap Min, "The Entrepreneurial Adaptation of Korean Immigrants," in *Origins and Destinies: Immigration, Race, and Ethnicity in America*, eds. Silvia Pedraza and Ruben G. Rumbaut (Belmont, CA: Wadsworth, 1996), 309.

5. Dinaw Mengestu, *The Beautiful Things That Heaven Bears* (New York: Riverhead Books, 2007), 16.

6. Ibid., 217.

7. W.E.B. Du Bois, *The Souls of Black Folk* (Boston: Boston Globe, 2005), 11.

8. Most recently, this has been evident in the media's depiction of black Katrina survivors as "refugees" and the questioning of President Obama's citizenship from the originators of the so-called Birther Movement. Similarly this has been the case with the policing of the Mexican borders rather than the Canadian borders.

9. Yoku Shaw-Taylor, "The Intersection of Assimilation, Race, Presentation of Self, and Transnationalism in America," in *The Other African Americans: Contemporary African and Caribbean Immigrants in the United States*, eds. Yoku Shaw-Taylor and Steven A. Tuch (Lanham: Rowman and Littlefield Publishers, 2007), 7.

10. Mengestu, 17–18.

11. For more reading, see Shaw-Taylor, Yoku and Steven A. Tuch, eds. *The Other African Americans: Contemporary African and Caribbean Immigrants in the United States* (Lanham: Rowman and Littlefield Publishers, 2007).

12. Mengestu, 41.

13. Ibid., 23.

14. 14 Ibid., 140.

15. Ibid., 116.

16. Ibid., 145.

17. Mengestu, 41.

18. Ibid., 23.

19. Often, as immigration scholar John Arthur attests, African immigrants even accent their foreignness in an attempt—albeit unsuccessful at times—to disassociate with native African Americans and gain an enhanced social and economic status. See Arthur, 4.

20. Bonacich, 585.

21. Dayo Olopade, "Go West, Young Men: Conspicuous Consumption" in Dinaw Mengestu's *The Beautiful Things That Heaven Bears*, as Prefigured by V.S. Naipaul's *A Bend in the River, Transition* 100 (2009), 135.

22. Mengestu, 110.

23. Ibid., 17.

24. Ibid., 188–189.

25. Ibid., 193.

26. Silvia Pedraza, "Origins and Destinies: Immigration, Race, and Ethnicity in America History," in *Origins and Destinies: Immigration, Race, and Ethnicity in America*, eds. Silvia Pedraza and Ruben G. Rumbaut (Belmont, CA: Wadsworth, 1996), 2.

27. Mengestu, 23.

28. Ibid., 23–24.

29. Ibid., 15.

30. Ibid., 52.

31. Iris Young, "The Five Faces of Oppression," *Oppression, Privilege, and Resistance: Theoretical Perspectives on Racism, Sexism, and Heterosexism*, eds. Lisa Heldke and Peg O'Connor (Boston: McGraw Hill, 2004), 48.

32. Ibid., 46.

33. Ibid., 46.

34. Mengestu, 58.

35. Ibid., 59–60.

36. Bonacich, 586.

37. Mengestu, 189.

38. Ibid., 192.

39. Ibid., 200.

40. Ibid., 197–198.

41. Ibid., 228.

Chapter 6

Beyond Racial Myths, Prejudices, and Stereotypes: Deconstructing African/Black Diaspora Studies in a Changing World

Okpeh Ochayi Okpeh, Jr.

The African Diaspora as a field of scholarly investigation has been studied for more than one hundred years. The interest in this field shows no sign of waning as the world becomes increasingly integrated. The struggle against racial and ethnic oppression and the strategies of resistance to exploitation that have characterized the African Diaspora for more than five centuries seem all the more relevant as contemporary ethnic and racial conflicts proliferate around the globe.[1] The increasing popularity of Africana studies is incontrovertible. The study of the African/Black Diaspora is a core and intrinsic part of world history.[2] From the research interests it has generated globally, to the passion it has engendered among scholars, the study of the African/Black Diaspora can no longer be neglected because it addresses the relationship of Blacks with Africa and with their newfound abodes in many parts of the world. Africana studies scholars have generated theories and concepts to test and interpret the social realities underpinning the existence of the African/Black Diaspora.

The purpose of this chapter is to examine the changes and continuities that have occurred within African/Black Diaspora studies, and the implications the changes have had on past and present knowledge of the African/Black Diaspora. From a historical perspective, this chapter argues that since African/Black Diaspora studies have always been multidimensional, it is necessary to shift the focus to more concrete interpretations hinged upon a multidisciplinary perspective that is underpinned by meta-theoretical, conceptual, methodological, and ideological commitment. This approach provides a platform from which African/ Black Diaspora studies can effectively assess the contested terrain of a fast changing world and the many challenges this is generating for humanity.

Trends in the Historiography of African/Black Diaspora Studies

The review, analysis, and understanding of African/Black Diaspora studies are not complete without a close examination of the trajectory of the African/ Black experience. To thoroughly comprehend this experience, this analysis should begin with Black slavery and the Atlantic Slave Trade. Slavery is as old as human history, but the enslavement of Black people in Africa and people of African descent in the Americas and Europe from the sixteenth century marked a watershed in the historical development of Africa and people of African descent, especially in their relationships with Euro-Americans.[3] The Atlantic Slave Trade and slavery determined, and sometimes dominated, virtually all major social, economic, and political activities in Africa and the African world both internally and externally. There were, for example, critical variables in the rise, development, and collapse of major African states. This also determined the nature and character of economic and political relations between African states and people, on the one hand, and between them and Europe and America, on the other.

Black slavery was also central to the emergence, consolidation, and ideological validation of Euro-American racism, a powerful force in world history since the eighteenth century, of which the Black world has remained perhaps the worst victim.[4] It is important to understand the basis of the sustained attention and provocative debates that Black slavery and the Atlantic Slave Trade have generated among scholars over the years: they constitute the crucibles of the global discourses on the African Diaspora. While the major goal of this chapter is not to reconstruct the history of the Atlantic Slave Trade, which has been adequately documented by many scholars,[5] it is important to point out that it has remained a core aspect of the African/Black Diaspora, in both the collective consciousness and material history of all Blacks.

Besides connecting the African Diaspora with its past, the memories of the Atlantic Slave Trade are a significant factor in their understanding of the multiple problems they confronted (and are still confronting) in the New World, and the implications of these on their identity construction and re-construction processes. As scholars on the slave trade such as Walter Rodney and Joseph

Inikori have insisted, the enslavement of Blacks and their forceful evacuation from Africa (as well as the consequences of these on their subsequent development), collectively constitute the matrix in which the conception, articulation, and consummation of the Black experience (as a strand of knowledge) is set.[6] The controversies generated by the global essence and significance of Blacks have become the building blocks for the development of African/Black Diaspora studies.

One area that has received attention is the myth of Black racial and cultural inferiority that underpinned the justification for the enslavement of Black people in the New World. Although race was not originally a factor in the ideology of slavery, during the course of the seventeenth and eighteenth centuries when slaves had become predominantly Black, slavery came to be rationalized on racial grounds.[7] In consequence, across Europe, the dubious notion that Africans were destined to be "hewers of wood and drawers of water" was unanimously accepted and popularized. This is evident from the views of European scholars such as David Hume, a Scottish scholar, who declared in 1768:

> I am apt to suspect the negroes to be naturally inferior to the white. There never was a civilized nation of any other complexion than white, nor even any individual eminent in action or speculation. No ingenious manufactures amongst them, no art, no science.[8]

Similarly in 1774, Edward Long, the Jamaican plantation historian contended that, "Blacks were a brutish, ignorant, idle, crafty, treacherous, bloody, thievish, mistrustful and superstitious people."[9] George W. Hegel, the internationally acclaimed German philosopher and historian in the nineteenth century, described Africa and its peoples as follows:

> It is manifest that want of self control distinguishes the character of the Negroes. This condition is capable of no development or culture, and as we have seen them at this day, such have they always been. At this point we leave Africa, not even to mention it again. For it is no historical part of the world; it has no movement or development to exhibit.[10]

The earliest known efforts at reconstructing the Black experience were therefore directed at questioning the preceding denigrating notions about Africans and Black people generally. This was the first major preoccupation in the historiography of African/Black Diaspora studies. Scholars such as Earl E. Thorpes and Eric E. Williams attempted through their works to discredit the racial stereotypes and prejudices against Blacks, and on this basis demonstrate to humanity the reality and global essence of African/Black civilization.[11] They justified this endeavor on the basis of the contributions of Africans/Blacks to the development of the New World. Accordingly, a leading figure of the time, George Washington Williams, contends that:

> A history of the Colored people of America was required because of the ample historically trustworthy material at hand; because the Colored people themselves have been the most vexatious problem in North America from the time of its discovery down to the present day; that in every attempt upon the life of the Nation, whether by foes from without or within, the Colored people had always displayed matchless patriotism and incomparable heroism; and because such history would give the world more correct ideas of the Colored people, and incite the latter to greater effort in the struggle for citizenship and manhood.[12]

For this generation of scholars, the study of the African/Black experience would have achieved a major landmark if it had reversed the racial stereotypes and prejudices against the Black people. This core objective informed its "drum and trumpet" methodology of dealing with the problem. Essentially, it sets out to glorify Great Africa and the contributions of its sons and daughters, in and outside the continent, to world civilization. Although these initial efforts achieved much, they suffered from a number of challenges. Uya, for example, points out an important missing link in the activities of this generation of scholars. According to him, they: ... were not trained historians but interested amateurs who identified history as a necessary weapon for the struggle for racial justice and equality in the New World. Inspired by their Christian beliefs, the egalitarian principles of the French and American Revolutions, and great faith in the future of "The Negro," these early writers wrote history to justify the need to emancipate the race.[13]

Related to the above was the narrow Eurocentric conception of history, which recognized only written records as sources of man's knowledge of the past. According to Mario Azevedo, since much of Africa had mostly non-literate languages, it was excluded from historical consideration.[14] In the attempt to demonstrate that Africa had a history, scholars were confronted with the problem of the dearth of written documents, which were needed to justify the mainstreaming of the African/Black experience in world history. Further, there were problems associated with the dynamics of the power relations involving Africa and Europe. In the construction of these power dynamics during the Atlantic Slave Trade and subsequently colonialism, Africans/Blacks became the major casualties. In such a situation, and for a fairly long time, they were unable to shape their own destiny.[15]

It is against this background that the intervention of early professional historians such as W.E.B DuBois, Carter G. Woodson, Charles S. Johnson, Ralph

Bunche, and later, Charles H. Wesley, Ira DeRied, Oliver Cromwell Cox, Marcus Garvey, and John H. Franklin represent a significant milepost in the historiography of the African/Black experience. Following his prophetic declaration that the problem of the twentieth century was "The Race Question," DuBois spent much of his time carrying out research and educating the world about the contributions of Black people to human civilization. Through such awareness, DuBois had hoped that the "Racial Question" would be resolved.[16] From his base at Atlanta University, DuBois devoted his scholarly activities to the analysis and appreciation of the American Negro and his African origins.

Ironically, it was the activities of Carter G. Woodson, the acclaimed "father of modern Black history" that gave an ideological tinge and substance to the African/Black Diaspora experience during this period. His thesis that race prejudice was merely the logical sequence of tradition (i.e. the inevitable outcome of thorough instruction to the effect that the Negro) has never contributed anything to the program of mankind. Woodson believed that a different variant of education, presenting the Negro in a more favorable light, was the basic solution to the so-called color problem, for it gave the African/Black experience the intellectual compass with which it navigated the contested terrain of knowledge at that time. As part of his project, Carter G. Woodson's scholarly works[17] made a positive impact on the changing image of Black people all over the world, particularly those in the western hemisphere.

Besides the debates he sparked, Carter G. Woodson's contributions in other areas of Black historiography are even more significant. He founded (along with his colleagues) The Association for the Study of Negro Life and History in 1915. Prior to the 1960s, this group was the major, if not the only, scholarly association exclusively devoted to the study of the Negro in Africa and the world.[18] Through its annual conferences and other activities, both Black and White scholars had the opportunity to interact and exchange ideas on the Black experience. Woodson also established and edited the *Journal of Negro History* beginning in 1916. Using this journal as an instrument for teaching, Woodson educated the world about the great exploits of Blacks throughout history. Accordingly, Uya notes that, "Since its first publication in 1916, the journal has remained the major outlet for most of the important scholarly works on Black people all over the world, but most especially, in the New World."[19] Woodson institutionalized the celebration of Negro History Week (now a month-long celebration each February) in the United States of America. Besides generating group consciousness and solidarity among Africans/Blacks around the world (particularly in the New World), Negro History Week drew national attention to the Negro Question and helped shape awareness about the significance of the Black experience through the popular media and the *Negro History*

Bulletin.[20] The basic objective became how to identify and showcase the immense contributions of Blacks in making and developing the New World. As Woodson argued:

> In our own particular history, we should not dim one bit the luster of any star in our firmament. Let no one be so thoughtless as to decry the record of the makers of the United States. Along with learning about Washington, one should also learn about "the three Thousand Negro Soldiers of the American Revolution" who helped to make "this father our country" possible.[21]

A major theme of African/Black studies by this time was the identification and eulogizing of Black heroes. The evidence used to justify this was the invaluable contributions of Blacks and their place in the history of the New World. Scholars of that generation consequently problematized African/Black studies in terms of its location, which was then on the periphery of the broader history of the New World, dominated by Europe and the activities of Europeans. Conceived within this context, the emphasis of African/Black studies was basically anchored on the contributions of Black people to the growth and development of the New World.

As an important aspect of these intellectual cross-currents, the question of improving racial interactions and understanding through the mainstreaming of the Black experience acquired pronounced importance in the New World, particularly in North America. Benjamin Quarles, and John Hope Franklin, the renowned Negro American historian of the 1950s and 1960s, became the staunchest defenders of this tradition. Articulating the basis of this new trend in the historiography of the African/Black experience, Franklin contends that:

> The new Negro history says to America that its rich heritage is the result of the struggles of all its peoples, playing the roles that conditions and circumstances have permitted them to play. These roles cannot be evaluated in terms of race. Rather, they must be judged in terms of their effect on the realization of the great American dream.[22]

This tradition stresses the point that the history of the New World in general, and the U.S. in particular, would be grossly inadequate without the recognition and incorporation of the Black experience in the making of that history. Russell L. Adams observes that scholars were challenged to interrogate this new trend and its implications for race relations in the New World.[23] It is important to point out that the Pan-African Movement strengthened this new wave of concern for the African condition in the New World by providing it with the context that allowed it to flourish and operate.[24] The leading characters of this era relied on and got their inspirations from the philosophy of Pan-Africanism espoused by its leaders, particularly Marcus Garvey.

This trend held sway until the rise of the Black Power Movement in the U.S. during the 1960s. The movement questioned the logic that informed the construction of the dominant social order and the place of Blacks in it. It underscored the need to understand Blacks as a distinct race in America.[25] Its consequence on the African/Black experience was revolutionary. Emphasizing this point, Uya opines that:

> Largely nationalistic in its political orientation, the Black Power Movement, which affected all parts of the world, questioned the dominance of the integrationist image of Black scholarship and challenged it, not as totally incorrect, but as largely inadequate. The nationalistic stance adopted by this movement demanded a historical image which insisted on the pluralistic as opposed to the "melting pot" emphasis on American and New World cultures....[26]

A number of variables aided the growth and development of this tendency. One of the factors was the urbanization of Black communities in the U.S., which brought into sharp focus the deplorable social conditions of Blacks and provided the impetus to protest them. Another factor was the rise of the Civil Rights Movement (CRM), which challenged the dominant social order in all its ramifications and emphasized the moral imperative to correct this in order to ameliorate the condition of Blacks in the interest of the future advancement of humanity. The eventual realization of institutionalizing African-American studies in the late 1960s arose from students' demands after the assassination of Dr. Martin Luther King, Jr.

The subsequent intellectual activities sparked by these developments revolutionized African/Black studies in many ways. First, they generated more debates, which through conferences, symposia, and workshops created the awareness of, and interest in, the African/Black Diaspora experience. Second, they gave rise to the development of alternative ways of studying this experience beyond the integrationist White Filter theoretical model. As a direct consequence of this, a new Black historical image emerged challenging conventional approaches. Third, African/Black Diaspora studies have been accepted as a strand of knowledge in its own right by scholars, who increasingly began to explore appropriate methodologies for its conception and interpretation.

Perspectives, Approaches, and Challenges

In the wake of the acceptance of African/Black autonomous experience as a field of academic study, a plethora of analytical perspectives and methodological approaches have emerged since the 1970s. Many of the features of this later analysis can be traced to the Melville Herskovits — E. Franklin Frazier polemics of the 1930s–1950s. Because of this, it is worthwhile to understand the basic assumptions and arguments of Herskovits and Frazier and the specific ways they influenced the construction of perspectives, theories, and methodological approaches to African/Black Diaspora studies.

On the assumption that because of their experience of slavery, Blacks had been cut off from their African roots, Frazier, in his scholarly works, concluded that Negro identities and institutions were forged and shaped in the discriminatory setting of the New World and therefore reflected the internal pathologies of that condition.[27] For Frazier, whatever cultural identities the Negro established in the New World had more to do with the realities of his existence in this new home than the extant ones he left behind in Africa. Arguing to the contrary, Herskovits drew the attention of scholars to the resilience of the African culture in the New World. Herskovits reasoned that the African linguistic traits, religious practices, patterns of family organization and modes of songs and dance survived the trauma of enslavement and should be given due emphasis in the reconstruction of the African/Black experience in the New World.[28]

Herskovits, however, warned that the major challenge of cultural research on Africans in the diaspora had to do with determining how, in what specific ways, and to what extent and degree the cultural elements of Europeans, Africans and Indians interacted with one another as both recipients and donors in the exchange. Anchoring his thesis on the anthropological concepts of acculturation and culture contact, interaction and interpretation, Herskovits consequently challenged scholars to examine the New World experience of Blacks within the context of their African cultural base.[29] It was in response to these new challenges (which gained widespread attention of scholars in the early 1970s) that the African/Black Diaspora experience was subjected to new and multiple perspectives, analytical methodologies, and theoretical approaches. For the purposes of on-going analysis, three dominant, influential, and popular perspectives are examined by assessing their significance in the development of African/Black Diaspora studies.

First is the Creolization perspective, which attempts to study the African/Black experience in the New World in terms of the new cultures and identities slaves created in their new habitats. In 1976, Sidney Mintz and Richard Price, in a seminal essay, argued that as a result of the intermittent and unsteady nature of the slave trade, the Africans uprooted to the New World were not made up of homogeneous groups that could be associated with a single, specific, and unifying culture traceable to their African roots; on the contrary, they were made up of heterogeneous groups and cultures.[30] As Falola and Childs observed in their review of this model, Mintz and Price did not ignore or even deny the cultural traditions that Africans brought with them to the New World, but they forcefully advocated the need to examine the emergence of a Creole culture in the New World on the basis of their initial common identity as slaves.[31] This perspective warns against the futility of looking for similarities between Old World and New World African traditions. Instead, scholars are encouraged to focus their research on the more rewarding areas of the inter-mixtures and coalescence of these diverse cultures, and the resulting new cultures and identities, or what is referred to as Creolization.

Accordingly, Mintz and Price challenged scholars to address the questions raised by the ways African slaves in the New World lived, the institutions they created, and how these impacted positively on their existence against the background of the encumbrances imposed on them by slavery.[32] It is important to note that this perspective's strong anthropological bent has made it very popular amongst those who study the African/Black diaspora experience from the cultural anthropological and sociological framework. As a result of this, the model influenced much of the research carried out on the Africa/Black experience in the late 1970s and 1980s. The major weakness is its near ahistorical assumptions about its subject matter.

What appeared to be new ground in the field of African/Black Diaspora studies appeared in the 1990s, when the fundamental assumptions of the Creolization model were challenged by a focus on the Atlantic Ocean as a baseline. This perspective challenged scholars to examine and analyze the African diaspora as a process determined by events and experiences on both sides of the Atlantic.[33] Falola and Childs again pointed out that subscribers to this analytical methodology "… emphasized that slaves who were forcefully transported to the Americas carried with them their own history, culture, and identity that decisively shaped their experience in the Americas."[34] Compared to the Creolization model, this perspective caught the fancy of many Afro-centric historians who, in responding to this fresh call to activism, deepened and broadened their studies of the Trans-Atlantic Slave Trade and its implications on the historical development of Africa and the New World.[35] Its Afro-centric basis enables it to focus attention on the dialectical relationship between the slave-exporting African countries and the European colonies importing them.

An interesting feature of this perspective that has contributed tremendously to the understanding of the African/Black experience is its focus on specific migration patterns from Africa to the Americas through the analysis of qualitative and quantitative sources. Its meta-theoretical and multidisciplinary approach has provided new insights to the diaspora phenomenon generally, and the African/Black experience in particular, and has strengthened scholars' interest and confidence in this field of study. Falola and Childs explain why this is precisely the case. According to them:

> Those who favor an Atlantic approach to Diasporic studies do not deny (and many even study) the cultural changes and innovations that were fundamental aspects of the experience of Africans in the Americas, but they do contend that in order to understand the history and struggles of Africans in the Americas it is indeed necessary to study both sides of the Atlantic.[36]

This Atlantic perspective has since become firmly established in the African/Black Diaspora studies as a veritable alternative analytical framework.

Beyond the preceding two seemingly contrasting perspectives, there is a third that attempts to bridge the Creolization and trans-Atlantic approaches. This new framework cautions against the mono-causal methodology implied in the first two perspectives, and tries to creatively bring them together as one useful tool for studying the African/Black experience. This echoes Paul Lovejoy's 1997 call for scholars to recognize the fact that the enslaved interpreted their lived experiences in terms of their personal histories, and in that sense the African side of the Atlantic continued to have meaning for them.[37] This perspective recognizes and appreciates the extent to which the African values held by slaves were altered as a result of the challenges they confronted in the New World.[38] What is important is not to emphasize the divergence of the two analytical approaches, but to understand their usefulness in the process of analyzing the African/Black experience in the New World. This perspective has become increasingly important not only because of its elasticity as an analytical approach to the study of the African/Black Diaspora studies, but also because of its ability to accommodate the changes and continuities that have been major features of this field. It studies the African/Black Diaspora from both sides of the Atlantic thus transcending the mere narrative that underpin such studies. Furthermore, this viewpoint approaches the African Diaspora studies from a holistic perspective, which enables it to capture and understand the African Diaspora from more than just one narrow point of view.

Since it first emerged as a perspective and method of analysis, a more detailed and better picture of the Black experience has begun to take shape. On this basis, it is possible to understand the variables that accounted for the resilience of the African cultures in the New World, as well as their implications in shaping the dynamics of the African identity. The perspective is also anchored first on history and then on other disciplines, making it multi-dimensional, multi-disciplinary, and analytically sophisticated. As a result, the reconstruction of the African/Black Diaspora experience has moved beyond racial myths, prejudices, stereotypes, and other anachronisms.

The African/Black Diaspora: Issues, Options, and Prospects

It has been proposed that the field of African/Black Diaspora is here to stay because it is an important knowledge portal. Furthermore, the point has been made that over the years, numerous analytical perspectives and methodological approaches have underpinned the articulation of the African/Black diasporic experience. What remains contentious, however, is the extent to which this field of study has been integrated in the broader category of diaspora studies. The polemic surrounding this matter is far from being settled, to say the least. Indeed, there are still those who strongly hold the view that Africa has not had diasporas, and therefore cannot claim that nomenclature to qualify what so many of her children have experienced in the history of her historical development over the past five hundred years. One important problem this poses is finding agreement in what exactly is meant and encompassed by the idea of diaspora in general, and the African Diaspora to be specific.

Robin Cohen partially dealt with this problem in 1997 in his classic magnum opus, where he identified nine features of a diaspora including: dispersal from an original homeland, often traumatically, to two or more foreign regions; the expansion from a homeland in search of work, in pursuit of trade, or to further colonial ambitions; and a collective memory and myth about the homeland, including its location, history, and achievements.[39] Going by the above qualifications, the African continent has clearly experienced the diaspora phenomenon, the history of which dates back several centuries before modern times. The African/Black Diasporas exist in North America, Europe, the Caribbean, Brazil, Latin America, the Middle East, and parts of Asia. This is in addition to their presence in all the major regions of the world.

A major challenge now confronted by scholars of the African/Black diaspora discourse is the development of a workable strategy for mapping out these numerous and culturally diverse African communities. Another important issue is the limitations imposed by scholars in their almost over blotted attention on the trans-Atlantic dimension of the African/Black diasporic experience. This has led to many scholarly studies on the English-speaking diaspora concentrated in North America and the Caribbean, and the contrasting neglect of the much larger African/Black Diaspora in Portuguese-speaking Brazil, Spanish-speaking Latin America, and parts of Europe.

This gap must be filled as part of the attempt to mainstream the African/Black experience in the broader global diaspora debate. As the globalization process continues to de-territorialize the world economically, politically, and socio-culturally, the African/Black experience would be better appreciated if scholars were to broaden their scope of analysis and deepen the understanding of their subject matter. They would then achieve mastery of the requirements, and application of the highest and most current research standards and techniques, all anchored in a multi-disciplinary approach.

There is also the question of delineating and understanding the contemporary African Diaspora and establishing the many ways it is different from the old experience. This has become increasingly important because of the many questions posed by modern demographic flows from the African continent to other parts of the world. A few of these are briefly mentioned here. First, there is the need to know if contemporary population movements from the African continent and the creation of new diasporic communities in parts of the world have linkages with the crisis of underdevelopment currently confronting the African continent. Second, it is also important for us to examine the relationship between the continent and its diasporas over the years. Third, there is now the urgent need to promote a dialogue between existing perspectives on this relationship and its consequences on the development of the African/ Black diaspora experience on the one hand, and on the African continent on the other.

As a corollary to the above, there is the issue of determining the role of the African diaspora in the development of the African continent. A careful analysis of the trajectory of these interactions suggest that they have been factored by changes in at least three inter-related areas, namely, the situation of, and developments in Africa; the status and influence of the African/Black diasporas; and the changing dynamics of the international system. Within the context of the emerging New World Order and the globalization process driving it, and against the background of the clash of civilization suggested by Samuel Huntington,[40] new diasporic identities are now being constructed that could impact on the development of the continent in the near future. In the words of Thandika Mkandawire:

> In Africa, as elsewhere, diasporas have played an important role in the reinvention and revitalization of the 'home country's' identity and sense of itself. And today, with the capacity to participate in political

life of their homelands, there can be no doubt that diasporic groups will be even more immediate in the rethinking of a new Africa.[41]

Scholars need to explore this process and come to terms with their significance in the contemporary history of the continent.

Conclusion

This chapter has examined the historiography of the field of African/Black Diaspora studies, as well as the variables that have factored in its development, from its emergence in the eighteenth century to its maturity as a full-fledged field of study in its own right. The analysis in this chapter has indicated that in the course of its development, African/Black Diaspora studies have been amenable to several analytical perspectives and theoretical approaches, which have impacted significantly on the qualities of the studies carried out by scholars and the ways they handled their subject matter. In examining this theme, however, this chapter has shown how racial stereotypes and prejudices have influenced the way African/Black Diaspora experience has been handled over the years, and why this necessarily has to be transcended by modern scholars as humanity advances. This chapter has made a case for mainstreaming the African/Black Diaspora experience within the broader category of global diaspora studies, articulated on the basis of a meta-theoretical and multi-disciplinary perspective, and an analytical approach. The fundamental issues of the African/Black experience should be examined against the background of the emerging New World Order and globalization.

The recommended methodological perspective in this chapter will go a long way in deepening the understanding of the contributions of the African/Black Diaspora to world civilization while at the same time providing an objective framework for analyzing their challenges and prospects in the New World Order of the twenty-first century. As the world becomes more globalized, and races, peoples, and cultures intersect, fuse and transform, it is time to move beyond orthodox stereotypes, prejudices, and fixations. The world is a place where cultures, races, and civilizations intermingle and coalesce for the progress of humanity. The experience of the African/Black Diaspora and their rich historiography provide an important field of study.

Notes

1. Toyin Falola and Matts D. Childs, eds., *The Yoruba Diaspora in the Atlantic World* (Bloomington, IN: Indiana University Press, 2004), ix.

2. This is evident in the increasing numbers of Black Studies Programs in many universities across the world, the rapid expansion in literature on African/Black Diaspora, and the overall debate it has generated concerning the fate of the Blackman in an increasingly dynamic world. For more of these and related issues consult the following works: Mario Azevedo, ed., *Africana Studies: A Survey of Africa and the African Diaspora*, Second Edition (Durham, NC: Carolina Academic Press, 1998); Roger Bastide, *African Civilizations in the New World* (New York: Harper and Row, 1971); Margaret E. Crahan and Franklin W. Knight, *Africa and the Caribbean: The Legacies of a Link* (Baltimore, MD: The Johns Hopkins University Press, 1979); Isidore Okpewho and Carole Boyce Davies, et al., eds., *The Black Diaspora: African Origins and New World Identities* (Bloomington, IN: Indian University Press, 1999); Linda M. Heywood, ed., *Central Africans and Cultural Transformations in the American Diaspora* (Cambridge: Cambridge University Press, 2002); and Okon E. Uya, *African Diaspora and the Experience in New World Slavery*, Third Edition (Calabar, Nigeria: Clear Lines Publications, 2005).

3. Okon Uya, *Contemporary Issues on Slavery and the Black World* (Calabar, Nigeria: CAT Publishers, 2003), 2–4.

4. Uya, 3. Also consult Carl Deglar, *Neither Black Nor White: Slavery and Race Relations in Brazil and the United States* (New York: The Macmillan Company, 1971); Walter Rodney, *How Europe Underdeveloped Africa* (Enugu, Nigeria: Ikengga Publishers, 1982); Joseph Inikori, ed., *Forced Migration: The Impact of the Export Slave Trade on African Societies* (London: Hutchinson University Library, 1983); W. O. Alli, ed., *Africa and African Diaspora: Aspects of an Experience* (Jos, Nigeria: Mazlink Nigerian Ltd, 1999); George M. Fredrickson, *Racism: A Short History* (Princeton, NJ: Princeton University Press, 2003); and Armstrong M. Adejo, *Reparations: Africa's Charge New Charge in a Changing World* (Makurdi, Nigeria: Peach Global Publications, 2004).

5. For details of this consult, Rodney, *How Europe Underdeveloped Africa*; Inikori, *Forced Migration*: Joseph Inikori and Stanley Engerman, eds., *The Atlantic Slave Trade: Effects on Economies, Societies and Peoples of in Africa, the Americas and Europe* (Durham, NC: Duke University Press, 1992); Joseph C. Miller, *The Way of Death: Merchant Capitalism and the Angolan Slave Trade, 1730–1830* (Madison, WI: University of Wisconsin Press, 1988); Paul Lovejoy, *Transformations in Slavery: A History of Slavery in Africa*, Second Edition (Cambridge: Cambridge Press, 2000).

6. Michael J. C. Echero, "An African Diaspora: The Ontological Project," in Isidone Okpewho, Boyce Davies, and Ali A. Mazuri, eds., *The African Diaspora*, 3–18; Earl E. Thorpe, *The Central of Black History* (Westport, CT: Greenwood Press, 1960); Henry Richards, ed., *Topics in Afro-American Studies* (Buffalo, New York, 1971); Daniel C. Thompson, *Sociology of the Black Experience* (Westport, CT: Greenwood Press, 1974); and Joseph E. Harris, ed., *Global Dimensions of the African Diaspora*, Second Edition (Washington, D C: Howard University Press, 1993).

7. Uya, 6–7.

8. Cited in Okon E. Uya, "Trends and Perspectives in African History," in *Perspectives and Methods of Studying African History*, ed., Erim O. Erim and Okon E. Uya (Enugu, Nige-

ria: Forth Dimension Publishing Company Ltd, 1984), 1.

9. Edward Long, cited in Uya, *African Diaspora and the Experience in New World Slavery*, 2.

10. See Uya, "Trends and Perspectives in African History," 1.

11. Earl E. Thorpes, *The Central Theme of Black History* (Westport, CT: Greenwood Press, 1960); Earl E. Thorpes, *Black Historians: A Critique* (New York: Vintage Books, 1971); Eric E. Williams, *British Historians and the West Indies* (New York: Africana Publishing Corporation, 1966).

12. George W. Williams, cited in *African Diaspora*, ed., Uya, 2.

13. Uya, *African Diaspora*, 2–3.

14. Mario Azevedo, "African Studies and the State of the Arts," in Azevedo, ed., *Africana Studies*, 6.

15. Festus Ohaegbulam, *Towards an Understanding of the African Experience from Contemporary and Historical Perspectives* (Lanham, MD: University Press of America, 1990).

16. W.E.B. Du Bios' earliest studies were directed at realizing this objective. For details see his *The Suppression of the Atlantic Slave Trade in the United States of America, 1638–1870* (Baton Rouge: Louisiana State University Press, 1996); *Black Reconstruction in America, 1860–1880;* (New York: The World Publishing Co., 1964); *The Philadelphia Negro* (Philadelphia: The University of Pennsylvania Press, 1899); and *The Souls of the Black Folk Then and Now* (New York: Penguin Books, 1989).

17. Such seminal works include *The Negro in Our History; The African Background Outlined* (Washington, DC: Negro University Press, 1968); and *The Mis-Education of the Negro* (Washington DC: The Associated Press, 1933). Through these, Woodson was able to generate engage the racial prejudices and stereotypes that were the dominant features of knowledge about the Black people.

18. Uya, 3–4.

19. He adds that Melville Herskovits' early scholarly articles on the relevance of an adequate knowledge of African History as the basis for understanding of the Blacks in the New World first appeared in the *Journal*. The *Journal* also published essays on the role of Black activities of Black explorers who accompanied the Spanish conquistadors to the New World before the advent of Black slavery. Uya, *African Diaspora*, 4.

20. Uya, 4. These activities played an important role in the emergence of the Black Power Movement of the 1960s.

21. Ibid.

22. Cited in Uya, 6.

23. Russell L. Adams, "Intellectual Questions and Imperatives in the Development of Afro-American Studies," *Journal of Negro Education,* Vol. 53, 3 (Summer, 1984), 201–225. Also see James E. Turner, ed., *The Next Decade: Theoretical and Research Issues in Africana Studies* (Itchaca, NY: Cornell University Africana Center, 1984).

24. Contrary to the widely held view by most historians of the Pan-African experience, there is proof that Pan-Africanists were the first to express deep concerns about the status of Blacks in the New World intellectual credence. Immanuel Geiss, *The Pan-African Movement: A History of Pan-Africanism in America, Europe and Africa* (New York: Africana, 1972); Tony Martin, *The Pan-African Connection: From Slavery to Garvey and Beyond* (Cambridge, MA: Schenkman, 1982); and Michael Williams, "The Pan-African Movement," in Azevedo, ed., 169–181.

25. Nathan Huggins, Martin Kilson, and Daniel Fox, eds., *Key Issues in the Afro-American Experience*, 2 Vols. (New York: Harcourt Brace Jovanovich, 1971); Vincent Harding, *There is a River: The Black Struggle for Freedom in America* (New York: Harcourt Brace Jovanovich, 1983); Rhoda Lois Blumberg, *Civil Rights: The 1960s Freedom Struggle* (Boston, MA: Twayne Publishers,1984); Lorraine Williams, ed., *Africa and the Afro-American Experience* (Washington DC: Howard University Press, 1981).

26. Uya, *African Diaspora*, 7; Sterling Stuckey, *The Ideological Origins Black Nationalism* (Boston, MA: Beacon Press, 1972); Lawrence W. Levine, *Black Culture and Black Consciousness: Afro-American Folk Thought from Slavery to Freedom* (New York: Oxford University Press, 1977).

27. E. Franklin Frazier, *The Negro in the United States* (New York: The Macmillan Co., 1947); James E. Turner, ed., *The Next Decade*; and John Blassingame, *New Perspectives on Black Studies*.

28. Melville J. Haskovits, "Acculturation and the American Negro," *Southwestern Political and Social Science Quarterly* 8 (1927), 211–412; and Melville J. Haskovits, *The Myth of a Negro Past* (Boston, MA: Beacon, 1958).

29. Uya, 16.

30. Sidney W. Mintz and Richard Price, *The Birth of African-American Culture: A Anthropological Perspective* (Boston, MA: Beacon, 1992), 18–19.

31. Falola and Childs, 4.

32. Mintz and Richard Price, 18–19.

33. John Thornton, *Africa and Africans in the Making of the Atlantic World, 1400–1680* (Cambridge: Cambridge University Press, 1992); Paul Gilroy, *The Black Atlantic: Modernity and Double Consciousness* (Cambridge, MA: Harvard University Press, 1993).

34. Falola and Childs, 4.

35. For examples of this see, Joseph Inikori and Stanley Engerman, eds., *The Atlantic Slave Trade: Effects on Economies, Societies and Peoples of in Africa, the Americas and Europe* (Durham, NC: Duke University Press, 1992); Okon Uya, *African Dimensions of American Cultures* (Calabar, Nigeria: University of Calabar Press, 1994); Joseph Miller, T*he Way of Death: Merchant Capitalism and the Angolan Slave Trade, 1730–1830* (Madison: University of Wisconsin Press, 1988); Paul Lovejoy, *Transformations in Slavery: A History of Slavery in Africa*, Second Edition (Cambridge: Cambridge Press, 2000).

36. Falola and Childs, 4.

37. Paul E. Lovejoy, "The African Diaspora: Revisionist Interpretations of Ethnicity, Culture, and Religion Under Slavery," *Studies in the World History of Slavery, Abolition, and Emancipation* 2, No. 1 (1997). This article is also available at http//www2.h-net.msu.edu/ -slavery/essaysesy9701love.html.

38. Falola and Childs; David Eltis, et al., eds., *The Trans-Atlantic Slave Trade: A Database on CD-ROM* (Cambridge: Cambridge University Press, 1999); and Paul E. Lovejoy, ed., "Identifying Enslaved Africans in the Diaspora," in *Identity in the Shadow of Slavery* (London: Continuum, 2000).

39. For other features, see Robin Cohen, *Global Diasporas: An Introduction* (London: Routledge, 1997), 26.

40. Samuel P. Huntington, "The Clash of Civilizations: The Debate," Council of Foreign Relations, United States, 1996, 1–25; Ali A. Mazrui, *Cultural Forces in World Politics* (Portsmouth, Heinemann, 1990); Yakubu A. Ochefu, "A Historical Perspective of Cultural

Stereotypes and its Implications for National Integration," in *Obudu Journal of Arts and Culture*, Vol. 2., No. 1., November 2000; and Okpeh O. Okpeh, Jr., "The New World Order, Diaspora Africans and the Racial Identity Question: A Historical Reflection on Some Emerging Issues," paper presented at the African Cultural Conference organized by African Cultural Institute, University of Lagos, October 7–10, 2003.

41. Cited in CODESRIA Multinational Working Groups, "Africa and Its Diasporas," Call for Proposals, 2005, 3.

Part II

The Modern African Diaspora and Black Identity

Chapter 7

Black Like Who? The Identity of an American President

Hettie V. Williams

Barack Obama, the 44th President of the U.S., projects an identity that is fragmented as opposed to an identity that is essentialist or unitary. In nearly every public setting where the issue of his race has been introduced, Obama routinely self-identifies as an African American.[1] He continuously acknowledges his mixed race heritage, and rarely fails to mention the gratitude he feels towards his white grandparents for raising him. In his autobiography he states that, "I can't even hold up my experience as being somehow representative of the black American experience."[2] Obama makes this statement in the same breath in which he claims to be writing about his life as a "black American."[3] Obama's self-identity, as based on his writings, speeches, and public statements, may be characterized as a type of hybrid fluidity as opposed to the hybrid fixity sometimes expressed in the black/white multiracial identity. In other words, hybrid fixity tends to focus on one's multiraciality as the primary vehicle for self-identification and actualization. Obama's identity includes a mixed race dimension as merely one component of a more encompassing hybridity, which also embraces his subjectivity as local (African American), and transnational (world citizen). His hybrid fluidity is deployed in his autobiographical writings.

These mutable subjectivities, often illustrated in ethnic autobiographies, are evidenced in Obama's two books. Michael M. J. Fischer contends that ethnic autobiography helps us to better understand contemporary society, because in these autobiographies, there is an illustration of a multifaceted or pluralist concept of the self that serves as a basis for a "wider social ethos of pluralism."[4] This chapter presents an understanding of Obama's autobiography as a specific genre of writing often used by members of distinct ethnic groups to express the inexpressible aspects of self-identity through memoir and trauma narrative. In these narratives, the autobiography functions as a mechanism through which ethno-racial subjectivity is materialized, negotiated, and sometimes reformed. Obama's *Dreams from My Father* as a form of ethnic self-life-writing is also a *bildungsroman* (coming of age story) that details his passage into blackness. This chapter also analyzes *Dreams from My Father* as a form of ethnic autobiography that helps to support the notion of Obama's hybrid-fluid sense of self-awareness.

Obama consistently negotiates a range of racial identity positionings that are at times reflective of the shifting understanding of race in contemporary America.[5] He has learned to negotiate the fluid contours of self-identity having been born and raised outside of African American culture, as expressed in his "many voices." In her analysis of *Dreams from My Father*, British-Jamaican novelist Zadie Smith (author of *White Teeth* and *On Beauty*), describes Obama as a "many-voiced man," because:

> the tale he tells is all about addition. His is the story of a genuinely many-voiced man. If it has a moral it is that each man must be true to his selves, plural.[6]

Americans have been forced to re-think race, blackness, and multiraciality in significant ways[7] since November 4, 2008. Smith's assessment of Obama's ethnic autobiographical writing, *Dreams*, helps to demonstrate the notion of Obama as having a fluid sense of self-awareness or "selves." This hybrid fluidity is best expressed in Obama's writings and sometimes in his everyday race talk, and is reflective of what Russian literary theorist Mikhail Bakhtin referred to as "double voice."

This chapter examines Barack Obama's journey to self-identity as a racialized subject by incorporating sociological, cultural, and feminist theory with variant forms of philosophical cosmopolitanism. The core argument of this chapter is twofold in that I am asserting the notion of (1) *other black* as contingent upon and in opposition to essentialist notions of blackness and the phrase (2) *hybrid fluidity* that incorporates multiple subjectivities such as multiraciality and cosmopolitanism. The term "other black" is borrowed from cultural studies theorist Shirley Ann Tate to illustrate the idea that Obama selects the identity category of black, and represents himself as a black man, while speaking back to blackness. The concept of *hybrid fluidity* includes multiracial identity and variant trajectories of cosmopolitanism. Taken together, these terms help to define Obama's composite sense of self-awareness as: *other black cosmopolitan*. In order to capture Obama's complex self-identity, a discussion of race and the multiracial movement, hybrid identities, linguistic subjectivity, and cosmopolitanism are necessary.

Obama and the Concept of "Other Black"

Obama is best described as an "other black"[8] cosmopolitan. He may also be considered a self-identified black man with a complex sense of self-awareness. This complex sense of self-awareness incorporates identities that go beyond blackness. In her book, *Black Skins, Black Masks: Hybridity, Dialogism, Performativity*, British cultural studies scholar Shirley Ann Tate utilizes the phrase "other black" to examine the lives of black/white biracial women in contemporary Britain. Applying the concept of "other black," Tate integrates the theories of Michel Foucault, Mikhail Bakhtin, and Homi Bhabha, among others, to advance her theory of the "hybridity of the everyday." Tate utilizes this concept to examine the daily speech patterns of black biracial women "who speak back" to blackness as illustrated in their everyday conversations about race.

Similarly, Obama's sense of self is shaped by his early social experiences; these were developed outside of the African American community because he was brought up in Hawaii and Indonesia by his white maternal grandparents and Asian step-father, along with his mother. He has constructed a composite self out of his mixed race background and transnational and multicultural experiences. Obama's self-perception is also in part fashioned in reaction to how he has been/is sometimes perceived by those outside of his immediate family: as a black man and a member of the black community. Yet, he occasionally speaks back to blackness.

Obama does not embrace a hybrid self that crystallizes in a multiracial identity, nor does his sense of self include identification with multiracial individuals as a part of his broad subjectivity (that is to say, hybrid or multiracial fixity is not the locus of his core identity). Rather, as an "other black cosmopolitan," he embraces a broader and more dynamic hybrid sense of self-awareness. He acknowledges his multiracial background, but embraces an identity that encompasses his transnational experiences while at the same time being grounded in the African diasporic experience through a visceral connection with the struggles of African Americans. Obama's "other" blackness challenges essentialist assumptions about blackness, race, and multiraciality by speaking back to blackness but not against blackness as primarily illustrated in his autobiographical narrative *Dreams*. Political scientists Valeria Sinclair-Chapman and Melanye Price, note that Obama's ability to articulate the self as "occupying liminal spaces" was integral to his success on the campaign trail.[9]

Moreover, Obama made an explicit connection to questions of his multiraciality in the statement "a lot of shelter dogs are mutts like me,"[10] which he made as President-elect during his first official news conference on November 7, 2008. However clumsily articulated, Obama found a way to acknowledge his mixed race heritage. He does this in his very first official performance as the forty-fourth president of the United States of America. Obama has been continuously referred to as "no drama Obama" by his campaign team. Thus, this statement was not necessarily a "clumsy" error on the part of a man who has come to be known as a more than elegant speaker. A brief overview of Obama's biography may help provide some insight into this statement.

Obama's mother, Stanley "Ann" Dunham, is of European-American descent, a white woman originally from Wichita, Kansas. He was raised by both his mother and maternal grandparents in Indonesia and Hawaii. He has siblings who would presumably self-identify as black-African, and a sister from his mother's second marriage to an Indonesian man who could/would easily self-identify as Asian (her husband is Chinese Canadian), but defines herself as "hybrid." In an interview with Deborah Solomon, Obama's sister Maya Soetoro-Ng was asked about her brother's race and responded in such a way:

> *Solomon*: Do you think of your brother as black?
> *Soetoro-Ng*: Yes, because that is how he has named himself. Each of us has a right to name ourselves as we will.
> *Solomon*: Do you think of yourself as white?
> *Soetoro-Ng*: No. I'm half white, half Asian. I think of myself as hybrid. People usually think I'm Latina when they meet me. That's what made me learn Spanish.[11]

Obama speaks quite evocatively of the brief union between his "white" American mother and his "black" African father, originally from Kenya, in his autobiography *Dreams from My Father: A Story of Race and Inheritance* (1995). The inheritance that Obama speaks of is that of a man with a mixed race ancestry or "divided inheritance" of race bequeathed to him by both his white American mother and black African father. It is in essence the search for a way to name himself "a race." Obama found a way to "name himself" black, as his sister states, without completely relinquishing his mixed race background. Obama explains in his memoirs how at the end of his parent's marriage, he was left in the space in between, "Even as that spell was broken and the worlds that they thought they'd left behind reclaimed each of them, I occupied the place where their dreams had been."[12] The narrative seems largely to be a story of maturation into a black identity, but "the place where their dreams had been" is the sanctuary of the hybrid that struggles for actualization through the racial inheritance of his mother and father.

Barack Obama therefore embraces his blackness, but at the same time he consistently celebrates his multiracial background. David Hollinger has commented on how visible Obama's whiteness is, and how Obama has made Americans aware of multiraciality:

> Press accounts of Obama's life, as well as Obama's own autobiographical writings, render Obama's whiteness hard to miss. No other figure, not even Tiger Woods, has done as much as Obama to make Americans of every education level and social surrounding aware of color-mixing in general.[13]

Obama's sense of self as understood in this examination is both fluid and contingent upon blackness while rejecting notions of essentialist hybridity (or hybrid fixity)[14] reflected in the "popular" multiracial movement. His counter to this is a hybrid fluidity that is illustrated in his autobiography, speeches, public statements, and other writings, and as a result of his lived experience.

Obama's multilayered identity is an intricate interweaving of the particular and the universal; his cosmopolitanism combines cultural, political, and visceral trajectories grounded in an identity shaped by his transnational experiences and mixed race background. He also has a sense of black cosmopolitanism or black collective subjectivity that transcends national and geographical specificity. Obama rejects what I call essentialist hybridity because he associates with the multiracial movement in general. Cultural and visceral cosmopolitanism[15] are more thoroughly examined in section six, while Obama's connection to his multiracial ancestry is further developed in the next section.

Race and the Multiracial Movement

The landmark text by Michael Omi and Howard Winant *Racial Formation in the United States from the 1960s to the 1980s* introduced a contemporary concept of racial formation theory. This theory asserts that race is a multidimensional process of competing race projects as produced in social relations. It is shaped by socio-political power structures, as well as subjective phenomena; these are articulated in racial identities shaped by perceptions about the body (phenotype) and cultural practices. The concept of "race" today has little to do with biology given the findings of social scientists, historians, and geneticists altogether. The race concept was initially manufactured to justify the enslavement of Africans and regulate black bodies in servitude. Historically, race has been an unstable concept. Most scholars have recognized that race continues to operate at the social level in U.S. society, but not as a concrete biological reality.

There remains no consensus among the biological sciences as to what race actually is, or how many races exist if human biology is to be considered in discussions about race. The genetic characteristics present in one population are not necessarily absent in another. The notion that race (or mixed race) can be simply understood as ancestry is problematical given the most recent research in human genetics. The idea of mixed race as ancestry may be explained away quite succinctly as Pilar Ossorio and Troy Duster assert:

> People whose skin color is perceived as white can have genetic profiles indicating that 80% of their recent ancestry is West African, and people whose skin color is perceived as black can have genetic profiles indicative of predominantly European ancestry. A person with substantial, recent African ancestry may pass as White and may have medically and psychologically consequential social advantages of whiteness. On the other hand, a person may pass as White but possess medically relevant alleles more commonly associated with Blacks or with African ancestry.[16]

Ancestry fails to serve as a firm moniker for race or "mixed race" from one generation to the next despite arguments to the contrary made by theorists of mixed race studies.

The case of a South African woman, Sandra Laing, born in 1955 with a markedly African phenotype of two white parents, was continuously reclassified as first white then as a person of color despite the circumstances of her "white" birth and European "ancestry." Her white parents fought to have her reclassified as white (her father attesting to his paternity in court), and there appeared no recent evidence of known African ancestry in her "white" parent's lineage. Scientists at the time argued the "genetic throwback" theory insisting that Laing's physical features were a result of an unknown "African" ancestor's DNA, having lain dormant for generations, manifested in Sandra thereby explaining the difference between nearly pure white parents with an "African" child.[17] Laing eventually selected to become reclassified as a person of color upon her romantic association and subsequent marriage to a man of "African," i.e. black, descent.

Troy Duster has further argued that understanding race involves a complex interplay of social and biological realities as coupled with ideology and myths about race as word and idea.[18] Duster continues:

> Rather, when race is used as a stratifying practice (which can be apprehended empirically and systematically), there is often a reciprocal interplay of biological outcomes that makes it impossible to disentangle the biological from the social.[19]

Duster notes that the empirical biological data is not uniformly consistent with the social, ideological, or cultural assumptions about race such as found in claims about ancestry.

Race operates at the social level and is based on perceptions about human bodies. Race and racism operated in the life of Obama as a man of mixed race[20] ancestry with a particular phenotype who could not pass for white. He articulates this in his autobiography when he describes his life as a child not yet realizing, "I needed a race."[21] As Michael Omi and Howard Winant have argued, racial projects have appeared throughout the modern history of humankind. As a result of these "projects," race, operating at both the micro-level of individual social experiences and at the macro level in racial classification systems, has been reconfigured, but has not disappeared.[22]

The 1960s activism of African Americans, coupled with changes in U.S. immigration laws and the global migration of non-whites into the U.S., helped to produce a new "racial project" predicated on a ternary racial order that acknowledges white, black, and other mono-racial identities as well as multiracial identities. G. Reginald Daniel, in his book *More Than Black*, contends that the emergence of the multiracial identity movement after 1967 can be understood as "a natural outgrowth" of the civil rights activism of the 1960s and is defined by individuals "who resist the one-drop rule and navigate the uncharted waters of multiracial identity."[23] The multiracial movement as advancing a new racial project should be briefly examined here before we can discuss how, and later why, Obama incorporates his multiracial background into his complex sense of self that rests upon a foundation of blackness.

The multiracial movement is a broad based scholarly, social, and cultural movement that includes a host of support groups, informational, and educational agencies. It engages both the scholars who have advanced mixed race studies (the fastest growing subfield within ethnic studies), in the academy, and dozens of groups such as I-Pride (Interracial/Intercultural Pride), founded in Berkeley, California in 1979; the Biracial Family Network (BFN), established in Chicago in 1980; the Interracial Family Alliance (IFA) of Houston; the Multiracial Americans of Southern California in Los Angeles (MASC); and Project RACE (Reclassify All Children Equally). The Association of Multiethnic Americans (AMEA) is a nationwide multiracial/ethnic organization based on existing local groups. It was developed in 1988, and is now centered in California.

Matt Kelley, a nineteen year-old college freshman at Wellesley University in Connecticut, created MAVIN magazine out of his college dorm room in 1999. The MAVIN Foundation as a 501(c) 3 nonprofit group became one of the most important associations dedicated to the support of projects and the dissemination of information related to the mixed race experience. The first major scholarly anthologies dedicated to the study of the mixed race experience were Maria P.P. Root's *Racially Mixed People in America*, which was followed by *The Multiracial Experience*. These anthologies included essays by some of the foundational scholars associated with the mixed race studies movement in academia.

The multiracial movement is not a monolith. There have also been proliferations of online journals, blogs, and forums such as "Interracial Voice" and "Mixed Chics" that exist alongside the aforementioned associations. There are an increasing number of scholarly texts by those who seek to advance knowledge about the mixed race experience. One of the major goals sought by advocacy groups such as the AMEA and the later Project RACE was to make it possible to collect data on multiracial identified individuals on official forms such as the U.S. census. In 2000, the U.S. Census did indeed allow for "a mark more than one" option. This was a significant victory for the multiracial movement in general. In his 2010 U.S. census form, Obama did not select "more than one" but instead chose the category Black/Negro/African American.

The advocates of a multiracial identity category tend to emphasize ancestry, experience, demographics, and personal expression to determine their identity that hinges upon a *hybrid fixity* (that is, the condition of being of two or more races as the axis of identity). Scholars in support of the multiracial identity label have helped to develop a definition of multiracial identity as determined by ancestry. This definition includes the labeling of "first generation" (one parent who is socially designated as black, and one parent who is socially designated as white), and "multigenerational" (those with parents or generations of ancestors with multiracial backgrounds who have resisted identifying only with the African American community), as multiracial.[24]

Challengers to the multiracial identity project label these scholars "pro-identity scholars."[25] Indeed, the emphasis by multiracial advocacy groups and some scholars on personal experience and hybrid "fixity" through ancestry (by drawing lines of delineation that create a distinct multiracial category out of ancestry and social experience) prompted Obama to reject MAVIN's overtures in such a way when meeting with the Generation Mix college students in his Senate offices April 25, 2005:

> Well you know, I don't think that you can consider the issue of mixed race outside of the issue of race. And I do think that racial relations have improved somewhat, and I think to the extent that people of mixed race can be part of those larger movements and those larger concerns then I think that they serve as a useful bridge between cultures .... What I am always cautious about is persons of mixed race focusing so narrowly on their own unique experiences that they are de-

tached from larger struggles, and I think it's important to try to avoid
that sense of exclusivity, and feeling that you're special in some way ...
ultimately the same challenges that all of you face a lot of young people face....[26]

Obama rejects the "exclusivity" of the multiracial category predicated upon
ancestry and experience. This does not mean that he has not found a way to
incorporate his own multiracial ancestry into his self presentation. His more
composite sense of self-awareness, rooted in blackness, is made abundantly
clear in his narrative writings. It has been noted by mixed race studies scholars that individuals of mixed race ancestry, such as Barack Obama, often, in
specific situations, embrace a range of identity formations.

Sociologists David Brunsma and Kerry Ann Rockquemore have demonstrated in their comprehensive cross-regional studies of black/white biracials
in the United States that identity formation for these individuals is customar-
ily multidimensional. That is, black/white biracial identity has a tendency towards the interactional and situational as shaped by social perceptions, personal
choice, and cultural assumptions. Brunsma has drawn a distinction between
the public categories and private identities of black/white multiracials stating
that, "black/white biracials understand themselves in a multitude of ways that
are rooted in their private and social worlds."[27]

Furthermore, Rockquemore contends that black/white biracial individual self-
understanding contains a range of identity categories such as singular (monoracial), border (biracial), protean (sometimes black, white, or biracial) and
transcendent (no single race identified).[28] Obama's core identity is thus clos-
est to a combined singular/border (that is at times strategically transcendent)
identity as coupled with notions of cosmopolitanism. He certainly does not
claim a distinct multiracial or biracial identity that supersedes his blackness. Indeed, Obama has routinely claimed to be black, and writes a memoir clearly
detailing his passage into a "functional" blackness despite his multiracial experience.

Consequently, the desire of many individuals associated with the multiracial movement to claim Obama as their own is at best highly speculative. This
of course does not diminish the choice made by those few individuals who do
indeed publically and privately embrace a multiracial identity. However, the notion that Obama is "at his core" multiracial is a gross misreading of *Dreams
from My Father*. The denial of Obama's self affirmation of blackness (in private or otherwise) seems dangerously close to white supremacist and anti-black
sentiments regarding African Americans more generally. This attempt to su-
perimpose *hybrid fixity* upon Obama tends to privilege mixed race identity,
and ultimately, whiteness.

Scholars and activists associated with the multiracial (identity) movement, that is, those that advance the notion of a distinct multiracial category, tend to promote a *hybrid fixity* that hinges upon bloodlines (ancestry) and personal experience. The construction of race as a stratifying practice that defines one as either "multiracial" or "monoracial" is a new race project that is both exclusionary and self-indulgent as is the nature of identity movements. Human ancestry is shared. Indeed, if ancestry overlaps with genetic inheritance (and it does), and mixed race identity is to be understood as determined by ancestry, "mixed race" constitutes the human community as a whole. Obama's deployment of self-identity is far more progressive than what has been promulgated by the multiracial movement in that he deploys a self awareness that is an on-going negotiation between multiple "I" positions that have no firm axis or point of "fixity."

The only evidence we have of Obama's sense of racial self-identity is to be found in his memoirs, his political treatise, and everyday race talk. *Dreams from My Father* is the most comprehensive discussion delivered by Obama, to date, concerning his personal notions of racial self-identity. To label Obama at his core bi-racial or mixed race is to call into question the man's own words, as he has consistently defined himself as a black man with a mixed race heritage or more composite sense of self-awareness (where the mixed race component is largely muted by choice). Indeed, Obama does speak of a mixed race experience in *Dreams* through the metaphor of "two-worlds," but it is an experience that ultimately reinforces his blackness, not a *mixed identity,* private or otherwise. Obama is clearly far too self-assured an individual to lurk around in private hiding his true "self" from the world despite the hegemony of the one-drop rule.

In one instance in *Dreams,* upon telling his sister Auma the story of a romantic relationship he had with a white woman, he affirms that to continue his involvement with a white woman was to agree to live in her world stating, "I knew that if we stayed together I'd eventually live in hers. After all, I'd been doing it most of my life. Between the two of us, I was the one who knew how to live as an outsider."[29] If indeed Obama tells us of his "mixed race experience" in *Dreams,* he also tells us of living the life of an *outsider* within that experience. Thus, what resonates with him most upon his trip to Africa and in his personal connections with African Americans is the struggle of black people and blackness despite having lived outside of African American culture.

This attempt to impose a multiracial identity upon Obama hinges upon a hybrid fixity that seeks to delineate the monoracial from the multiracial as predicated upon a "feeling of in-between" and blood lines. To foist upon Obama a private multiracial identity is a form of sophistry that seeks to make Obama a type of multiracial mascot for a new race project. The film *Invasion of the*

Body Snatchers comes to mind here as based on the Jack Finney novel *The Body Snatchers* published in 1954. We know the plot well: imposter simulacrums grown from giant plant like pods invade suburbia masquerading as the people we know. Obama has the typical experience of a mixed race person, but has repeatedly chosen to self-identify as a black man and has consistently called himself black. To believe that he is at his core or in private a mixed race identified person is tantamount to believing that he is a type of imposter black man or black simulacrum who is hiding his mixed race identity only to be revealed in private.

If we are to believe the notion that Obama has been forced to capitulate to the one drop rule that defines anyone as black with one drop of black blood, we must also take into account that perhaps Obama may have indeed chosen to call himself black in reaction to white racism. That is, Obama's refusal to identify with mixed race categories might very well be a type of reactionary disassociation with whiteness (his white ancestry) and white supremacist beliefs that hold blackness in contempt. Though he does not live it, what resonates with Obama the most is the black experience. Therefore, given the disdain for blackness present in U.S. society, it seems more plausible (as blackness is more often than not determined by phenotype) that Obama found community in blackness and black people not through his mixed race experience, and does not identify himself as merely mixed race in private or public. Despite the "archetypes" and "tropes" of the mixed race experience that appear in Obama's autobiography, he found greater comfort and camaraderie with people who look like him (as he so states).

Tanya Hernandez, among others, contends that U.S. society is increasingly adopting a "multiracial matrix" similar to that found in Latin America in which mixed race identity serves as a moniker of racial transcendence.[30] This is not to infer that the "multiracial matrix" present throughout Latin American countries affords equality to people of color; on the contrary, the myth of racial democracy in places such as Brazil has long been abandoned by scholars. One can infer that the one-drop rule is becoming less hegemonic in U.S. society. Much like the popular multiracial movement, there seems to be a fixation on mixed race identity like never before in U.S. history as mixed race people by the millions have begun to self-identify. This is not necessarily a climate in which a mixed race president of the most powerful nation on the planet would hide his "true" core identity from the world.

Certainly, had Obama's phenotype been lighter or nearly white, his choice may have been different. The question of phenotype tends to complicate the whole notion of a mixed race experience for black/white multiracial individuals. Indeed, Obama embarks on a search for "his people" (i.e. African Americans) at an early age while feeling like a stranger among white people in *Another Country.*[31] This is the story he tells us in his own words.

Obama relates to us, in his memoirs, a story of blackness as a "doing" and a "becoming." His own sister tells us that she considers herself "hybrid," but her brother has chosen to name himself black. For most individuals, self-identity tends to be fixed while identification is about process. At the same time, identification with one or more "selves" threatens to unseat the very notion of identity. Obama's biography is clearly the story of a man searching for a way to name himself black, while maintaining a connection to his multiracial background whenever possible. The title *Dreams from My Father: A Story of Race and Inheritance* is enunciated through the story he tells us: that the racial inheritance bequeathed to him from his father is blackness. This notion of Obama as a black man is continuously reinforced in his memoirs, and ever present in his autobiography. At the very end of *Dreams,* he states his claim to blackness, saying "the pain I felt was my father's pain. My questions were my brother's questions. Their struggle, my birthright."[32] Obama's personal biography is examined in the following section.

The Obama Biography in Perspective[33]

Barack Obama was born August 4, 1961 in Honolulu, Hawaii to a white American mother, Stanley "Ann" Dunham, and a black Kenyan father, Barack Hussein Obama, Sr. His parents were students at the East-West Center of the University of Hawaii at Manoa during the time of Obama's birth. He has seven siblings including Maya Soetoro Ng, from his mother's second marriage to an Indonesian man, Lolo Soetoro, and a total of six more from his father's marriages to other women (one African wife and a Jewish American woman). Obama was raised primarily by his white American mother and grandparents in Hawaii after his father left to pursue doctoral studies at Harvard, and later returned to Kenya, when Barack, Jr. was two years old. Ann Dunham married Lolo Soetoro in 1967, another student at the East-West Center, when Barack was six years old. The family relocated to Jakarta, Indonesia after Soetoro was forced to return home due to unrest in Indonesia. Obama's sister Maya was born August 15, 1970 in Jakarta, Indonesia. Obama attended schools in Indonesia until he was ten years old, when his mother sent him back to Hawaii in 1971 to be raised primarily by his grandparents. He would only see his father once more. Although they corresponded with one another, in 1982, when Barack was twenty-one years old, his father was killed in a car accident in Nairobi, Kenya.

Historian Paul Spickard has noted that Pacific Islander Americans who inhabit Hawaii have complex multiethnic identities based on ancestry, family, practice, and place. They have a "greater consciousness" than other American groups of mixed peoples having multiple ethnicities including Samoan, Tongan, Marquesan, Tahitian, Maori, and European.[34] Pacific Islanders are more successful at balancing multiple ethnicities while being "deeply involved" with more than one of these identities at the same time; therefore, Pacific Islander American identity is ultimately situational.[35] In his historical and ethnographic studies of Pacific Islander ethnicity, Spickard has provided several examples of how multiple identities are balanced and negotiated in Hawaii. Barack Obama, coming of age in Hawaiian culture, would have learned to balance his multiple selves more proficiently as opposed to if he had come of age on the U.S. mainland. Indeed, his memoir suggests that he found ways to incorporate his "multiple selves" into a composite self that included his biracial background, which he developed in a multiethnic setting that encourages the "balancing" of more than one ethno-racial identity.

The hybrid Obama came of age in Indonesia and the multicultural setting in Hawaii, where he struggled to name himself black. In his memoirs, Obama mentioned that becoming black in his formative years was, at times, a difficult process. On several occasions, he illustrates to his reader the process of being/becoming black out of the sometimes awkward relationship with white people and whiteness (including the grandparents who raised him). Obama speaks of a search for self and manhood in his early years that could not come from his grandfather, but rather from "some other source."[36] He found a way to become black by watching *Soul Train* and going to the basketball courts where he met a cohort of sometimes angry black youths. In *Dreams from My Father*, he reveals that:

> TV movies, the radio; those were the places to start. Pop culture was color coded, after all, an arcade of images from which you could cop a walk, a talk, a step, a style. I couldn't croon like Marvin Gaye, but I could learn to dance all the *Soul Train* steps. I couldn't pack a gun like Shaft or Superfly, but I could sure enough curse like Richard Pryor. And I could play basketball, with a consuming passion ....[37]

Obama found camaraderie and community among his black boyhood friends in Hawaii, "it was there [the basketball court near his grandparents home] that I would meet Ray and the other blacks close to my age who had begun to trickle into the islands, teenagers whose confusion and anger would help shape my own."[38]

Obama, the college student, continued to search for a sense of self until he moved to Chicago, where he became black. He was made aware at an early age that he needed both a race and a community, as asserted in his autobiographical narrative *Dreams from My Father*. Two years after graduating from High School, he was still pondering the question "Where do I belong?"[39] He articulates this upon receiving a letter from his father:

> Two years from graduation, I had no idea what I was going to do with my life, or even where I would live. Hawaii lay behind me like a child-hood dream; I could no longer imagine settling there. Whatever my father might say, I knew it was too late to ever truly claim Africa as my home. And if I had come to understand myself as a black American, and was understood as such, that understanding remained unanchored to place. What I needed was a community, I realized, a community that cut deeper than the common despair that black friends and I shared when reading the latest crime statistics, or the high fives I might ex-change on a basketball court. A place where I could put down stakes and test my commitments.[40]

Obama "named" himself black before leaving Hawaii for the mainland in pur-suing his college studies at Occidental College, but remained "unanchored" in blackness.

In his writings, Obama trots out a succession of black friends from child-hood to the college years, including Ray, Reggie, Marcus, and Regina in an at-tempt to legitimate to his readers, and possibly to himself: see, "I have black friends." His quest for place in blackness is at times painful during his more awk-ward early years from grade school through college and ultimately law school. Indeed, Obama characterizes his early college experience as a time when he, par-ticularly in his first year at Occidental, felt as if he were "living a lie" and con-tinuously "running around in circles" trying to "cover his tracks" when interacting with his black friends.[41] On one occasion he tells Regina, after giving a public address in association with the divestment campaign against South Africa or-ganized by black students on campus, that he has no "business speaking for black folks."[42] It is through Regina's stories that his romanticized vision of black life and community takes shape:

> She [Regina] told me about evenings in the kitchen with uncles and cousins and grandparents, the stew of voices bubbling up in laugh-ter. Her voice evoked a vision of black life in all its possibility, a vision that filled me with longing-for place, and a fixed and definite history. As we were getting up to leave, I told Regina I envied her:[43]

"For what?"

"I don't know. For your memories, I guess."[44]

Obama's quest for self seemed to be ultimately stifled at Occidental. Was he to be forever consigned to live vicariously through Regina's, and other friends, memories and experiences of blackness in his personal attainment of a black self? This pursuit of self eventually continued beyond Occidental, and took him to another space.

The search for community and "place" brought Obama to New York City and Columbia University where he began to further conceptualize himself as a black man:

> And so, when I heard about a transfer program that Occidental had arranged with Columbia University, I'd been quick to apply. I figured that if there weren't any more black students at Columbia than there were at Oxy, I'd at least be in the heart of a true city, with black neighborhoods in close proximity.[45]

It was while attending Columbia University that Obama became acutely aware of the structural inequalities in American society, which he understood to have a deep impact on the ability of African Americans to progress:

> But whether because of New York's density or because of its scale, it was only now that I began to grasp the almost mathematical precision with which America's race and class problems joined; the depth, the ferocity, of resulting tribal wars; the bile that flowed freely not just out on the streets but in the stalls of Columbia's bathrooms as well, where no matter how many times the administration tried to paint them over, the walls remained scratched with blunt correspondence between niggers and kikes.[46]

Obama's musings on black people and his search for community in blackness, at times, are romanticized and seem paternalistic. Nonetheless, his journey into blackness is consummated in New York City. The second Obama, as a black man anchored in place, comes of age in Chicago. Indeed, Obama became black in Chicago. He confirmed his entrenchment in blackness through endogamy having met and married a dark skinned black woman named Michelle Obama with roots in Chicago's Southside. The following section examines how Obama came to balance his hybrid self with a functional blackness grounded in the black community,[47] while never completely dismissing his mixed race heritage as articulated in both his memoir and political biography *The Audacity of Hope.*

Race, Hybridity, and Functional Blackness

Shirley Ann Tate postulates in her book *Black Skins, Black Masks* a space where black as a category is constantly recouped, transformed, and reformed. Obama is both performer and producer of an "other black" identity that is sometimes in opposition to positionings within the larger discourses of blackness. The "larger" discourses about blackness are predicated upon experiences that Obama does not have. It is clear that Obama, with his "African" features, and skin tone, could never pass for white. Obama was not completely at ease in his blackness until he learned the language, gesture, and "ways" of his two worlds on his path to self development.

His embodiment of blackness can be seen in representations of his public self and language. His musical sense of language and his ability to harness the creative power of the word *nommo*,[48] reveal a black identity deeply connected to the African American experience. Yet, his journey into blackness took place within a multicultural setting where he learned to appropriate the languages of his "two worlds."[49] His blackness is, in part, performance. He learned to speak, talk, and perform blackness on his journey into adulthood.[50] This homogenizing trajectory[51] into blackness has never been completely divorced from Obama's multiracial self as shaped by his upbringing in multicultural Hawaii. Further, Obama's blackness is contingent upon, and in opposition to essentialist concepts of race while also being connected to his hybrid cosmopolitan subjectivity.

Cultural studies theoretician Homi K. Bhabha postulates hybridity as a "third space" subject position or indeterminate space, where a constant blurring and questioning of essentialist boundaries occurs.[52] Further, Bhabha asserts that this "third space" may be characterized as an "interruptive, interrogative, and enunciative" space where the process of identification takes shape "through another object, an object of otherness."[53] For Obama, blackness, as understood in a multicultural setting by a man with a multiracial background, is at first an object of otherness. Tate, utilizing the theories of Bhabha, has argued that the third space of hybridity is a "dialogical space where speakers thread together discourses to identify with and through objects of otherness."[54] Tate examines the discussions by mixed race women "who speak back to their positioning within blackness" to establish her premise that hybridity is about "the ongoing assemblage of identifications."[55]

Neither Bhabha nor Tate understands hybridity as a fixed identity, but rather as a situational process of identification. Obama's blackness is in part a type of hybrid blackness as understood in relation to his multiracial background and cosmopolitan outlook. Hybridity, as Naomi Pabst contends, "enables us to conceive of a blackness that crosscuts, overlaps, and blends with other categories, racial and otherwise."[56] Obama's blackness blends with other categories.

This process of identification through dialogue is ongoing and not merely about selecting a moniker of self-identity such as "multiracial" or "black" on a public form. Obama repeatedly speaks back to his positioning within blackness from the standpoint of his biracial and multicultural experience through his memoir, political writings, and public speeches. He embodies the "experience" but not the identity of a multiracial person on many occasions.[57] He may have become black through endogamy and by situating himself within the black community, married to a black woman with dark skin, but his composite identity is far more complex than "black," "white," or "multiracial." The self for Obama is framed broadly, as opposed to a unitary or essentialist space. Bhabha contends that the hybrid "third space" is an ambivalent space where there exists no unity or fixity.[58] This notion of the hybrid pertains to Obama's blackness, which may be seen as the foundation of the self but not the end of the self.

Indeed, blackness does not constitute the beginning, end, or composite of the self for this U.S. president. This blackness is neither unitary nor fixed, given that Obama is at times in dialogue with blackness. Obama's black identity may be seen as political or public in that he does indeed situate the self as grounded in the black community; he claims a black/African American identity that seems much more nuanced when coupled with his writings, speeches, and everyday race talk. Given that Americans continue to see race through a binary lens, Obama understood that he needed a race (as he states in his memoirs) to become president of the United States. This many-voiced man spoke the language of an "other black"[59] to secure the highest position in the land.

Obama's blackness has been hotly debated since he entered the political arena. Critics of his blackness have included Stanley Crouch, who wrote a piece in the *New York Daily News* detailing why he believed Obama was not "black like me;" Debra Dickerson, who insisted that Obama did not meet the proper criteria for blackness because he did not descend from African slaves; and the *New Republic* columnist Peter Beinart, who defined Obama as a "good black." Questions of Obama's identity have engaged both the far right and liberal Democrats. Joe Biden (who later became Obama's choice for Vice-President) described Obama as "clean and articulate," while Democratic Senate Majority Leader Harry Reid defined Obama's blackness in similar ways when he remarked on his ability to speak as a proper "Negro."

In an interview with Charlie Rose, Obama himself commented on his blackness, "If I'm outside your building trying to catch a cab," he told Rose, "they're not saying, oh there's a mixed race guy." It is interesting to note that Obama's critics on the far right have blackened Obama further as he has become president. Indeed, many on the far right contend that Obama is an alien non-citizen born in Africa. Yale race scholar Naomi Pabst has noted that to question a person's blackness is to admit the very blackness of the person under scrutiny stating that, "you have to be black by some definition in order to be 'not really black.'"[60]

Obama's blackness may also be understood as a doing and a becoming as evidenced in his biographical narratives. One can sense this "otherness" in several excerpts from his memoir *Dreams from My Father* that exemplify his dialogue with "blackness," and to a lesser extent, in his book *The Audacity of Hope*, through the rhetoric of racial transcendence. Although Obama consistently defines himself as an African American, it is through his writings that we see him struggle with his racial self; as Carly Fraser asserts, "Obama writes in a way that emphasizes the complexities of his background and his desire to embrace all aspects of it."[61] This struggle with his racial self is an attempt by Obama to construct a composite identity that includes blackness, mixed race ancestry, and his transnational experiences. To illustrate this further, it is necessary to examine Obama as linguistic subject.

Obama as Linguistic Subject

In his autobiography, Obama stated, "I learned to slip back and forth between my black and white worlds, understanding that each possessed its own language and customs and structures of meaning, convinced that with a bit of translation on my part the two worlds would eventually cohere."[62] This statement encapsulates Obama as linguistic subject. The French linguist Emile Benveniste (1902–1976) argued that it is "in and through language that man constitutes himself as a subject." The understanding of individual self-identity through the study of language has been the concern of psychology, philosophy, and literary theory for some time. Russian philosopher and literary critic Mikhail Bakhtin (1895–1975) studied literature to examine how human social identity is materialized through language and voice. Bakhtin's ideas are directly applicable to Obama as linguistic subject.

Bakhtin's research led him to coin phrases such as "heteroglossia" and "dialogism." The term heteroglossia is a combination of the Latin term *hetero* for different, and the Greek word *glossa* for tongue/language. This term "heteroglossia" as utilized by Bakhtin, connotes "different-speech-ness," "another's speech in another language," or the coexistence of distinct varieties of speech within a single linguistic code. More succinctly, heteroglossia constitutes the existence of conflicting discourses within any field of linguistic activity such as with a work of literature (a novel or memoir) or a diversity of voices, styles of discourse, or points of view. The Obama narratives *Dreams from My Father* and *Audacity of Hope* contain an often conflicting discourse on Obama's racial identity while Obama himself "speaks in tongues" throughout much of *Dreams.* Dorthy J. Hale contends that African American linguistic identity contains a powerful heteroglossia that may be equated with Du Boisian double consciousness.[63] Hale has argued that scholars of African American literature and culture have found a way to read Du Boisian double consciousness through Bakhtinian double voice, thereby "transforming the Du Boisian crisis of subaltern invisibility into a Bakhtinian triumph of self-articulation."[64] Obama's journey to self-articulation evolves in his *Dreams from My Father.*

On the one hand, *Dreams* is about Obama's journey into blackness, but on the other hand he continuously tells his reader how he learned to appropriate the language of his two worlds while running around in circles and tripping over his tongue when lamenting the crimes of "white folks." Further, in his political treatise *Audacity of Hope*, he tells us again how he has never completely harnessed a singular ethno-racial identity through which to understand himself in the world as a "black man of mixed race heritage." He states that, "I've never had the option of restricting my loyalties on the basis of race, or measuring my worth on the basis of tribe."[65]

Bakhtin studied novels because it was his contention that the novelist best illustrated the social voices present in language. Bakhtin often understood voice as accent, ventriloquation (internal dialogue of voices or a process through which self-understanding of experience receive linguistic formulation), refraction, or inflection. Voice as a property of language allows for an understanding of human identity as both self-selected and socially determined (both individual and collective). For Bakhtin, human subjects are both voiced and have the ability to "voice." The quality of being "voiced" illustrates the language that speaks the subject into society, while the subject's use of *voice* may be used to speak back to the dominant discourses concerning identity. Obama's use of the terms "mutt" and more recently "mongrel" could perhaps be analyzed through Bakhtinian theories of language and subjectivity. For Bakhtin, all language appears dialogic. That is, everything anyone says always exists in response to things that have been said before and in anticipation of things that will be said. Obama's thinking is highly strategic if not anticipatory on questions of race.

The Dutch psychologist Herbert Hermans utilized the theories of Bakhtin to develop Dialogical Self Theory (DST). This theory illustrates the mind's ability to imagine different positions in a dialogue moving beyond the self-other dichotomy infusing the internal with the external. DST considers the existence of a dynamic multiplicity of relatively autonomous I-positions. In this theory, "I" moves from one spatial position to another in accordance with changes in situation and time. Obama exhibits a composite self that incorporates a multiplicity of "I" positions as opposed to a singular core self identity. For Obama, "I" moves from one spatial position to another in accordance with changes in situation and time (such as with both the "mutt" and "mongrel" statements). He may have lived a mixed race experience, but he does not invest his self-identity in a singular racial self, be it mixed race or black. His autobiographical narratives are replete with hybrid utterances or passages that may employ a single speaker, but one or more "voices."

Obama has straddled his two worlds in his early development and as a political figure from his speech at the Democratic National Convention in 2004, to his first two years as President through 2010. It is as candidate, and later President, that we see Barack H. Obama harness the language of his "two worlds" best. There is a marked difference that speaks to the "many-voiced" man that Obama is, between a speech that he gave at the Opening Convocation at Howard University, and the Commencement address that he gave at Southern New Hampshire University while on the campaign trail in 2007. The international addresses connect us more to the cosmopolitan Obama (for obvious reasons), while in his speeches to the American public there seem to be greater variations of the black/white Obama navigating between his "two worlds" depending on context and situation. Indeed, his public persona in these public forums presents a self that is at times contradictory. Zadie Smith notes Obama's talent for dialogue as evidenced in his memoir in such a way:

> In *Dreams from My Father*, the new president displays an enviable facility for dialogue, and puts it to good use, animating a cast every bit as various as the one James Baldwin—an obvious influence—conjured for his own many-voiced novel *Another Country*. Obama can do young Jewish male, black old lady from the South Side, white woman from Kansas, Kenyan elders, white Harvard nerds.... This new president doesn't just speak *for* his people. He can *speak* them. It is a disorienting talent in a president; we're so unused to it.[66]

Smith notes, as too few others have, that Obama with his "many-voiced" narrative articulates a plural self with multiple ethno-racial and transnational allegiances. She goes on to state that because Obama, as a mixed race man born in the space where his parents dreams ended, had no choice but to "speak in tongues" like all others born in this place "betwixt and between."[67] Smith writes:

> Naturally, Obama was born there. So was I. When your personal multiplicity is printed on your face, in an almost too obviously thematic

manner, in your DNA, in your hair and in the neither this nor that beige of your skin-well, anyone can see you come from Dream City .... You have no choice but to cross borders and speak in tongues.[68]

Obama utilizes his "many-voices" to connect with all people beyond the U.S. when he speaks. This is evidenced in Obama as linguistic subject. Obama's identity is connected to a cosmopolitanism that accepts broad notions of self-identity, but neither rejects nor discards subjective racial identities.

Conclusion

Barack Obama may be seen by some as a calculating individual. He is a savvy, shrewd, and pragmatic politician who gives himself to no one and everyone at the same time. Obama unceremoniously dismissed Reverend Jeremiah Wright and Shirley Sherrod amid racial controversies. Wright, Obama's former pastor for twenty years, was discarded for his audacious articulation of black liberation theology. The now famous Obama speech on race was delivered specifically to salvage his campaign (again, Obama responds out of necessity) after an incendiary speech by Reverend Wright "damning America" surfaced on YouTube. Obama was forced to divest himself of Wright, the quintessential "angry black man," or run the risk of irreparable damage to his carefully crafted bid for president. Sherrod, an African American U.S. Department of Agriculture administrator in Georgia, was asked to resign for her alleged mistreatment of white farmers on the basis of race. There have been other casualties, such as former White House special advisor on green jobs Van Jones, who was forced to resign when he was branded a "black nationalist" and "communist" following clips of an inflammatory speech he had given appeared on YouTube. Interestingly enough, these same charges have been continuously hurled at Obama by the far right.

Obama is not the first politician of African American descent to use a strategy of racial transcendence to win an election. Obama's rhetoric of transcendence is often strategically deployed and never completely anchored in black social justice claims.[69] Of course, his campaign for president may have utilized some of the same techniques as those who came before him, such as Shirley Chisholm, Harold Washington, or Jesse Jackson, in terms of his connections to the black community through the Black Church and his community organizing experience. However, his deployment of racial ambiguity through his many voices, as opposed to a "black-centered" rhetoric of social justice, gained him more white votes than any other black candidate on the national scene, ultimately helping him to secure the highest office in the land.[70]

Obama articulated in his now famous race speech the grievances harbored by African Americans with the demands of "all people" or all Americans, while at the same time giving voice to "legitimate" white resentment. While this technique flagrantly diminishes the real structural inequalities faced by African Americans past and present, it nonetheless proved successful for candidate Obama with a campaign team that was made up of mostly white operatives of the Democratic Party outside of the black community. The Obama campaign was not a traditional "black" campaign. His deployment of the rhetoric of racial transcendence mirrored the composite self that he has managed to forge.

Obama's nuanced and dispassionate engagement with race has been interpreted by some as a type of silence. The Obama administration's decision to boycott the United Nation's Durban Review Conference on racism known as "Durban II" held in Geneva in April 2009 was a signal to some that Obama was unwilling to deal directly and honestly with issues of race unless they significantly impacted his campaign (such as with the race speech) or administration. The civil rights activist and writer Juan Santos delivered a widely circulated critique of Obama during his run for President in 2008 in which he predicted that Obama as President would become "a silenced black ruler" and "muzzled black emperor" unwilling to talk about race honestly and directly.[71]

Naomi Klein has remarked that, "no matter how race-neutral Obama tries to be, his actions will be viewed by a large part of the country through the lens of its racial obsessions."[72] The far right has fueled enough white racial anxiety about Obama since his election, including the "birthers," "deathers," and "tea-baggers," that fears about his "otherness" have not been quelled. Indeed, according to some national statistics, a large number of Americans continue to believe that Obama is a Muslim and that he was not born in the United States. Klein goes on to state that because "his most modest, Band-Aid measures are going to be greeted as if he is waging a full-on race war,"[73] Obama has nothing to lose by engaging issues of race head on.

Obama has, perhaps naively, attempted to use his diverse background to engage wider questions of race, ethnicity, and community. This approach has neither sustained nor assuaged white fears about his perceived "foreign" or "alien" character. Indeed, his perceived "otherness" has been exploited by extremists and the far right for the purpose of inciting white rage and personal political gain. Obama occupied the space where his parents' dreams of a lifelong union failed to take shape. The pursuit of self by Obama as the U.S. President reflects the nation's long struggle with race and racism.

Notes

1. Oscar Avila, "Obama's Census form Choice: Black," *Los Angeles Times,* April 4, 2010, latimes.com, http://articles.latimes.com/2010/apr/04/nation/la-na-obama-census4-2010apr04 (Accessed: 7/17/10). Several reports of Obama's census choice appeared in leading American newspapers after the White House released a statement indicating the President's choice. It is a well known fact that Obama selected the African American/Negro/Black category on his U.S. census form.

2. Barack Obama, *Dreams from My Father: A Story of Race and Inheritance,* (New York: Three Rivers Press, 1995), xvi.

3. Ibid.

4. Michael M.J. Fischer, "Ethnicity and the Post-Modern Arts of Memory," in *Writing Culture: The Poetics and Politics of Ethnography,* eds., James Clifford. (Berkeley: University of California Press, 1986), 194–233.

5. The notion of human identities as partial, contradictory, strategic and ultimately fragmented is not new and has long been associated with feminist, cultural, and post colonial theory. The work of Donna Haraway (1991) in the "Cyborg Manifesto," Nancy Hartsock's writings on feminist historical materialism (1983), and Chela Sandoval's work on "oppositional consciousness" (1991) in one way or another engage the concept of identity as a complex affair. Haraway's assertions on identity infer that subjects negotiate a series of positionings that are never completely fixed on a given positioning (partial), that these positionings may be in conflict (contradictory), and that a subject positions herself/himself according to context or situation at a given moment. Feminist Standpoint theory, which understands knowledge as particular rather than universal, defines subjects as constructed by relational forces rather than as transcendent; Nancy Hartsock argues that some perceptions of reality are partial and Sandoval views the world as a type of topography where groups and individuals may produce themselves as oppositional subjects.

6. Zadie Smith, "Speaking in Tongues," Nybooks.com, February 26, 2009. http://www.nybooks.com/articles/archives/2009/feb/26/speaking-in-tongues-2/.

7. Kimberly McClain DaCosta, "Interracial Intimacies, Barack Obama, and the Politics of Multiracialism," *The Black Scholar 39, No. ¾,* (September 22, 2009): 4–5.

8. In her book *Black Skins, Black Masks: Hybridity, Dialogism, Performativity* (2005) Shirley Ann Tate conceptualizes the notion of an "other black" identity in the lives of mixed-race women of black/white parentage in contemporary England through an examination of the everyday "talk" of these women. Tate utilizes the work of Mikhail Bakhtin, Homi K. Bhabha, Paul Gilroy, Stuart Hall, Franz Fanon and Gayatri Spivak to articulate her notion of the "other black" in her discussion of language as hybrid and performativity in hybridity. The women in Tate's study project a multidimensional sense of self by simultaneously deploying blackness and mixedness in an interactional "hybridity of the everyday." My use of this term advances the notion of Barack Obama as an "other black" cosmopolitan as he embraces a public blackness while his narratives and other writings (and statements) present a more complex sense of self through a "dialogical space" (written and spoken).

9. Valeria Sinclair-Chapman, Melanye Price, "Black Politics, the 2008 Election, and the (Im)Possibility of Race Transcendence," *Political Science and Politics* (October 2008): 739–745.

10. Lauren Kornreich, "Obama: New Dog Could be Mutt Like Me," Politicalticker.blogs.

cnn.com, November 7, 2008. http://politicalticker.blogs.cnn.com/2008/11/07/obama-new-dog-could-be-mutt-like-me/?fbid=6ya-SUWVgiG (Accessed: 7/17/10).

11. Deborah Solomon, "All in the Family." *New York Times.* January 20, 2008. http://nytimes.com/2008/01/20/magazine/20wwln-Q4-t.html_r=1&pagewanted=print (Accessed: 3/11/10).

12. Barack H. Obama, *Dreams from My Father: A Story of Race and Inheritance,* (New York: Three Rivers Press, 1995), 27.

13. David Hollinger, "Obama, the Instability of Color Lines and the Promise of a Postethnic Future," *Callaloo 31.4* (2008): 1033–1037.

14. The term "essentialist hybridity" will be defined in conjunction with my notion of "fluid hybridity" later in this chapter.

15. Mica Nava, *Visceral Cosmopolitanism: Gender, Culture and the Normalization of Difference*, (New York: Berg, 2007), 3–5. Here I adopt the phrase "visceral cosmopolitanism" coined by cultural studies theorist Mica Nava in her groundbreaking work that explores the imaginative and empathetic aspects of engagement with race, culture, and racial difference. This phrase will be deployed later in the chapter in the section on cosmopolitanism.

16. 8 Pilar Ossorio and Troy Duster, "Race and Genetics: Controversies in Biomedical, Behavioral, and Forensic Sciences," *American Psychologist* 60 (January 2005), 116–118.

17. Sandra Laing's story has been made the subject of books, documentaries, and feature films such as with the recently released movie "Skin" and the documentary "Skin Deep: The Sandra Laing Story."

18. Troy Duster, "Buried Alive: The Concept of Race in Science." In *Genetic Nature/Culture: Anthropology and Science beyond the Two-Culture Divide*, ed. Alan H. Goodman, Deborah Heath, and M. Susan Lindee (Berkeley: University of California Press, 2003), 259–262.

19. Ibid.

20. Here again the term mixed-race is used to connote largely the social understanding of the term as based on claims about ancestry by self-identified multiracial activists and scholars.

21. Barack Obama, *Dreams from My Father: A Story of Race and Inheritance,* (New York: Three Rivers Press, 1995), 27.

22. See Michael Omi and Howard Winant, *Racial Formation in the United States: From the 1960s to the 1990s* (London: Routledge, second edition, 1994).

23. G. Reginald Daniel, *More Than Black: Multiracial Identity and the New Racial Order,* (Philadelphia: Temple University Press, 2002), 124.

24. Ibid, 6–7.

25. Rainier Spencer, *Challenging Multiracial Identity,* (Boulder: Lynne Rienner Publishers, 2006), 91–93.

26. This statement was made by Barak Obama to the Generation Mix college students while on tour through 2005. They were invited to his Senate offices and the scene also appears in the film "Changing Daybreak."

27. David L. Brunsma, "Public Categories, Private Identities: Exploring Regional Differences in the Biracial Experience," *Social Science Research* 35 (2006), 555–576.

28. Kerry Ann Rockquemore and David L. Brunsma, "Socially Embedded Identities: Theories, Typologies, and Processes of Racial Identity among Black/White Biracials," *The Sociological Quarterly 43, No. 3* (Summer 2002), 335–356.

29. Barack Obama, *Dreams from my Father,* 211.

30. See Tanya Hernandez "Multiracial Matrix: The Role of Race Ideology in the Enforcement of Anti-discrimination Laws, A United States Latin America Comparison," in the *Cornell Law Review* (2002).

31. Many scholars, including Zadie Smith, have remarked how Obama's own memoirs are clearly influenced by James Baldwin's work titled in *Another Country*.

32. Obama, *Dreams from my father*, 430.

33. G. Reginald Daniel, and Hettie V. Williams, "Barack Obama and Multiraciality," *Encyclopedia of African American History*, ed. Joe Trotter (New York: Facts on File, forthcoming in 2010). Some of the information in this section, in terms of the generic biographical material on Barack Obama, was co-authored by this author and G. Reginald Daniel for a forthcoming publication that includes a biographical essay of Barack Obama in relation to his multiracial background.

34. Paul R. Spickard, and Rowena Fong, "Pacific Islander Americans and Multiethnicity: A Vision of America's Future?" *Social Forces 73, No. 4,* (June 1995): 1365–1383.

35. Ibid.

36. Obama, *Dreams*, 78.

37. Ibid.

38. Obama, 80.

39. Obama, *Dreams,* 115.

40. Ibid.

41. Obama, *Dreams*, 102.

42. Ibid., 108.

43. Ibid., 104.

44. Ibid.

45. Obama, *Dreams*, 115.

46. Obama, *Dreams,* 120–121.

47. Reginald Daniel makes the argument in his essay contained in this volume that though Obama may be understood as hybrid it is a hybridity that extends outward from the location of a black identity rooted in the black community.

48. Sheena C. Howard, "Facility of Nommo: Afrocentric Rhetorical Analysis of Barack Obama," unpublished paper delivered at the 2009 annual conference of the National Association of African American Studies (NAAAS), 1–3.

49. Barack H. Obama, *Dreams from my Father: A Story of Race and Inheritance* (New York: Three Rivers Press, 1995), 82–83.

50. Ibid.

51. Georgiana Banita, "Home Squared: Barack Obama's Transnational Self-Reliance," *Biography 33,* No. 1, (Winter 2010): 24.

52. Homi K. Bhabha is considered one of the chief architects of understanding hybridity in postcolonial theory. He develops his notion of hybridity in the interview titled "The Third Space" that appears in the text *Identity, Community, Culture, Difference* (1990) with such works as *The Location of Culture* (1994), and in "Frontliners/Borderposts" in *Displacements: Cultural Identity in Question* (1994).

53. See Homi K. Bhabha in "The Third Space-Interview with Homi Bhabha" in *Identity, Community, Culture, Difference* edited by J. Rutherford, (1990) 207–221.

54. Shirley Ann Tate, *Black Skins, Black Masks: Hybridity, Dialogism, Performativity* (Burlington, VT: Ashgate, 2005), 59.

55. Ibid.

56. Naomi Pabst, "An Unexpected Blackness: Musings on Diasporic Encounters and Hybrid Engagements." *Transition 100* 2009, 112–132.

57. In both *Dreams of my Father* and the *Audacity of Hope* we find that Obama makes repeated inferences to his mixed heritage and multicultural experience while at the same time claiming a black identity that is not rooted in the "typical" experience of most African Americans. He does this on the opening pages of *Dreams* and once again in the early chapters of *Audacity of Hope.*

58. Homi Bhabha *The Location of Culture* (1994) and "Frontliners/Borderposts" in *Displacements: Cultural Identification in Question* (1994).

59. Shirley Ann Tate utilized the phrase "other black" as applied to her study of mixed race women in the UK in her text *Black Skins, Black Masks* in the development of her important thesis of hybridity as a dialogical space where these women fashion for themselves a "hybridity of the everyday" through everyday "talk." I appropriate the phrase "other black" from Tate, and apply it to the life and writings of Barack H. Obama while also understanding that hybridity is about dialogue and "dialogical space" (Tate utilizes the notion that language or dialogue is hybrid from the Russian philosopher Mikhail Bakhtin) as evidenced in the writings and speeches of Obama. Further, I postulate that Obama frames the self within a transnational and cosmopolitan context—henceforth my notion of Obama as "other black cosmopolitan" is unique in that it presents Obama as having a complex multilayered sense of self that is both dependent upon a public essentialism *and* hybridity *at the same time* within a larger cosmopolitan frame.

60. Pabst, 115.

61. Carly Fraser, "Race, Post-Black Politics, and the Democratic Presidential Candidacy of Barack Obama," *Souls* July 1, 2009, 19–40.

62. Obama, *Dreams,* 82.

63. Dorothy J. Hale, "Bakhtin in African American Literary Theory," *English Literary History* 61, No. 2, (Summer 1994), 445–471.

64. Ibid.

65. Obama, *The Audacity of Hope: Thoughts on Reclaiming the American Dream.* (New York: Vintage Books, 2006), 14, 274.

66. Zadie Smith, "Speaking in Tongues," http://nybooks.com/articles/archives/2009/feb/26/speaking-in-tongues-2/.

67. The use of this phrase "betwixt and between" connotes notions of liminality first advanced by the German born French ethnographer and folklorist Arnold Van Gennep in his important text *Les Rites de Passage* (1909) later borrowed, expanded, and enhanced by anthropologist Victor Turner in his work "Betwixt and Between: The Liminal Period in Rites de Passage," that appeared in *The Forest of Symbols: Aspects of Ndembu Ritual* (1967). G. Reginald has applied the concept of liminality understood as a place "betwixt and between" to the multiracial experience in various writings such as with his landmark text *More than Black: Multiracial Identity and the New Racial Order* (2001).

68. Zadie Smith, "Speaking in Tongues."

69. Valeria Sinclair Chapman and Melanye Price, "Black Politics, the 2008 Election, and the (Im)Possibility of Race Transcendence," *Political Science and Politics* (October 2008): 739–745.

70. Ibid.

71. Juan Santos, "Barack Obama and the End of Racism," February 12, 2008, Countercurrents.com, http://www.countercurrents.org/santo/20208.htm (Accessed: 7/25/10).

72. Naomi Klein, "Obama's Big Silence: the Race Question," September 12, 2009, Guardian.co.uk, http://guardian.co.uk/global/2009/sep/12/barack-obama-the-race-question-kle ... (Accessed: 9/16/09).

73. Ibid.

Chapter 8

Black First, But Not Only: Racial Identity Formation in a Changing Black 'Hood'

Barbara H. Combs

Migration and the slave trade have created a diverse African Diaspora. Historian William Wright argues that while ethnically distinct, all of the groups comprising the vast African Diaspora are part of the black race.[1] Black racial identity in America is complicated by often competing notions of regional and national identity. People identify with the places they live in and where they are from, making areas undergoing black gentrification compelling sites to study the dynamics of black unity and solidarity, as well as conflicts and tensions in the black community. There are multiple bases of identity construction and formation. Race, ethnicity, class, gender, religion, culture, and nationality are some of the more important foundations of human identity. Essentialist notions of blackness posit a homogeneous and monolithic black culture. In an era where identity construction is composed from both without and within, these defining features of self and communal identity often converge, conflate, and compete, which can result in identity crises.

This chapter examines the role of place in identity formation, and the role gender and class play in the crisis and convergence of identity in two historic black gentrifying in-town Atlanta neighborhoods—the Old Fourth Ward and the West End. Despite a deep sense of responsibility felt by some black gentrifiers, the literature points out a tension which often develops in black gentrifying spaces as residents, new and old, struggle to find a sense of identity and group cohesion amidst disparate representations of blackness. In the larger black gentrification literature, a black identity is often a simple matter of race; however, sometimes there are disputes about "authentic" representations of blackness.

The two Atlanta neighborhoods under study are in flux. Location is one of each neighborhood's strongest attributes. Located on the Westside of Atlanta, the West End neighborhood sits near the historic Atlanta University Center (AUC). The nearby AUC houses several African American institutions, including Spelman College, Morehouse College, Clark Atlanta University, and Interdenominational Theological Center. West End Atlanta is twelve minutes away from Hartsfield Jackson International Airport, five minutes from downtown, and three minutes from the Georgia Dome. In recent years, the appeal of the West End area has grown, which has made it somewhat vulnerable. According to official Federal Bureau of Investigation Mortgage Fraud reports, each year from 2006–2010, the West End, once a center of black consciousness in the city, has boasted one of the highest mortgage fraud rates in the nation. Adjacent to Downtown Atlanta, Old Fourth Ward Atlanta is also centrally located. The area is also rich in history and important sites in African American cultural heritage. These include the birth home of Dr. Martin Luther King Jr., the Center for Non-Violent Social Change, Auburn Avenue (once termed by Fortune magazine as the richest "Negro street in the world"), and the Atlanta Life Insurance Company.

Both neighborhoods are widely perceived by residents and outsiders as "black spaces," and this distinct sense of place impacts individuals' sense of identity—both shared and individual. Recent research suggests that in addition to race, class, and gender, place is an important basis of identity construction among individuals.[2] Sociologist Thomas Gieryn notes, "[S]ociologists should perhaps add place to race, class, and gender, as a wellspring of identity drawn upon to decide just who we are in an always unsettled way."[3] For this reason, historic, black-gentrifying locations are compelling sites to study the potential for physical location (i.e., place) to impact how social identity (neighborhood, group, and individual level) develops and is evaluated and understood amidst class and lifestyle fractures in the black community.

Black Gentrification Literature Review

In the last twenty years, a growing body of research concerning black gentrification has emerged.[4] Political scientist Michelle Boyd defines gentrification as "the process through which poor and working-class neighborhoods in the inner city are refurbished via an influx of private capital and middle-class homebuyers and renters."[5] Black gentrification follows the same pattern as mainstream gentrification with one notable exception: both the poor residents who resided in the community prior to its "gentrification" and the new residents of greater economic means are black.[6]

A distinguishing feature of "black gentrification" is the deep sense of responsibility many black gentrifiers feel for the larger black community.[7] In the black gentrification literature, this sometimes manifests as "racial uplift." Despite the deep sense of "responsibility" felt by some black gentrifiers, the literature points out a tension that often develops in black gentrifying spaces as residents, new and old, struggle to find a sense of identity and group cohesion amidst disparate representations of blackness.[8] In sociologist Kesha Moore's examination of class and racial identity formation in a low income black gentrifying North Philadelphia neighborhood, she concludes that whilst living side by side with the urban black poor, the returning black middle class often develops a "multi-class" identity which "embodies the unreconciled class tension between the middle and lower classes ... [and] lead[s] to confusing and contradictory behavior."[9] Studies in Harlem and Chicago unearth a similar phenomenon.[10] As a result, solidarity and conflict are ideas that recur throughout the black gentrification literature.

While intra-racial conflict is present in gentrifying areas, race can also be the basis for the formation of class.[11] In American societies, racial identities are pervasive. The construct of race commonly erects artificial divisions based largely upon physical markers such as skin color and hair type. Ethnicity, on the other hand, is a social construct-dividing people who share a common culture (for example, language, religion, region, nationality, etc.) into even smaller, discrete social groups.[12] According to Stephen Cornell and Douglas Hartmann, "Races ... are not established by some set of natural forces but are products of human perception and classification. They are social constructs."[13] Race categorises certain people as "the Others," while ethnicity unites with a common sense of the "we." A sense of "we-ness" only becomes possible because of the "binary them." Thus race can be viewed as a social class.

There is no monolithic black experience. However, African Americans form a distinct community or class because they share a common history that works to create the perception of a common experience. The limits of this perceived black solidarity are often tested. Sociologist Mary Pattillo acknowledges that boundaries exist in the black community, but these same boundaries "work from without to contain its members within a community of solidarity."[14] This community of solidarity contains schisms and gradations.

Conflict is a common theme in early gentrification literature. A great deal of the conflict outlined in the larger body of gentrification literature was previously framed as inter-racial in nature, when researchers began to examine "black gentrification" as a phenomenon, some were surprised to find that tensions, disagreements, and conflict were still prominent themes. The conflict sometimes consists of black "old-timers" versus black "newcomers" embroiled over competing ideas about the identity of a community in transition. In other cases, it involves intra-racial class-based conflict, or disputes over acceptable uses of community space. Thus, the age old notion of competing interests rooted in a hierarchical stratification system is present. The intra-racial dynamics of black gentrification of course are not limited just to conflict. Researchers have documented motives and actions infused with cooperation and solidarity among the varied residents of these neighborhoods.

Race and class are important social identities in American society. Many Americans use race and class to define themselves, and their positions in society. Because U.S. society conflates race and class, they become important as either. Pattillo studies how the middle class residents of the black gentrifying area of North Kenwood-Oakland in Chicago broker the precarious position of belonging to two worlds—one white (accessible to the black middle class by virtue of their economic status and educational attainment level) and one black (accessible to them by virtue of race/ethnicity).[15] Pattillo explains:

> The black middleman occupies a classic liminal position. Much of life is lived *on the border* rather than fully in the worlds on either side: in the car between a predominately white workplace and a predominately black neighborhood, in a sentence that uses 'ain't' but crisply pronounces all the '-ing' endings, walking across the stage to receive a bachelor's degree to give to mom, who dropped out of high school. Straddling these two worlds, black middlemen take up new positions within the black community and vis-à-vis the man.[16]

Those in the middle form an identity that is both race and class based. Pattillo argues that the "precariousness of the 'middle'" adds a complexity to gentrification studies that merits more attention in the literature.[17]

In black gentrification literature, the black middle-class has multiple interpretations, but all concur with the belief that some members of the black middle class are able to identify with the black poor, thereby straddling two worlds. Pattillo's concept of "middleness" is akin to W.E.B. DuBois' notion of double consciousness, which suggests that black identity is doubly constrained by internal and external forces. In his seminal work, DuBois, observes that the position of blacks in the larger society compels the formation of a sort of "second sight" which compels African Americans to look at themselves "through the eyes of others."[18] Pattillo terms such blacks "middlemen," but Kesha Moore calls those who express solidarity across class lines "multi-class," and juxtaposes "multi-class identity" against what she labels "middle-class minded."[19] Moore believes a multi-class black identity crosses class, in that "multi-class identity values the continuation of a connectedness to lower-income members of the black community."[20] The neighborhood development efforts in multi-class black neighborhoods affirm black identity and consciousness.

Some researchers find the concept of "the middle" a useful category, while others do not. In *Harlemworld,* cultural anthropologist John L. Jackson acknowledges that economic stratification exists among the black residents of his study area in Harlem, but he suggests that the stratification cannot be understood through the use of labels like "middle class," "underclass," and "lower class."[21] While African Americans recognize class and its markers, their understanding of class is much broader than the aforementioned labels suggest.[22]

Explicitly or implicitly, the literature on black gentrification reveals that there is no monolithic black experience or singular authentic representation of blackness. Jackson touts black gentrifying spaces, such as Harlem, as places where multiple black identities can co-exist. He writes, "The space of a gentrifying community reveals a collision of economics, politics, and culture that signals multiple meanings of the types of blackness available in Harlem."[23] These multiple identities to which Jackson refers can manifest at will. Researchers Moore, Boyd, and Pattillo suggest that the concept of middleness is seminal to the black gentry's ability to access multiple meanings of and types of blackness.[24] Where multiple meanings and identities are available, the possibility of borders (existence on the fringe) exists too.

Attitudes and Perceptions about Race, Class, and Gender Dynamics

This section moves from a general discussion of the black gentrification literature, to a specific discussion of the role of race, class, and gender in identity formation in the study neighborhoods—Atlanta's Old Fourth Ward and West End. A total of 56 respondents were surveyed. Pseudonyms are used for all respondents in the study. Respondents include business owners, residents, and stakeholders.

The language respondents use to describe the neighborhoods presents the areas as distinct black spaces. Historically, both neighborhoods have had a mix of African Americans and Caucasians While in the course of the last thirty years the black majority in the West End has solidified (94.8%), the overwhelming black majority in the Old Fourth Ward (63%) has declined.[25] In both the West End and the Old Fourth Ward, respondents of all races describe the areas as "a black neighborhood," a "black community," or "a black area." Some of this vision of the neighborhoods is rooted in the past. West End resident Brian Simpsons has lived in the area for over twenty years. Simpsons says:

> In 1991 it was a cohesive black African-American community … it's different now …. And let me say, let me qualify too. The reason why I say it's different is because of … [diversity] … the Muslim community has always been a part of this community. They have not always been attuned to the, you know, this voting and kinds of things so they …. So that's why I say it's very diverse. And there are other religious groups here also that do not necessarily participate in that kind.[26]

Simpsons still perceives the area as "a black community" but one with fractures. His comments suggest that those fractures are a result of diverse religious, economic, cultural, educational, and civic mentalities among the populous.

Race, class, and gender influence social processes in the neighborhood; while the Old Fourth Ward and West End, Atlanta are largely black communities, people of a variety of racial and ethnic contexts live, work, play, and do business in the areas. According to the 2000 Census data, over 63% of the population of the Old Fourth Ward is African American. However, because the Census data used herein is broken down at the tract level, and tract lines do not follow neighborhood lines, the actual percentage of the study neighborhood which is black is likely much higher. According to the 2000 Census data, approximately 95% of the West End identifies itself as African American. Amidst the multiethnic background of a place like the King Center, respondents notice salient characteristics such as race, class, gender, and age.

Race Consciousness

In the historic Old Fourth Ward, the answer to the question 'does race matter?' is as varied as the people who inhabit the social space. Race is a central part of the neighborhood's past. There is less certainty about the role race plays in the future of the neighborhoods. People see and feel race in the neighborhoods. Visible markers of race include street signs bearing the names of important Civil Rights leaders, businesses with phrases like "Sweet Auburn," and "Shrine of the Black Madonna." There are multiple "felt" elements of race including the sounds, sights, and smells that fill the air.

Long time Old Fourth Ward resident Elizabeth self identifies as African American, despite the fact that her mother is white, and her father is black. Ms. Battle moved to the Old Fourth Ward almost thirty years ago when her daughter was school aged. At the time, she placed her in a predominately white private school.[27] Regarding her decision to move her child to the predominately black Atlanta public school system, she says: "[I thought] you know what; I think I need to take her out of this school just because I wanted a sense of blackness to her."[28] This "sense of blackness" she communicates is the same reason for her move to "a black neighborhood."

Some of the people who view the Old Fourth Ward as a distinctly black space are its white residents. Daniel Tepee is a white man in his early fifties who has lived and worked in the Old Fourth Ward for over ten years. Tepee describes himself as "your basic Caucasian."[29] He describes the Old Fourth Ward as "a black community." Most of his substantial holdings and investments are in the Old Fourth Ward. His enterprises include owning real estate and developing property, and he is also part owner of a coffeehouse. Naomi Goldman is a 35-year-old Jewish woman who has resided in the Old Fourth Ward for almost three years. Goldman echoes Dan's sentiments, and utilizes even stronger words to set forth her premise that the Old Fourth Ward is a black neighborhood.

> In a larger context, I think I feel I'm intruding a little bit, which is fine with me because to me this is a historical neighborhood that I think should belong to African Americans. I don't think white people should take this over. So, I have no problem with it [feeling unwelcome], but I don't feel welcome sometimes.[30]

Goldman believes that there are many indications that the community just serves African Americans. These indications include things such as clothing, food, and hair care options available in the community. According to Goldman, these indicia mark the space as black territory.

Goldman's comments indicate that she views both people and places as potential threats to her acceptance in, and of, the community. There are a number of places in the Old Fourth Ward community where Naomi Goldman feels welcome, and not labeled. Daniel Tepee's coffeehouse is one of those places. However, there are a number of places where she feels like an outsider.[31] Naomi Goldman remarks on one such experience:

> I used to volunteer at the Samaritan House … used to.[32] [I stopped because]I had a big fight with the chef. Was it the chef? Yeah, it was the chef. He was two hours late, and because he had to drive miles and miles and miles away and I was doing all his work … he only lasted there for a very short time. So, it wasn't just me. But there were other things that bothered me.… I think that's an example of not feeling welcome. I didn't feel welcome [there] …. It's because of the color of my skin, yeah. Yeah. Like the chef … he's a different chef.[33]

Some of the labels Goldman disclosed include "newcomer," "white woman," "outsider," "interloper," and "gentrifier." The varied labels cross race, class, and gender lines.

Goldman perceives that people there treat her differently because of her race. Goldman says she endured this treatment for almost two years before she decided to stop volunteering at the organization. No one was overtly hurtful to her, but no one made her feel welcome in the organization either. Many other businesses in the community do not make her feel welcome, but none of her experiences have been as overt as the one at the Samaritan House.

Racial dynamics are complex. Goldman's perceptions about the community may not be without merit, but perception is a two way street. The problems Goldman details seem to begin with her negative encounter with the first chef. As a white, upper middle-class woman, Goldman exhibits very fixed perceptions about time; while, in the African American community, time is often a more fluid concept. She became concerned because of the chef's "extreme" tardiness, and admittedly, she does not hide this. Race may have played a role in the social dynamics present at Samaritan House, but it is possible that the public argument Goldman had with the chef and his later dismissal played a role in how others interacted with her. When interviewed, it appears that this possibility does not occur to her. In her mind, race is the only possible dynamic that can account for her disparate treatment.

Despite a deliberate attempt to build a broad community and a sense of solidarity, West End residents are not colorblind. Race still matters. In a myriad of ways, respondents observe, feel, and communicate race. Thirty-seven years ago when Ruth Marshall and her family (African American) moved to one of the community's premiere streets, there was no welcoming committee.[34] Her white neighbors did notice her, but they did not stop to talk to her. Marshall recalls approaching her neighbors and her initial conversation:

> When I moved in I introduced myself to them and if they didn't say anything I would let it go .... If they listened, I let them know .... We wasn't going to bother them, and I said we're not going to come in and hurt you. We're not going to steal from you because that's what they think, and I said my kids are not going to bother you.[35]

Not all of the white neighbors were unwelcoming; but it was tense enough that Marshall still recalls that when the second black family moved into the neighborhood, she shouted and told all her friends, "I've got black neighbors!"[36]

The racial mix in the West End is changing. According to the 2000 Census, African Americans comprised almost 95% of the West End's total population. In the period from 1990 to 2000, the black population of the West End stayed constant, while the number of white residents dropped from 170 to 104. The Asian population rose from 2 to 51 (an increase of 2450 %,), and the Hispanic population increased from 17 to 78 (i.e. by 359%). The community had a total population of 5058. Despite these changes, most residents still view the West End as a black community. Lauren Murphy has resided in the community for 2½ years; her partner, Samantha, is a fourteen year resident of the West End.[37] In her short tenure in the community, Murphy has already noticed an increase in the white population in the community.

> I don't know if they're moving here from other cities. I see more Caucasians, most likely maybe yuppies, younger generation. People who ride bikes to work. I won't say I've seen them actually going to work. They may have a backpack,[38] people exercising, maybe a mother with a child with a certain type of stroller, jogging, walking dogs, jogging with dogs.[39]

Murphy's comment illustrate that she perceives the Caucasians moving into the neighborhood as distinct from the current population on a number of levels. Besides the obvious racial distinctions, Murphy notes that the newer white residents' consumption pattern vary from the African American residents she knows. Murphy perceives differences between the way the white population of the West End and its black residents dress, as well as their interests.

Six-year resident West End Zaniah Ford has observed changing demographics in the community too, but she still views the West End as a black neighborhood.[40] She explains:

> [the community] Seems pretty black to me, and I was interested in the range of cultural expressions going on. The religious communities ... I thought the Hebrews, the Israelites were kind of fascinating as were the sort of Sunni Muslim community in this place, and it's just kind of .... Seems kind of in some ways like my neighborhood in Brooklyn, except the West Indians here live in Stone Mountain.[41]

For Ford, the range of black cultural and religious expressions present in the West End gives the community a sort of racial "authenticity." She seeks a place where there is a diversity of black identities and experiences. For her, the West End is such a community. Although Ford views the community as a black community and hopes it will remain such, she has a surprising appreciation for the recent influx of white residents. She explains this by saying, "I think the more diversity you have in a black neighborhood, the better."[42]

The racial history of the neighborhoods comprising this study is complicated. Since the turn of the century, some racial diversity has always existed in both neighborhoods.[43] For example, although in varying numbers, whites have always been in the West End.[44] The community started as a white community, and even as the black population grew, some whites remained. Many white newcomers to the West End occupy the dwellings they own. Even those who want the community to remain "black" recognize a need to occupy and stabilize the housing force so that the community survives. The act of whites buying and occupying the homes engenders a certain amount of respect from some in the community.

Various community members' ideas about race are somewhat fluid, but in the coming years, green may be the color that best determines the life chances of black residents of the West End.[45] At least that is what Amina Charles, president of the local neighborhood association, thinks.[46] Charles views "green" as a proxy for other things. According to Charles, the demographics that matter in the West End are not black and white; instead they are "education and income," proxies for social class.

> One of my neighbors said, "The Caucasians are coming in and now they're [the Caucasians] saying 'We're here. We're here!'" And I said to them, yeah they say they are here, but they're also here doing stuff. They started the patrol …. As long as they're doing stuff … I don't care if you're black, blue, green, or yellow, as long as you are helping to elevate West End, I don't give a damn what you are.[47]

Charles has resided in the West End for ten years. As she reflects back on her decade-old history with the community, she observes that early on, the community seemed kind of stuck in a "black vs. white mentality." Now, Charles believes there is a strong willingness to bridge ties across racial and economic divides in an attempt to do what is good for the West End.

Class Consciousness

During the years that Atlanta was a racially segregated city, the Old Fourth Ward was a vertically integrated neighborhood. Segregation forced low income, middle income, and even a few affluent blacks to live together in an economically diverse neighborhood because they were not welcome anywhere else. Today, as the Old Fourth Ward neighborhood wrestles with the challenge of finding a way for all social classes to coexist, it struggles with the ghost of its past. Some people seek to recreate what they "remember" as a harmonious past, but times have changed. In the last two decades, the middle and upper middle class have returned to the Old Fourth Ward. The poor and working class never left. As a result, some distrust, resentment, and caution exists on the part of the returning gentry and those who remained.

Class matters loom under the surface of any discussion of neighborhood level interactions in the Old Fourth Ward. For example, many of the interviewees expressed an appreciation for the advantages of urban living, and a tolerance of the disadvantages. The disadvantages most commonly outlined— drugs and drug dealers, homeless and panhandlers, home and car break ins, inferior schools and substandard infrastructure—are strongly correlated with socio-economic factors. Class is the unspoken differentiator present in seemingly innocuous comments like Elizabeth Battle's statement, "we're in it, but not of it, and not above it."[48] Battle is a middle-class African American woman. Her comments elucidate an acknowledgement that she resides in the inner city of a major metropolitan city. They also evidence an awareness of her "middleness" in the class hierarchy.

There are a number of ways to communicate class standing. We use dress as a proxy for social class. Despite spending a lot of time on the streets of the Old Fourth Ward, Kevin Washington takes care to make sure he dresses well. In doing this, he is deliberately attempting to avoid marking himself as overtly homeless. In spite of his efforts to present himself in a way that does not identify his homeless status, the police stop Washington from time to time. Oftentimes, they pat him down to see if he has drugs. According to Washington, it bothers him when they stop him, but he does not believe there is anything he can do about it. Washington says the community in general is not very welcoming to people like him.[49] When he enters local business establishments looking for work, people "act like they are scared" of him. Here, Washington draws a distinction, and says that the black owned businesses do not tend to treat him that way.[50] Some of the local black restaurants even allow him to work in their kitchens from time to time.[51] Conversely, non-black business owners have kicked him out of several of their establishments. While Washington dresses up to garner respect in the community, Councilman Martin has learned that dressing down can have the same impact.[52] He says:

> There are a lot of parts in various cities that have been lost in the glamour, the shimmer, the shine, and for various other ethnic groups or demographic groups here you may have that. But the core and the base [here] is really real. It's really real. Although I wear suits every day, [on] any given day at any given time you might see me dressed down, and I still deliver the service that I'm supposed to deliver, [the same] that I would deliver out in a suit, and the same is true for every-

one else here. And sometimes if you're not without the suit, you don't garner the same level of respect and trust.[53]

Martin's comments suggest that appearance is a tool to either place others at ease, or induce discomfort. Additionally, Martin's comments suggest that dressing down can help upper class African Americans to posit an authentic black racial identity in the neighborhood. Dress proves to be a very uncertain proxy for social class. Consider the comments of Melinda Galveston, an upper middle class black Old Fourth Ward resident who states:

> I'd consider it [Old Fourth Ward] as one of the best neighborhoods, but you know what, public opinion will probably call things because of what they think they see on Boulevard. Plus, not to be racist, but the youth culture with the baggy pants and the cap and all of that, everybody wears that. If you're dark skinned and you have that on ... people make a lot of assumptions about you .... People make a lot of assumptions .... People make a whole lot of assumptions, and some of what they see is not drug dealers, but they look the same. They just see the kids that don't have anywhere else to be but outside on the streets because of the hood.[54]

Now, many college students are on Auburn Avenue as well. This is due, in part, to the expansion of Georgia State University. Georgia State, termed by one respondent as "the university that ate Atlanta," is a downtown urban university. The university built a new dormitory in the nearby Old Fourth Ward community, and they have acquired additional property in the neighborhood. As Galveston notes, many of the young college students dress in a manner which residents previously associated with the drug dealers in the area.

Class matters in the Old Fourth Ward, and residents express it in a number of spoken and unspoken ways. Individuals seem to feel the need to mark themselves as a part of a distinct group, or to distinguish themselves from less desirable group affiliations. In so doing, they claim membership and allegiance, not only to the various social groups or classes they might occupy, but they also legitimate their claims to the neighborhood itself.

Faith Howard is a middle class, college educated black woman who settled in the West End (from Brooklyn, NY) about ten years ago.[55] Despite her length of time in the community, in some ways, she still feels like an outsider. As a black woman, the majority of the people in the neighborhood look like Howard. In her interview, she espouses a level of kinship with the blacks in the neighborhood, but on some level she sees herself and her family as different from the community. Howard describes that West End as a "broke down neighborhood" and discusses some of the "risk for my family," but she also espouses a deeply felt desire to elevate the community and the black race. Her college educated status and class standing seem to separate her from many residents of the West End. Although her earlier comments illustrate a respect for the efforts of the oldtimers, there is an inherent assumption in her comments that her ways and efforts are both needed to make the neighborhood better and superior to any efforts that the oldtimers might craft. Howard's comments illustrate ageism in her suggestion that both the seniors in Brooklyn and the West End need saving.

Oldtimers feel that there is very little appreciation or knowledge of how things were done in the past. This struggle accentuates class tensions, as a distinct percentage of oldtimers lack a college education, and are lower in social class than the many newcomers who are middle class and college educated. Underlying all of this there seems to be a sincere desire to help the black community to which Howard feels inextricably tied. It is a form of racial uplift often discussed in the black gentrification literature. All of these tensions are present in Faith Howard's comments.

The African American residents of West End and Old Fourth Ward, Atlanta engage in many activities stratified by class status. No time is this more evident than on Sunday mornings. Some of the middle to upper class respondents' express overt negative opinions of their neighbors of lower socio-economic means, but upper class standing does not make one immune to negative perceptions by others in the neighborhood. Nigel Walters, a working class African American resident of the West End, describes his perception of a congregation of black men and women attending a newly formed church meeting in the neighborhood.[56] Walters says:

> I've never went [there]. Like I said, I just noticed that when it started at first, when it opened, it seemed like it was more of an invitation [to] people that were trying to become more financially equipped, so to speak. So it seemed like those semi boogey blacks were attending the church.[57]

Walters' comment illustrates his belief that the congregants' black authenticity is somewhat compromised by their middle class status. Even though church members went door to door in inviting neighborhood residents to the service, Walters felt the "invitation" was not open to him or people like him (in terms of their economic means). When the church began holding services at the local middle school, it made an already constrained parking situation even worse, as "everybody" in the church seemed to drive a car and park it on Walters' street. Neighborhood people could walk to the church, but none seemed to attend.

Gender-Based Consciousness

While gender is arguably as readily identifiable as race, in the largely racially homogeneous black gentrifying West End neighborhood, gender consciousness is less pronounced than race consciousness. Despite this distinction, gender based attitudes (predicated on a gender consciousness) do prevail in the West End. Some of those attitudes seem benign in nature and some not, but in subtle and unsubtle ways, gender based attitudes exist in the community.

Overt gender discussions are most noticeable by their absence in the neighborhood. In my discussions with residents, business owners, and stakeholders in the area, respondents were more apt to bring up issues of race and class than gender. In analyzing this absence, it is concluded that inside the "matrix of domination" that sociologist Patricia Collins discusses, the residents of this black gentrifying neighborhood perceive gender as a lesser axis of discrimination than either race or class.[58] Several examples from my interviews typify this belief.

Bedford Pines is a privately owned housing project which does not run out of housing credits until 2015, so despite the Atlanta Housing Authority's decision to raise all the public housing projects in Atlanta, it still stands. The facility is run down, but centrally located. Pines is a housing project populated by young (most are under 21), black mothers. In discussions about Pines, respondents recognize that multiple forces or sources of oppression work together to disadvantage the residents of that housing project; however, respondents as sources of oppression commonly mention only race, class, and age, not gender. Similarly, discussions about sexuality (an issue directly related to gender), are often secondary to those about class and often race. Tony Miller is an upper class African American resident of the Old Fourth Ward. Earlier in Miller's interview, he comments about the range of racial, ethnic, and sexual orientations represented among his neighbors, going on to discuss the only group he would like to be "rid of."[59] He says:

> There are obvious drug deals and dealers in the neighborhood. I used to tease people and say they were running a horizontal corporation. You can go out there [and see]. They have shift changes. They have uniforms. They have regimen. Me and my neighbors talk about it all the time. You know who the drug dealers are. You watch them do their busi-

ness. And that's one thing that frustrates us is that if we know all of this, then why can't the police stop it?[60]

Miller is less bothered by the sexual orientation of his neighbors than he is by their means of employment. Johnetta Hope, Old Fourth Ward resident, believes that she can be open with those in the community about her sexual orientation. She says:

> I don't have to hide it [that I am a lesbian]. I am very open about that. There are a number of couples in the neighborhood. I know that there are people that feel that gays and lesbians are a problem, especially when gay men, gay white men come into a neighborhood and change things. And that's an issue, well for some that's an issue.[61]

Hope's comments hint at a gender issue. Her comments primarily illustrate that while sexual orientation is a problem for some in the neighborhood, the issue is aggravated when the individuals involved are white. In black gentrifying neighborhoods like the Old Fourth Ward, discussions of gendered experiences and gendered space seem inextricably tied to issues of safety and perceptions of crime. The discussion, however, is more complex than just an analysis of the perspectives of men and women. Issues of age, upbringing, race, and even class further complicate the analysis. Survival requires what field of academic discipline? Elijah Anderson terms it a "code of the streets."

Identities are varied and complex. According to Peter Burke, identities are "meanings a person attributes to the self as an object in a social situation or social role."[62] Among other possible sources of identity formation, identities can be race, class, gender, and/or place-based. There are multiple bases of identity formation, and every basis upon which individuals form their identity is mediated by society and our social interactions. David Demo and Michael Hughes contend that "one psychological consequence of being black is black group identity, the intensity of which should vary with the nature of role experiences."[63] Despite fractures and factions, the residents of the neighborhoods under study possess such a sense of "black group identity."

Conclusion

American society conflates race, class, and gender. As a result, all three become important to respondents as either intersecting or competing avenues of identity construction. In sociologist Patricia Hill Collins' 1990 *Black Feminist Thought: Knowledge, Consciousness, and the Politics of Empowerment,*[64]

Collins makes clear that race, class, and gender operate as overlapping systems of oppression. Collins states:

> In addition to being structured along axes such as race, gender, and social class, the matrix of domination is structured on several levels. People experience and resist oppression on three levels: the level of personal biography; the group or community level of the cultural context created by race, class, and gender; and the systemic level of social institutions.[65]

Inside the "matrix of domination" that Collins outlines, the residents, business owners, and stakeholders of Atlanta's Old Fourth Ward and West End neighborhoods exhibit a consciousness of race, class, and gender as separate axes of oppression. However, in the neighborhoods under study, race seems to operate dually. Race is a vehicle through which oppression can be experienced; however, in the black gentrifying areas under study, race is more commonly used as a means through which to resist oppression. The respondents' deliberate efforts to remember and maintain the neighborhoods as "black" areas are a form of resistance, one in which the African American racial identity is embraced and heralded, rather than viewed negatively.

Race, class, gender, and age, as well as intersections of any two or more of these factors, impact neighborhood level interactions and perceptions of the neighborhood space. West End and the Old Fourth Ward respondents identify, group, and delineate others on the basis of race. Respondents refer to "the Chinese lady" on the corner, the "crazy white man," "Snow White" and other names. Sometimes, the names are intentionally derogatory, but more often than not, they are simple means of classifying individuals into readily identifiable groups. The labels also provide other important social clues regarding individuals' social standing and status as insiders or outsiders.

Social identities in the neighborhoods (including race-based identities) are constantly in flux, and while issues of race, class, and gender often overlap, in respondents' reflections about who they are, race comes through most poignantly. Respondents describe race as the single most important factor that defines them, the neighborhood, and their relationships to other people, places, and social/cultural institutions in the space. Race is often what binds people to the study neighborhoods, and, ultimately the tie that binds them to each other. West End resident Cheryl Simpson says:

> Again, racism is still real. Now, we always talk about the intersection of race and class. The reality is you're still black and you're still white even if you're on the same class line. And my daughter can speak about

that more than I can because she has more white friends than I do, although I do have more white friends than most of my black friends, but I'm always black first.[66]

A number of respondents echo sentiments similar to those of Simpson. Whether spoken or not, there is a keen awareness of race present in the study neighborhoods. In Simpson's case, this cognizance manifests itself in a self-awareness and identification of belonging to the African American racial group, but also awareness that others also perceive her as African American.

Notes

1. William D. Wright, *Black History and Black Identity: A Call for a New Historiography* (Westport, CT: Praeger, 2002).

2. Thomas F. Gieryn, "A Space for Place in Sociology," *Annual Review of Sociology* 26 (2009): 463–496.

3. Ibid, 481.

4. Mary Pattillo, "Negotiating Blackness, For Richer or Poorer," *Ethnography* 4(1) (2003): 61–93l; Mary Pattillo, "Black Middle-Class Neighborhoods," *Annual Review of Sociology* 31 (2005): 305–329; Mary Pattillo, *Black on the Block: The Politics of Race and Class in the City* (Chicago: University of Chicago Press, 2007); Mary Pattillo-McCoy, *Black Picket Fences: Privilege and Peril among the Black Middle Class* (Chicago: University of Chicago Press, 1999); Derek S. Hyra, "Racial Uplift: Intra-Racial Class Conflict and the Economic Revitalization of Harlem and Bronzeville," *City & Community* 5(1) (2006): 71–92; Michelle Boyd, "Reconstructing Bronzeville: Racial Nostalgia and Neighborhood Redevelopment," *Journal of Urban Affairs* 22(2) (2000): 107–122; Michelle Boyd, "The Downside of Racial Uplift: The Meaning of Gentrification in an African American Neighborhood," *City & Community* 17(2) (2005): 265–288; Kesha S. Moore, "What's Class Got to do with It? Community Development and Racial Identity," *Journal of Urban Affairs*, 27 (2005): 437–451.

5. Boyd, "The Downside of Racial Uplift," 266.

6. Pattillo, "Black Middle Class Neighborhoods" and Pattillo *Black on the Block*.

7. Hyra, "Racial Uplift" 85–86 and Boyd, "The Downside of Racial Uplift," 82.

8. In the literature, a black identity is often a simple matter of race; however, sometimes there are disputes about "authentic" representations of blackness.

9. Moore, "What's Class Got to do with it?" 447.

10. For work on Harlem, see Jackson, *Harlemworld* and Taylor, *Harlem*. Works on Chicago include Hyra, *The New Urban Renewal* and "Racial Uplift"; Pattillo, "Black Middle Class Neighborhoods" and *Black on the Block*; and Boyd, "The Downside of Racial Uplift" and "Reconstructing Bronzeville."

11. Pattillo, "Negotiating Blackness" and Moore, "What's Class Got to do with it?"

12. Michael Omi and Howard Winant, *Racial Formation in the United States*, Second Edition (New York: Routledge, 1994), 14–23.

13. Stephen Cornell and Douglas Hartmann, *Ethnicity and Race: Making Identities in a Changing World* (Pine Forge Press/A Sage Publication Company, 1988) 21–34.

14. Pattillo, *Black on the Block,* 20.

15. Ibid.

16. Ibid, 117.

17. Ibid, 304.

18. W.E.B. DuBois, *The Souls of Black Folks* (Greenwich, CT: Fawcett, [1903] 1961), 7.

19. Moore, 442–443.

20. Ibid, 443.

21. Jackson, *Harlemworld,* 86.

22. Ibid, 86–87.

23. Ibid, 176.

24. Moore; Boyd, "The Downside of Racial Uplift"; and Pattillo, *Black on the Block*.

25. U.S. Bureau of the Census. *Census of Population and Housing,* 2000.

26. Brian Simpson, personal interview with author, May 28, 2009.

27. Elizabeth Battle, personal interview with author, December 20, 2008.

28. Ibid.

29. B.H. Combs, "The Ties that Bind: The Role of Place in Racial Identity Formation, Accord, and Discord in Two Historic, Black Gentrifying Atlanta Neighborhoods" (Ph.D. Dissertation, Georgia State University, 2010), 73.

30. Ibid, 74.

31. Naomi Goldman, interview with author, March 13, 2009.

32. Samaritan House is located in the Old Fourth Ward. The organization helps homeless men and women to become self-sufficient. Café 458 is one of its outreach programs. The Café is located in the Sweet Auburn area, and its motto is "where eating out can be your good deed for the day." It offers gourmet menu selections prepared by an "award winning chef" at reasonable prices, and the proceeds benefit Samaritan House.

33. Combs, 74.

34. Ruth Marshall, interview with author, April 17, 2009.

35. Combs, 154.

36. Ruth Marshall, interview with author, April 17, 2009.

37. Lauren Murphy, interview with author, June 14, 2009.

38. Ibid.

39. Combs, 157.

40. Zaniah Ford, interview with author, June 17, 2009.

41. Combs, 157.

42. Ibid, 158.

43. U.S. Census Bureau. Housing and Population Census. 1990–2000.

44. Timothy Crimmins, "West End: Metamorphosis from Suburban Town to Intown Neighborhood." *The Atlanta Historical Journal* XXVI (1982): 35–50.

45. William Julius Wilson, *The Declining Significance of Race: Blacks and Changing American Institutions* (University of Chicago, 1990), 120.

46. Amina Charles, interview with author, June 16, 2009.

47. Combs, 61.

48. Ibid, 92.

49. Kevin Washington, interview with author, February 10, 2009.

50. Ibid.

51. Ibid.

52. Councilman Denzel Martin, interview with author, March 19, 2009.

53. Combs, 105.

54. Ibid., 106.

55. Faith Howard, interview with author, May 26, 2009.

56. Combs, 310.

57. Ibid, 149.

58. Patricia Hill Collins, *Black Feminist Thought: Knowledge, Consciousness, and the Politics of Empowerment* (New York: Routledge, 1990), 221–238.

59. Tony Miller, interview with author, January 30, 2009.

60. Combs, 107.

61. Ibid, 107–108.

62. Peter J. Burke, "The Self Measurements Requirements from an Interactionist Per-

spective," *Social Psychology Quarterly* 43 (1990), 18.

63. David Demo and Michael Hughes, "Socialization and Racial Identity among Black Americans," *Social Psychology Quarterly* 53:4 (1990), 364.

64. Collins, *Black Feminist Thought*, 221–238.

65. Ibid.

66. Cheryl Simpson, interview with author, May 28, 2009.

Chapter 9

The African Diaspora in the U.S.: Cultural Clash and Identity Challenges[1]

Julius O. Adekunle

Immigration is the process by which a person enters and settles as a permanent resident in another country. From a historical perspective, immigration has been a continuing global phenomenon; from the past to the present, people continue to cross international borders. People have different reasons for moving from one locality to another. Some move as a result of war or political problems, some move for economic or ecological reasons, and others move for personal reasons. Usually, immigrants move in search of better living conditions. Immigration occurs in mainly two ways: forced immigration, such as the trans-Atlantic slave trade that brought Africans to the New World, and voluntary immigration, which is responsible for the African Diaspora in the United States (U.S.) in modern times. An estimated one billion people in the three centuries since the Industrial Revolution have settled in countries beyond their place of birth. This has dramatically modified global social geography. The United Nations Organization (UNO) sponsored Global Commission on International Migration Study that was published in 2005 indicates that 150 million people (an estimated 3% of the world's population) reside outside of their country of birth. The Commission has also determined that transnational migrations doubled between the years 1980 to 2000, and that migrants "depart from and arrive in" every country of the world as of 2005.[2]

Most of the world's developed countries have become diverse multi-ethnic societies since the 1950s. Many of these migrants have left Africa for Europe, Canada, and the United States. According to the U.S. Census Bureau, America will become a nation dominated by ethnic minorities by the year 2040 with those of primarily European ancestry comprising only about 46% of the total

U.S. population.[3] Today's immigration process involves regulations—for example, visas are issued to ensure that the immigrant has legal entry, and work authorization is then given to allow the immigrant to work. Over the centuries of its existence, the U.S. has witnessed a series of waves of migrations from different parts of the world. With the long history of this transnational network, the U.S. has become a land for all nations, and a place for all cultural identities.

The influx of people has brought about cultural clashes and challenges of identity for many immigrants. Because of their long stay in the U.S., many immigrants have been fully integrated, or completely "Americanized." They have lost some of their life-long cultural identities and imbibed new ones. The process of assimilation has been markedly different between white immigrants and immigrants from Africa. In particular, the process of immigration for people of African descent has been characterized by the retention of distinct aspects of African culture. Africans have succeeded in retaining specific aspects of their original cultural roots. The people of the contemporary African Diaspora, as described in this chapter, face a clash of culture and identity challenges as they try to maintain a strong link with their homeland.[4] As much as possible, they try to retain some of their identity, and continue on with some of the practices of their original culture. Through oral interviews, surveys, and other primary sources, this chapter analyzes the clash of culture and challenges of identity of the African Diaspora in the U.S.

The idea of converging identities is not totally new in African history. In many parts of Africa, people converged in fertile areas and established political and economic connections. In the interlacustrine region in east-central Africa, there was a convergence of people around the Great Lakes. The discovery of iron became a revolutionary factor that changed the technological culture and economy of Africans. For example, iron smelting in ancient Carthage was partly responsible for the increase in population and economic growth of the region in the period B.C. Similarly, in the Niger-Benue Confluence area in central Nigeria where the Nok Culture was developed, the agricultural population used iron and stone tools. Iron smelting began in that area and spread to other parts of West Africa. Based on archaeological and linguistic evidence, Ade Obayemi suggested that in the Niger-Benue Confluence, a "cluster of languages within the larger Kwa group" was formed and "the separations between the units of this cluster vary between 2,000 years ... and 6,000 years...."[5] The Bantu expansion from Cameroon to central and eastern Africa led to the establishment of kingdoms and diffusion of iron technology in the sixth century B.C. While these examples were not on a global scale, they epitomized the concept of converging identities as a result of migration and cultural continuity.

In explaining how Africans came to the United States, historians do not ignore the terrible and horrific practice of human trafficking that took place between the fifteenth and nineteenth centuries—the Transatlantic Slave Trade. This unfortunate episode has been solely responsible for the African-U.S. link, and the beginning of African settlement in the U.S. As a result of the flourishing slave trade, the U.S. became a place of converging identities. Starting with the arrival of the English people who were in search of gold, and the subsequent domination of the native people, followed by the arrival of African slaves, the U.S. eventually became a land of many identities. The first set of African slaves in Virginia came from Angola in the first half of the seventeenth century. Unable to find gold, the English people established tobacco plantations which required heavy and intensive labor. While at first the planters relied on white servants, it became apparent that African slaves were a better labor investment. The immigrants from Europe and slaves from Africa eventually transported their different cultures to the U.S., but they had to change their names. Some African slaves were given names such as Coffe, Longo, Moccafunke, Mongo, Transport, and Zambo. However, while names changed, the African attitude toward enslavement and interest to practice their own culture did not wane.

In North America, slaves from Nigeria, the Gold Coast, and Sierra Leone in West Africa met slaves from the Bight of Benin and West Central Africa. Michael Gomez, in his *Exchanging Our Country Marks*, points out that "the Igbo contingent to North America ... accounted for nearly one-quarter of the number of Africans imported into North America, placing it in a virtual first-place tie with West Central Africa."[6] However, irrespective of their number and places of origin, all the slaves encountered similar experiences and challenges. The rapidly growing population of Africans in the U.S. had an impact on their culture and identity. According to Gomez:

> A number of principal groups comprised the African presence in America. Arriving at different times and in different volumes, they tended to be concentrated in respective locations; their relative rates of entry, population sizes, and distribution patterns within the South are therefore critical to understanding the consequent African American identity. Of course, they brought with them their culture and worldviews, the blending of which varied from state to state and was dependent upon ethnic configurations specific to the area in question. All, however, passed through certain stages in moving from ethnicity to race.[7]

As a result of continuity and increase in the African population, the argument can be made that African cultures in the U.S. today follow the pattern of the slavery era. Joseph E. Harris contends that "the African Diaspora assumes the character of a dynamic, continuous and complex phenomenon stretching across time, geography, class, and gender."[8] The continuity and the dynamism of the African Diasporan culture help to explain the uniqueness of their identity in a converging environment such as the U.S. On the one hand, the slave trade was partly responsible for the African presence and the convergence of African cultural identity in the U.S. in modern times. The long and complex history of racial and ethnic interaction and intermixture cannot be easily erased. On the other hand, the former enslaved population has been associated with the identity crisis that many people of African descent experienced in the past. The new waves of migration and new experiences also create challenges of identity for the African Diaspora in contemporary times. Not surprisingly, the African Diaspora faces some cultural challenges that force immigrants to go through cultural adaptation and cultural transformation. As Africans come to the U.S., they come with high hopes of success—both educational and financial. While some have initial struggles adjusting and adapting, others quickly settle down to reinforce or improve their educational standard in order to fit properly into the American society. The beginning may be rough, but with perseverance and hard work, many end up realizing their dreams and hopes.

The modern African Diaspora in the U.S. is divided into two periods—the pre-September 11, 2001, and the post-September 2001.[9] The table below shows

Table 1. Total and African Foreign-Born Populations, 1960–2007

Year	Foreign Born	Share of All Foreign Born	African Born
1960	9,738,091	0.4%	35,355
1970	9,619,302	0.8%	80,143
1980	14,078,906	1.4%	199,733
1990	19,797,316	1.8%	363,819
2000	31,107,889	2.8%	881,300
2007	38,059,555	3.7%	1,419,317

Source: Data for 2000 from the 2000 Census; 2007 data from the American Community Survey 2007. http://www.migrationinformation.org/usfocus/display.cfm?ID=719#1.

how significantly the number of the African Diaspora has increased in the U.S. between 1960 and 2007.

Table 2. African Diaspora in the U.S.

Region	Number of Immigrants	Percentage
Western Africa	542,032	36.3 percent
Eastern Africa	423,298	28.4 percent
Northern Africa	264,536	17.7 percent
Southern Africa	85,145	5.7 percent
Central Africa	65,457	4.4 percent
Others	112,317	7.5 percent (information on origin not available)

The census figure in 2009 put the foreign-immigrants at 38,517, 104 and African-born at 1,492,785, which is 3.9% of the total foreign-born.[10] According to the table below, most of the African Diaspora came from West Africa.

The top five countries of origin for the 1.5 million African immigrants in the U.S. were:[11]

Nigeria	209,908	14.1 percent of all African immigrants
Ethiopia	148,221	9.9 percent
Egypt	138,194	9.3 percent
Ghana	108,647	7.3 percent
Kenya	87,267	5.8 percent

No individually reported country accounted for more than 14.1 percent of the African immigrant population. Some Africans came to the U.S. to seek asylum; Ethiopia Liberia, Somalia, and Sudan top the asylum list. According to the statistics, Ethiopia had 11,421, and Cameroon had 7,300 asylum seekers in the US in 2010.[12] As Anna Miller indicates, seekers:

Must prove refugee status—they must show that past persecution or a well-founded fear of future persecution prevents them from returning to their home countries, and that such persecution is based on race, religion, nationality, political opinion, or membership in a particular social group.[13]

In *What is History?* E.H. Carr points out that there is "an unending dialogue between the present and the past."[14] The experiences of the African Diaspora in the U.S. may differ in some respects, but they still attest to the fact that the present cannot be devoid of the past. Enslaved Africans were engaged in all kinds of odd jobs, providing long hours of agricultural labor, planting, and picking cotton. Some worked on plantations, and others served as artisans and constructions workers. They all had little or no education, as white slave owners did not encourage education for slaves. Hence, education was not synonymous with blackness. In a similar way, many Africans in diaspora first begin working all kinds of odd jobs. While some come with a good education, others struggle to advance themselves in order to rise from the lowest rung of the ladder toward the top for a better life.

While the early demographic movements of Africans were driven by slave labor, the modern African-U.S. migration is motivated by economic reasons, especially job opportunities. Immigrants seek better educations, reunions with family members, and political asylum. To distinguish between the past and present demography, some Africans describe their stay in the U.S. or any other country outside Africa as "voluntary slavery." The idea of voluntary slavery presumably emanates from the nature of jobs most of them do, and the long hours they spend at work, particularly when they first arrive.

Africans and Education

Education is a high priority to the people of the African Diaspora. It is considered to be the key to success in life, and allows access to good jobs. That is why many Africans immigrate to the U.S. in order to receive a sound and stable education. Although African immigrants come to the U.S. from different African countries and speak different languages, they share a common goal— they want to secure well-paid jobs and live a comfortable life. However, many of them (especially those not from Anglophone areas) do not speak fluent English. There are immigrants who have little education at the time of their arrival, while some have college degrees and still others come with advanced degrees. They all find ways of improving themselves academically. A Nigerian female who responded to the survey for this chapter came to the U.S. with a Nigerian teachers' certificate (the National Certificate in Education), had the desire to integrate into American society and enter into the competitive job market. While doing all kinds of odd jobs such as stuffing letters in envelopes for a company and working in nursing homes, making minimum wage, she went to school and received her first degree, became a registered nurse, and proceeded to obtain a Master's of Science in Nursing. She became a nurse practitioner. Another example is that of a Nigerian family where the father is a university professor of history and the mother is a nurse practitioner pursuing her doctorate in science. One of their daughters is a medical doctor, the other is pursuing her doctorate in geography, and their son is a computer engineer.

A study published in 1996 based on the U.S Census affirms that African-born residents were "the most highly educated members" of both the U.S. and British societies. It is stated in the article that:

> Of all foreign-born U.S. residents, those who came from Africa had the highest level of educational attainment. Nearly 90 percent of African-born U.S. residents over the age of 25 are high school graduates. More than 47 percent of African-born U.S. residents have completed college. In comparison, only 23 percent of U.S. residents born in the United Kingdom and 38 percent of U.S. residents born in Asia (including China and Japan) are college graduates.... More than 22 percent of all African-born U.S. residents hold a graduate degree and 4 percent hold a Ph.D. Only 2.7 percent of U.S. residents from all of Asia and 2 percent of all immigrants from Japan hold a doctorate. Immigrants from Africa also have far higher levels of educational attainment than does the entire white population of the United States—including immigrants and native-born whites.[15]

Dr. Kefa M. Otiso, Associate Professor of Geography at the University of Minnesota, corroborates with the U.S. Census study in his own research conducted in 2000. According to his findings, "African immigrants perform better than the rest of the U.S. population in education and employment." He states that:

> Because these immigrants come from a continent that is often cast in an unfavorable light in the U.S. media, there is a tendency for many Americans to miss the vital contribution of these immigrants to meeting critical U.S. domestic labor needs, enhancing American global economic and technological competitiveness and helping America build critical economic, cultural and diplomatic links with the increasingly strategic African continent.[16]

In another study published in the *Houston Chronicle* in 2008, it was noted that Nigerians were the most educated in the U.S. The article states "Nigerian immigrants have the highest levels of education in this city [Houston] and the nation, surpassing whites and Asians, according to Census data bolstered by an analysis of 13 annual Houston-area surveys conducted by Rice University."[17] In the same article, Amadu Jacky Kaba (an associate professor at Seton Hall University), contends that "many Africans pursue higher levels of education as an unintended consequence of navigating the tricky minefield of immigration."[18] Africans in general are education-driven; they set high standards not only for themselves, but also for their children because they believe that education is a major key to good jobs and to success in life.

The African Work Experience

The U.S. is a vastly growing industrial nation, which allows people to be employed in various sectors of the economy. Having overcome significant levels of discrimination since the 1960s as a result of Civil Rights legislation (such as the Civil Rights Act of 1964), many African Americans and immigrants of the African Diaspora take advantage of the educational and job opportunities that the U.S. has to offer. According to Dr. Asopuru Okemgbo, an environmentalist in the U.S., "Life in America is good. For African people in America, it is very challenging because you have to prove yourself beyond your equals, in order to come to the top. But there in America, the basic needs—water, food, access roads, and transportation—are not issues, but you have to sweat for every dollar you earn."[19] While some Africans in diaspora have positioned themselves in politics, others made considerable contributions to the economic and social development of the communities in which they live. The economic group of the African Diaspora range from odd job workers to business people, and to professionals. All, in various ways, have made impacts on local or national economy. Isaac and Elizabeth Osei of New York typify the early struggles and success as well as the identity issue of people of the African Diaspora in the U.S. Isaac Osei came to the U.S. from Ghana in West Africa. He and his wife were cab drivers, but later owned a restaurant and cab company. In the U.S., the couple is like other Africans, but in Ghana, Osei is a chief in charge of five towns.[20] When they leave the U.S. for Ghana:

> their roles will suddenly and drastically shift. As they cross the Atlantic Ocean, Mr. Osei will become Nana Gyensare V, a chief of the Akwamu people, who oversees the residents of five towns across the

Eastern Region. After arriving in Accra, the capital of Ghana, he will don a delicate gold crown, take a seat on his throne or stool and work 20-hour days out of his 10-room palace. Rather than focus on taxi tune-ups and inspections, Mr. Osei will assume judicial and other powers, like mediating family disputes. Ms. Osei, who is happiest talking about chassis and alternators, will have to fulfill the responsibilities of a chief's wife by running women's groups in each town ....[21]

Some reasons can be adduced for the brain drain that is affecting African countries. First, there is the absence of good jobs and poor living wages. From undergraduates to doctorate degree holders and medical doctors, the wages are not attractive and the living conditions are not favorable. At the point of leaving, the immediate thought of the migrants of the African Diaspora is not underdeveloping their individual countries. They left to develop themselves and to find "greener pastures." Second, there is the problem of maintenance culture. Many of the facilities and instruments that should have been used in development programs have been abandoned or are not adequately maintained. Houses have collapsed and instruments have been wasted because of the lack of technological education or power to maintain them. Third, the complacency of dependency bites hard on African governments. Dependence on foreigners and foreign goods hinders or slows down domestic development. This has been the trend in history.

The growth of capitalism led to economic exploitation and underdevelopment of Africa and Africans. Walter Rodney points out that in the pre-colonial times, "Western Europe and Africa had a relationship which insured the transfer of wealth from Africa to Europe."[22] The era of imperialism, further "underdeveloped" Africa and made Europe an economically dominant world power. Admittedly, Africa lacks neither economic nor human resources—rather, it lacks the technology and industrialization needed to develop and make its people gainfully employed instead of immigrating to industrialized countries. Imperialism and differences in industrial development brings an imbalance to the global economy.

Because of the inequalities in the global economy, wealthy countries recruit the best experts (in various fields) from all over the world. Not surprisingly, the U.S. has become an attractive and popular place for many Africans with special skills. Until African governments improve their attitude towards development, and provide the necessary tools for people to work with, the issue of brain drain will most likely continue.

Culture and Adaptation

Africans are not the only diaspora people who bring their culture to the U.S. Historically, cultures travel with immigrants. During the Atlantic Slave Trade slaves were not permitted to practice their African culture in the New World or in the Americas; but that position has changed in modern times. Freedom, modernity, and respect for other people's cultures have now made it possible for Africans not only to transport, but also to practice some aspects of their culture in the U.S. while adapting to or being assimilated into new ones. John Arthur indicates that "assimilation and integration into the affairs of the host society varies significantly among immigrants." Among the factors for the variations are: "age, country of origin, racial and ethnic identification, immigrant normative and cultural values, and the presence of relatives already settled in the United States."[23]

Some Africans went from one country to the other before finally settling down in the U.S. Some lived in Europe and others in the Middle East. A Nigerian woman indicated that her family first lived in Canada before relocating to the U.S. Thus, after having lived in Canada and being exposed to North America culture, it was relatively easy to adapt. It would have been more difficult if she had come directly from Nigeria; the issue of food and lifestyle would have been difficult to adapt to. Another immigrant indicated that he did not have much difficulty in adapting because a "friend who had lived and worked in the U.S., gave me his honest opinion of what it is like in the U.S. His information prepared my mind for the worst, but the rosy image of 'America the Beautiful' refused to go. I had a wonderful, forthright and hospitable host—he was a shepherd."[24]

In this period of globalization, it is important for the migrants of the African Diaspora to be fully aware of cultural adaptation. The intersection of two or more cultures calls for adaptation in order to conform to the norms and expectations of the whole society. Promoting multiculturalism, which involves peaceful inter-ethnic and inter-racial relations, is one of the core values of African societies. Cultural adaptation involves a person's cultural heritage, language, and ethnicity. Adapting to new cultures helps an individual to understand and respect other people and their cultural practices and belief systems. Similarly, it is important for the African Diaspora to be cognizant of the cultural nuances in the U.S.

Unlike the first generation of the African Diaspora who experience "culture shock" when they first arrive in the U.S., cultural adaptation seems to be easier for the next generation. Indeed, the reverse adaptation applies to these children because they were born into an environment that is different from their parents' and they are just beginning to learn their African culture and language. However, they too may experience culture shock when they face challenges of a new environment and lose their familiar cultural milieu. Africans indicated that they were shocked about children not being disciplined by their parents as they were in Africa. Many were baffled by the high rate of marital divorce; some marveled about a drive-through for fast food; several were taken aback seeing people kissing in public; many experienced shock when a woman announced that she is pregnant; others were appalled by the way Americans dress, especially the young ones.

There is also the idea of gender equality, which is a global phenomenon. Historically, African men have been dominant, but the female liberation movement world-wide is changing that perspective. African women are now more prominent in politics and economics, contributing significantly to the development of their respective countries. Africa can now boast of two female presidents (in Liberia and Malawi), women in the majority in the Rwandan parliament, and women occupying top political positions in many countries. Culture and tradition may be maintained in some respects, but women in the African Diaspora feel more liberated; many of them are educated and engaged in jobs that bring economic convenience for the family.

Migration and its attendant culture shock often contribute to stress, anxiety, and depression for many immigrants. Immigrants sometimes feel frustrated and become homesick. According to psychiatrists Dinesh Bhugra and Oyedeji Ayonrinde, culture shock is "a stress reaction arising from the uncertainty of important physical and psychological rewards." They referred to Kalervo Oberg, who identified six aspects of culture shock: strain; a sense of loss or feelings of deprivation; rejection by members of the new culture; role expectation and role confusion; surprise, anxiety and indignation; and feelings of impotence.[25] To deal with the situation, immigrants need to understand the new cultural environment and have to develop adaptation mechanisms such as being open-minded, keeping active, seeking help from people, and belonging to socio-cultural organizations.

African Diaspora and Raising a Family

The parents in the African Diaspora face many challenges in living in the U.S., one being how to raise their children. Many African parents are of the opinion that raising children in the U.S. is a daunting and challenging task that is sometimes frustrating because American society allows many practices that African cultures do not permit. The Africans in diaspora come from their community-oriented life style and must deal with the concept of individualism. The African Diaspora, according to Vivian Yenika-Agbaw, "prefer to distance themselves from a [American] culture they often perceive as promoting individualism, materialism, racial polarization, and violence."[26] They come to the U.S. with the idea of strict discipline only to struggle against not spanking—otherwise the child would dial 9-1-1. As Victor Dike eloquently puts it:

> Torn between two cultures, African parents are therefore in a dilemma as to where to raise their children. Those who have the infrastructure and courage to send their children back home to Africa (in the care of their relatives) to get familiarized with the African culture have many things to be thankful for.... In traditional African societies parents have the power to straighten up or punish their children when they go astray. In the United States one often avoids that for fear of being branded a child molester .... There is no substitute for education anchored on traditional African values.[27]

Vivian Yenika-Agbaw also asserts that African parents have a tough time raising children in the U.S. She argues that the problem is "complicated by issues related to racial and ethnic identities in addition to their children's reality as first generation American born."[28] In an attempt to ease the problem, parents teach their children their African language and culture, especially with an emphasis on the need for discipline. Parents make them realize that discipline is part of African culture that builds the character and personality of the individual, and that they only restrain from using corporal punishment to avoid unpleasant legal issues. There are examples of African parents who went overboard in disciplining their children in the "African way," and have been prosecuted.

Parenting becomes more complicated if the parents do not have the same cultural background or identity. This happens in an interracial marriage or where only one of the parents is from Africa. An attempt to impose African values on the children may create problems between the parents. Many Africans in diaspora adjust very well to this situation, realizing that heavy discipline or punishment may have a lasting negative impact on the child. A Nigerian immigrant, married to an African American, decided to send their daughter to Nigeria for discipline and to learn Nigerian culture in 1995. The first year was difficult for the girl, but she reportedly adjusted, enjoyed her three-year stay, and loves to go back to Nigeria to visit.[29] Not all cases of sending the child to Africa end up in a success story or with a pleasant experience. Some of the children come back to the U.S. with illness, especially malaria fever. There are Africans in diaspora who do believe that sending the children back to Africa for whatever reason is counter-productive, especially for the children.

Africans allow their spiritual beliefs or upbringing to come to play in raising their children. They come from their respective countries and religious backgrounds to live in a very secular society. It becomes difficult from parents when their children choose to practice other religions or none at all because of the secular nature of the American society. The lifestyles from Africa therefore pose many challenges of cultural adaptation and conflicts. Removed from their cultural background, parents have to adjust to and adopt a new culture in which their children will be raised. Immigrant families undergo a process of acculturation and transformation. Having to oscillate between attending school to improve themselves and work, parenting becomes a hard combination.

African Diaspora and Associations

Wherever they settle, migrants of the African Diaspora form cultural, economic, and social organizations to support each other or to help their people in Africa. Associations provide network opportunities and they are sources of empowerment for the African Diaspora.[30] For example, there is the Association for the Advancement of Africa (AAA), a U.S.-based non-profit organization. One of its objectives is "to help first-generation Africans assimilate into American society while aiming at strengthening and enhancing the fundamental relationship between Africans of the diaspora and Africa." Its mission is "to mobilize and unite Africans of the Diaspora, Africans in Africa, and all friends of Africa to address the cultural, economic, educational, civic, immigration, health, scientific, and social needs of African societies, domestic and international."[31] There is also the Association of Nigerian Physicians in the Americas (ANPA), a group of licensed medical doctors practicing in the Americas and Canada who hold annual conferences. The BINI Association of Northern California promotes African cultural practices and raises funds to aid in the treatment of HIV/AIDS, especially in Edo State of Nigeria.

Even where no formal associations exist, Africans support each other in times of crisis. For example, a university professor was denied tenure, and his African colleagues rallied round to provide financial support for his legal fees. Another example is that of an African man who died in the U.S. His fellow Africans contributed money so that the family could send the body home for proper burial. These examples illustrate that in times of crisis, an African does not feel alone and abandoned. In times of celebrations such as wedding ceremonies, Africans rally round each other as well. This type of organized tradition of assistance, which was brought to the U.S. during the slavery era, is also found among African Americans. It is part of the culture and value system that

Africans in diaspora do not forget or ignore.[32] Belonging to associations or so-cial circles is not limited to fellow Africans in diaspora. While some Africans find it easy to associate with Asians because of the cultural and religious sim-ilarities, the second generation, relate well with their Hispanic neighbors and friends at school.

Reconnecting with Homeland

Africans are, by culture, hospitable. This is demonstrated by their concept of gift-giving. Europeans who visited Africa in the nineteenth century attested to African hospitality and gift-giving cultural practices. For example, Hugh Clapperton a Scottish explorer, reported of the Yoruba, "We were received with much kindness and attention.... He [the Alaafin of Oyo] presented us with gooro [kola] nuts. The king never comes to us empty-handed."[33] Richard and John Lander, English explorers to West Africa, asserted that "we were lib-erally regaled with water from a calabash, which is a compliment the natives pay to all strangers ...."[34] W. H. Clarke, an American Baptist missionary who visited Yorubaland remarked that he enjoyed "the hospitality of the kind-hearted chief of Igboho [who was] the very embodiment of humour." He stated further, "I could but feel that I was among those who loved me because their eyes, countenance, action, and words, all expressed a decided welcome."[35] As recent as 2011, Amanda Lichtenstein remarked on her experience in Zanz-ibar. She wrote:

> I realized that gift-giving is a major thread in the great tapestry of Swahili coastal culture. The gift is the heartbeat of an intricate system of social exchange. Notions of gift-giving along the Swahili coast stem from traditions and customs rooted in African and Arab worlds, both realms known for their over-the-top hospitality. It's the generous ges-ture, the thoughtfully tied sack of flour, the signature bundle of shillings that, when exchanged rightfully, is a bond that seals Swahili friendships.[36]

Thus, because it is an integral part of their gift-giving culture, Africans in diaspora do not hesitate to remit money to their family members and friends. They send huge sums of money to their respective to alleviate the poverty that is rampart in many African countries. While on annual vacation, the African in diaspora becomes the financial problem-solver for many family members. There are stories of Africans in diaspora who had to borrow money to return to the U.S. or who had to cut short their vacation time because they ran out of funds. An African in the U.S. narrated his experience when he went to wire money to a brother in Nigeria. Looking at the records of the people this Nigerian man has been sending money to, the Money Gram agent said, "you are Santa Claus" in reference to the giver's generosity. However, the Nigerian saw it as part of the cultural practice of gift-giving, especially because of the poor economic situation in Nigeria. The same story goes for other African immigrants.

Although the remittance of money was directed at assisting a family member, it is also generally and significantly contributing to the macroeconomics of the African countries. Dilip Ratha, manager of the Migration and Remittances unit at the World Bank, indicates that:

> Remittances are a critical lifeline for families and entire communities across Africa, especially in the aftermath of the global crisis. The fact that remittances are so large, come in foreign currency, and go directly to households, means that these transfers have a significant impact on poverty reduction, funding for housing and education, basic essential needs, and even business investments.[37]

Egypt and Morocco in North Africa, Somalia in East Africa, and Nigeria in West Africa are the leading countries with high remittance. According to a report, the inflow of remittance to Africa rose to nearly $40 billion between 1990 and 2010, constituting approximately 2.6 percent of Gross Domestic Product (GDP).[38] African governments recognize the importance and contributions of the African Diaspora to socio-economic developments in their respective countries. For example, the Federal Government of Nigeria, through Vice President Mohammed Namadi Sambo, described Nigerians in the diaspora as "valuable assets and catalysts in the drive to achieve its transformation agenda." Sambo indicated that "the diaspora constitutes a force for positive change which should be maximally harnessed for the development of our homeland."[39]

Africans in diaspora maintain close connections with their homeland not only through remittance of money, but also by going home for vacations or to attend funerals or wedding ceremonies of loved ones. Furthermore, many of them have substantial investments and properties that they hope to fall back on when they retire in the U.S. and relocate to their home country. Sulaimon Olanrewaju asserts that:

> Apart from helping individual families, the fund from Nigerians in the diaspora has also contributed greatly to the macroeconomics of the nation at large. Some Nigerians living abroad have set up small scale businesses for their relations in Nigeria. Some have also invested greatly in properties, thus contributing to alleviating the nation's housing problem. Some have invested in transportation and education as

well as other sectors of the economy. But in the last one year or so, the contribution of this category of Nigerians living abroad has slowed down.[40]

The global economic decline since 2008 has forced Africans in diaspora to limit their remittance to their home countries. The condition has gotten worse for many who have been forced to return home. The most affected people were those who lost their homes and jobs, and found living in the U.S. continuously difficult. A recent study reveals that Nigerians in diaspora who are in bad economic situations have to ask their relatives in Nigeria to send money to them. This is a reverse financial assistance.[41] Some Africans in the diaspora have chosen to go back to their countries to participate in politics or engage in business ventures, believing that no matter how prosperous a foreign land may be, there is always the desire to connect with home.[42]

Opportunities and Challenges

The U.S. has been recognized as a land of opportunities. This means that there are freedoms and opportunities for people (citizens as well as foreigners) to achieve their desired goals through education and work. The U.S. is regarded as the "land flowing with milk and honey." Hence, immigrants come for the economic and other opportunities that the U.S. has to offer. It is also clear that once in the U.S., economic opportunities provide social mobility, although immigrants have to make a lot of sacrifices in order to achieve their dreams. In spite of the recent economic downturn, it is not surprising that the U.S. remains a place of opportunity for many in the African Diaspora whose indigenous countries are experiencing severe economic difficulties. For example, in the Horn of Africa, countries such as Djibouti, Ethiopia, Kenya, and Somalia have been experiencing drought; there have been civil wars in the Chad, Democratic Republic of Congo, and Sudan; political instability in Egypt, Libya, and Tunisia; and insecurity in Nigeria as a result of suicide bombings and kidnapping. As discussed elsewhere, political stability and economic growth go hand in hand.[43] Corroborating this view is an International Monetary Fund (IMF) working paper that states:

> Political instability is regarded by economists as a serious malaise harmful to economic performance. Political instability is likely to shorten policymakers' horizons leading to suboptimal short term macroeconomic policies. It may also lead to a more frequent switch of policies, creating volatility and thus, negatively affecting macroeconomic performance.[44]

As far as African countries are concerned, poor leadership, natural climatic disasters, and political instability significantly inhibit economic growth and job opportunities; they dictate why Africans immigrate to the U.S. in "search of the golden fleece."[45] As Rodney argued, this is also a product of how Europe underdeveloped Africa.

The first generation of the African Diaspora enjoys some of the opportunities (not accessible to them in their countries of origin), but they also face a variety of challenges. Some of them feel that because they come from economically disadvantaged countries and reside in a white-dominated country that they are regarded as "second class people." They therefore work hard to prove themselves. Many of those who responded to the survey for this chapter claim that although they visit home on a regular basis and have investments in their home countries in preparation for retirement, they still try to preserve their African culture and identity in the U.S. This is an indication that they are not completely assimilated into the American culture.[46] The second generation of the African Diaspora does not have this challenge in the same magnitude of their parents because they are more Americanized or more integrated into American society. In another sense, there is the problem of identity because white Americans often identify Africans as African Americans. Africans in diaspora do not identify as African Americans, but as Africans in America.

As a result of the recent events going on in their respective countries, Africans in diaspora sometimes face specific challenges of acceptance into the U.S. community. For example, piracy in Somalia has become a global concern, putting the Somalis in the U.S. in a challenging situation. This is well demonstrated in *Welcome to Shelbyville*, a documentary on immigration directed by Kim Snyder. The documentary powerfully shows the uneasiness of Americans in welcoming the Somalis who came to settle in Shelbyville, Tennessee as refugees. Being predominantly Muslims, and given the psychological impact of September 11, 2001, there was the fear that these immigrants "want to kill us." A former mayor of Shelbyville was quoted as saying, "We don't know what diseases they have."[47] While the host neighbors entertained some fear, the immigrants had great expectations of a better life in the U.S. Hawo Siyard, one of the Somali refugees, declared, "I always imagined America as a place where I could work, find a better education, and live peacefully."[48] Siyard attests that they have not come to the U.S. to kill, but to enjoy the opportunities that the U.S. has to offer. Similarly, kidnapping, terrorism, and financial scams in Nigeria have created an environment of insecurity for foreigners and have put Nigerians in diaspora in a difficult situation in the U.S. Also, Umar Farouk Abdulmutallab's unsuccessful attempt to blow up a Detroit-bound jetliner on Christmas Day in 2009 caused more distrust of Nigerians in the U.S.

The challenges of racial discrimination, in subtle or blatant ways, cannot be ignored. As John Arthur points out, Africans are eager to come to the U.S., but they face the reality of discrimination, which they did not expect. He asserts:

> Now that they have had the opportunity to engage in the affairs of American society, the majority of them are convinced that the racial polarization and the institutionalized patterns of discrimination in America are antithetical to what American stands for: freedom, equality, and justice for all. Over time, the African immigrants adjust their attitudes about race relations. The adjustment takes into account the reality that the immigrants are powerless to alter the balance of racial relations in their favor.[49]

Some of the problems of the African Diaspora do not affect their children. The children have more educational and job opportunities than their parents, but they face cultural challenges and identity crises. The children are more connected to American cultural and education systems. Being in the U.S., they are able to receive sound and stable educations while their counterparts in Africa experience financial hardships and are not able to pay their way to college. In some African countries where education is unstable, students know when they will begin college or university, but they do not know when they will finish; this is partly because of political instability and incessant strikes by university professors. Many African colleges and universities are owned by the government. Hence, due to the poor economy, professors frequently demand higher salaries from the government. However, while the children are the inescapable victims of cultural conflict in the U.S., they value some of the African cultural practices of their parents. They appreciate their parents' hard work, discipline, respect, and African traditional clothing. Although some of them cannot speak their African languages fluently, they do understand when their parents speak.

Conclusion

When Africans come to the U.S., they come with high hopes of success—educational and financial. The beginning may be rough, but with perseverance and hard work, many end up realizing their hopes and dreams. Africans transport their culture of living in a community to their host countries through the tradition of support systems. In times of crises or celebrations, Africans support each other in ways similar to their home countries. They sur-round themselves when there is a death in the family, especially when the bereaved is unable to go back to Africa. Life in Africa is community-based. Hence, Africans in the diaspora do not totally practice individualism, but continue to relate to their fellow Africans in various ways.

Many Africans in diaspora claim they do not experience cultural clash or have identity challenges. Understandably, many of them do not identify themselves as African Americans because they were either not born in the U.S. or their parents were not born in the U.S. They simply identify themselves as Africans in the U.S. They claim that they cannot redefine their identity or radically alter their culture. While their culture does not change, their identity depends on how they see themselves—either as Africans or as Africans in America. In the U.S. today, there is a stigma attached to blackness and the question of identity is often difficult to answer. The U.S. is a very diverse country, making it difficult to be exact in determining the countries of the Black people merely through their physical appearances. While some came from Africa, others came from the Caribbean or West indies thus creating challenges of identity. The people of the African Diaspora continue to add to the cultural, identity, and racial dynamism in the U.S. as their numbers grow.

Notes

1. This chapter benefits from oral interviews and a survey conducted between 2010 and 2012. The author acknowledges the several Africans in diaspora who granted oral interviews and those who responded to the survey.

2. "Global Commission on International Migration," *International Organization for Immigration*, http://www.iom.int/jahia/Jahia/gcim (Accessed June 8, 2012).

3. Ibid.

4. In the survey conducted for this paper, those who responded came from Cameroon, Ghana, Kenya, Nigeria, Sierra Leone, South Africa, and Uganda at various times, but ranging from 1985 to 2011. Among these are first and second generations of immigrants. Some came through the Diversity Immigrant Visa (DV), drawn through lottery. The Immigration Act of 1990 made provision for approximately 55,000 citizens of selected foreign countries to seek entry to the U.S. The program, which began in 1995, was aimed at diversifying the immigrant population of the U.S.

5. Ade Obayemi, "The Yoruba and Edo-speaking Peoples and their Neighbours before 1600," in *History of West Africa*, Vol. One, Second Edition, ed., J. F. Ade Ajayi and Michael Crowder (London: Longman Group, 1976), 200.

6. Michael A. Gomez, *Exchange Our Country Marks: The Transformation of African Identities in the Colonial and Antebellum South* (Chapel Hill, NC: The University of North Carolina Press, 1998), Chapter 6.

7. Ibid., 13.

8. J. E. Harris, ed., *Global Dimensions of the African Diaspora* (Washington, DC: Howard University Press, 1993), 5.

9. There have been several African Diasporas from the prehistoric period to modern time, but this chapter focuses on the voluntary diaspora in the post WWII era.

10. Kristen McCabe, "African Immigrants in the United States," Information Migration Source, 2011, http://www.migrationinformation.org/USFocus/display.cfm?ID=847.

11. Ibid.

12. China has the highest number with 54,599 followed by Columbia with 25,607. Miller, 24.

13. Anna Miller, "Prescriptions for Sanctuary," *Medical and Health: The George Washington University School of Medicine and Health Sciences*, Fall 2011, 24.

14. E.H. Carr, *What is History?* (New York: Vintage Books, 1961), 35.

15. "African-Born U.S. Residents are the Most Highly Educated Group in American Society," *The Journal of Blacks in Higher Education*, No. 13 (Autumn, 1996), 33–34. http://www.aracorporation.org/files/14._africans_most_educated.pdf.

16. "African immigrants most educated immigrants in the US," http://www.thestudentroom.co.uk/showthread.php?t=1044361, originally published in *Mshale*, a Minneapolis-based newspaper for African people.

17. Leslie Casimir, "Data show Nigerians the most educated in the U.S.," *Houston Chronicle*, May 20, 2008, http://www.chron.com/news/article/Data-show-Nigerians-the-most-educated-in-the-U-S-1600808.php.

18. Ibid.

19. Robert Obioha and Vincent Ukpongkalu, "Why Some Nigerians are trapped in America," http://odili.net/news/source/2011/jul/10/502.html, Saturday, July 10, 2011.

20. "An African Chief in Cabby's Clothing," http://www.nytimes.com/2011/08/14/nyregion/isaac-osei-taxi-driver-in-new-york-and-chief-in-ghana.html?src=me&ref=nyregion.

21. Ibid.

22. Walter Rodney, *How Europe Underdeveloped Africa* (Washington, D.C.: Howard University Press, 1982), 75.

23. John A. Arthur, *Invisible Sojourners: African Immigrant Diaspora in the United States* (Westport, CT: Praeger Publishers, 2000), 69–70.

24. Interview with Mr. Bayo Olabisi, a Nigerian in New Jersey.

25. Dinesh Bhugra and Oyedeji Ayonrinde, "Depression in Migrants and Ethnic Minorities," *Advances in Psychiatric Treatment*, 2004, 13–17. Retrieved from http://apt.rcpsych.org/content/10/1/13.full#ref-19.

26. Quoted from, *In Motion: The African American Migration Experience*. The Schomburg Center for research in Black Culture, New York. [exhibit] April 2006.

27. Victor Dike, "The Dilemma of Raising their Children Abroad," *Vanguard* newspapers, September 21, 2004, http://allafrica.com/stories/200409210314.html.

28. Vivian Yenika-Agbaw, "African Child Rearing in the Diaspora: A Mother's Perspective," *The Journal of Pan African Studies*, vol.3, no.4, December 2009, 1–14.

29. Discussion with Mr. Tunde Awolola, Chicago, U.S., 2011.

30. Some of the associations are: Association des Senegalais d'Amerique, Bini Club of Northern California, Bini Club of Southern California, Nigerians In Diaspora Organization (NIDO), Egbe Isokan Yoruba, Washington DC, Egbe Omo Yoruba Greater New York, Egbe Ilosiwaju Omo Yoruba Ni Kolorado (The Progressive Association of Yorubas in Colorado), Kenyan Cultural Association, Kenyan Women's Association, and Moghamoan Group (Cameroon). School Alumni associations are also formed.

31. Dr. Sunday-Joseph Otengho of Uganda formed the association in 2000. Serving under Idi Amin's repressive regime, he sought political asylum in the United States in January 1981. http://www.advanceafrica.com/index2.htm.

32. See Gomez, Chapter.

33. Hugh Clapperton, *Journal of a Second Expedition into the Interior of Africa from Bight of Benin to Soccattoo* (London: Frank Cass, 1966), 27.

34. See Robin Hallet, ed., *The Niger Journal of Richard and John Lander* (London: Routledge and Kegan Paul, 1965), 56.

35. W. H. Clarke, Travels and Explorations in Yorubaland (1854–1858), ed., J. A. Atanda (Ibadan, Nigeria: Ibadan University Press, 1972), 66–71.

36. Amanda Leigh Lichtenstein, "5 Reasons to Give a Gift: Zawadi Culture in Zanzibar," http://matadornetwork.com/abroad/5-reasons-to-give-a-gift-zawadi-culture-in-zanzibar/. March 21, 2011.

37. "Remittances to Africa Resilient Despite Global Financial Crisis—World Bank Study," http://web.worldbank.org/WBSITE/EXTERNAL/COUNTRIES/AFRICAEXT/0,,content-MDK:22759320~menuPK:2246551~pagePK:2865106~piPK:2865128~the-SitePK:258644,00.html.

38. Dilip Ratha, Sanket Mohapatra, Çağlar Özden, Sonia Plaza, William Shaw, Adebe Shimles, "Leveraging Migration for Africa:Remittances, Skills, and Investments," *The World Bank*, Washington, DC, March 2011, 4.

39. Sunday Ode, "Diaspora, Asset for Transformation Agenda—Sambo," *New Nigerian* Online Edition, July 26, 2011, http://www.newnigeriannews.com/cover_2.htm.

40. Sulaimon Olanrewaju, "Moaning as Remittances from Abroad Decline," *Nigerian Tribune*, December 19, 2011, http://odili.net/news/source/2011/dec/19/600.html.

41. Ibid.

42. For example, some Nigerians who studied and worked in the U.S. have gone back to participate in politics with the objective of developing their own communities. For example, Prof. Julius Ihonvbere, a political scientist and professor in the U.S., served as a Special Adviser on Project Monitoring in the Olusegun Obasanjo administration and remains active in Nigerian politics. Also, Dr. Kayode Fayemi, who was Strategy Development Adviser at London's City Challenge and research fellow at the African Research and Information Bureau in London, is now the governor of Ekiti State. In Ghana, there is the Fihankra community of Africans from the diaspora. See Godfrey Mwakikagile, Relations Between Africans and African Americans: Misconceptions, Myths and Realities (Grand Rapids, Michigan: National Academic Press, 2005), Chapter 8.

43. Julius O. Adekunle, "Political Violence, Democracy, and the Nigerian Economy," in *Democracy in Africa: Political Changes and Challenges*, eds., Saliba Sarsar and Julius O. Adekunle (Durham, NC: Carolina Academic Press, 2012), 89–110.

44. Ari Aisen and Francisco Jose Veiga, "How Does Political Instability Affect Economic Growth?" *IMF Working Paper*, 2010, 3, http://www.imf.org/external/pubs/ft/wp/2011/wp1112.pdf.

45. Segun Adelakun, a Nigerian Lawyer in the U.S.

46. See John. A. Arthur, *Invisible Sojourners: African Immigrant Diaspora in the United States* (Westport, CT: Praeger Publishers, 2000).

47. Tom Jacobs, "Loving, and Fearing, thy Neighbors," *Miller-McCune: Smart Journalism. Real Solutions*, May/June 2011, 76–77.

48. Ibid.

49. Arthur, 75.

Chapter 10

The Things They Carried: From West Africa to Low Country Georgia, 1750–1800

Karen Cook Bell

Lucia, a young girl transported to the Georgia low country during the 1760s, brought with her a deft understanding of her provenance. Prior to her forced migration, her father established her identity by placing "a black stroke over each of her cheeks" as a mark of her ethnicity.[1] Her family's conception of their historical reality no doubt included reverence for naming ceremonies, secret societies, and the rituals associated with such societies, gendered roles, warrior traditions, and untrammeled freedom. For Lucia, running away was the final act of resistance to enslavement. It was a Pyrrhic victory against a system that sought to subsume her traditions and knowledge of herself. Within this system of inhuman bondage, however, enslaved Africans such as Lucia remained free. They retained a sense of themselves and relied upon an informal network of both enslaved and free Africans for support, including the quasi maroon communities developed by Africans who escaped enslavement.

The ideology of freedom can be discerned through eighteenth century fugitive slave advertisements which reveal that enslaved Africans carried hidden and explicit ideologies of knowledge and resistance. These overt and covert ideologies of knowledge and resistance created a public and private culture within the community of the enslaved, which made their discursive reality discernible. As a central epistemological category of the human experience, narratives, reflected in slave advertisements, represent a body of ideas that help to explain relations, structures, and the conjuncture of discourse and power.[2]

This chapter is written against the "master narratives" of slavery to reveal the individual oral narratives of enslaved men and women. It tells of their engagement with slavery and freedom in a region where slavery received legal sanction two decades before the Revolutionary War began in 1775. In this context, this chapter argues that the fissures within slavery provided opportunities for symbolic moves in an essentially polemic and strategic confrontation that persisted throughout the era of North American slavery. First, the slave trade to Georgia will be examined and reconstructed, and then the various manifestations of resistance (with a focus on running away) will be analyzed.

The Subaltern's Landscape

Within transatlantic communities, resistance to enslavement became an integral part of the landscape. As discrete communities based on shared transatlantic pasts, these groups were linked by regional origins, American destinations, and New World cultural developments. By examining colonial records, a composite picture of the enslavement, forced migration, and resistance of Africans emerges. The examination of colonial records also illuminates the extent of the transference of African cultures and knowledge systems in the low country. Slave ship manifests, published documents of the slave trade, advertisements of the arrival of slave ships from the Rice and Grain Coast in the *Georgia Gazette* reveal a great deal about slave life in the Georgia low country. The accounts of planters and merchants such as Joseph Clay demonstrate that the forced migration of specific populations from West Africa transferred the technology and culture of rice production to the low country. Moreover, through an examination of the origins of rice production in Africa, the forced migration of enslaved Africans (from rice growing regions in West Africa to South Carolina and Georgia) and similarities between the technology and culture of rice production in West Africa and North America may be compared. This has been demonstrated in the work of scholars such as Daniel Littlefield, Judith Carney, and Edda Fields-Black. These scholars have illuminated the process by which African origin and ethnicity informed rice cultivation in the Americas.[3]

In this chapter, political activity is understood as an organized collective action that affects power relations. Sterling Stuckey, Lawrence Levine, and Eugene Genovese have each looked beyond subversive acts for evidence of the deeper cultural and social resistance found in folkways, religious practices, and family life.[4] Enslaved Africans in the Georgia low country retained much of their African cultural identities as a result of three inwardly related factors. First, the ratio of the African and African American population to the white population remained disproportionately high in several low country counties in 1790. This pattern continued throughout the slavery era (see Table 1). Second, the continued importation of new Africans in the years following the

Table 1. Population of Low Country Georgia, 1790

County	Slave/Free Black*	White	%Black Population
Chatham	8,313	2,426	77%
Liberty	4,052	1,303	75%
Glynn	220	193	53%
Camden	84	221	27%

* There were 112 free blacks in Chatham County; 27 in Liberty County; five in Glynn County; and 14 in Camden County. By 1820, 65 percent of Camden County population was black. The fifth low country county, McIntosh County, was separated from Liberty County in 1793.

Source: *United States Population Census, 1790.*

1808 ban on the slave trade persisted, which reinforced African cultural traditions and reduced assimilation. Third, the low country environment with its string of barrier islands separated the island communities from the mainland white population and this reinforced the collective identity and consciousness of enslaved Africans in the Georgia low country.[5]

By 1790, three principal transatlantic communities had emerged: the Savannah-Ogeechee District (located between the Savannah and Ogeechee Rivers containing Chatham County), The Midway District (located between the Savannah and Altamaha Rivers and containing Liberty and McIntosh Counties), and the Altamaha District (from the Atlantic between the Altamaha and St. Mary's Rivers) that contained Glynn and Camden Counties. These communities served as watersheds, which by definition is the land area which contributes surface water to a river or other body of water. Consequently, settlement in watershed areas is characterized by a complex system involving social, ecological, and physical factors.[6] The regions five large rivers, Savannah, Ogeechee, Altamaha, Satilla, and St. Mary's, were vital to the growth of rice and served as the focal point for settlement.[7]

The arrival of over 13,000 Africans in low country Georgia led to the creation of a new language structure, the Gullah/Geechee language, which had a common semantic and stylistic form. This shared language made possible the reclamation of a territory to establish a sense of place. The cultural identity of these forced transatlantic communities emanated from shared traditions, perspectives; and intersecting relations and languages.[8] Building on both their African background and American experience, Africans in low country Georgia retained their African culture and established cultural resistance to their enslavement. Cultural resistance represented a salient form of opposition to federally sanctioned enslavement. The establishment of rice plantations along the coastal and inland areas of Georgia in the eighteenth century created a unique environment for enslaved Africans to re-create social and cultural institutions. Functioning within the constraints of an inhumane system, Africans and African Americans established familial bonds, preserved agricultural techniques, re-created artistic expressions, maintained Islamic practices, and syncretized African religious beliefs with Christianity.

The legalization of slavery in Georgia in 1750 and the concomitant expansion of the Transatlantic Slave Trade shaped the evolution of African slave communities in the low country. In low country Georgia, as well as in other parts of the New World, enslaved Africans perceived themselves as part of a community that had distinct ethnic and national roots. Randomization was not a function of the Middle Passage. Although slave ships traversed the coast of Africa to secure Africans, in some instances, slave ships also drew their cargo from only one principal port. These ports included the Island of Gorée, Bonny, Calabar, Elmina, and the Biafra.[9] Slave ships bound for Georgia included captive Africans who shared a similar linguistic heritage; for example, Mande speakers such as the Malinke and Serer. To a large extent, the Transatlantic Middle Passage in the North Atlantic defined and shaped African perceptions of kinship, ethnicity, and community, although the voices of captive Africans have been difficult to "hear."[10] With few exceptions, their words and thoughts are absent from extant archival records. Constructing a cultural map of the Transatlantic Slave Trade to Georgia to establish the geographical dimensions of the trade, the cultivation of rice as the primary plantation crop, and African cultural resistance provides an important historical frame of reference for "hearing" the voices of enslaved Africans.[11]

The demand for African slave labor increased with the establishment of rice and Sea Island cotton plantations during the late eighteenth century. As rice became a profitable export crop in coastal Georgia, merchants in Savannah imported Africans from the Rice and Grain Coast of West Africa, which extended from the Senegambian region to Sierra Leone.[12] From 1755–1767, 53 percent of slaves imported into Savannah originated from the Caribbean, while 35 percent came directly from the Rice and Grain Coast.[13] Comparatively, during the intermediate period from 1768–1780, 68 percent of slaves imported into Savannah originated from the Rice and Grain Coast.[14] From 1784–1798, West African captives from rice growing regions accounted for 45 percent of slaves imported to Savannah (see Tables 2–5).[15]

Most voyages across the Atlantic Ocean from West Africa to Savannah occurred during the period from April to September. Merchants believed that seasonal changes affected the health of captive Africans considerably, and thus

Table 2. Savannah Planter Merchants Who Received and Sold West
Africans from Rice Growing Regions, 1765–1771

Name of Firm	Origin of Africans	Quantity Sold
Ingliss and Hall	Gambia and Sierra Leone	667
Clay and Habersham	Gambia	320
John Graham/Ingliss and Hall	Rice Coast	340
John Graham	Sierra Leone	200
Craig, MacLeod, and Co.	Isle of Banana (Sierra Leone)	237
Joseph Clay	Gambia	170
Robert Watts	Bance Island, Africa	95
Cowper and Telfair	Windward Coast	90
Robert Watts	Gorée Island (Senegal)	84
Broughton and Smith	Senegal	78

Source: *Georgia Gazette*, 1765–1771; Inward Slave.

preferred to arrange for vessels to arrive during the relatively mild spring and
summer months. In 1766, all five of the slave vessels from Africa arrived between April and October. This pattern continued, with few exceptions, through
the decade of the 1790s. The duration of the voyage combined with the pro-
longed confinement of enslaved Africans increased the spread of infectious
diseases. To prevent the spread of infectious diseases in Savannah, city officials in 1767 authorized the construction of a nine-story quarantine facility, a
"Lazaretto" (pest house, in Italian) on the west end of Tybee Island. Prior to
entering the Savannah port, slaves brought directly from West Africa remained
quarantined at Lazaretto where they were inspected by a physician who determined if they harbored infectious diseases. Diseased slaves remained at the facility. Slaves who died of infectious diseases were buried on the west end of
Tybee Island.[16]

Transatlantic Transformations and African Resistance

The Middle Passage can be characterized as a space of "in betweeness" with
its links to the origins of captive Africans.[17] As a voyage through death, the

Table 3. Slaves Imported into Savannah by Origin and Time Period, Early Period, 1755–1767

Island	Number	Percent of Africans
Montseratt	137	4%
St. Kitts	156	13%
St. Croix	76	2%
Curacao	92	3%
Grenada	75	2%
Other Islands	166	5%
Arrivals from U.S.	120	4%
Total	3,318 (822)	33%

Table 4. Slaves Imported into Savannah by Origin and Time Period, Middle Period, 1768–1780

Origin	Number	Percent of Africans
Gambia, Senegal, Sierra Leone, Windward Coast	2,932	68%
Gold Coast	287	6%
Angola and West Central Africa	500	12%
Origin Unknown	280	6%
Caribbean	337	8%
Total	4,336	100%

Table 5. Slaves Imported into Savannah by Origin and Time Period, Final Period, 1784–1798

Origin	Number	Percent of Africans
Gorée Island (Senegal), Gambia, Sierra Leone, Windward Coast	2,829	45.4%
Gold Coast	1,518	24.3%
Origin Unknown	1,146	18.3%
Total	5,493	88%

Source: Inward Slave Manifests, Savannah, RG 36, NARA, Washington, D.C.; Donnan, *Documents Illustrative of the History of the Slave Trade,* Vol. 4, 612–663; Eltis et al., *The Transatlantic Slave Trade Database,* http://www.slavevoyages.org.

Middle Passage paradoxically asserted life through its destructive process.[18] Through the marginal spaces of slave ships, captive Africans forged bonds of kinship and created forced transatlantic communities under desperate conditions. Captive Africans such as Lempster, James, Peter, Fanny, and Silvia, who may have arrived on the same slave vessel, survived the Middle Passage and labored on the Ogeechee rice plantation of James Read. Identified as Gola slaves, they maintained ethnic and kinship ties through their forced migration, settlement, and collective escape from slavery. The ethnic and cultural make-up of the African supply zones for the Georgia low country in the late eighteenth century included the Fula, Igbo, Gola, and Mande speakers—the Malinke, Bambara, and Serer, all in West Africa.[19]

The late eighteenth century represented a critical watershed period for West Africa. The thirty-year period from 1760–1790 represented the most violent phase of conflict in the hinterland region of Futa Jallon, the interior of present day Guinea. Internecine wars, caused by an alliance of Fulbe and Jallonke Muslims against non-Muslims, resulted in a greater than 100 percent per annum increase in slave exports from the region. From 1760–1780, the Transatlantic Slave Trade peaked with 65,500 captive Africans reaching the Americas annually. Walter Rodney estimated that 75 percent of the eighteenth century trade came from the interior.[20] From 1778–1783, the hostilities between the American colonists and the British extended to Africa, as a result of a French alliance with the North American colonies in 1778. This alliance exacerbated hostilities between Great Britain and France, in Africa to maintain zones of influence over important slave forts along the West African coast, such as Saint James (in the Gambia), Saint Louis in Senegal, and Gorée Island off the coast of Senegal.

The Senegambian supply zone provided the greatest number of African captives during the middle period of direct importation to Savannah. Extending from the Senegal River to the Casamance River and from the Atlantic coast to the upper and middle Niger valleys, this area produced three conduits for the capture and sale of Africans. During the 1760s and 1770s, Africans shipped from the Gambia and Senegal came from sources closer to the coast. Beginning in the second half of the 1780s, and continuing through the next decade, Senegambia became a major center for the Transatlantic Slave Trade to North America.[21] The two most important staging zones for this trade were the coastal areas from the lower Senegal to the lower Casamance valleys, and the mid-range area encompassing the middle and upper Senegal and Gambia valley. The Wolof dominated these regions and maintained strong political centers in the coastal states of Waalo, Kajor, and Baol.[22]

Islamic reform movements, which originated in Morocco and spread into Senegambia during the first half of the eighteenth century, had a significant impact on the coastal states of the Senegambian region and the direct trade to Savannah and other parts of the Americas. Islamic expeditions coincided with periods of the worst climatic crisis. Low rainfall caused a series of famines that spread throughout Senegambia between 1700s and 1760. This period witnessed depopulation in Senegambia as famine and the export slave trade took a heavy toll on the region. The second half of the eighteenth century saw a general improvement in both climate and disease, with the exception of low rainfall in the south bank region of the Gambia and the hinterland of the southern rivers in 1786.[23]

In Waalo, continuous conflict with North African Muslims from neighboring Trarza culminated in a series of devastating raids between 1775 and 1776. The North African Muslims, who were subsidized by the French and English, captured between 9,000 and 10,000 West Africans during this period.[24] These raids invariably extended southward into Kajor. Wars and raids resulted in the enslavement of large numbers of people from within Waalo and Kajor, and from border-states during the late eighteenth century.[25] Rulers even preferred to integrate captives into their societies. Some kings in Futa, who objected to the massive export of males in the slave trade, retained men who were captured in raids.[26]

The second staging area for the trade, the upper Senegal and Gambia valley, produced a significant number of slave exports from the Senegambian region. The slave trade from Gajaaga and the Gambia reached its peak in the 1780s, when one-third of the slaves exported came from the interior beyond Gajaaga, and two-thirds came from the Gambia. During this period of escalation in the slave trade, the demand for slaves from the Senegambian region increased. Savannah merchant Joseph Clay asserted in 1775 that Gambian slaves were preferable to the "Ibos, Conga's, Cape Mounts, and Angola Negroes," because of their knowledge of rice cultivation.[27] Although Igbos were not preferred, slave traders captured Igbos like Carolina Underwood of Sapelo Island as a young man in Guinea. During the eighteenth century, Igbos became significant actors in the Transatlantic Slave Trade, regulating trade and generating captives for the slave trade.[28]

The Transatlantic Slave Trade imposed serious restraints on agricultural production, and paradoxically, served to reinforce domestic slavery in West Africa. In the Fouta Djalon territories controlled by the Fulas, Mandingos, and Susus, enslaved Africans not purchased by European traders cultivated rice and other commodities when their average prices fell.[29] These local captives engaged in intense agricultural activities. An indication of the production of rice in Sierra Leone, the secondary slave supply zone, is provided by Major A.G. Laing who traveled in the region. Major Laing observed that the capital of the Sulima Susus, Falaba, had its own slave town, Konkodoogoree. Laing found the fields of the area the best tilled and best laid out than any other region observed throughout his travels.[30] Similarly, Chief William Cleveland, a powerful mulatto slave trader near the Banana Islands of Sierra Leone, maintained extensive rice fields cultivated by enslaved Africans.[31] Early accounts of West African rice culture demonstrate the range of cultivation techniques employed. These techniques included the construction of earthen embankments, canals, and sluices; the use of tides, flood recession, and rainfall for planting; specialized implements for preparing heavy soils; as well as the seasonal rotation in land use between rice field and cattle pasture.[32]

Recent scholarship by David Eltis, Philip Morgan, and David Richardson has challenged the contributions of diasporic Africans to rice production in North America. Based upon an examination of slave ships from *The Transatlantic Slave Trade: A Database on CD-ROM*, they argue that enslaved Africans from rice growing regions had very little impact on the rice industry in South Carolina and Georgia.[33] According to Eltis, Morgan, and Richardson, the Rice and Grain Coast was a secondary slave supply zone that supplied enslaved Africans to the tobacco-producing Chesapeake region, as well as the South Carolina and Georgia coast. However, an examination of extant ship manifests from the *Transatlantic Slave Trade Database of Slave Voyages* reveal that 60 percent of slave vessels which arrived in Georgia brought slaves from rice producing regions in West Africa from 1755–1858.[34] The Senegambia, Sierra Leone, and the Windward Coast provided the largest percentage of slaves over a 108-year period. Although it may be difficult to determine the exact number of vessels that disembarked from West Africa, and embarked in Georgia, records of extant slave voyages underscore a pattern of securing slaves from rice producing regions.[35]

In assessing the validity of the arguments presented by Eltis, Morgan, and Richardson, Gwendolyn Midlo Hall and Walter Hawthorne contend that a major problem with the *Transatlantic Slave Trade Database of Slave Voyages* is the exclusion of data on specific ethnicities that arrived in rice producing regions of the Americas.[36] Without such data, the overarching conclusions reached by Eltis, Morgan, and Richardson are flawed. The Mandinka, Bambara, and Wolof were rice producing ethnicities from the Upper Guinea Coast who constituted a significant presence in rice producing districts in Louisiana, Maranhão, Brazil, and low country Georgia.[37] Moreover, the reliance on quantification without considering other qualitative forms of evidence, such as Carney's "geographic perspective" and Fields-Black sociolinguistic evidence creates an asymmetrical view of human transformations.[38]

Indeed, African technology created and sustained rice cultivation in West Africa and North America. African rice cultivation systems received recognition from

French botanist August Chevalier who hypothesized in 1914 that *Oryza glabberima* represented a separate and African specie of rice. Receiving its appellation from German Botanist Ernst Gottleib Studel in 1855, the *Oryza Glabberima* specie formed the nucleus of a sophisticated knowledge system that enabled the adaptation of the crop to lowland and upland environments. Cultivation cycles ranged from three to six months and included such techniques as direct seeding, broadcasting (which refers to the process of planting rice seedlings to intensify their growth), and transplanting.

Women were central to the planting, milling, and processing of rice. In Senegambia and other areas settled by the Mandinka, rice was a women's crop, and women's labor informed the diverse microenvironments (e.g. water availability, the influence of salinity, flooding levels, and soil conditions). Milling rice with a mortar and pestle and winnowing rice in fanner baskets represented a transfer of specialized technology to the low country and constituted a significant component of female farming systems in West African societies. Similarly, in low country Georgia, the labor force for cultivating rice was disproportionately female as women were valued for their productive and reproductive abilities.[39] In this context, women such as Katie Brown, who continued to cultivate rice as a "money crop" during the early twentieth century, retained specialized knowledge of rice cultivation as did previous generations of Sapelo Island women.[40]

Enslaved Africans labored on barrier islands that were on the periphery of time and space. For nearly a century, they produced rice and Sea Island cotton within the confines of an isolated environment on Georgia's six largest offshore islands, Cumberland, Jekyll, St. Simons, Sapelo, St. Catherines, and Ossabaw Islands. These Africans were living in a state of distance from the larger society.[41] Two of the larger barrier islands are St. Simon's Island and Jekyll Island. St. Simon's Island lies eighteen miles east of Brunswick, Georgia. It is approximately thirteen miles long and two miles wide. Jekyll Island lies south of St. Simon's Island and is ten miles long and consists of 11,000 acres.[42] This region is divided into six natural ecosystems, which include barrier islands, coastal marine, estuaries and sounds, mainland upland, rivers, and swamps. A culture of strategic resistance permeated the marshlands and tidal rivers of low country Georgia. This landscape also included a host of smaller barrier islands and inland rice districts such as Skidaway, Butler, Argyle, and Whitemarsh Islands.[43]

Within transatlantic communities, the oral narratives of escaped Africans, which reveal acts of strategic resistance, were central to the expression of human agency.[44] Illustrative of this is Ben and Nancy who escaped their enslavement on James Read's rice plantation in early December 1789 by crossing the Ogeechee

River with several other captives. Prior to their escape, Ben and Nancy had married. Their marriage and plans to escape slavery by making their way to Spanish settlements in Florida underscored the determination of enslaved Africans to subvert slavery and the structures and powers, which perpetuated the system.[45] Like Ben and Nancy, Patty and Daniel (of William Stephens Bewlie's rice plantation) planned to escape slavery by running away to Spanish Florida. Nine months earlier, Patty had given birth to a son, Abram. Wearing a green wrapper and coat, and carrying additional clothing with which to change, Patty carried her son through the swamps of the Ogeechee Neck in route to Florida and freedom.[46]

Invariably, women fugitives sought out a town as the place to pursue diverse objectives for running away.[47] Savannah and the outlying areas of the city proved an opportune environment for runaways. In Sunbury, a "negro girl, 16 years old and Guiney born," escaped from the Ogeechee River ferry en route to Savannah still wearing handcuffs.[48] Similarly, Sally and her two mulatto children found refuge in the woods near Savannah as their owner, Alexander Wylly, promised severe prosecution to any person harboring or concealing them.[49] From the 1730s to 1805, one out of five runaways, or 18 percent, were women.[50]

In several instances, newly arrived Africans saw enslavement as a problem to be solved collectively. In August 1764, two "new negroe men, both branded on the right breast" with the initials IB, escaped from the plantation of Alexander Wylly on the Savannah River.[51] Proximity to rivers and other bodies of water facilitated get-away as runaways usurped canoes to make their escape. Both Colerain and Derry, branded with the initials IB, absconded from Wylly's plantation with a canoe in February 1765. By all accounts, Colerain was a repeat offender and perhaps the organizer of planned escapes as his name and a description of him, along with other Africans, reappear in advertisements submitted by Alexander Wylly over a period of several months.[52] For newly enslaved Africans, planning an escape involved utilizing networks on the plantation. These networks centered upon shared occupations as well as shared origins. On Mark Carr's plantation near Sunbury, Bridgee, a "prime sawyer," who spoke fluent Portuguese and Spanish, organized other sawyers on the Carr plantation. He also included his wife Celia in his plans to escape slavery.[53] After inflicting "several outrages" near the ferry, the group cut away a chained canoe at the Sunbury wharf and made their escape northward.[54]

Resistance in the low country represented a formative process which involved a tension between what the enslaved thought and what they lived. Runaway slave advertisements and oral narratives provide a window for examining the thought and aspirations of enslaved Africans. In this context, the act of running away marked the establishment of a dialectical relationship with the environment in which captive Africans lived. Between the 1730s and 1805, 816 men and 182 women were runaway slaves in Georgia low country.[55] An examination of 270 advertisements for runaway slaves, reveal that 126 advertisers designated fugitive Africans by nationality and included detailed descriptions of country markings.[56] Sydney, a young woman whose country marks were evident on her breast and arms, and who spoke "no English," took flight from the home of Elizabeth Anderson, well dressed with a cloth gown and coat.[57] Like many other new Africans, Sydney was unfamiliar with the environment in which she lived. She perceived a successful flight from the oppression of bondage in the city and deftly concealed her country marks and her identity as a fugitive as she moved through the city of Savannah. Similarly, "a stout young negroe [sic] fellow named Africa," who was well known in and about the city of Savannah, retained a consciousness of his African origins as he fled his enslavement and never relinquished re-gaining his freedom.[58]

The belief that the enslaved could transcend their physical oppression by returning to Africa symbolized a reversed transatlantic migration to escape an abhorrent reality.[59] Oral narratives of flight back to Africa preserved as intergenerational narratives within transatlantic communities, underscoring the persistence of Africa in the consciousness of the enslaved. Illustrative of this was Ryna Johnson; a persistent memory of her as an enslaved woman on Hopeton plantation in the Altamaha district (as well as several others in the St. Simons Island and Sapelo Island communities), was the legend of Butler's Island Africans who, resentful of the overseer's lash, flew back to Africa.[60] The narratives of Prince Sneed, Serina Hall, and Solomon Gibson, whose ancestors labored on St. Catherines Island, also revealed a parallel flight migration to Africa. The metaphor of returning to Africa expressed a determination to dream of and hope for a better life literally and symbolically beyond their present situation in slavery. The historical re-envisioning of returning to Africa remained a persistent theme in the consciousness of African Americans who lived within the Georgia-South Carolina low country continuum. Phyllis Green, a former slave in Charleston, South Carolina, described a similar event that took place on James Island in which Africans who refused to submit to the "seasoning" process feigned accommodation, and began their flight back to Africa. These oft-repeated oral narratives were represented as actual lived experiences, underscoring several forms of resistance such as refusing to assimilate, plotting return back to Africa, pretending to accommodate, and flying home to freedom.[61]

In a similar vein, oral narratives of freedom through death provided the theoretical underpinnings for an alternate conception of historical reality. On

St. Simons Island, newly purchased captive Africans (sold to John Couper and Thomas Spalding by the Savannah firm of Mein and Mackey), endured a second "voyage through death" down the coast from Savannah in 1803. Their confinement below deck created the conditions which led to a revolt against the crew and Couper's overseer. Landing near the marshlands, the Igbos began singing and wading through the waters of the Altamaha River, where twelve drowned in an attempt to reverse their forced migration.[62]

The historical memory of the descendants of enslaved African Americans provides an important window in which to examine their traditions in the discourse and cultural logics of the slavery era. The emergence of a dissident subculture within transatlantic communities embodied by a complex system of traditions represented the second form of resistance along the South Carolina-Georgia continuum. The traditions developed by low country African Americans emerged as a central component in their ontological praxis. The communitarian character of the slaves' traditions provides salient insights into how enslaved men and women understood and communicated their experiences and struggles through their use of language. Their symbolic and metaphorical traditions provide crystalline insights into the ways in which they transformed their experiences into images that tell their stories of both oppression and liberation.[63] In this context, spirituals from the low country, interpreted as oral texts, reveal the intertextuality of the lived experiences of enslaved men and women through artistic expression. Dublin Scribben, an African born slave in Liberty County, fused English with his native language to express both the oppression of the Middle Passage and the symbolic rebirth of the individual in the slave song "Freewillum" [Freewill]. The ocean served as a metaphor for rebirth and freedom (reproduced without phonetic exaggeration):

> Going home to see the ocean religion told New Jerusalem I bring good news, a-tatta-ho! My soul seen the ocean.[64]

Similarly, expressions of freedom through death represented the ultimate conception of freedom from physical bondage. In Liberty County, Abraham Scriven expressed profound grief upon being sold and separated from his wife, children, and parents. He vowed to meet in heaven if he could not rejoin them in this world.[65]

Both the First and Second Great Awakenings shaped the extent to which Africans embraced Christianity. Although the process of conversion varied according to the local environment and African ethnicities, Christianity appealed to low country enslaved Africans for two principal reasons. First, Christian customs, rituals, and beliefs paralleled West African religious beliefs. This was true of the sacrament of baptism, which conformed to their beliefs about bodies of water which they regarded as sacred, and the African circle dance they performed known as the "ring shout" at funerals.[66] Christianity's "life after death" concept also meant that the enslaved would eventually join their ancestors in Africa.[67] West African religious thoughts and practices shaped their lives even after their conversion to Christianity. As in other U.S. and New World enslaved communities, they syncretized elements of Christianity with their sacred beliefs and traditions and in doing so, informed the contours of American religious culture.[68] In this context, African traditional religions adhered to a form of monotheism.

According to John Mbiti, within the African ontology, there was always a Supreme Creator. In Akan, the creator was *Onyame*; in Bantu—*Nzambi*, Mende—*Ngewo*, and in Gola—*Daya*. Second in the hierarchy were spirits capable of appearing within the world as living guardians. Men, animals, and objects constituted the penultimate forces in the African cosmology.[69] Creation stories, Supreme Being, spirits, and priest-healers were central to African religions and enslaved Africans found similar features in Christianity that intensified conversion.[70] The demographic figures for Darien Baptist Church in McIntosh County near Sapelo Island reveal that a significant number of enslaved Africans (943), attended services by 1860.[71] Similarly, in Liberty County, enslaved African Americans such as Lucy, who converted to Christianity while a slave of Reverend Charles C. Jones, embraced Christianity because it nurtured and kept alive the promise of equality and freedom and thus had both a liberatory and political meaning.[72]

Within low country communities, slave preachers risked their lives to preach a message of liberation and resistance. Preacher George received a threat of 500 lashes from his master if he continued to preach subversive messages to slaves. George disregarded his master's threat and continued to preach. After the discovery of George's activities, he was forced to flee across the Savannah River. He was captured after hiding in a nearby barn and burned alive with an assembly of slaves forced to travel twenty miles to the Greenville town square to watch what Moses Roper, a former slave and abolitionist, described as a "horrid spectacle."[73] Attending unsupervised religious slave meetings led to the imposition of severe forms of punishment. Enslaved men and women risked punishment and death if they undermined the power of the planter and the system of slavery. Tom Bucknie, a slave in Chatham County, received 150 lashes, "washed with brine," for attending religious meetings.[74] Bucknie continued to "attend the meetings and pray for his master," despite repeated threats and severe whippings.[75] As the nineteenth century progressed, planters became increasingly concerned with controlling the religious expression of their captive population.

The number of Christian converts among the slave population increased rapidly. It was a result of their desire to embrace an Africanized version of Christianity, and of a post 1830 campaign within the "militant South" to use religion as a means of social control. By 1860, 4,727 free and enslaved African Americans belonged to the African and Colored Baptist churches in low country Georgia.[76] As Africanized Christianity (which interlocked African traditional and Christian religious beliefs) emerged, Islam in the low country underwent a transformation. This transformation interlocked Christian and Islamic identities as evidenced by the practices of a peripatetic preacher belonging to Sapelo Island's First African Baptist Church in 1866, "Preacher Little." The countenances of Preacher Little and other low country African Americans who were described as "tall, lean and resembling Arab sheiks," epitomized this fusion.[77]

Conclusion

Within transatlantic communities, enslaved Africans expressed a unique political will to resist enslavement and maintain dignity. Their dislocation reinforced the tragedy of the slave trade and simultaneously fostered cultural resistance to enslavement, which began during the Middle Passage and continued upon arrival in Georgia. The cross-current of events that promoted the acquisition of rice and grain coast slaves transformed the landscape of low country Georgia. As enslaved Africans altered the physical environment, African socio-cultural practices such as kinship, religion, and cultural processes transformed New World slavery. They kept a collective memory of West Africa, which survived across the Middle Passage and created a distinct African identity shaped by the North Atlantic.

The varied discourses of slave resistance illustrate that enslaved men and women created alternate geographies for themselves in low country Georgia. Enslaved Africans brought their bodies, their minds, and their cultures to the Americas, and employed all three to address conflicting ideas of slavery and freedom. They carved out marginal spaces within slavery to engage in strategic resistance, and established alliances based upon ethnicity, occupation, kinship, and mutual oppression to contest their bondage. In several cases, women, who lingered furthest from the center of organizing and planning strategic resistance, emerged as leaders of planned escapes. Slave insubordination crystallized into open defiance as they sought to gain individual and collective freedom by challenging the fissures within slavery. During this critical period, enslaved men and women reimagined, reformulated, and transformed the legal contexts in which they lived.[78] They carried their blackness and many aspects of their culture from their original home in West Africa to Low Country Georgia where they became the first core of the African Diaspora.

Notes

1. *Savannah Georgia Gazzette*, November 19, 1766, i. Georgia Writers Project, Rosanna Williams, Tatemville and Ophelia Baker, Sandfly, Ga. in *Drums and Shadows: Survival Stories Among the Georgia Coastal Negroes* (Athens, GA., rept. 1986), 71 and 91.

2. Anthony Balcomb, "The Power of Narrative: Constituting Reality through Storytelling," in *Orality, Memory, and the Past: Listening to the Voices of Black Clergy under Colonization and Apartheid*, ed., Philippe Denis (Pietermaritzburg, South Africa, 2001), 49–53.

3. Daniel Littlefield, *Rice and Slaves: Ethnicity and the Slave Trade in Colonial South Carolina* (Baton Rouge, LA: Louisiana University Press, c1981); Judith Carney, *Black Rice: The African Origins of Rice Cultivation in the Americas,* (Cambridge, MA, Harvard University Press, 2001); Edda Fields-Black, *Deep Roots: Rice Farmers in West Africa and the African Diaspora* (Bloomington, IN., 2008).

4. Gervase Phillips, "Slave Resistance in the Antebellum South," *History Review* (December 2007): 34–35.

5. *U.S. Population Census, 1790, 1830, 1860*; *The Transatlantic Slave Trade Voyages Database*, accessible at www.slavevoyages.org, see entries 41892 *Tentativa*, 1817; 41893, *Politena*, 1817; 41895 *Sirena* 1817; 41896, *Antelope*, 1820; 4974, *Wanderer*, 1858; Record Group 21 (hereinafter cited as RG 21) Records of the District Courts of the United States, *Tentativa, Politena, Sirena, Antelope*, Box 22, 23, 26, 28, National Archives and Records Administration (hereinafter cited as NARA), Southeast Region, Atlanta, Georgia; W.E.B. DuBois, *The Suppression of the African Slave Trade to the United States of America, 1638–1870*, Appendix D (New York: 1970).

6. Gwen McKee, ed., *A Guide to the Georgia Coast* (Georgia Conservancy, 1993), Chapter. 1; Michael Mann, *Sources of Social Power* (New York: Cambridge University Press, 1986), Chap. 2; Leland Ferguson, *Uncommon Ground: Archaeology and Early African American, 1650–1800* (Washington, D.C.: Smithsonian Books, 2004), 118.

7. Sam B. Hilliard, "Antebellum Tidewater Rice Culture in South Carolina and Georgia," in *European Settlement and Development in North America: Essays on Geographical Change in Honour and Memory of Andrew Hill Clark*, ed., James R. Gibson (Toronto, Canada: Dawson Publishing, 1978), 97–104.

8. Inward Slave Manifests, Savannah, Bureau of Customs, Record Group 36 (hereinafter cited as RG 36), NARA, Washington, D.C.; Elizabeth Donnan, *Documents Illustrative of the History of the Slave Trade*, Vol. 4 (Washington, D.C.: Carnegie Institution of Washington, 1930), 612–663.

9. *Georgia Gazette*, April 13, 1768, John Stirk; *Georgia Gazette*, July 13, 1774, James Read; *Georgia Gazette*, March 29, 1775, James Mossman in Windley, *Runaway Slave Advertisements*, 29, 53, 62; *The Transatlantic Slave Trade Voyages Database*, accessible at www.slavevoyages.org.

10. First hand accounts of the Middle Passage by Africans are scant. Narratives by Olaudah Equiano and Mary Prince are the best known. Additional voices are accessible at http://www.awesomestories.com/history/slave_voices_ch1.htm.

11. Dimmock Charlton, in John Blassingame, *Slave Testimony: Two Centuries of Letters, Speeches, Interviews, and Autobiographies* (Baton Rouge, LA: Louisiana State University Press, 1977), 325–338, note 11. According to Charlton, he "was born in a country called Kissee." The Kissi lived in Guinea and were ethnologically and culturally related to the Malinke.

Maria Diedrich, Henry Louis Gates, Jr., Carl Pederson, eds. *Black Imagination and the Middle Passage* (New York, Oxford University Press, 1999), 5–10. See also Bailey, *African Voices of the Atlantic Slave Trade* (Boston, MA: Beacon Press, 2005).

12. Inward Slave Manifests, Savannah, Bureau of Customs, RG 36, NARA, Washington, D.C.; Donnan, *Documents*, 612–663. Donnan provides regional documentation which includes listings of slave vessels, merchant or agent's name, owner of vessel, and where the vessel was built. Shipbuilding emerged as a significant industry in Savannah with West Indian linkages.

13. Inward Slave Manifests, Savannah, Bureau of Customs, RG 36, NARA, Washington, D.C.; Donnan, *Documents*, 612–663.

14. Donnan, *Documents Illustrative of the History of the Slave Trade*, Vol. 4, 612–663.

15. Inward Slave Manifests, Savannah, Bureau of Customs, RG 36, NARA, Washington, D.C.; Donnan, *Documents Illustrative of the History of the Slave Trade*, Vol. 4, 612–663; *The Transatlantic Slave Trade Voyages Database*, accessible at www.slavevoyages.org, see entries for Georgia.

16. *Georgia Gazette*, July 27, 1768 in Windley, *Runaway Slave Advertisements*, 31; Allen D. Candler and Lucian Lamar Knight eds., *Colonial Records of Georgia*, vol. 18 (New York: 1970): 792–794; *The Transatlantic Slave Trade Voyages Database*, accessible at www.slavevoyages.org, see entries for Georgia; Darold D. Wax, "New Negroes Are Always in Demand," *Georgia Historical Quarterly* (Summer 1984): 209.

17. Françoise Charras, "Robert Hayden's and Kamau Brathwaite's Poetic Renderings of the Middle Passage in Comparative Perspective," in Maria Diedrich, Henry Louis Gates, and Carl Pederson, *Black Imagination and the Middle Passage* (New York, Oxford University Press, 1999), 57–68.

18. Françoise Charras, "Robert Hayden's and Kamau Brathwaite's Poetic Renderings of the Middle Passage in Comparative Perspective," 57–68. For a discussion of slave insurrections see Eric Robert Taylor, *If We Must Die: Shipboard Insurrections in the Era of the Atlantic Slave Trade* (Baton Rouge, LA: Louisiana State University Press, 2006).

19. *Georgia Gazette*, July 13, 1774, James Read in Windley, *Runaway Slave Advertisements*, 53; Donnan, *Documents*, 612–663; Lempster, James, Peter, Fanny, and Silvia successfully ran away from James Read's plantation. *The Transatlantic Slave Trade Voyages Database*, accessible at www.slavevoyages.org, see entries for Georgia.

20. Boubacar Barry, *Senegambia and the Atlantic Slave Trade* (New York: Cambridge University Press, 1998), 61–80; Philip Curtin, *Economic Change in Precolonial Africa: Senegambia in the Era of the Slave Trade* (Madison, WI: University of Wisconsin Press, 1975), 177; See also Walter Rodney, *History of the Upper Guinea Coast, 1545–1800* (New York: Monthly Review Press, 1970). According to Selwyn H. H. Carrington, figures from the British National Archives put this figure at 104,000. Other figures quote 47,500. Carrington, *The Sugar Industry and the Abolition of the Slave Trade, 1775–1810.*

21. Walter Rodney, *A History of the Upper Guinea Coast*, 112, 244–55; Becker, "La Sénégambie dans la Traite atlantique du XVIIIe siècle," 63–103; W.E.B. DuBois, *The Suppression of the African Slave Trade* (Gainesville, FL: University Press of Florida, 2002), 46–48; Barry, *Senegambia and the Atlantic Slave Trade*, 49, 79. See also, J.E. Inikori and Stanley Engerman, eds. *The Atlantic Slave Trade* (Durham, N.C.: Duke University Press, 1992), Chap. 1–3.

22. Barry, *Senegambia and the Atlantic Slave Trade*, Chap. 5; Paul E. Lovejoy, *Transfor-*

mations in Slavery: A History of Slavery in Africa (Cambridge: Cambridge University Press, 1983), 59.

23. Curtin, *Economic Change*, 54–55, 180.

24. Ibid.

25. Boubacar Barry, *Le Royaume du Waalo, 1659–1859: Le Sénégal avant la conquête*, 190; Barry, *Senegambia and the Atlantic Slave Trade*, 81–112; Inikori, "Underpopulation in Nineteenth Century West Africa: The Role of the Export Slave Trade," 25–308. Establishing concrete demographic patterns for Waalo, Kajor, and Baol in the late eighteenth century is problematic since records are incomplete or non-existent for this period. However, the accounts of French and English officials who resided in the coastal regions combined with the extant studies of the slave trade's impact on Senegambia provide a partial reconstruction of the population. See Pelletan, *Mémoire sur la colonie française du Sénégal avec quelques considérations historiques et politiques sur la traite des Nègres*, 14.

26. Charles Becker and Victor Martin, "Kayor and Baol: Senegalese Kingdoms and the Slave Trade in the Eighteenth Century," in J.E. Inikori, ed., *Forced Migration: The Impact of the Export Slave Trade on African Societies* (New York: Africana Publishing Company, 1992), 119; Stephanie Smallwood, *Saltwater Slavery: A Middle Passage from Africa to American Diaspora* (Cambridge, MA: Harvard University Press, 2007), 103.

27. *Letters of Joseph Clay, Merchant of Savannah, 1776–1798* (Georgia Historical Society, Collections VIII), 187; Aland D. Candler and Lucian Lamar Knight, eds. *Colonial Records of the State of Georgia*, Vol. 22 (Atlanta, Ga: Franklin Printing, 1904–1916), 420, 465; Wax, "New Negroes Are Always in Demand: The Slave Trade in Eighteenth Century Georgia," 207.

28. Carolina Underwood, Family No. 136, "Sapelo Island Families," Genealogical Source Book, copy provided by Dr. Carolyn Douse, Sapelo Island Historical and Genealogical Society (SICARS), Sapelo Island, Georgia; David K. Northrup, *Trade Without Rulers, Precolonial Economic Development in South-eastern Nigeria* (Clarendon, UK: Clarendon Press, 1978). Carolina and Hannah Underwood were both listed on the 1870 Census of McIntosh County as being 95 years old and born in Guinea. Their descendants recounted their Ibo origins and Carolina's capture by slavers as a small boy.

29. Becker and Martin, "Kayor and Baol," 101–102; Curtin, *Economic Change*, 187. Juula traders established a network which brought captive Africans from the interior; Rodney, "African Slavery and Other Forms of Social Oppression on the Upper Guinea Coast in the Context of the Atlantic Slave Trade," in Inikori, *Forced Migration*, 61–68.

30. A.G. Laing, *Travels in the Timanee, Kooranko, and Soolima Countries* (London: John Murray, 1825), 221; Charlotte Quinn, *Mandingo Kingdoms of the Senegambia: Traditionalism, Islam, and European Expansion,* (Evanston, IL., 1972) 9–22.

31. John Atkins, *A Voyage to Guinea, Brazil, and the West Indies* (1735; reprint, London, Taylor & Francis, 1970), 49. William Bosman, *A New and Accurate Description of the Coast of Guinea* (London: Routledge, 1705; reprint 1967), 359. Atkins observed that a peck of rice yielded above forty bushels which suggests a high level of output.

32. Fields-Black, *Deep Roots: Rice Farmers in West Africa and the Africa Diaspora*, 107–133; Carney, *Black Rice: The African Origins of Rice Cultivation in the Americas*, 28. See Littlefield, *Rice and Slaves: Ethnicities and the Slave Trade in Colonial South Carolina;* For a discussion of the emergence of rice culture in South Carolina, see Peter Wood, *Black Majority: Negroes in Colonial South Carolina from 1670 through the Stono Rebellion* (New York: W. W. Nor-

ton & Company, 1974).

33. David Eltis, Philip Morgan, and David Richardson, "Agency and Diaspora in Atlantic History: Reassessing the African Contribution to Rice Cultivation in the Americas," *American Historical Review* 112 (December 2007): 1335–43.

34. *The Transatlantic Slave Trade Voyages Database*, accessible at www.slavevoyages.org.

35. Additionally, evidence of the desirability of securing specific Africans from the Rice and Grain Coast is revealed in advertisements from Georgia's colonial newspaper, the *Georgia Gazette*. These announcements, which appeared with frequency throughout Georgia's involvement in the transatlantic slave trade, provided planters, who were establishing and expanding rice plantations, with relevant information concerning the origin and ethnicity of captive Africans. *Georgia Gazette*, 1765–1771; *Royal Georgia Gazette*, 1779–1782; *Gazette of the State of Georgia*, 1783–1788; *Georgia Gazette*, 1788–1790.

36. Gwendolyn Midlo Hall, "Africa and Africans in African Diaspora: The Uses of Relational Databases," *American Historical Review* 115 (February 2010):139; Walter Hawthorne, "From 'Black Rice' to 'Brown': Rethinking the History of Risiculture in the Seventeenth and Eighteenth-Century Atlantic," *American Historical Review* 115 (February 2010): 154.

37. Hall, Africa and Africans in African Diaspora, 142; Hawthorne, "From 'Black Rice' to 'Brown': Rethinking the History of Risiculture in the Seventeenth and Eighteenth Century Atlantic," 155; *Georgia Gazette, 1765–1771.*

38. Carney, *Black Rice: The African Origins of Rice Cultivation in the Americas*; Edda Fields-Black, *Deep* Roots: *Rice Farmers in West Africa and the Africa Diaspora* (Bloomington, IN: Indiana University Press, 2008).

39. Account Book of Stephen Habersham, Grove Plantation Near Savannah, June 1858–July 11, 1864, M432, Roll 89, Georgia Historical Society, (hereinafter cited as GHS), Savannah, Georgia; James Postell, "Kelvin Grove Plantation Book, 1853," Margaret Davis Cate Collection, Hargrett Rare Book and Manuscript Library, University of Georgia Libraries; Berry, " 'She Do a Heap of Work:' Female Slave Labor on Glynn County Rice and Cotton Plantations," *Georgia Historical Quarterly*, 82 No. 4 (Winter 1998): 707–734.

40. Interview with Dr. Benjamin Lewis, February 3, 2001, Savannah, Georgia. Dr. Lewis is the grandson of Sapelo Island resident Katie Brown, who is featured in the Georgia Writer's Project, *Drums and Shadows: Survival Stories Among the Georgia Coastal Negroes;* and Parrish, *Slave Songs in the Georgia Sea Islands* (Athens, Ga: University of Georgia Press, 1992). Born during slavery, Mrs. Brown cultivated rice on Sapelo Island, as did previous generations of women. Dr. Lewis described rice as his grandmother's "money crop."

41. Inward Slave Manifests, Savannah, RG 36, NARA, Washington, D.C.; Donnan, *Documents Illustrative of the History of the Slave Trade*, Vol. 4, 612–663.

42. Hazzard, *St. Simon's Island Georgia, Brunswick, and Vicinity* (c. 1825; reprint, Belmont, MA: Oak Hill Press, 1974).

43. McKee, ed., *A Guide to the Georgia Coast*; Kenneth K. Krakow, *Georgia Place Names* (Macon, Ga: Winship Press, 1975), 120, 199–200.

44. Balcomb, "The Power of Narrative: Constituting Reality through Storytelling," 49–53. Narratives have been central to the study of slavery. See, for example, William F. Andrews, *To Tell a Free Story: The First Century of Afro-American Autobiography, 1760–1865* (Urbana, IL: University of Illinois Press, 1986).

45. *Georgia Gazette*, December 10, 1789, David Leion [sic]; Ben and Nancy were 25 years old. Nancy was blind In her right eye; see the case of Betty, *Georgia Gazette*, Decem-

ber 22, 1788, Benjamin Gobert; the case of Patra, Mary, and Judy, *Georgia Gazette*, January 29, 1789, J.M. Delarocque; the case of Patty and Daniel, *Georgia Gazette*, May 21, 1789, Peter Henry Morel, in Windley, *Runaway Slave Advertisements*, 161–62, 172.

46. *Georgia Gazette*, May 21, 1789, Peter Henry Morel in Windley, *Runaway Slave Advertisements*, 166.

47. Michael Mullin, *Africa in America: Slave Acculturation and Resistance in the American South and British Caribbean, 1736–1831* (Urbana, IL: University of Illinois Press, 1992), 290.

48. *Georgia Gazette*, April 12, 1764, Thomas Cater in Windley, *Runaway Slave Advertisements*, 5.

49. *Georgia Gazette*, May 10, 1764, Alexander Wylly in Windley, *Runaway Slave Advertisements*, 6.

50. Mullin, *Africa in America*, 290.

51. *Georgia Gazette*, August 16, 1764, Johnson and Wylly in Windley, *Runaway Slave Advertisements*, 7.

52. *Georgia Gazette*, February 7, 1765, Alexander Wylly; *Georgia Gazette*, July 18, 1765, Alexander Wylly, in Windley, *Runaway Slave Advertisements*, 10, 14.

53. *Georgia Gazette*, July 2, 1766, Mark Carr in Windley, *Runaway Slave Advertisements*, 17.

54. Ibid.

55. Mullin, 289.

56. Ibid., Appendix II, 289.

57. *Georgia Gazette*, March 7, 1765, Elizabeth Anderson in Windley, *Runaway Slave Advertisements*, 10.

58. *Georgia Gazette*, November 15, 1764, Jemima Love in Windley, *Runaway Slave Advertisements*, 8.

59. Karen B. Bell, "Narratives of Freedom: Communities of Resistance in Low Country Georgia, 1798–1898," Ph.D. Dissertation, Howard University, 2008, 58.

60. Cuffy Wilson, Currytown, Savannah; Floyd White, St. Simons Island; Ryna Johnson, St. Simons Island, in Georgia Writer's Project, *Drums and Shadows: Survival Stories Among the Georgia Coastal Negroes*, 32, 169, 175–77, 184.

61. Cuffy Wilson, Currytown, Savannah; Floyd White, St. Simons Island; Ryna Johnson, St. Simons Island, in Georgia Writer's Project, *Drums and Shadows: Survival Stories Among the Georgia Coastal Negroes*.

62. Prince Sneed, White Bluff; Serina Hall, White Bluff; Bruurs [sic] Butler, Grimballs Point; Floyd White, St. Simons Island, in Georgia Writer's Project, *Drums and Shadows: Survival Stories Among the Georgia Coastal Negroes*, 79, 81, 99, 185; George P. Rawick, *The American Slave: A Composite Autobiography, Supplement 1*, Vol. 11 (Westport, Conn.: Greenwood Press, 1977), 179; William Mein to Pierce Butler, May 24, 1803, Butler Family Papers, Historical Society of Pennsylvania; Bell, *Major Butler's Legacy: Five Generations of a Slave Holding Family* (Athens: University of Georgia Press, 1987), 132; Robert Hayden, "Middle Passage," 444–446. Although the Georgia state legislature banned the slave trade in 1798, ten years before the national ban in 1808, an active illegal slave trade persisted until 1858.

63. Will Coleman, "Coming through 'Ligion': Metaphor in Non-Christian and Christian Experiences with the Sprit(s) in African American Slave Narratives," in *Cut Loose Your Stammering Tongue*, ed., Hopkins and C.L. Cummings, 66–67.

64. Lydia Parrish, *Slave Songs of the Georgia Sea Islands* (Athens, GA: 1992) 45–46. See, W. Jeffrey Bolster, *Black Jacks: African American Seamen in the Age of Sail* (Cambridge, MA: First Harvard University Press, 1997), which discusses the significance of rivers and bodies of water as sources of spiritual power in the cosmology of Africans.

65. Abream [*sic*] Scriven to Dinah Jones, September 19, 1858, Savannah, in Starobin ed., *Blacks in Bondage: The Letters of American Slaves* (New York: M. Wiener, 1974), 58.

66. Art Rosenbaum, *Shout Because You're Free: The African American Ring Shout Tradition in Coastal Georgia* (Athens, Ga: University of Georgia Press, 1998).

67. John Mbiti, *Introduction to African Religion* (London: Heinemann, 1991), 116–124.

68. Josephine Stephens, Harris Neck; Charles Hunter, St. Simons Island; Lawrence Baker, Darien in Georgia Writer's Project, *Drums and Shadows: Survival Stories Among the Georgia Coastal Negroes*, 127, 155–56; 177; Bailey, *God, Dr. Buzzard, and the Bolito Man: A Saltwater Geechee Talks About Life on Sapelo Island* (New York: Doubleday, 2000), Chapter Sixteen; Sylvia Frey and Betty Wood, *Come Shouting to Zion: African American Protestantism in the American South and British Caribbean to 1830* (Chapel Hill, The University of North Carolina Press, 1998).

69. Mbiti, 35.

70. Ibid.

71. Mechal Sobel, *Trabel'in On: The Slaves Journey to an Afro-Baptist Faith* (Princeton, NJ: Princeton University Press, 1998) 314–331.

72. Lucy to Charles C. Jones, December 30, 1850, in John W. Blassingame, *Slave Testimony: Two Centuries of Letters, Speeches, Interviews, and Autobiographies* (Baton Rouge, LA: Louisiana State University Press, 1977) 90–91; Andrew to Rev. Charles C. Jones, Sept. 10, 1852, Maybank, in Starobin, *Blacks in Bondage: The Letters of American Slaves*, 52. Andrew's daughter, Dinah, joined the Baptist church established for slaves in Sunbury. For a discussion of the intersection of religion and the informal African American economy see, Wood, *Women's Work, Men's Work, The Informal Slave Economies of Low Country Georgia* (Athens, Ga: University of Georgia Press, 1995), 160–176.

73. Moses Roper to Thomas Price, London, June 27, 1836 in Blassingame, *Slave Testimony: Two Centuries of Letters, Speeches, Interviews, and Autobiographies*, 23.

74. *Liberator*, February 4, 1837; Blassingame, *Slave Testimony: Two Centuries of Letters, Speeches, Interviews, and Autobiographies*, 124–25.

75. Ibid., 25.

76. Sobel, *Trabel'in On: The Slave Journey to an Afro-Baptist Faith*, 314–331. For a discussion of slave missions in the Baptist church, see Janet Duitsman Cornelius, *Slave Missions and the Baptist Church in the Antebellum South* (Columbia, SC: University of South Carolina Press, 1999).

77. Parrish, *Slave Songs of the Georgia Sea Islands*, 158; Michael Gomez, "Muslims in Early America," *The Journal of Southern History*, Vol. 40, No. 4 (November 1994), 708–709.

78. Lauren DuBois and Julius Scott, *Origins of the Black Atlantic: Rewriting Histories* (New York: Routledge Press, 2009), 1–5.

Chapter 11

Is the Negro Like Other People?: Race, Religion, and the Didactic Oratory of Henry McNeal Turner

Andre E. Johnson

Henry McNeal Turner delivered the lecture, "The Negro in All Ages" at the Second Baptist Church in Savannah, Georgia on April 8, 1873. As with many of Turner's speeches, there is no historical evidence of Turner's thoughts while he drafted the speech or responses to the speech,[1] but there is evidence that he gave this lecture at least once before. In his autobiography, William Heard writes that in January of 1867, he heard Turner give a speech entitled "The Negro in All Ages" in Augusta, Georgia. William Heard wrote, "he spoke for two hours and I was so impressed with the pictures and historic facts he presented of the Race in the past ages and of the men of the present, that my life is largely what it is because of the impressions made at this meeting. I returned to my home in Elberton, and began my future work."[2] The lecture was billed as an "examination into several abominable, anti-scriptural, and pseudo-philosophical theories" that was "designed as a degradation to humanity," and on the surface, the speech can be classified as a refutation. However, just calling it a refutation limits the speech's impact and power because Turner was doing much more in the speech than just refuting the "pseudo-philosophical theories" of his day.

This chapter examines how Henry McNeal Turner engaged didactic oratory. By offering a close reading of the lecture, the chapter explores the ways that Turner navigated the intersections of race and religion; and furthermore, how he adopted a prophetic persona to refute much of the science of the day that was injurious to the African American identity.

Henry McNeal Turner

Born on February 1, 1834 as a free black in New Berry Court House, South Carolina,[3] Turner still experienced the harsh reality of prejudice and racism. As a child, Turner worked in cotton fields alongside enslaved people as well as in a blacksmith shop under some of the harshest overseers.[4] He fancied having an education, but South Carolina state laws at the time did not allow blacks to attend school or learn how to read and write. After obtaining a spelling book, he attempted to teach himself, but ultimately credited a divine "dream teacher" in helping him to read and write.[5] At age fifteen, he had read the entire Bible five times, and started a habit of memorizing lengthy passages of scripture, which helped him to develop a strong memory.[6]

It was also at this time that Turner found employment at a law office in Abbeville, South Carolina. The lawyers took notice of his quick mind and eagerness to learn and furthered his education by teaching him other subjects such as arithmetic, history, law, and theology.[7] Turner attended revival services with his mother, and joined the Methodist church in 1848. However, his conversion would not come until three years later in 1851 under the preaching of plantation missionary Samuel Leard in a camp meeting at Sharon Camp Ground. Soon after his conversion, Turner accepted the call to preach.

Licensed to preach in the Southern Methodist Church at the age of nineteen, Turner preached to large integrated audiences all over the South.[8] He found it frustrating that the Southern Methodist Church would never ordain him and that as a licensed exhorter he had already achieved the highest level a black person could attain in the denomination. After discovering a Methodist denomination that had black bishops, Turner joined the African Methodist Episcopal Church (AME) in 1858. As an AME minister, not only was Turner ordained, but he also became a regular correspondent for the *Christian Recorder*, the AME weekly newspaper. In 1862, he also became pastor of the influential Israel AME church in Washington D.C. During the Civil War, 1861–1865, Abraham Lincoln commissioned Turner to the office of Chaplain in the Union Army, making him the first black chaplain in any branch of the military. He also became a war correspondent, publishing many articles in the *Christian Recorder* about the trials and tribulations of the First Regiment U.S. Colored Troops.

After his service in the military, Turner focused his attention on politics. During the period of Reconstruction (1865–1877), and while working with the Freedmen's Bureau, he became a Republican Party organizer and helped recruit and organized black voters throughout Georgia. He helped establish the first Republican State Convention in 1867, helped draft a new Constitution of Georgia, and served as a Georgia State Representative in 1868. However, his victory was short-lived because on September 3, 1868, white members of the state legislature voted to disqualify blacks from holding elected office. After his ouster from the Georgia state legislature, Turner became United States Postmaster in Macon, Georgia. He was the first black ever to hold this position. However, pressures began to mount on the federal government to dismiss him "based on trumped up improprieties."[9] Fired after only two weeks in office, he took a position as a customs inspector in Savannah, Georgia. He held this position for several years, but eventually resigned from this position because of increasing demands of the church.

Turner focused his efforts on building the AME church in the South after resigning from his position as customs inspector. His primary effort was to increase AME membership. By 1876, he became publications manager for the AME church. This allowed him to travel to all the districts and meet the pastors and leaders of local churches. During the four years he served as publications manager, he developed a following that led to his election in 1880 as one of the twelve bishops of the church. In his role as a bishop with the AME church, Turner had a national platform to espouse his ideas on race, politics, lynching, and other issues of the day. As racism became more of an issue for blacks, Turner increasingly became a proponent of emigration.

Near the end of the nineteenth and the beginning of the twentieth century, Turner's influence began to wane with the rise of Booker T. Washington and W.E.B. Dubois as leaders in the black community. Though not perceived as a relevant leader, Turner remained active. He founded the *Southern Recorder* newspaper in 1888 as well as edited two others—the *Voice of Missions* (1893–1900) and the *Voice of the People* (1901–1904). He served as the Chair of the Board of Morris Brown College from 1896–1908, and kept a busy schedule up until the end of his life. While in Windsor, Ontario, at the General Conference of the AME church in 1915, he suffered a massive stroke. He died hours later at a Windsor hospital.

The Study of Ethnology and Didactic Oratory

Didactic oratory was an important rhetorical strategy for African Americans. Coming out of slavery, African Americans faced a double-edge sword when it came to receiving an education. There was a strong desire of the recently emancipated slaves to acquire an education. At the time, there was a strong belief in the black community that the road to freedom came by way of education. Therefore, learning how to read, write, and gain access to public education was paramount for African Americans. However, much that was taught and deemed educational was aimed at keeping African Americans in subservient positions. The development of a field called ethnology during the nineteenth century reveals such a preoccupation.

The discipline of *ethnology* started in America with the 1839 publication of Samuel George Morton's *Crania Americana*, "a compendious report on the author's researches into the size and shape of skulls from around the world."[10] Morton believed that by measuring cranium size, one could provide an accurate analysis of moral and mental capabilities of each racial group. Science had made it official—since Caucasians had the largest skulls and blacks the smallest, whites were superior in moral and mental capabilities than blacks. Blackness became synonomous with inferiority.

It was only a matter of time before Morton's research began to ask the question, "Why are blacks inferior?" While there were many answers to the question regarding the supposed inferiority of blacks, the one that gained scientific credibility was that blacks were a wholly distinctive race, with a separate origin than whites—which led to the conclusion that blacks were not part of the human family. Known as the theory of *polygenesis*, it argued for the plurality of origins because Morton had argued that the different races had not changed scientifically over time. According to Stephen Browne, "Ethnology had revealed the several races to be diverse, fixed, and as embodying essential traits, physical, mental, and social."[11] The prevailing sentiment of the times was that whites were superior to blacks as based on phenotype, traits, and culture.

Though profoundly discredited today, it is important to understand the rhetorical force behind the study of ethnology. Its rhetorical power lay in two areas. Ethnology was cloaked in science and scientific justification. The American School of Ethnology, as it began to be called, was comprised of some of the most prestigious people of the day. Many of the proponents of the science held posts at colleges and universities in America; for example, Morton was a professor of anatomy at the University of Pennsylvania. Morton's disciples, Josiah Nutt and George R. Glidden, published lectures that supported Black inferiority.[12] With any of his findings, these scholars could easily hide behind the cloak of authority by claiming scientific non-partiality.

Since polygenesists grounded their work in science, this gave whites the authority to pronounce without shame the inferiority of blacks. Much of this thinking came from whites who were also confessing Christians who normally would have a problem with scientific theories that attacked the monogenesis creation story found in the Bible. However, the belief of racial superiority and inferiority proved to be too strong to ignore. When it came to ethnology, many whites did accept the main thrust of the argument about black inferiority, and rejected the theory of polygenesis. In other words, whites knew that blacks were inferior, so it really did not matter to them how they were inferior, or what caused the inferiority. With science as an aid to racism, blacks were further assigned a subservient place in society.

Understanding that they were under attack by this line of thinking and belief, blacks begin to study ethnology to offer rebuttals to these racist theories. Many black writers and orators such as John Russwurm, David Walker, Robert Benjamin Lewis Hosea Easton, John Rock, James McCune Smith, Martin Delaney, Frederick Douglass, and Frances Ellen Watkins Harper all offered ethnology driven theories of their own that affirmed African American humanity.[13] To offer a full account of black ethnologic study here is beyond the scope of this essay, however, just a cursory reading of ethnographic books, pamphlets and materials produced by African Americans offers similar rhetorical features.

First, blacks offered *a rhetoric of vindication*. Drawing from anthropologist St. Clair Drake, Moses stated that a rhetoric of vindication involved the "defending of black people from the charge that they have made little or no contribution to the history of human progress." Further he wrote, "Vindicationism has often been concerned with presenting African history in a heroic or monumental mode. It emphasizes the spectacular past and monumental contributions of the ancient civilizations of the Nile, including Ethiopia, Egypt, and Meroe."[14]

Second, black ethnology offered *a rhetoric of redemption*. As Wilson noted, this rhetoric was often associated with "Ethiopianism."[15] The rhetoric offered African Americans as a "redeemer race" because of their peaceful demeanor and long-suffering, and they had "unique characteristics that would put them at the forefront of the human race come Judgment Day."[16] Third, there was *a rhetoric of explanation*. Much of black ethnology consisted of a detailed explanation of the color of the races. Many black ethologic discourses sought to refute the claim that blacks were inferior simply because they were black, and therefore grounded much of their arguments in the science of climatology. Climatology, or environmentalism, simply maintained that blacks and whites were different colors because of their different climate conditions. Fourth, there was *a rhetoric of distinction*. While arguing in the equality of the races, much black ethnologic literature maintained "significant distinctions" about the races. According to Mia Bay:

> What was distinctive about black ethnology, then, was not its mixture of scientific and religious ideas but its emphasis on two not always compatible themes: human sameness and racial distinctions. Whether

they celebrated their race's redemptive qualities, bemoaned the present-day condition of African American, or attacked the character of the white race, black thinkers invariably conceded that blacks and whites were not quite the same, while simultaneously insisting that they were equal.[17]

It is within the context of ethnology and African American responses that *Negro in All Ages* should be interpreted. While a typical African American response is available to him, Turner did not adopt this four-fold strategy. He engaged in a rhetoric of vindication, and to a small degree, a rhetoric of "explanation." What is remarkably absent in Turner's speech is the rhetoric of redemption and distinction. His aim was not to name any group a "redeemer group," or to set distinctions among the races, but to prove that all humans were the same.

Mark Bernard White calls our attention to didactic literature within the African American literary tradition. He writes that literature can be considered didactic when one of its principle aims is to transform its audience by way of teaching, and it should not be surprising that a "substantial portion—perhaps most—of the African American literary tradition is preeminently didactic."[18] White argues that even though didactic literature "represents a richly diverse and immeasurably significant part of African American communication, culture and history," this "discourse has largely been neglected by both rhetorical and literary critics."[19] Didactic literature is "discourse" that "calls forth an imaginative experience that moves the heart and enlarges the understanding" while occupying "a vast middle ground between artistic and instrumental communication." For White, didactic literature "performs serious business and addresses serious issues of the real world."[20]

While White limits the didactic to the African American literary tradition in his essay, the same can be said about the African American oratorical tradition as well. Therefore, drawing upon White's definition of didactic, it may be suggested that Turner's *Negro in All Ages* speech was an example of didactic prophecy because his main rhetorical aim was to transform his audience by way of teaching and by presenting new facts to his audience that would serve as foundations for understanding and learning.

The use of a didactic speech was not foreign to Turner because the didactic sermon had been the primary type of discourse for the instruction of Christian principles. While this speech was delivered in a church and from the pulpit, it was not a sermon—but a lecture designed to teach and to transform his audience into believing in its own personhood and identity. However, by Turner's time, the problem with the didactic—especially the didactic sermon was that, even though many pastors preached them, they were associated with being boring—the hearers were passive participants. Didactic sermons also were associated with lack of feeling and for having "unimpassioned" deliveries.[21] In short, these sermons had the possibility of not being received well because of the theories associated with the genre.

Turner was immediately faced with a rhetorical problem—how does he present this teaching and transformative rhetoric to an audience that had grown weary of the didactic? There are two ways to respond to this question. By adopting the prophetic persona,[22] Turner immediately strengthened his ethos as prophet, which gave him more credibility with the audience. He was a leading spokesperson for the African American community; he was no longer just a pastor, but seen as a prophetic orator. His teaching was thought to have divine origin and worthy of intense attention. It is immaterial that he did not explicitly say this in the speech; he did not need to—the assumption was already there when he began his speech. More importantly for the purposes of this chapter, was what Turner did within the speech. While he adopted the prophetic persona, which presented him in the role of prophet, he still had to deliver the speech. He was on the lecture circuit, and there was an expectation associated with being on the circuit. Reputation or prophetic status could only carry one so far—the speaker must, in the final analysis, be able to speak.

Turner's lecture was meant to inspire and transform by way of teaching. The speech consisted of an introduction in which he contrasted scientific discovery and what he considered sacred truth. He grounded himself in the sacred by claiming the sacredness of humanity along with the bible. He offered prophetic critiques of *Darwinism,* the *Curse of Noah,* and the beliefs about Africa. After Turner answered the question, "Is the negro like other people," he offered hope and encouragement to his audience for a brighter future.

Lecture: The Negro in All Ages

Turner began his speech with an apparent appreciation of science. By acknowledging that "we live in an age of investigation, scrutiny and moral and intellectual enlightenment," he felt comfortable with his assertion that "we lived in the Laboratory Age."[23] There was something more important than scientific discovery—the discovery of truth. For Turner:

> Truth regards not the opinions of illustrious authorities, nor does she pity the mistaken dupes of false theories, however honest to their convictions the devotees may be…. Truth, however, has to fight its way,

inch by inch, and foot by foot, for the forces of error have been large, vigilant, alertive, and unutterably presumptuous, encouraged by innumerable votaries, error with shameless voracity strode in every direction, and with an insatiable greed sought to destroy the last vestige of truth....[24]

While acknowledging that "truth" has to "fight" (ostensibly to be heard), Turner indicated how deep cultural knowledge is weaved into the fabric of everyday living and existence. Truth is at war with the "forces of error," which have as their goal the utter destruction of "truth." Creating their own "self-evident truisms," the forces of error are "marshalled" against "teachings of nature" and also against "simple revelations of Holy Writ." These "forces" have as their leader the "vile foe who assaulted Omnipotence upon his throne" and "who served hell as an attorney" when the "son of God" fasted "forty days." Therefore, since Satan is really at the helm, Turner charged that no one should be surprised about truth being under attack, even in this "illuminated age."

Turner's descriptions are meant to serve two points. First, he emphasized what was at stake. Science was interpreted as truth, which did not bode well for African Americans. As the next part of the speech indicates, some people believed that African Americans did not "have a soul" and "were not part of the human family."[25] This is supported by scientific discovery acting as truth. By framing his argument this way, Turner implies that, while appreciating science and all it does, there is a difference between science and "truth." Second, Turner's strong descriptions indicate a keen sense of how rhetoric helped construct cultural knowledge. He understood that science had constructed a version of truth, and if left unabated and unchecked, it would continue to be used against African Americans. However, he had a twofold rhetorical problem. First, how could he enter into a scientific debate to critique scientific discovery while not having any scientific credentials; and second, how did he critique science while still having an appreciation for science and scientific discovery in this "Laboratory Age" since he did not classify himself as an anti-intellectual?

Turner did this by adopting a prophetic persona that allowed him to elevate his status so that his notion and conception of truth could be just as valid (or more so in his own assessment) as scientists capitulating to the "forces of error." Instead of attacking the study of ethnology directly, Turner offered his audience both a version and a reinterpretation of truth grounded not in scientific discovery, but in sacred beliefs that the audience readily accepted as truth. Once Turner's truth is established, he could argue his case on this perceived "truth."

Although he did not explicitly say it, Turner, by engaging the realm of scientific discovery and applying a reinterpretive analysis and understanding of truth, understood that whatever is deemed truth is profoundly rhetorical. Therefore, he could talk on this subject and address the question "Is the Negro like other people?" He assumed that African Americans were, and went about to prove his argument. He refuted his critics only after he established himself as an expert who could discuss the subject. However, the rhetorical tools Turner used were not scientific, but sacred.

Sacred Identity and the Sacredness of the Bible

To project his version of truth, Turner grounded himself in the sacred identity of humankind, and the sacredness of the Bible:

> I assume upon the authority of Holy Writ, that all men sprang from one original source. This is most explicitly (sic) set forth in the following declaration of the Bible. "God that made the world and all things therein, hath made of one blood all nations of men; for to dwell on the face of the earth, and hath determined the times before appointed and the bounds of their inhabitation ...." Here you see you see Christianity encounters human philosophy, invades its hoary maxims and asserts one of its cardinal doctrines to be the emanation of all men from a single source; having a unity of blood-relationship, which implies a oneness of origin.[26]

Much is at work with this declaration. First, Turner grounded his truth in the "authority" of Holy Writ that all people "sprang from one original source." He countered the polygenesis arguments by grounding himself not in his own authority, but in the authority of the Bible. It is through this authority that Turner found a place in the debate. Finding his authority in the Bible, Turner drew from scripture to offer other proofs, Acts 17:26—"God hath made of one blood all the nations of men." By drawing upon and invoking this scripture, Turner had made God the centerpiece of creation and had elevated his argument from the earthly to the spiritual realm in which he, as God's representative, had authority to speak.

Second, Turner offered a historical contextualization of the passage for rhetorical effect. Biblical tradition has indicated that Paul spoke to Epicurean and Stoic philosophers at a meeting of the Areopagus.[27] What Turner attempted to do was demonstrate the mythic story of creation—that God, who made of one blood all nations of people, was not far removed from the Greek creation story that people were birth from the "sacred soil of Attica." Turner's goal was not to get into a debate of whether the Greeks or Paul had it right or wrong, but to show similarity of these stories to highlight the "oneness of origin." By framing the argument this way, Turner showed how Christianity "encounters human philosophy" that demonstrates the "unity of blood relationship" of humankind. He argued that if one believed in either Paul's or the Greek's accounts of creation, then there was one source that brought forth the creation of humankind.

It was through this argument that Turner could claim race unity. However, he was not talking about African American or white race unity, but human race unity. If all people were created from a single source, then all people are in union with one another. This would be a foundational belief for him throughout his life, which would also eventually become the impetus for his emigration ideas.[28] Through the Apostle Paul, Turner argued that the "unity of the human race" was a key component in Christianity. By comparing this belief and placing it alongside the "God-head," he meant to emphasize this relationship as a cardinal doctrine to the faith. What he implied through his analysis was that if one does not believe in this cardinal doctrine of the "unity of the human race," then one cannot be called a Christian.

Turner's belief in human race unity was important for another reason. Without this belief, white supremacists placed other African Americans outside of the human race into a category called "non-historic races." He situated this part of his lecture by offering several scripture references or "proof-texts" about the nature of Adam, and the redemptive powers of Christ. It was through Adam that he argued "many were made sinners," and it is through Christ "shall many be made righteous." Furthermore, Turner said:

> As Adam is the actual head of all that transgressed, all who die, and all who feel the curse; so Christ is the spiritual head of all that are saved from sin and the sting of death. The universal headship of the one, finds its parallel in the universal headship of the other, thus the path to Eden is the same to all so far as we can glean from biblical authority.... For salvation is restricted to the sons of Adam; and whoever proves himself a son of Adam, proves his title to salvation, and whoever proves his right to salvation by the operation of the Holy Spirit proves that he is a son of Adam.[29]

By offering this orthodox interpretation of the Christian doctrine of redemption, Turner attempted to place African Americans into the "historic race" category. He did this by grounding himself again in the unity of the human race with his goal being to prove "himself as a son of Adam." It was important for Turner to prove this because since Adam is considered by Christians as one of the first humans on the planet (Eve being the other) and since all races are unified, all people are human. This enthymeme would not be lost on Turner's primary African American audience because to prove kinship with Adam would not only prove that African Americans are part of the "historic race," but also would prove that they too are benefactors of the salvation of Christ and therefore part of the Christian community. For Turner and his mainly African American Christian audience, salvation can only be given through Christ, and that salvation can be only given to descendents of Adam. Moreover, if descendents of Adam are in the "historic races" category, this will also include African Americans since they are also recipients of the salvation that only Christ provides.

Therefore, Turner claimed Adamic priority to prove African American humanness. Grounded in the sacred creation story of Christianity and the Christian redemption story, Turner refuted arguments of his opponents. He refuted the arguments of the "naturalists" who would accept the "Mosaic Record," yet placed African Americans in the "non-historic" category. To accept the "Mosaic Record" was to accept the unity of the races—one origin, and one beginning—and to accept this truth was to include African Americans as part of the "historic" races, and therefore accept them as humans.

Turner later said, "I wish I could however, trace my race to some other source, than the fallen and unfortunate Adam: I wish I could give both him and mother Eve to our white friends if they desire it, but I can't; he is my daddy too."[30] He pushed for the logical conclusion of "historic" and "non-historic" theories. If African Americans are not descendents of Adam, and thus non-historic; they do not by logical conclusion have a part in "the Fall."[31] If African Americans are not part of "the Fall," then there is no need to worry about salvation from Christ or anyone in the line of Adam because African Americans are not in need of redemption since they are not "fallen." Only those who are descendents of Adam are in need of redemption. Turner, in wishing that he could trace his "race to some other source than the fallen and unfortunate Adam," demonstrated the hypocrisy of his Christian opponents who promote polygenesis as a doctrine of the faith. Turner found his place in a scientific debate.

Major Critiques

Arguing this way allowed Turner to establish a foundation which gave him an ability to offer critiques of contemporary ideology—the beliefs that are allowed to penetrate the minds and the hearts of his immediate audience as well as society in general. For him, these ideologies or "heresies" posed a big problem for African Americans because they promoted the general idea that blacks were inferior. The first of these critiques comes by way of a scathing critique of Darwinism:

> During the last decade and a half, a parcel of self-constituted Anthropologists have sprung up with a great flourish, and have tried to shake heaven and earth with new tidings from the scientific arena. Their theory is that man is the culmination of the ape, monkey, orang-outang (sic) or some baboon species. That by some process he lost his hairy hide and long tail, and have thus by a series of upward gradations rose to the status of man and womanhood. This monstrous theory is not only at variance with the Mosaic record, but is infinitely worse than the opinions which prevailed in Greece.... Again, these wise timber heads who trace man's origin to the monkey tribe, invariably identify the negro race, with him especially.... The negro they say, sprung from the monkey, or in other words, is an elevated monkey an higher order of monkey.[32]

Turner's critique of Darwinism is two-fold. First, the "theory" is at "variance" with the "Mosaic record." This is important for him because his argument that African Americans are human is grounded in the Mosaic record that believes God made humankind in God's own image. Any attempt to discredit biblical teaching of the origin of humankind would not only render the faith moot, but also place these "self-constituted anthropologists" at the forefront of the debate and allow their version of truth to spread unabated. Second, the "theory" was invariably used against African Americans. Whatever Charles Darwin actually meant when he developed his theory, Darwinism had been reduced to a theory that could be used effectively against African Americans. These "wise timber heads" are scientists who promoted this theory, and for Turner, the theory is null and void because it was used to identify the "negro" with the monkey.

Turner argued that this theory cannot be trusted because it inherently affirms the inferiority of African Americans, and any theory that does this is naturally against the "Mosaic record"—or biblical truth. Moreover, the "Mosaic record" is not only the word of God, because any fair reading and interpretation of it must lead the reader to a doctrine of equality of all races. Turner argued that Darwinism allows, under the guise of science, the hierarchal structure of races cloaked in scientific approval. Turner's critique of Darwinism is grounded primarily in the fact that its supporters use the theory to prove the subordination of African Americans. Therefore, his critique is actually that of how Darwin's work has been interpreted, as much as it is a critique of the work itself.

Turner's second major critique offers a reinterpretation of the Curse of Noah.[33] After being seen naked by his son Ham, Noah cursed Ham's son Canaan to be "servants of servants" to Noah's other two sons Shem and Japheth. It is the primary story that not only justified slavery, but after emancipation, it justified the inferior treatment of African Americans. Interestingly, the curse had no biblical justification or explanation as to why Canaan was singled out to bear the brunt of Ham's "sin," or why it was only African Americans who were affected by the curse. To demonstrate the rhetorical force of this biblical doctrine, one only have to read the words of former slave Gus "Jabbo" Rogers when interviewed in 1938:

> God gave it [religion] to Adam and took it away from Adam and gave it to Noah, and you know, Miss, Noah had three sons and when Noah got drunk on wine, one of his sons laughed at him, and the other took a sheet and walked backwards and threw it over Noah. Noah told the one who laughed, "Your children will be hewers of wood and drawers of water for the other two children, and they will be known by their hair and their skin being dark." So, Miss, there we are, and that is the way *God meant it to be*. We have always had to follow the white folks and do what we saw them do, and that's all there is to it. *You just can't get away from what the Lord said.*[34]

Knowing his audience heard similar sentiments and possibly began to believe them, Turner addressed this story which became for many a doctrine of faith. Interestingly, Turner did this. Turner did not start by attacking the story itself; rather, he offered a critique of the interpretation of the story. By drawing from the work of Alexander Crummell,[35] he argued:

> Mr. Crummell, after proving by both sacred and profane history that the malediction or curse of Noah never effected any of Ham's children, except Canaan, and that the curse was exhausted in the extermination of the Canaanites by the children of Israel after their introduction into the promised land, proceeds to say, "that Africa was originally settled by the descendents of Ham, excepting his son Canaan." Ham himself is supposed to have emigrated to Egypt, and Egypt in scripture is called the "land of Ham."[36]

This functions rhetorically in two ways. By drawing on the work of Alexander Crummell, Turner attempted to stimulate a sense of pride for his primarily black audience to hear from an African American who had studied and contributed significantly to this debate. Again, drawing from Crummell, Turner advanced the argument that the curse really never affected any of Ham's children, except Canaan. This is important for two reasons. First, if the curse only affected Canaan, according to Crummell, the curse is over because of the "extermination of the Canaanites by the children of Israel." Second, Canaan did not settle in Africa anyway; only Ham settled there with his children Cush, Mizraim, and Phut. What Turner attempted to do here through the writings of Crummell is to prove that since Canaan did not settle in Africa, Canaan could not have been black because the common belief was that only black people resided or came from Africa. Turner's aim is clear—if Canaan did not settle in Africa, and African Americans came from Africa, then African Americans could not be part of the curse.

This led Turner to participate in a rhetoric of vindication where he lists for his audience a long line of "African" accomplishments which his primarily African American audience could take some pride in hearing.[37] However, it was not long before Turner turned his attention back to Canaan:

> But we must not desert Canaan. He too was a child of Ham; we are bound to him by the consanguineous laws of nature. He is our brother with all his faults and misfortunes, and a noble brother too. The Canaanites can boast a long line of illustrious personages.[38]

By saying "we must not desert Canaan," Turner was doing two things. He was acknowledging that all the Canaanites were not totally exterminated as Crummell believed. However, his rhetorical strategy was much bigger than mildly opposing Crummell. Turner used his objection as a foundation to present a much bigger argument. Since Canaan was also a child of Ham, that makes Cush, Mirizam, Phut, and Cannan brothers.

If all of Ham's children (except Canaan) went to different parts of Africa, and they were the "fathers" of the African people, where did Canaan go, and who are his descendents? Turner, in a departure from Crummell, believed that "hundreds" of Canaanites escaped to "Phoenicia" and built cities in Greek countries. They eventually would move to Ireland and Spain and father the Irish and English peoples.[39] In short, Turner argued that Canaan was the father of European or white people.

By framing his argument in this way, Turner drew the line between black and white. While the conventional wisdom of his day was to imply that Noah's curse subjugated black people for eternity, he, through a reinterpretation of this story, placed white people as the descendents of Canaan. Thus, to believe in the curse of Noah was to believe that white people and not black people were cursed eternally. While Turner could have grounded the rest of the speech in this line of thinking, he did not. He believed that Canaan being also a son of Ham makes both blacks and whites brothers and sisters. Therefore, just as he offered a rhetoric of vindication for African descendents, he did the same for the descendents of Canaan by saying:

I think, however, that I have shown conclusively that the Noachian malediction neither effected their complexion, their intellects, their morals, their religion, their industry and ingenuity, nor their size, for in the days of Moses and Joshua, there were giants in their midst.[40]

Turner attempted to place his opponents in a rhetorical predicament. First, if one believed in the curse and all of its implications, one would have to believe that whites instead of blacks were the ones cursed. Second, if one believed in the curse, it did not stop those who were supposedly cursed from achieving great things. Offering a rhetoric of vindication for both blacks and whites demonstrated that both races are capable of producing and achieving great things even if one particular race was supposedly cursed. By doing so, he nullified the curse, and concluded: "For the Lord's sake let old Pa (Noah) rest."[41]

Turner also included a critique of Africa in his speeches as a major concern. He did not critique what whites thought about Africa, because his critique focused on what blacks thought about Africa. He critiqued comments made by Frederick Douglass who commented on one of Turner earlier speeches:

A few weeks since, Hon. Frederick Douglass animadverted through his organ severely; upon a paragraph, he saw in one of my speeches in regard to Africa. Wherein I stated that I did not believe this country would be the ultimate home of the negro race, that I believed our race would one day turn their attention to Africa and go to it. Mr. Douglass accused me of clandestinely aiding the Colonization Society and hurled his philippics at me in a most frightful manner. Since then, I have given the Colonization scheme some attention: I have read one or two works which have opened my eyes and enlarged my store of information, and has enabled me to form an opinion.[42]

Using the words "animadverted" and "philippics" demonstrated that he felt personally attacked by Douglass' comments. He argued that Douglass charged him with "clandestinely aiding the Colonization Society" (ACS), which would have been a direct challenge to Turner's credibility, and would have called his leadership and position into question. Many African Americans believed that the American Colonization Society was made up of white men who advocated the emigration of blacks to Africa only because of their racists beliefs. Charging Turner as secretly plotting with them would have made his advice and leadership suspect. Thus he used this as an opportunity to strengthen his credibility and character.

In order to strengthen his standing, Turner positioned himself as the one under attack. He stated that Douglass commented on one of his speeches "in regard to Africa," while Douglass attacked him in the "most frightful manner" about his "clandestine" relationship with the Colonization Society. By framing his argument in this way, Turner revealed Douglass' attack as being erroneous. Because of Douglass' false assertion on the Society, Turner had the time to "read" up on "one or two works" from the Society, and gather more information in order to "form an opinion."

Turner's aim was to restore his ethos, and demonstrate that he had the capability to serve as a trusted leader with the best interests of his people at heart. However, his desire was not just to be just a leader, but to be a prophetic leader—one who reads, one who has an open mind, and one that is willing to learn and form opinions after discerning all the options. Through this argument, Turner not only placed himself as an informed and enlightened person, but also declared that Douglass was not be as informed as he should be. It is within this framework that Turner, with strengthened ethos, was further able to address what he felt was the real situation or issue.

After honoring Douglass as a "great champion of human rights," Turner still declared him wrong on his "obstinate and irreconcilable repugnance" to the Colonization Society.[43] In defense of the Society, Turner believed that the group "has done good, is doing good and will ultimately be adored by unborn millions."[44] Turner's belief in this prophecy came from his more earthly belief that the Society had opened up communication between "here and our fatherland" and without the Society there would be no medium through which to convey the waters of life to that famishing people.[45] Turner revealed the real reason behind the hatred of the Colonization Society was that people despised Africa. He said:

> Why should we despise Africa because the whites do? Let them despise their own fatherland. Whenever I hear the Irish ridiculing Ireland, the English England, the French France, the Germans Germany, the Italians Italy, and the Spanish Spain, then will I, as a descendent of Africa, consider the propriety of ridiculing Africa. I do not wish it understood I am advocating African emigration, but I believe it is our duty to civilize our fatherland, and the only way to civilize a people is to move into their midst and live among them.[46]

Turner's rhetorical question "why should we despise Africa because the whites do" addressed many of the problems blacks had with the ACS and Africa. For many blacks, the ACS was not only a racist organization that did not have black interests at heart, but also their plans to send African Americans to Africa was seen as sending them to an uncivilized and heathen infested place. This opinion of Africa developed not from African Americans, but from white people.

What Turner argued was that white people constructed an idea about Africa in the minds of blacks, and this was so strong that it made them despise their own homeland, and by further implication, it made African Americans despise themselves.

Turner also addressed the issue of self-identity, which featured prominently in his later speeches and writings. By listing several ethnic groups that are in America, and appreciating how they did not despise their homelands, Turner wanted his audience to identify with Africa and to appreciate their homeland as well. By identifying with Africa, Turner believed that not only would African Americans learn to appreciate Africa, and learn to appreciate themselves, but that they would also learn to appreciate what the ACS was trying to do. Turner later argued that even if blacks believed that the "prime movers" in the ACS were not "noted friends of the race," it did not matter, because "Providence over-rules evil for good."[47] He saw the ACS as doing God's bidding by helping African Americans return to Africa.

Turner did not call for a total African emigration—although he felt that some African Americans should go to Africa to civilize the people. Evidently, Turner's critique of other African Americans fell upon him as well—with the only difference that Turner did not despise Africa, and was in favor of sending missionaries there. Turner believed, along with many African Americans, that Africa was uncivilized and needed the influence of Christianity to become a continent worthy of respect. He believed that this process should be "slow and gradual."[48]

Turner's Hope and Encouragement

At the end of his speech, Turner offered hope and encouragement in two places. First, he indicated that there was hope for Africa:

> O! Africa there is hope for you yet, there are better days in store for thee! These are the days of your small things, "but they are not to be despised"; for the pregnant words of the poet: there is a light in the window for thee, brother, there is a light in the window for thee.[49]

Turner's proclamation of "better days" for Africa was grounded in his belief that the ACS would help African Americans return to Africa where his plan of establishing civilization would take place. He drew from an old hymn of the day that "there is a light in the window" for Africa. Once again, hope for Africa was grounded in the ACS and African Americans working together to civilize and evangelize the "fatherland." There was no reason for blacks to despise or criticize Africa, because Africa was to be redeemed and become an "enlightened and civilized nation with posterity who are now sleeping in the womb of the future."[50]

After a roll call of important contemporary African Americans, Turner encouraged his audience at the end of his speech with his declaration that the "negro is a human being." He said:

> I think I hear the voice of God and reason say: Hold! Hold!! Hold your peace, enough have been said! The negro is a human being, the negro has capacities susceptible of eternal evolutions—he too is a man bearing the undoubted impress of his maker. And to those monomaniacs who would rob him of his manhood—seek to defame his name and eclipse his glory I now leave to the wormwood and the gall, and hell must chant their dreadful requiem, and finish the sad story, for I have no organ that can give utterance to the rest.[51]

Turner believed that blacks are human because first, their capacities are susceptible to "eternal evolutions" and constantly evolving. Second, because blacks were created in the image of God, they must be human. He would not engage his opponents in discussion of whether or not blacks are human, because the case is self-evident.

Two points are important here, that both God and reason declared blacks human. Unlike many of his contemporaries who had issues with God and reason standing side by side with one another, he had no problem with this at all. Stephen Angell noted that Turner had moved away from a literal interpretation of scripture, to a more metaphoric one which allowed him to appreciate the discoveries of science and all that it had to offer—especially when it was not grounded in what he would have believed was racist ideology.[52] Turner's encouragement was geared towards his primarily African American audience to take pride in who they were. He encouraged them to believe and understand that no one could take away the fact that they too were human.

Conclusion

Turner believed that identity rested in a belief that God created humankind in God's own image. With this foundational belief, Turner refuted many of the scientific and theological arguments of the day. By adopting a prophetic persona, Turner rose above his critics and opponents, and argued on a morality that concluded with a love for Africa and a charge for his audience to recognize their own humanness.

Turner saw that this argument, grounded in the sacredness of God, needed expansion and discovered that theology itself was racist. To counter this argument, his theology became increasingly contextual and poignantly focused on questions of how theology works to help African Americans cope with the struggles they face on a daily basis. He found that the theology studied, discussed, and proclaimed throughout America did not help with the self-esteem of African Americans. He began to question all of the hymns that were sung to the adulation of whites and the contempt of blacks. He was tired of African American preachers who preached from their pulpits that when they died, they would turn white, and God would accept them in heaven. This led Turner to boldly proclaim at the first National Baptist Convention in 1895 that, "God is a Negro," and began a movement that culminated in James Cone's Black Theology. Through his didactic oratory, Turner proved that religion can be used for race and identity.

Notes

1. Just as many African American orators during this time, Turner spoke extemporaneously—without a prepared manuscript or notes.

2. William Heard, *William H Heard: From Slavery to the Bishopric in the AME Church. An Autobiography* (Philadelphia, PA: AME Book Concern, 1928), 90.

3. There has been some discrepancy in the actual year of Turner's birth. See Stephen Ward Angell's *Bishop Henry McNeal Turner and African American Religion in the South*, footnote, 278.

4. Andre E. Johnson, *An African American Pastor Before and During the American Civil War: The Literary Archive of Henry McNeal Turner,* Vol. 1. (New York: Mellen Press, 2010), vii.

5. Ibid., vii.

6. Ibid., viii.

7. Ibid.

8. For a more detailed summary of Turner's iterant preaching, see Stephen Ward Angell, especially Chapter 1.

9. Johnson, xi.

10. Stephen Browne, "Counter Science: African American Historians and the Critique of Ethnology in the Nineteenth-Century America," *Western Journal of Communication,* 64 (Summer 2000): 3, 270.

11. Ibid., 271.

12. See Josiah Nutt, *Two Lectures on the Natural History of the Caucasian and Negro Races (1844)* and *Two Lectures on the Connection between the Biblical and Physical History of Man.* See George R. Glidden, *Discourses on Egyptian Archeology, (1849).*

13. For a fuller detail account of Black Ethnology, see chapters 1–3 of Mia Bay's *The White Image in the Black Mind: African American Ideas about White People, 1830–1925* (New York: Oxford University Press, 2000).

14. Wilson Moses, *Afrotopia: The Roots of African American Popular History* (Melbourne: Cambridge University Press, 1998), 21, 24.

15. Moses, 26, based on the biblical verse found in Psalms 68:31, "Princes shall come out of Egypt: Ethiopia shall soon stretch forth her hands unto God."

16. Bay, 49.

17. Ibid., 54.

18. Mark Bernard White, "The Rhetoric of Edification: African American Didactic Literature and the Ethical Function of Epideictic," *Howard Journal of Communications* 9 (April 1998), 126, 128.

19. Ibid., 125.

20. Ibid., 127.

21. For comments on didactic sermons see William Russell's *Pulpit Elocution* Second edition (Boston, MA: Draper and Halliday, 1869), and Henry J. Ripley's *Sacred Rhetoric or Composition and Delivery of Sermons,* Fifth Edition (Boston, MA: Gould and Lincoln, 1869).

22. Elsewhere I defined prophetic rhetoric and prophetic persona. See "Will We Have Ears to Hear: the African American Prophetic Tradition in the Age of Obama." *African American Pulpit,* Spring, 2010 (10–14) and "The Prophetic Persona of James Cone and the Rhetorical Theology of Black Theology." *Black Theology Journal,* Vol. 8.3, 2010, 266–285.

23. Henry McNeal Turner, *The Negro in All Ages: A Lecture Delivered in the Second Baptist Church of Savannah, Georgia*, April 8, 1873, *Savannah*, 1873, 5.

24. Turner, 5–6.

25. Ibid., 6.

26. Ibid., 8.

27. The Holy Bible, Acts 17:26.

28. Many have traditional misunderstood Turner's emigration ideas. His emigration policy derived from his strong belief in racial egalitarianism. He always believed that humans were made equal; however, since he also believed that equality would never happen in America for African Americans, he suggested that blacks who wanted to emigrate to Africa should and begin to live up to the egalitarian ideals that America suggested but never placed into practice.

29. Turner, 8–9.

30. Ibid., 22.

31. The doctrine of "the Fall derives from the story of how Adam and Eve were removed from the Garden of Eden. For Christians, it expresses the idea that human nature has 'fallen' from its original state." See Alister E. McGrath's *Christian Theology: An Introduction* (Oxford: Blackwell Publishing, 1994).

32. Turner, 12–13.

33. Found in Genesis 9:21–27, the curse of Noah (or the curse of Canaan) describes the story of Noah.

34. Forrest G. Wood, *The Arrogance of Faith: Christianity and Race in America from the Colonial Era to the Twentieth Century* (Place of publication Northeastern University Press, 1991), 84.

35. For a complete examination of Crummell's work on the Curse of Noah, see "The Negro Race Not Under a Curse: An Examination of Genesis," 9:25. *Christian Observer London, 1850.*

36. Turner, 19.

37. Ibid., 23–24.

38. Ibid., 25.

39. Ibid., 27.

40. Ibid., 28.

41. Ibid., 27.

42. The speech referred to was Turner's *"Present Duties and the Future Destiny of the Negro Race."* 28.

43. Ibid., 28.

44. Ibid.

45. Ibid., 28–29.

46. Ibid.,.

47. Turner, 29.

48. Ibid., 29.

49. Ibid.

50. Ibid., 28.

51. Ibid., 31.

52. See Stephen Angell's *Bishop Henry McNeal Turner and African-American Religion in the South* (Knoxville, TN: University of Tennessee Press, 1992), Chapter 12.

Part III

The Black Diaspora in Latin American Identity and Culture

Chapter 12

"*Pardo*" and "*Preto*" into "*Negro*": Blackness in Contemporary Brazil[1]

G. Reginald Daniel

Brazil and the United States (U.S.) have accorded whites privileged status relative to other racial groups. Their racial orders followed different trajectories in terms of white-black relations. The U.S. implemented a binary racial order distinguishing blacks from whites by reference to the "one-drop rule."[2] This device defines as black everyone of African descent, and has supported legal and informal barriers to racial equality, which culminated in Jim Crow segregation. In Brazil, by contrast, pervasive miscegenation and the absence of legal barriers to racial equality earned it the reputation of being a "racial democracy," with a ternary racial order that designated the population as white (branco), multiracial (pardo), and black (preto). This supported the idea that social inequities were primarily based on class and culture rather than race. In recent decades, Brazil's Black Movement has sought to replace the categories of *preto* and *pardo* with the category of *negro* (African Brazilian) to heighten awareness of and mobilize against the real racial discrimination that exists in Brazil.[3]

This chapter examines the Black Movement's impact on black-white relations, given the history of African slavery and unique legacy of attitudes and policies that have crystallized around individuals of African descent in terms of Brazil's racial order and national identity. Drawing from Michael Omi and Howard Winant's *Racial Formation in the United States from the 1960s to 1990s* (1994), the Black Movement may be defined as a racial "project," which is simultaneously a cultural and political initiative seeking to bring about social structural change. This has taken the form of projects in which singular actors are the agents of resistance. It also has been manifest in collective action that has called upon the state to play a significant role. The cultural initiative is an interpretation and representation of racial dynamics by means of identity politics; the political initiative is most evident in appeals for changes in official racial categories and the collection of racial data, as in the census, challenging institutions, policies, conditions, and rules directly and indirectly based on and supporting Brazil's racial order.[4]

Brazil's racial democracy was popularized in the work of Gilberto Freyre: *The Masters and the Slaves* (1933), *The Mansions and the Shanties* (1936), and *Order and Progress* (1959).[5] Freyre argued that the Portuguese colonizers, as compared to their Anglo-North America counterparts, displayed an exceptional receptivity to miscegenation as well as generosity in differentiating multiracials from blacks. However, throughout the Americas, these phenomena were motivated primarily by self-interest, and closely related to the ratio of European men to women and the ratio of whites to blacks.[6]

In Brazil, the colonizing Europeans were a minority and mostly single males. The preponderance of African slaves, in conjunction with the fact that few Portuguese women immigrated to Brazil, gave rise to miscegenation between white men and women of African descent, as had been the case with attitudes towards liaisons with Native American women. This phenomenon historically originated in relationships that were largely consummated through coercion and violence such as rape, fleeting extramarital relations, and extended concubinage rather than through mutual consent and peaceful means.

Whether interracial intimacy involved coercion or mutual consent, Portuguese civil and ecclesiastical authorities condemned miscegenation. Interracial marriages in the Southern and some Northern colonies in Anglo-North America were proscribed and stigmatized where they were not legally prohibited. The interracial family in colonial Brazil was informally legitimized notwithstanding the legal barriers to racial intermarriage. Official reprimands failed to have the desired effect, such that authorities tended to turn a blind eye to interracial intimacy.[7] In practice, common-law unions involving European men and women of color produced "legitimate" offspring alongside more widespread clandestine and fleeting liaisons involving births outside of wedlock. Moreover, the financial expenditure in contracting legal marriages was a disincentive for individuals throughout the racial spectrum.[8] Seventeenth-century Portuguese law recognized "common law" marriage as one of "virtually every kind of union"[9] approved to increase the population. By the end of the eighteenth century, marriages of whites with Native Americans and *mamelucos* (multiracial individuals of European and Native American descent) were encouraged by the state as a means of assimilating the indigenous inhabitants.[10] Marriages with African Brazilians continued to be stigmatized. These circumstances had ended by the time of Brazil's independence for Portugal in 1822.

Moreover, informal relationships between white males of all social classes and women of color continued to be widespread.[11]

In Brazil, where blacks greatly outnumbered whites, multiracials occupied an intermediate social location in the racial order. Multiracial slave offspring were often assigned tasks as domestics and artisans. The scarcity of white women mitigated opposition from the legal wife and enhanced the likelihood that these offspring would receive socially tolerated demonstrations of affection, as well as economic and educational support. Multiracials were given preferential liberation over blacks, who overwhelmingly were slaves. They entered the free classes early in the colonial period, where they filled interstitial roles in the economy, particularly in the artisanal and skilled trades. This was due to both a shortage of European labor and the need for workers in situations where slave labor was considered impractical.

Because of the shortage of whites, multiracials, who were a majority of Free Coloreds, also performed a critical role in the civilian militia. The monarchs in Portugal often viewed Free Colored militia as a means of expanding the frontier. They also secured Portugal's territorial borders against foreign interlopers and attacks by Native Americans, while also providing a military brake on the ambitions of independence-minded whites. Given the large number of mulattoes among Free Coloreds, whites also viewed them as natural allies against the black slave majority. So reliable were Free Coloreds, that Brazilian slaveholders used Free Colored militias to suppress slave uprisings, as well as catch and return fugitive slaves. The incorporation of Free Coloreds into the security apparatus of the colonial state, however, contributed as much to their own circumscribed status as to the superordinate position of whites. Free Colored militia could hardly have hoped to overthrow whites and simultaneously hold slaves in their place. Any attempt at revolt would have brought them into opposition to the Crown as well as the colonial government, resulting in reprisals in the event of defeat.[12]

Free Colored urban artisans, long before abolition, advanced into the arts, letters, and liberal professions. However, they were barred from holding public office, entering high status occupations in the clergy and governmental bureaucracy, experienced limitations on educational attainment, and were denied equal rights in various categories. Free Coloreds did not advance through competition in the open market. Rather, their mobility was generally facilitated through (and controlled by) patrons in the white elite.[13] European Brazilians granted multiracials (who were a majority of Free Coloreds), a social location that was somewhat superior to that of blacks, but significantly inferior to that of whites. They won their loyalty to exclude blacks from power while at the same time avoiding the undermining of white domination and control. The process of abolition sealed this racial contact. Whites relied on multiracial support long after slavery ended. John Burdick argues that as long as blacks were retained in the least remunerative sectors of the secondary labor force, multiracials settled for token integration into the skilled trades, the petty bourgeoisie, intelligentsia, and primary labor force.[14]

The Brazilian racial order has assured that African Brazilians are collectively denied the privileges of whites. Multiracials are at the same time rewarded in proportion to their phenotypical and cultural approximation to the European ideal through what Carl Degler refers to as the "mulatto escape hatch."[15] Degler does not imply, as many have argued, that the multiracial masses gain access carte blanche to the prestigious ranks of whites by virtue of the fact that they are multiracial as opposed to black. Rather, his central argument is that the escape hatch is an informal social mechanism through which a few "visibly" multiracial individuals (because of talent, culture, or education), have been allowed token vertical mobility, and with it the rank of situational "whiteness."

The escape hatch has broader implications. This device has allowed millions of individuals who have African ancestry, but who are phenotypically white, or near-white, to become socially designated and self-identified as such. This indicates that the social construction of whiteness—as well as the extension of white racial privilege in Brazil—is more inclusive compared to the U.S., where the one-drop rule ascertains that an individual who appears white is black. This also guarantees that many individuals who possess the sociocultural capital to serve as voices in the African Brazilian struggle are co-opted into silence. This in turn has retarded, if not prevented, mobilization along racial lines that allows de facto white control to continue.

If miscegenation and the escape hatch have made the line between black and white imprecise at best, and became a central tenet in the twentieth-century evolution of Brazil's racial democracy ideology, then racial and cultural blending was not posited on egalitarian integration (Figure 1.a). In this scenario, equal value would be attached to each of these racial and cultural constituents through a reciprocal *transracial/transcultural* process. Rather, it was a process of inegalitarian integration (or *assimilation* in disguise) that *perpetuated* only one—the European—with the goal of presenting a whiter national image (Figure 1.b).[16] If, according to nineteenth-century scientific racism espoused by European and European American thinkers, miscegenation and cultural blending were the disease, whitening through miscegenation and the Europeanization of Brazilian culture was the elite's prescription for a cure. The state thus encouraged and indeed subsidized European immigration and passed waves of legislation restricting that of blacks.[17]

Figure 1. Pluralist and Integrationist Dynamics

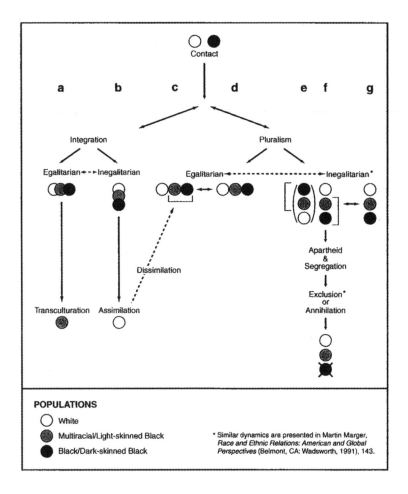

The Contemporary Racial Order

In the context of the scientific racism of the 1930s and 1940s (which culminated in Hitler's Third Reich), Freyre's works formalized Brazil's image as a racial democracy and gave it the legitimacy of a social scientist's stamp. A group of Brazilian and foreign social scientists was commissioned with funds from the United Nations Educational, Scientific, and Cultural Organization (UNESCO) to discover the formula for Brazil's impressive achievement. Empirical data about Brazilian race relations did not, however, correspond to their expectations. Their findings revealed that discrimination was based on a complex interweaving of class, culture, and physical appearance, rather than ancestry, as in the United States. There was a consensus that Brazilians who were phenotypically more African were disproportionately found at the bottom of social order.[18] This evidence not only made the Brazilian elite cautious about discussing race relations, but also made the racial democracy ideology even more crucial as a form of social control. It was defended by the ruling elite and reinforced by the military dictatorships that dominated the Brazilian political scene between 1964 and 1985.

During military rule, political organizing was violently suppressed. Efforts to mobilize along racial lines were deemed "racist," "subversive," and a threat to national security, and were punishable by detention, imprisonment, and even torture. Individuals who organized to address a problem that the state declared nonexistent were viewed as troublemakers, and accused of having been infected with a contagion imported from the United States. Many individuals were imprisoned; others emigrated or were exiled.[19] The censorship of public discussion on racial issues was paralleled by the fact that no racial data were collected in the 1970 census. State officials argued that racial categories were so ambiguous as to be meaningless. Actually, they were seeking to promote the notion that racial criteria were insignificant in determining social stratification by depriving researchers of figures that would confirm how poorly African Brazilians fared in terms of key social indicators.[20]

The veil of silence on the discussion of racial inequality was lifted beginning in the 1970s with the gradual return to civilian rule. This democratic opening (*abertura democrática*) provided political space to reformulate racial meanings, forge an oppositional racial ideology, and constitute alternative racial institutions. It was thus catalytic in rekindling the militancy of the Black Front (*A Frente Negra*, FNB) and the Black Experimental Theater (*Teatro Experimental do Negro*, TEN) of the 1930s and 1940s before they reached their nadir during the dictatorship of Getúlio Vargas (1937–1945). Racial mobilization was also fueled by the growing racial tension in Brazil, the U.S. civil rights movement, the decolonization of African countries—particularly the Portuguese colonies of Angola, Guinea-Bissau, and Mozambique—and the shift in foreign policy when Brazil launched its drive for new markets in Africa.

With the democratic opening, black consciousness first emerged in "cultural" phenomena, which were less threatening to military authorities. These included the urban "Black Soul" movement composed of underemployed working class African Brazilian youth who were inspired by U.S. cultural developments in music (e.g., James Brown, Isaac Hayes, and Aretha Franklin). They also filled movie theaters to see "Black" American films (for example, Wattstax, Claudine, Superfly, and Shaft). They adopted English-language phrases such as "soul" and "Black-power kids," colorful clothes, elaborate handshakes, and "Afro" hairstyles as part of an evolving culture of opposition that rejected traditional African Brazilian culture, now seen as co-opted by European Brazilian society and central to maintaining racial democracy.[21]

The same period that gave rise to "Black Soul" also witnessed a rebirth of traditional African Brazilian cultural expression through the formation of carnival groups such as *blocos afros* (Olodúm and Ihê Aiyê). Beginning in the 1970s, samba schools began dealing explicitly with racial inequality and were no longer willing to use racial democracy as a theme. The music, dance, and lyrics of samba, along with *capoeira*, became important conduits of black consciousness and affirmed a culture of opposition, particularly among African Brazilian workers. In addition, African Brazilian religious practices that had also been co-opted, such as *candomblé* and *umbanda*, became vehicles for black consciousness.[22]

The growing covert racial tension in Brazil in the early 1970s set the stage for the formation of the Unified Black Movement (*O Movimento Negro Unificado*, MNU). The MNU emerged out of protests in May 1978 on the steps of São Paulo's Municipal Theater. Coinciding with the anniversary of the abolition of slavery, African Brazilians organized in several major cities. They specifically protested the murder by police of an African Brazilian taxi driver named Robson Luiz and the expulsion of three African Brazilian youths from a yacht club where they were playing as part of a volleyball team. These events were not unusual, but were catalytic in the formation of the MNU. In addition, exiled life-long African Brazilian activists Guerreiro Ramos, as well as Abdias do Nascimento, who co-founded the MNU, returned to Brazil.[23]

The MNU enjoyed a flurry of publicity in the late 1970s and early 1980s. It gained greater attention from academics abroad than in Brazil. The MNU's interrogation of the dominant assimilationist ideology was met with hostility from sectors of the political and cultural establishment. At best, their tactics were deemed "un-Brazilian" and mindless imitations of the U.S. civil rights movement. Indeed, activists were influenced by that movement, attributable in part to the awareness of transnational racial formations facilitated by the growing forces of globalization, particularly in the media. At worst, the MNU's agenda was described as racist in the manner of a reverse type of apartheid (Figure 1.e on p. 235).[24]

The MNU's efforts were aided by a new generation of (mostly white) social scientists who helped reinstate the race question on the 1980 census. They provided a rigorous analysis of the 1940, 1950, and 1980 censuses, and the National Household Surveys of the 1970s and 1980s, which documented glaring disparities in terms of health, income, and education between whites (54 percent of the population) and African Brazilians (46 percent of the population).[25] The 1980 census data indicate that the overall socioeconomic divide is primarily located between whites and non-whites. Inequalities in employment and earnings reveal that African Brazilians achieved lower financial returns than whites on their investments in education, particularly at higher educational levels. In addition, African Brazilians have a lesser chance of entering university and have higher rates of infant mortality and incarceration.[26] Moreover, African Brazilians are handicapped by the cumulative disadvantages of persistent racial discrimination.

A key objective of African Brazilian activists was to contest the racial democracy ideology. In support of this aim, on May 11, 1988, two days before the official celebration of the centennial for the abolition of Brazilian slavery, they organized a public protest composed of several thousand individuals, who marched through downtown Rio de Janeiro chanting the slogans "Cem anos sem abolição" (One hundred years without abolition!) and "We are still enslaved! Racial democracy is a lie!"[27] This demonstration was met with the greatest display of police force since the end of the military dictatorship.

The 1988 Constitution, for the first time, declared racial discrimination to be a crime without bail or statute of limitation, and punishable by imprisonment.[28] The antiracist article in the constitution, like the 1951 Afonso Arinos Law, seemed more rhetoric than a societal commitment.[29] Also, civil rights attorneys have found it challenging to establish a legal basis for their criminal complaints even with the passage in 1989 of the necessary constitutional enabling statute—Law 7716—commonly referred to as the Lei Caó (Caó Law).[30] According to Guimarães this is due in part to the fact that racism as defined by the statute (and interpreted by the judiciary) is limited to acts of "segregation or exclusion based on skin color or race,"[31] particularly in terms of public services and business establishments. This type of blatant discrimination is rare in Brazil. When it occurs, the "racial" motive is hidden beneath a complex set of informal rules and processes, and is often disguised with a variety of "code words" (e.g., "good appearance," "service elevator").[32]

The Brazilian judicial system can present formidable obstacles to litigating criminal cases involving charges of racism, as well as obtaining favorable outcomes. Police officials frequently do not take complaints seriously. Sometimes they fail to conduct preliminary investigations. When evidence is gathered, police often neglect to forward it to the public prosecutor's office. Prosecutors have been known to settle cases with financial penalties that are so small that they fall short of either compensating the aggrieved parties or deterring future racially discriminatory behavior. Although cases are more publicized and investigated, they can take years before final resolution.[33]

The MNU garnered support from intellectuals, the church, and workers' organizations. Yet, many social justice advocates viewed African Brazilians as part of a transracial working class; they believed that race-specific policies would deviate from the main course of social reform.[34] Moreover, class divisions within the MNU's ranks arose as a result of the primarily urban bourgeoisie leadership, which prevented it from garnering support from the larger African Brazilian community. The MNU and similar political organizations are, nonetheless, part of a larger Black Movement encompassing a variety of social, cultural, and political organizations and activities. Prominent African Brazilians have spoken out publicly about their experiences with racial discrimination. It is unlikely that large numbers of individuals will join African Brazilian political organizations. Many embrace the notion of a distinct African Brazilian culture and experience. For example, *Black People* (English title, Portuguese text), which was launched in 1993, and *Raça: A Revista dos Negros Brasileiros* (Race: The Magazine of African Brazilians), which emerged in October 1996, have been among glossy magazines targeting an African Brazilian audience.[35]

Beauty salons specializing in *cabelo crespo* ("kinky" hair) have sprung up in urban areas, and on city streets women are wearing nontraditional hairstyles, including rasta dreads, braids, and Afro permanents.[36] There has also been a revitalization of African-derived religious and musical expression, as well as a growth in African Brazilian literature.[37] According to Livio Sansone, African Brazilians still display a "thin" sense of themselves as a racial collectivity, while at the same time articulating a "thick" black cultural identity (which is itself to some extent part of the global interchange of black cultural symbols increasingly shared by large numbers of individuals in the African diaspora, particularly the Black Atlantic).[38] Advertisers exploring the market for "black" products have become aware of the financial potential of targeting an African Brazilian audience. Others have included African Brazilians in television commercials for more mainstream products.[39]

Even with these gains, African Brazilians are noticeably absent from television, newspapers, and magazines. The same Eurocentric bias that plagues the U.S. media, entertainment industry, and the world of high fashion is even more evident in Brazil.[40] Women representing Brazil in international beauty pageants such as Miss Universe exemplify this phenomenon. The slender white female, preferably with auburn hair and light eyes, has historically been the norm. Miss Brazil contestants of obvious African descent in the Miss Universe pageant are anomalies and even rarer than black Miss Americas. The Brazilian public's reaction has been decidedly racist, ranging from "murmurings of distress"[41] in the case of Vera Lúcia Couto dos Santos (who was third in 1964), to blatant scorn in the case of Deise Nunes de Souza (1986).[42] Despite this public outcry, the two African Brazilian women ever crowned Miss Brazil were multiracial, not black. Based on their phenotypes, body types, hairstyles, and attire, they represent the absorption, validation, and commodification of blackness that is an acceptable reproduction of whiteness. No African Brazilian has won the title of Miss Brazil displaying "strong" West African facial features or wearing an Afro, braids, or dreadlocks.[43]

Since the 1990s, Brazilians have become increasingly aware of racism.[44] In June 1995, the newspaper *Folha de São Paulo* published a special Sunday supplement entitled "Racismo cordial: A mais completa análise sobre preconceito de côr no Brasil" (Cordial Racism: The Most Comprehensive Analysis of Color Prejudice in Brazil). The study was based on a Datafolha survey that polled five thousand individuals who were questioned about color terminology and self-identification as well as the prevalence of racism.[45] The data indicated that 89 percent of white respondents agreed that African Brazilians were the targets of racism. Only 10 or 11 percent stated they themselves were prejudiced or behaved in discriminatory ways.[46] France Twine and others have noted that individuals commonly toe the "politically correct" line about racism, yet have difficulty identifying racism in their own thoughts, behavior, or experience. They speak of individual rather than structural (or institutional) racism and do nothing to interrupt either.[47] Activists questioned whether the Datafolha findings reflected any fundamental change, which they argued would require major reforms.[48]

In the Black: The Racial State, the Census, and Public Policy

The Black Movement has challenged institutions, policies, and conditions based on Brazil's racial democracy ideology, ternary racial order, and mulatto escape hatch. Among other things, the movement's cultural initiative involves an explanation of racial dynamics by means of identity politics. Activists have rearticulated a "new" African Brazilian identity that dichotomizes whiteness and blackness as two distinct categories to dismantle the hierarchical relationship of the former over the latter. The goal is to replace the color distinctions of *pardo* and *preto* with an African Brazilian identifier such as *negro* (meaning *Afrodescendente* or African-descended) by sensitizing individuals to ethno-racial origins.[49] Many activists believe the U.S. binary racial thinking should be adopted in Brazil, for this would enable the mass mobilization of African Brazilians. Activists argue that the absence of the original negative factor of legal discrimination, typified by the U.S., along with miscegenation and fluid racial identities, have undermined unity in the antiracist struggle and social progress of African Brazilians.[50]

The Movement's political initiative has focused considerable attention of changing official racial categories, as in the census. Activists have called upon the state to implement a *negro* identifier in the federal standard for data collection. By so doing, they have forced recognition and discussion of the state's role in maintaining racial categories and the formation of identities. In 1980, based on an analysis of the 1976 Household Survey (*Pesquisa Nacional por Amostra de Domicílios* PNAD) and 1980 census, the Brazilian Institute of Geography and Statistics (IBGE) documented the social inequities between whites and nonwhites when it began analyzing and publishing racial data in binary, rather than ternary, form.[51] This change in procedure was a response in part to demands made by African Brazilian activists and by the new generation of social scientists. Previously, the IBGE had advanced policy decisions to serve the national project aimed at unifying Brazil's three parent racial groups—European, African, and Native American—to project a more integrated (albeit whiter) national image. The IBGE had not abandoned the traditional three-category concept of color—or four, if one includes the category of yellow (*amarelo*) used to designate individuals of Asian ancestry—in the actual collecting of data. It had moved conceptually closer to U.S. racial formation. Accordingly, *pretos* and *pardos* were combined as a single nonwhite group. Activists have placed great emphasis on these and other survey data as a confirmation of their argument that the socioeconomic status of *pretos* and *pardos* is similar.[52]

In 1990, Black movement activists organized a formal campaign to change procedures for collecting official racial data based on these findings. Movement discourse and writing largely employs the term *negro* as an expanded definition of blackness that relies on African ancestry. Individuals who identify as *preto* on the census had never surpassed 10 percent of the population. If this 10 percent is combined with the roughly 42 percent who identified as *pardo*, the total surpasses 50 percent. Activists claimed that the percentage of African Brazilians ranges from 50 to as high as 80 percent, making it possible for the movement to identify its constituency as a numerical majority.[53]

The Black Movement was unsuccessful in getting the IBGE to use the term *negro* on the 1990 census (which was actually delayed until 1991). The term conveyed a politicized identity mobilized against the state and long-entrenched patterns deemed fundamental to maintaining racial civility and social cohesion. The IBGE considered retaining the term *pardo* with a sub-option that would allow individuals to acknowledge African ancestry. *Branco*, *preto*, *amarelo*, and *Indígena* (Native American) would be retained. President Cardoso called upon the IBGE to continue combining *pretos* and *pardos* for the purposes of certain statistical work. In terms of public presentation, the relevant categories would be "white" and "non-white."[54]

As was the case with the 1990 census, activists were unsuccessful in getting the term *negro* added to the 2000 census. Moreover, color data on both censuses were consistent with previous statistics.[55] In 1991, the percentage of Brazilians identified as *branco* still remained slightly more than half of the population (52 percent). Those who identified as *preto* decreased from 5.9 percent in 1980 to 5 percent in 1991. The percentage of individuals identifying as *pardo* increased from 38.8 percent in 1980 to 42.6 percent in 1991. The 2000 data indicated that 6.2 percent of the respondents identified as *preto*, a slight increase over the 5 percent on the 1991 census; 0.5 percent as *amarelo*, and 0.4 percent as *Indígena*. At the same time, there was a decrease in the number of individuals who identified as *pardo* (42.6 percent in 1991 to 39.1 percent in 2000). The majority of Brazilians (53.7 percent) still identified as *branco*.[56]

Beginning in the 1990s, during the administration of President Cardoso, there was increased discussion of affirmative action. Since then, state agencies began announcing affirmative action policies. Some entities, including several ministries and universities, have established percentages (or quotas) of positions that must be reserved for African Brazilians.[57] After taking office in 2003, President Luiz Inácio Lula took steps, both practical and symbolic, stressing his commitment to racial equality. His cabinet included four African Brazilians, among them the minister of a newly created Secretariat for the Promotion of Racial Equality. The most prominent African Brazilian member of the cabinet is the minister of culture, Gilberto Gil, an internationally renowned musician who is outspoken on issues of African cultural heritage. Lula appointed the first African Brazilian Supreme Court judge, Joaquim Benedito Barbosa Gomes. He created a racial equality committee and ordered three ministries to recruit African Brazilians to fill at least 20 percent of senior posts. Lula also promised that African Brazilians would account for at least one-third of the federal government within five years.[58]

Affirmative action policies were not yet accompanied by the necessary federal legislation and implementation.[59] Also, opponents have argued that race-based affirmative action has no place in Brazil.[60] These initiatives are viewed as a solution imported from the United States—where racial definitions and relations are different—and will exacerbate rather than ameliorate the situation in Brazil. The most egregious racial inequalities, they argue, can be eradicated with class-based policies aimed at eradicating poverty. Moreover, they believe that universal initiatives supporting improved public elementary and high school education, sanitation, medical and dental care, affordable housing, employment, and land distribution for the poor would proportionally benefit more African Brazilians than whites, given that the majority of the former are poor.[61] Race-specific policies that expand access to university education, job promotion, and so on would primarily benefit the small African Brazilian middle class, which already has the qualifications to attend college, operate a company, or supply needed goods or services.[62] Supporters respond that racial quotas are a legitimate means of expanding educational and other opportunities for all African Brazilians, despite imperfections.[63]

A key site for the affirmative action debate has been policies at several of Brazil's most prestigious universities: The State University of Rio de Janeiro State University (UERJ), the Northern Fluminense State University (UENF), and the University of Brasilia (UnB). Of the 1.4 million students admitted to universities each year, only 3 percent have typically identified as African Brazilian and only 18 percent have come from public schools, where most African Brazilians are enrolled. The enrollment of African Brazilian students in elite institutions has doubled (and in some cases tripled) as a result of affirmative action initiatives.[64]

UEJR and UENF became the first public institutions to comply with October 2, 2001 legislation in the state of Rio de Janeiro requiring universities to reserve a 40 percent quota for African Brazilians in its 2003 entering class. This figure corresponded to the fact that roughly 45 percent of Brazil's 175 million (currently 191 million) people identified as African Brazilian. The legislation also mandated a 50 percent quota for graduates from public secondary schools, which are overcrowded, underfunded, and of lesser quality as compared to the private schools, which are attended by the children of middle class, wealthy, and mostly white Brazilians.[65] At UnB, racial quotas were first proposed in 1999 by two of faculty in the Department of Anthropology and, after much internal debate (and influenced by the UERJ experience), approved in 2002 by an internal committee.[66]

Despite similarities with the U.S., the affirmative action debate in Brazil is markedly different. The question of who is African American was settled long ago (although U.S. definitions of racial categories are now being challenged).[67] By contrast, Brazil is being forced to grapple with formally defining racial categories. The results have been ambiguous. Racial quotas provide individuals with an incentive to accommodate a wide range of phenotypes or emphasize ancestry over phenotype as means of identifying as African Brazilian. Indeed, some university applicants who were typically white-designated and white-identified did this to increase their chances of admission.[68] The potential for "fraud" is real since many whites have some African phenotypical traits and large numbers have African ancestry. UERJ and UnB thus intervened to clarify the intended targets for affirmative action.[69]

In terms of UERJ, state officials and representatives, university administrators, and Black Movement activists negotiated two modifications of the original quota law, which conditioned eligibility on applicants who identified as either *negro* or *pardo*. The modifications eliminated the term *pardo*, which was presumed to be included within *negro*. There was also the fear that many *brancos* would feel comfortable identifying as *pardo*. In addition, the new law restricted quota eligibility to low-income students, thus taking into consideration the importance of class. Otherwise, affluent African Brazilians would be the primary beneficiaries since they had the necessary sociocultural and academic capital to score high on the entrance exam. State legislators thus recommended that students benefiting from racial quotas must prove their families earn no more than 300 *reais* a month (about US$100).[70] As for UnB, the only term used from the very beginning was *negro*. Moreover, in contradistinction to UERJ, the university privileged racial over class criteria as there were no income limits or quotas for public school students. UnB's solution to potential abuse was to require candidates seeking admission under the quotas to have their photographs examined by a committee of "experts." Due to intense public opposition, UnB recently substituted photographs with an interview.[71]

More than 70 percent of Brazil's 98 public universities have affirmative action programs. Most rely exclusively on students' self-identification. Some employ the census categories of *preto* and *pardo*.[72] Many include additional socioeconomic criteria, or restrict eligibility to public school students. Although affirmative action in higher education appears promising, critics have expressed concerns about student test scores. For example, the average score for individuals admitted into UERJ law school in 2002 was nearly 81 percent; under the quota system, the average score was 64 percent. Many interpreted this as a lowering of academic standards. Supporters counter that racial quotas are not the problem. The focus should be on improving education in primary and secondary schools as well as college preparation. If increased African Brazilian admission rates further the goal of equal opportunity, retention and equal outcome are quite another matter.[73]

Support for affirmative action has grown considerably since former president Cardoso introduced goals for the development and implementation of such policies. Lula's government fully supported the Racial Equality Statute, which outlined plans and allotted resources for programs that would benefit African Brazilians. This legislation was submitted to Congress in 1998, but was not approved by the Senate until 2005.[74] On November 25, 2005, the legislation went to the House of Representatives for a vote, but was met with resistance. The statute recommended a 20 percent quota for African Brazilians in government jobs and public universities, enterprises with more than twenty employees, and actors in television programming (including television soap operas and commercials). In addition, 30 percent of political party candidates were to be African Brazilians.[75] In order to reach a compromise with the House's conservative members, and concerns about the constitutionality of mandated racial quotas, a watered down version of the original proposal passed in the House on September 9, 2010.

The approved statute removed mandated quotas in universities and the media, along with the public health care system's requirement to identify patients by race. The racial quota for political parties was reduced from 30 percent to 10 percent. The statute did establish the promotion of racial equality in guaranteeing spaces, if not actual quotas, in high schools and colleges for African Brazilians. It also mandated teaching African and African Brazilian history and culture in the public schools, providing government incentives for businesses with more than 20 employees and whose work force is at least 20 percent African Brazilian, and a term of up to three years in prison for those who practice racism on the Internet. The ruling also provided for a special office to accompany the implementation of the law, as well as prosecute violent police actions against African Brazilians.[76] On April 25, 2012, Brazil's Supreme Court in a 10 to 0 vote ruled in favor of racial quotas in public universities and in combating racial inequality more generally. This ruling ends the first of several legal challenges to programs at many of the Brazil's elite universities. The case was brought against the University of Brasilia in 1999 by the conservative Democratas Party (DEM). At least two challenges are outstanding against other universities. However the Supreme Court ruling should set a precedent.[77]

Conclusion

The Black Movement's articulation of an identity grounded in a positive valuation of blackness interrogates Brazil's whitening ideology and the European aesthetic bias that continues to permeate mass culture and holds sway over the public imagination in determining an individual's perceived worth. Activists seek to implement a binary racial order that distinguishes blacks (*negros*) from whites (*brancos*) in a manner similar to the U.S. one-drop rule.[78] They emphasize African ancestry and employ the term *negro* to replace the terms *preto* and *pardo* (although the latter is rarely used outside interactions with bureaucracies).[79]

Black Movement political organizations require de facto that participants identify as *negro*. They view multiracial identifiers as a strategy used by the white elite to undermine African Brazilian unity. Activists overlook, or outright re-

ject, the possibility of a multiracial identity formulated on egalitarian or antiracist premises.[80] This may also keep at bay individuals who sympathize with
Black Movement goals and unequivocally acknowledge they are the descendents of slaves, but cannot translate these sentiments into adopting *negro* as an
appropriate means of self-identification. Burdick suggests that this may orig-
inate in the awareness that their experiences have differed from darker-skinned
individuals. Schwartzman indicates that in everyday parlance, the term *negro*
is not consistently used to encompass both *pretos* and *pardos*. It is often restricted to individuals at the darker end of the phenotypical spectrum, and is
thus synonymous with *preto*.[81]

The one-drop rule was implemented to deny equality to African Americans,
but also had the unintended consequence of forging group identity. This, in
turn, enabled African Americans to mobilize in the Civil Rights Movement of
the 1950s and 1960s, which dismantled Jim Crow segregation and achieved
the passage of legislation ending legalized racial discrimination. Brazilian activists argue that the absence of the negative factor of legal discrimination and
the one-drop rule in Brazil has undermined African Brazilian unity in the
struggle against racism. Imposing ancestral definitions of racial identity in
Brazil is fraught with irreconcilable contradictions. African ancestry (not to
mention African phenotypical traits) is widespread, including among many
self-identified and socially designated whites.[82]

The 2010 census indicates that *brancos* decreased from 54 percent in 2000
to 48 percent in the 2010; the numbers of *pardos* increased from 40 percent in
2000 to 43 percent in 2010. The small increase in the numbers of *pretos* from
6.2 percent in 2000 to 7.6 percent in 2010 does not indicate a significant change
in normative racial identification.[83] These data do indicate that Brazil has an
African Brazilian (or non-white) majority. But *brancos* still compose almost
half of the population. Moreover, *pardos* make up the overwhelming majority of African Brazilians. Some attribute the growth in the numbers of African
Brazilians to the Black Movement's identity initiatives. Others consider this
more an opportunistic response to the perceived benefits of affirmative action.
Whatever the case, the Black Movement's identity politics has had a limited
impact on the masses.

The Black Movement has succeeded in undermining the racial democracy
ideology. Political discourse now includes references to "racial diversity" and
"multiculturalism" (egalitarian pluralism) instead of the traditional reference
to "racial unity" (egalitarian integration).[84] Group pluralism premised on a
distinct African Brazilian center of reference is considered a legitimate aspect
Brazil's racial order, compared to the traditional image of integration. In contrast to the Black Front and the Black Experimental Theater, group pluralism

is considered a tactic for dismantling (rather than fulfilling) the racial democracy ideology. Contemporary strategies seek the integration of African Brazilians as equals in terms of occupation, income, education, and political representation.

While Brazil has made progress in closing the gap between rich and poor, the nation's wealth remains highly concentrated. As the world's 10th largest economy, Brazil still has 53 million citizens living below the poverty line. More than 16.2 million individuals or 8.5 percent of the population live in extreme poverty, defined as family per capita income of 70 *reis* (US$43.70) or less per month. Statistics indicate that 63 percent of the 53 million individuals living in poverty and over 70 percent of those in extreme poverty are black and multiracial. These findings call attention to the primacy of race in determining social inequality.[85] Stanley Bailey and Edward Telles found, nevertheless, that some Brazilians cling to the myth of racial democracy, while others consider racial democracy an unfilled potential that may be realized in the future.[86]

Notes

1. This chapter borrows from G. Reginald Daniel's *Race and Multiraciality in Brazil and the United States: Converging Paths?* (University Park, PA: Pennsylvania State University Press, 2006).

2. The one-drop rule did not become a normative part of the legal apparatus in the U.S. until the early twentieth century (circa 1915) but gained currency as the informal or "commonsense" definition of blackness over the course of the seventeenth and eighteenth centuries. This was increasingly the case during the nineteenth century and definitively so by the 1920s (Daniel, viii–ix).

3. Oracy Nogueira, "Preconceito racial de marca e preconceito racial de origem (Sugestão de um quadro de referência para a interpretação do material sobre relações raciais no Brasil)," in *Tanto preto quanto branco: Estudo de relações racias,* ed. Oracy Nogueira (São Paulo: T.A. Queiroz, 1954, 1985), 78–9. *Preto, branco,* and *mulatto* are used in everyday parlance to refer respectively to black, white, and multiracial individuals. *Pardo* (which literally means brown) is more of an official term used to refer to multiracial individuals, particularly mulattoes.

4. Michael Omi and Howard Winant, *Racial Formation in the United States: From the 1960s to the 1990s.* 2nd edition (New York: Routledge, 1994), 55–56, 71–91.

5. Gilberto Freyre, *The Mansions and the Shanties.* Translated by Harriet de Onís (New York: Alfred A. Knopf, 1963a); Gilberto Freyre, *The Masters and the Slaves.* Translated by Harriet de Onís (New York: Alfred A. Knopf, 1963b); Gilberto Freyre, *Order and Progress.* Translated and edited by Rod W. Horton (New York: Alfred A. Knopf, 1970).

6. Oliver Cox, *Caste, Class, and Race: A Study in Social Dynamics* (New York: Monthly Review Press, 1970), 351–76; Carl N. Degler, *Neither Black nor White: Slavery and Race Relations in Brazil and the United States* (Madison, WI: University of Wisconsin Press, 1971), 213–38; Marvin Harris, *Patterns of Race in the Americas* (New York: Walker, 1964), 54–64, 79–94.

7. Degler, 213–38; Muriel Nazzari, "Concubinage in Colonial Brazil: the Inequalities of Race, Class, and Gender," *Journal of the Family* 21, No. 2 (April 1996): 108–24; Anthony John R. Russell-Wood, *The Black Man in Slavery and Freedom in Colonial Brazil* (London, Palgrave Macmillan, 1982), 30, 173, Júnia Ferreira Furtado, *Chica da Silva: A Brazilian Slave of the Eighteenth Century* (New York: Cambridge University Press, 2008), 65–68.

8. Nazzari, "Concubinage," 107–24; Russell-Wood, *The Black Man,* 176.

9. Donald Pierson, *Negroes in Brazil: A Study of Race Contact at Bahia* (Carbondale, IL: Southern Illinois University Press, 1967), 113.

10. John Hemming, *Amazon Frontier: The Defeat of the Brazilian Indians.* (London: Macmillan, 1987), 1–2; Anthony John R. Russell-Wood, "Colonial Brazil," in *Neither Slave nor Free: The Freemen of African Descent in the Slave Societies of the New World*, ed. David W. Cohen and Jack P. Greene (Baltimore, MD: Johns Hopkins University Press), 93, 109.

11. Degler, 213, 214, 226–38.

12. Herbert S. Klein, "Nineteenth-Century Brazil," in *Neither Slave nor Free: The Freemen of African Descent in the Slave Societies of the New World,* ed. David. W. Cohen and Jack P. Greene (Baltimore, MD: Johns Hopkins University Press, 1972), 309–34; Russell-Wood, "Colonial Brazil," 84–133.

13. Emilia Viotti da Costa, *The Brazilian Empire: Myths and History* (Chicago, IL: Uni-

versity of Chicago Press, 1985), 239–43.

14. John Burdick, "The Myth of Racial Democracy," *North American Congress on Latin America Report on the Americas* 25, no. 4 (February 1992): 40–42; Klein, "Nineteenth-Century Brazil," 309–34; Hartimus Hoetink *Slavery and Race Relations in the Americas: Comparative Notes on Their Nature and Nexus.* New York: Harper and Row, 1973, 108, Russell-Wood, "Colonial Brazil," 84–133.

15. Degler, 140. Hoetink, 197–98, 200, 201.

16. Anani Dzidzienyo, *The Position of Blacks in Brazilian and Cuban Society* (Minority Group Rights Reports, no. 7. London: Minority Rights Group), 1979, 2–11; Abdias do Nascimento, *Mixture or Massacre? Essays on the Genocide of a Black People.* Translated by Elisa Larkin Nascimento (Buffalo: Puerto Rican Studies and Research Center, State University of New York at Buffalo, 1979), 74–80; Thomas Skidmore, *Black into White: Race and Nationality in Brazilian Thought* (New York: Oxford University Press), 64–77.

17. Most European immigrants came from Italy, followed by Portugal and Spain, with Germany as a distant fourth. There were also arrivals from Syria, Lebanon, China, and Japan. These latter groups were outside the historical black-white framework; they had to carve out spaces that were largely unscripted. Some sought to achieve integration into the racial order as close as possible to whiteness and its privileges. Others formed pluralistic enclaves that sought to maintain distinct societies, or maintained identities as "hyphenated" Brazilians through various combinations of both of these trends. See Jeffrey H. Lesser, *Negotiating National Identity: Immigrants, Minorities, and the Struggle for Ethnicity in Brazil* (Durham: Duke University Press, 1999), 1–12, 168–73; Jeffrey H. Lesser, "Are African-Americans African or American?: Brazilian Immigration Policy in the 1920s," *Review of Latin American Studies* 4:1 (1991), 115–37; Teresa Meade and Gregory Alonso Pirio, "In Search of the Afro-American Eldorado: Attempts by North American Blacks to Enter Brazil in the 1920s," in *Luso-Brazilian Review* 25, No. 1 (Summer 1988): 58–110.

18. Charles H. Wood and José Alberto Magno de Carvalho, *The Demography of Inequality in Brazil* (New York: Cambridge University Press, 1988), 135–53.

19. Darien Davis, *Avoiding the Dark: Race and the Forging of National Culture in Modern Brazil* (Aldershot: Ashgate, 1999), 203; Skidmore, *Black into White,* 49–57.

20. Peggy Lovell-Webster, "The Myth of Racial Equality: A Study of Race and Mortality in Northeast Brazil," *Latinamericanist* (May 1987): 1–6; Thomas Skidmore, "Race and Class in Brazil: A Historical Perspective," in *Race, Class and Power in Brazil,* ed. Pierre-Michel Fontaine (Los Angeles: UCLA Center for African American Studies, 1985), 11–24.

21. John Burdick, "Brazil's Black Consciousness Movement." *North American Congress on Latin America Report on the Americas* 25, No. 4 (February 1992): 27; Pierre-Michel Fontaine, "Transnational Relations and Racial Mobilization: Emerging Black Movements," in *Ethnic Identities in a Transnational World,* ed. John F. Stack (Westport, CT: Greenwood Press, 1981), 141–62; Michael George Hanchard, *Orpheus and Power: The Movimento Negro of Rio de Janeiro and São Paulo, Brazil, 1945–1988* (Princeton, NJ: Princeton University Press, 1994), 111–19.

22. John Burdick, *Blessed Anastácia: Women, Race, and Popular Christianity in Brazil* (New York: Routledge, 1998), 60.

23. George Reid Andrews, *Blacks and White in São Paulo, Brazil, 1888–1988* (Madison, WI: University of Wisconsin Press, 1991), 146–56; Lelia González, "The Unified Black Movement: A New Stage in Black Mobilization," in *Race, Class and Power in Brazil,* ed.

Pierre-Michel Fontaine (Los Angeles: UCLA Center for African American Studies, 1985), 120–34; Hanchard, *Black Orpheus*, 104–29; Michael Mitchell, "Blacks and the Abertura Democrática," in *Race, Class and Power in Brazil*, ed. Pierre-Michel Fontaine (Los Angeles: UCLA Center for African American Studies, 1985), 120–34.

24. Thomas A. Skidmore, "Race Relations in Brazil." *Camões Center Quarterly* 4, No. 3-4 (1992–1993): 49–57.

25. Mac Margolis, "The Invisible Issue: Race in Brazil." *Ford Foundation Report* 23, No. 2 (Summer 1992): 3–7; Rebecca Reichmann, "Brazil's Denial of Race." *North American Congress on Latin America Report on the Americas* 28, No. 6 (1995) 35–45; Regina Domingues, "The Color of a Majority Without Citizenship." *Conexões: African Diaspora Research Project, Michigan State University* 4, No. 2 (November 1992): 6–7; Carlos Hasenbalg, "Race and Socioeconomic Inequalities in Brazil," in *Race, Class and Power in Brazil*, ed. Pierre-Michel Fontaine (Los Angeles: UCLA Center for African American Studies, 1985), 25–41.

26. Nelson do Valle Silva, "Updating the Cost of Not Being White in Brazil," in *Race, Class, and Power in Brazil*, ed. Pierre-Michel Fontaine (Los Angeles: UCLA Center for African American Studies, 1985), 42–55; Nelson do Valle Silva, "Racial Differences in Income in Brazil," in *Race Relations in Contemporary Brazil: From Indifference to Inequality*, ed. Rebecca Reichmann (University Park: Pennsylvania State University Press, 1999), 67–82; Nelson do Valle Silva and Carlos A. Hasenbalg, "Race and Educational Opportunity in Brazil," in *Race Relations in Contemporary Brazil: From Indifference to Equality*, ed. Rebecca Reichmann (University Park, PA: Pennsylvania State University Press, 1999), 53–66.

27. Burdick, "Brazil's Black Consciousness Movement," 23–27.

28. Antonio Sérgio Alfredo Guimarães, "Measures to Combat Discrimination and Racial Inequality in Brazil," in *Race Relations in Contemporary Brazil: From Indifference to Equality*, ed. Rebecca Reichmann (University Park, PA: Pennsylvania State University Press, 1999), 140; Edna Roland, "The Soda Cracker Dilemma," in *Race Relations in Contemporary Brazil*, 195–206; Skidmore, "Race Relations in Brazil," 55.

29. Congressman Afonso Arinos de Mello Franco introduced antidiscrimination legislation that prohibited racial discrimination in public accommodations. The bill passed as Law No. 1390 and became known as the 1951 Afonso Arinos Law. The law contained a very restricted definition of racial discrimination and treated infractions as misdemeanors rather than felonies. The law was in response to an incident involving Katherine Dunham, an internationally recognized African American dancer, while visiting São Paulo on tour in 1950. Dunham had advance reservations at a hotel, which had been confirmed in person by her white secretary. Yet she was denied entrance to the hotel (Daniel, *Race and Multiraciality*, 74, 240).

30. Guimarães, "Measures to Combat Discrimination," 140; Hasenbalg, "O negro nas vésperas do centenário," 79–96; Nobles, *Shades of Citizenship*, 109; Skidmore, "Race Relations in Brazil," 49–57. The constitution also affirmed protection of African Brazilian cultural practices and granted land titles to surviving occupants of *quilombos*, communities established by runaway slaves prior to emancipation in 1888 (See Htun 2005, 21).

31. Guimarães, "Measures to Combat Discrimination," 140.

32. Ibid., 140–41.

33. Benjamin Hensler, "Nao vale a pena (Not Worth the Trouble?) Afro-Brazilian Workers and Brazilian Anti-Discrimination Law," 30, No. 3, *Hastings International and Comparative Law Review* (Spring 2007), 267–346.

34. Dzidzienyo, *The Position of Blacks*, 9; Jan Rocha, "A Hundred Years of Servitude." *South* (August 1988), 21–25; Skidmore, "Race Relations in Brazil," 49–57.

35. Stephen Buckley, "Brazil's Racial Awakening: Multihued Nation Takes a New Look at Prejudice and Inequalities." *World News*, (June 12, 2000), A12; Burdick, *Blessed Anastácia*, 3; Nobles, *Shades of Citizenship*, 124.

36. Mark Wells, "Down in Black Bahia." *Brazzil*, June 2001 http://www.brazzil.com/pages/blajun01.htm/. The *Afro Permanente* is not a natural in the sense of wearing an Afro. It is more akin to the "Jheri Curl" of the 1970s and 1980s in the U.S. It turns "kinky hair" into a wet curly look that is achieved with a chemical treatment similar to that used in hair straightening.

37. Luiz Silva, "The Black Stream in Brazilian Literature." *Conexões: African Diaspora Research Project, Michigan State University* 4, No. 2 (1992), 12–13; Skidmore, "Race Relations in Brazil," 49–57.

38. Stephen Cornell and Douglas Hartmann, *Ethnicity and Race: Making Identities in a Changing World* (Thousand Oaks, CA: Pine Forge Press, 1998), 82; Livio Sansone, *Blackness Without Ethnicity* (New York: Palgrave Macmillan, 2003), 5, 16, 87–92, 104.

39. Buckley, "Brazil's Racial Awakening"; Ellis Cose, "Shaking Up 'Paradise': Brazil's Vocal Black-Identity Movement Creates a New Politics of Race." *Newsweek*, (March 9, 1998), 42–46; Diana Jean Schemo, "Among Glossy Blondes, A Showcase for Brazil's Black Faces." *New York Times*, (October 18, 1996), A13.

40. Zelbert Moore, "Reflections on Blacks in Contemporary Brazilian Popular Culture in the 1980s." *Studies in Latin American Popular Culture* 7 (1988): 213–26; Edward E. Telles, *Race in Another America: The Significance of Skin Color in Brazil* (Princeton, NJ: Princeton University Press, 2006), 155–56.

41. Era Bell Thompson, "Amalgamation Work in Brazil?" *Ebony*, (August 27–30, 1965), 32–34, 41.

42. "Crowning of Country's 1st Black Miss Brazil." *Jet*, (August, 29, 1986), 29. Jean (Gina) McPherson was a semi-finalist in 1960 but her racial designation is unclear.

43. Ann duCille, *The Skin Trade* (Cambridge: Harvard University Press, 1996), 27–28.

44. Stanley Bailey, "The Race Construct and Public Opinion: Understanding Brazilian Beliefs About Racial Inequality and Their Determinants." *American Journal of Sociology* 108, No. 2 (September 2002): 406–39; Burdick, *Blessed Anastácia*, 3, 32; Htun, "Racial Quotas for a Racial Democracy," 20–25.

45. Nobles, 124–26.

46. Nobles, 124–26; Reichmann, "Introduction," 5.

47. France Winddance Twine, *Racism in a Racial Democracy: The Maintenance of White Supremacy in Brazil* (New Brunswick, NJ: Rutgers University Press. 1997), 45, 53, 58–59, 61–63; Burdick, *Blessed Anastácia*, 3.

48. Burdick, *Blessed Anastácia*, 3; Nobles, *Shades of Citizenship*, 123–25, 127–28.

49. Daniel, 245.

50. Ibid., 244–46.

51. Elvira Oliveira, "Dia nacional da consciencia negra." *Nova Escola*, (November 1993): 23–25; Lori S. Robinson. "The Two Faces of Brazil; A Black Movement Gives Voice to an Invisible Majority," *Emerge* (October 1994), 38–42.

52. Skidmore, "Race Relations in Brazil," 49–57.

53. Burdick, *Blessed Anastácia*, 150.

54. Nobles, *Shades of Citizenship*, 123, 171–72.

55. In everyday parlance this is reflected in the increasing popular term *moreno* (or brunette). It can be used to describe a wide variety of phenotypes, including individuals who are designated as *preto, pardo,* or *branco* (if the latter have dark hair and eyes). See Nobles, *Shades of Citizenship*, 125. In polite conversation the term *moreno* is often used as a euphemism to avoid more specifically racialized terminology. For some, this may be an attempt to remove social bias from color designations. For others it may an attempt at whitening. See Edith Piza and Fúlvia Rosemberg, "Color in the Brazilian Census," in *Race Relations in Contemporary Brazil: From Indifference to Equality,* ed. Rebecca Reichmann (University Park, PA: Pennsylvania State University Press, 1999), 51.

56. Francisco Neves, "Two Brazils." *Brazzil,* May 1, 2002. http://www.brazzil.com/content/view/2562/68/; Marcelo Paixão, "Waiting for the Sun: Account of the (Precarious) Social Situation of the African Descendant Population in Contemporary Brazil." *Journal of Black Studies* 34, No. 6 (July 2004): 747–48; Instituto Brasileiro de Geografia e Estadísticas (IBGE). *Censo Demográfico 2000. Características gerais da população. Resultados da amostra. tabelas de resultados.* Rio de Janeiro: Fundação IBGE, 2000.

57. Marta Alvin, "Mixed Race, Mixed Up Feelings." *Brazzil,* (March 2002). http://www.brazzil.com/pages/cvr02.htm/; Kevin Hall, "Brazil Program Will Set Aside Jobs for Blacks: Government Plans to Address Inequities." *Detroit Free Press,* (June 21, 2002). http://www.freep.com/news/nw/nbrazil11_20011001/.

58. Htun, "Racial Quotas for a Racial Democracy," 2005, 24; Nobles, *Shades of Citizenship*, 123–24, 127; Reichmann, "Introduction," 23; Larry Rohter, "Racial Quotas in Brazil Touch Off Fierce Debate." *New York Times,* April 5, 2003. http://www.nytimes.com/2003/04/05/international/Americas/05BRAZ.html/; Telles, *Race in Another Country*, 76–77, 238, 261.

59. Guimarães, "Measures to Combat Discrimination," 143–53.

60. Pueng Vongs, J. Prakash, Marcelo Ballve, and Sandip Roy, "Around the World, Countries Grapple with Affirmative Action." *Pacific News Service,* July 11, 2003. http://news.pacificnews.org/news/view_article.html?article_id=3e26118fcdf4fba57da467da3eeb43d0/; Vongs et al. 2003.

61. Guimarães, "Measures to Combat Discrimination," 147–48; Sales Augusto dos Santos, "Ação afirmativa e mérito individual," in *Ações afirmativas: Políticas contra as desigualdades raciais,* ed. Renato Emerson dos Santos and Fátima Lobato (Rio de Janeiro: DP&A Editora, 2003), 83–126.

62. Guimarães, "Measures to Combat Discrimination," 147–48.

63. Jon Jeter, "Affirmative Action Debate Forces Brazil to Take Look in the Mirror." *Washington Post,* June 16 2003; Ricardo Rochetti, "Not as Easy as Black and White: The Implications of the University of Rio de Janeiro's Quota-Based Admissions Policy on Affirmative Action." *Vanderbilt Journal of Transnational Law* 37, No. 1423 (November 2004), http://web.lexisnexis.com/universe/document?_m=5eb66ec1eb9aff3afe64e92c41a1df60_docnum=3&wchp=dGLbVlb-zSkVb&_md5=0571753367a1a6b0fa45e7841eee1b9b/; Rohter, "Racial Quotas in Brazil Touch Off Fierce Debate."

64. Jeter, "Affirmative Action Debate"; Rohter, "Racial Quotas in Brazil."

65. Antonio Sérgio Alfredo Guimarães, "Ações afirmativas para a população negra nas universidades brasileiras," in *Ações afirmativas: Políticas públicas contra as desigualdades raciais,* ed. Renato Emerson dos Santos and Fátima Lobato (Rio de Janeiro: DP&A Editora,

2003), 75–82; Daniela Galdino and Larissa Santos Pereira, "Acesso à Universidade: Condições de Produção de um Discurso Facioso," in *Levando a raça a aério: Ação afirmativa e universidade*, ed. Joaze Bernardino and Daniela Galdino (Rio de Janeiro: P&A Editora, 2003), 157–72.

66. Luisa Farah Schwartzman, "Who are the Blacks? The Question of Racial Classification in Brazilian Affirmative Action Policies in Higher Education," *Cahiers de la Recherche sur l'Éducation et les Savoirs*, No. 7 (October 2008), 27–48.

67. The U.S. multiracial movement, which emerged since the dismantling of Jim Crow segregation, including the last laws against racial intermarriage in 1967, has moved the U.S. closer to a ternary racial order that has typified Brazil. By the 2000 census, this movement succeeded in making it possible for individuals to embrace a multiracial identity by checking more than one box in the census race question (See Daniel, 141–174, 201–236, 259–298).

68. Jeter; Rochetti, "Not as Easy as Black and White."

69. "Race in Brazil, Out of Eden"; Luisa Farah Schwartzman, "Seeing Like Citizens: Unofficial Understandings of Official Racial Categories in a Brazilian University," *Journal of Latin American Studies*, Vol. 41, Part 2, (May 2009): 221–250; Schwartzman, "Who are the Blacks?" 27–48.

70. Michael Astor, "Brazil Tries Quotas to Get Racial Equality." *Los Angeles Times*, February 29, A3, 2004; Raquel Villardi, "Acesso à universiadade por meio de ações afirmativas: Estudo da situação dos estudantes com matrícula em 2003 e 2004 (Junho)." UERJ (Universidade do Estado do Rio de Janeiro) Report, 2004, 3.

71. Schwartzman, "Seeing Like Citizens," 221–250; Schwartzman, "Who are the Blacks?" 27–48.

72. Schwartzman, "Seeing Like Citizens," 221–250; Schwartzman, "Who are the Blacks?" 27–48.

73. Jon Jeter, "Affirmative Action Debate Forces Brazil to Take Look in the Mirror." *Washington Post*, June 16, 2003.

74. Mario Osava, "Rights—Brazil: Blacks Demand Adoption of Promised Measures," Inter-Press Service News Agency, November 16, 2005. http://www.ipsnews.net/news.asp?id-news=31051/.

75. Michelle Amaral, "Brazil's New Racial Equality Law Is Watered Down. But Blacks Are Not Complaining," *Brazzil*, October 15, 2009, http://www.brazzil.com/component/content/article/209-october-2009/10278-brazils-new-racial-equality-law-is-watered-down-but-blacks-are-not-complaining.html.

76. Amaral, "Brazil's New Racial Equality Law"; Annie Gaisner, "Brazil Passes Racial Equality Law But Fails to Endorse Affirmative Action," *Guardian*, June 29 2010, http://www.guardian.co.uk/world/2010/jun/29/brazil-race.

77. Mari Hayman, "Brazilian Supreme Court Approves Racial Quotas in University," *The Latin American Dispatch* (April 29, 2012) http://latindispatch.com/2012/04/29/brazilian-supreme-court-approves-racial-quotas-in-university/.

78. Pierre Bourdieu and Loïc Wacquant, "On the Cunning of Imperialist Reason," *Theory, Culture, and Society* 16, No. 1: 41–58.

79. Schwartzman, "Seeing Like Citizens," 236.

80. Daniel, 293–4; Burdick, "The Lost Constituency," 150–52.

81. Schwartzman, "Seeing Like Citizens," 248.

82. Ali Kamel, *Não somos racistas: Uma reação aos que querem nos transformar numa*

nação bicolor. 2a impressão (Rio de Janeiro: Editora Nova Fronteira, 2006), 17–41, 49–57; Peter Fry and Yvonne Maggie, "Política Social de Alto Risco," in *Divisões perigosas: Políticas raciais no Brasil contemporâneo,* ed. Peter Fry and Yvonne Maggie, Marcos Chor Maio, Simone Monteiro, and Ricardo Ventura Santos (Rio de Janeiro: Civilização Brasileira, 2007), 277–81; Mike DeWitt and Adam Stepan, "Brazil in Black and White," http://www.pbs.org/wnet/wideangle/shows/brazil2/, 2007.

83. Taylor Barnes, "For the First Time, Blacks Outnumber Whites in Brazil." (May 24, 2011), http://www.miamiherald.com/2011/05/23/v-fullstory/2231323/for-the-first-time-blacks-outnumber.html#ixzz1Vjw8qUwa.

84. Nobles, *Shades of Citizenship,* 123–24, 127; Stanley R. Bailey, *Legacies of Race: Identities, Attitudes, and Politics in Brazil* (Stanford University Press, 2009), 190–224; Bailey, "The Race Construct and Public Opinion," 406–39.

85. Juliana Barbassa, "Brazil launches program to end extreme poverty," *The Boston Globe,* (June 2, 2011), http://www.boston.com/business/articles/2011/06/02/brazil_launches_program_to_end_extreme_poverty/; Ford Foundation 2011 http://www.fordfoundation.org/regions/brazil; Luciana Marques, "Um em cada dez brasileiros é extremamente pobre: Governo estabelece renda familiar per capita de 70 reais por mês como piso abaixo do qual cidadão já se encontra em situação de miséria." *Veja,* March 3, 2011, http://veja.abril.com.br/noticia/brasil/governo-define-valor-de-70-reais-para-extrema-pobreza; Ford Foundation. "Brazil: Overview," (2011), http://www.fordfoundation.org/regions/brazil.

86. Bailey, *Legacies of Race,* 119–226; Telles, 76–77.

Chapter 13

Afro-Puerto Ricans and Afro-Dominicans Online: Constructing Identities in Cyberspace

Ashley D. Aaron

In an age where for some, the internet is a part of everyday life, it is not surprising that many people use the World Wide Web as a space to freely articulate how they choose to define and identify themselves.[1] In particular, Afro-Latina/os have been making use of the internet as a platform to discuss their own history, culture, and identities. Lisa Nakamura, a leading scholar in both visual and digital studies, points out that "the internet as a privileged and extremely rich site for the creation and distribution of hegemonic and counterhegemonic ... images of racialized bodies."[2] This creation and distribution of counterhegemonic imagery is crucial to the construction of Afro-Latina/o identity, for its very presence is often contested in dominant discourse. It is counterhegemonic to proclaim existence within narratives which seek to erase Black bodies from Latinidad, or erase Latinidad from Black bodies.[3] To claim this space, whether online or in the 'real world,' is to claim visibility, to claim membership, and to claim *reality*. In this chapter, it is argued that the internet is filling a gap in the discourse of *Afrolatinidad*. The chapter examines how current theories about cultural production on the internet relate to the ways in which Afro-Latina/os online are discussing their identities.

Identity on the Internet

In their landmark book and study, *Web Theory*, Robert Burnett and David Marshall theorize that on the internet, " … a group of people of whatever size could easily express themselves, quickly acquire and convey knowledge [and] overcome misunderstandings."[4] In this respect, U.S. Afro-Latina/os on the web can connect with each other and with the larger society, combat invisibility, and document and express their own particularities of living *Afrolatinidad* in the United States. Burnett and Marshall also state that " … the internet allow[s] for the storage of large amounts of data from various sources that can be retrieved in turn by individuals at random who select only the information that interests them."[5] This has tremendous meaning for Afro-Latina/os seeking to explore and express their identity through the platform of the *World Wide Web*. One can 'virtually' come into contact with people, who, because of similar geopolitical spaces, cultures, and histories, reconceptualize and build communities based upon a shared participation in an experience of identity and identification. Furthermore, "The Web allows anyone to be a sender or a receiver, anyone can send or receive personal or mass messages, and information can be provided by many and accessed by many as a mass audience" but also "personal Web pages [or blogs] are an important component in the production of culture thesis, in that they allow individuals to become producers of media content [and] write the possibility of access to a mass audience that they normally would be unable to reach."[6] The mass audience attempting to be reached can be read as being other Afro-Latina/os, non-Black Latina/os, non-Latina/o Blacks, as well as the larger society in general. Afro-Latina/os have increasingly become producers of cultural content that documents and critiques their experiences of identity and identification in the United States. This use of the web as a social space to express and develop identities agrees with the " … conceptualization of the [internet as a tool or medium] of cultural production."[7]

Race on the Web

Although web theory attempts to tackle identity on the web, and understands that the internet, "is an elaborate hub for the formation of new collective identities," it does not interrogate what this means for racialized groups.[8] Its analysis is mostly limited to the identity 'tropes' of anonymity, language, narcissism, and gender—but does not interrogate how race and racial formation figure into the context/arena of cultural production on the internet. Nakamura expands the discourse by claiming that women and people of color are using the internet to dynamically articulate their communities, and express their own conceptions of their ethno-racial identities.[9] This chapter argues that Afro-Latina/os use the internet to vigorously express and narrate the particularities of their identities and identification in the United States.

In *Cultures of Internet: Virtual Spaces, Real Histories, Living Bodies*, Rob Shields acknowledges the internet both as increasing, " … a kind of empowerment to produce" in addition to " … becoming the preferred venue for pre-publication of articles, the airing of views and testing of ideas."[10] Indeed, a number of these Afro-Latina/os had published, were in the process of, or contemplating publishing some type of work [documentary, creative work, autobiographical, or testimony] that in some way relate to their experiences, identities, and ideas of *Afrolatinidades*. While conducting research for this chapter, one Afro-Latina had her work, *Hija de mi Madre*, self-published. The underground popularity of her work was due mainly to its proliferation and advertisement through various Afro-Latina/o blogs.

Afro-Latina/os Online

The following section will provide examples of eleven Afro-Latina/os who articulate *Afrolatinidad* online in ways which cover a range of issues relevant to Afro-Latina/o communities and their constructions of multi-faceted identities. These issues of *Afrolatinidad* usually express or engage a variety of topics that relate to their identity formation. These include how the concept of an Afro-Latina/o identity has empowered them in some way; a historic articulation and appreciation of the African presence in Latin America and their country of ancestry; a resistance to a state sponsored discourse which makes an Afro-Latina/o presence invisible; the relationship between colonization and a 'denial of Blackness'; an investigation of the ways in which racialization, Blackness or a Black consciousness are key components of the Afro-Latina/o experience; how *Afrolatinidad* displays an identity that is both Black and Latina/o and therefore transcends notions of mutual exclusivity; how *Afrolatinidad* is most often a transformative 'process' of identity development (and not something static), "which already exists, transcending place, time, history and culture;" and that claiming an Afro-Latina/o identity or consciousness is often both counter-hegemonic and liberating.[11]

The following section will provide eleven examples of personal online blogs that situate concepts of *Afrolatinidad* within their dialogues and narratives. These blogs have been chosen because of the ways the authors navigate fully integrated Black Latina/o identities in the United States. These sites also reveal that Afro-Latina/o identities are heavily influences by social realities and racialized experiences.

Afro-Latina/os in their Own Voices

Writer, activist, and blogger Alicia Anabel Santos describes how accepting an Afro-Latina/o identity empowered her, and gave her pride in both her heritage and her humanity. In her compelling testimony to *Afrolatinidad*, the author speaks of the ways *Afrolatinidad* is a revolutionary concept of identity dedicated to uncovering the invisibility of positive imagery of the African descended populations in the Dominican Republic's history, agenda, and nationalist discourse. What is more is that many Dominicans are often unaware of the cultural contributions of the African past in the Dominican Republic.[12] In writing that, "I am going to use Afrolatino, AfroDominican, Black Latina, Dominicana [as terms of self-identification]—all of it … because I am proud of what those labels mean to me," Santos is negotiating a sense of identity that returns the Afro-descended portion of her ancestry to the forefront.[13] To Santos, acknowledging and privileging her Afro-Dominican ancestry is a way in which in to speak back to certain discourses that would rather keep Blackness 'behind the ears' of the Dominican national imaginary.[14] While articulating her expression of what it means to 'claim' an Afro-Latina/o identity further, the writer asserts:

> YES—I do claim the AfroLatino definition! The definition as I understand it and as defined by the experts immersed and dedicated to this movement is the study of the African influence in Latino/Hispanic countries and the contributions of [B]lack people throughout Spanish speaking nations. I absolutely claim it and wear it with an incredible amount of pride that no one can take from me.[15]

In this narrative, Santos historicizes the African presence in her country of origin, a country which has traditionally concealed this part of their history from the national discourse. She also proudly claims the Afro-descended population's influence upon Dominican society and Dominican heritage. Santos demonstrates that for her, a privileging of *Afrodominicanidad* is a source of liberation, as well as a resistance to those who would rather her deny it. As an illustration of this statement, Santos has even used this empowerment as a catalyst for the creation of media which is committed to making the histories, contributions, and cultures of Afro-Latina/os visible. She further articulates that her multilayered [African, Spanish, indigenous Taino] heritage is something that strengthens and influences the conception of her identity. Santos centers her African ancestry as a point of departure in her ethnic formation, and claims that, "part of the strength that runs through my veins comes from the enslaved African who built our countries and those slaves that managed to hold on to their culture and faith in the face of a horrific history." [16]

Other Afro-Latina/os have been using the internet to speak back to discourse of another sort. Afro-Puertorriqueñas, such as Rebecca Lucret, use the internet as a platform to challenge and speak back to African Americans who have attempted to create a construction of Blackness, which excludes Black Latina/os from a definition of [or participation in] Blackness because of their dominant language use, cultural differences, and country of origin. The blogger readily exposes that the anti-Black racialization attributed to her mistreatment has been no different from the similar experiences of African Americans. Lucret declares:

> You tell me that I don't know what it's like to be Black in America. Oh but how I do! When most people see me, they see a Black face in America. They do not think that this dark-skinned woman is Afro-Latina. They do not see a Mexican in America. They do not see a Panamanian in America. They do not see a Colombian in America nor a Puerto Rican in America. They see my skin and there have been times, many in fact that I am treated unfairly because of it.[17]

In this critique, Lucret speaks of the ways in which Latinidad is racialized most commonly as *mestiza/o*, and as a result this *Puertorriqueña* is most often read as Black. She has endured the same anti-Black discrimination and prejudice felt by other Afro-descendants—it is not solely a trauma felt by African Americans. This testimony gives credence to the fact that African Americans are not the only ethnic group in the United States who experience and live Blackness in their everyday lives. In addition, Blackness is not synonymous with Black Americans. Many Black Caribbean, Afro-Latina/o, continental Black Africans, and others of African descent experience similar difficulties associated with anti-Black racism in the United States.

Afro-Latina/os and Residual Colonization

In addition to unveiling and exploring the anti-Black racism prevalent in their communities, other Afro-Latina/o authors/bloggers use online blogs to give exposure to the ways in which the residue of colonization continues to promote the glorification and privileging of all things Hispanic. As a result, colonized peoples have often internalized racist notions of the inferiority of African descent, and still try to distance themselves from it. This has been particularly widespread in Afro-Latina/o communities throughout the diaspora.[18] *Afro-Puertorriqueña* blogger Alicia Sanchez Gil describes this occurrence in a testimony with a fellow "very—I mean—very brown skinned Puerto Rican brother" who refused to acknowledge any part of his African or Black heritage or ancestry:

> We as Afro Latinos have such an influential history, and legacy! Do you think Columbus … created bomba, plena, or salsa y merengue? Hell no!! We did it! Yet with all of our insight and knowledge, we are so often slighted, just like much of the diaspora. We are taught to assimilate, and de-emphasize our African Roots![19]

She uses this experience as a transitionary opening, and proceeds to discuss the ways in which Afro-Latina/os have contributed tremendously to the history, culture, and traditions of Latin America, and how taking steps to re-claim and relearn this knowledge and heritage is a tool of empowerment.

What is particularly interesting to note about Gil's analysis of the Afro-Latina/o experience is her understanding of the often contrary notions of identity that abound in the different communities of African descendants in the diaspora. Though she also discusses the contributions of African descendants to the cultural productions and cultural traditions of Puerto Rico as astute and illuminated, her most sharp assessment is the ways in which racist colonial projects have been constructed to divide and separate Black populations in the Americas. She cites the differing racial projects of Haitians, native Black Americans, and those of African descent in the Spanish-speaking Caribbean. While Haitians and African Americans have been considerably more assured of their Blackness and Black-affirmed identities through memories of enslavement and membership in an African Diaspora—those of African descent from the Spanish-speaking Caribbean often lived a different reality and historical memory. These groups are much more likely to identify themselves as 'Spanish' because of their cultural traditions, colonial societies, and linguistic use.

Haitians, Gil remarks upon, do not see themselves as solely 'French,' and neither do African Americans [or Jamaicans and Trinidadians] see themselves as 'British' [or as White Americans do]. Gil finds this reverence to Spanish identity problematic, and describes the way this has achieved and promoted on the basis of colonial masters, language, and particularities of culture. Gil's testimony reflects her deconstruction of the period of enslavement and post-abolition being integrally apart of the racialization process in the Spanish-speaking Caribbean [though specifically Puerto Rico]. She remarks upon how the colonial project produced a distancing from an enslaved [and therefore African] past and the privileging of all things Hispanic, even to the extent of claiming it as one's sole racial and cultural identity.

Many Spanish-controlled colonies practiced miscegenation on a much higher scale than either French or British controlled colonies in the Americas. But Gil reasons that this does not excuse the wide scale rejection of an African ancestry and past. Many African Americans, like many Latina/os, do not have purely African ancestry as a component of their heritage—yet unlike African Americans, many African descended peoples from the Spanish-speaking Caribbean do not acknowledge a Black identity.[20] By acknowledging this "denial of [race] and race-issues," Gil speaks directly to those Latina/os of African descent who would rather deny its existence:

> Obviously, dismantling structures, policies and views about Black people that took more than 350 years to create (not to mention reinforcement throughout USA's continued colonization) cannot be undone in 100 years, especially when denial of race-issues is so fervent.[21]

In proclaiming her pride in her *Afrolatinidad*, Gil also impresses upon the reader that the colonization of the mind that has contributed to these issues have been constantly reinforced through Western notions of beauty, civilization, and history being told through the lens of the conqueror [Hispanic and other European powers]. Only by coming to terms with these "misconceptions about race and ignorance," and reeducating ourselves can we move "forward with a revolution, to expose to dishonesty in history and the racism that still exists."[22] Only by doing this, Gil claims, can we revolutionize ourselves.

Gil describes how Afro-Latina/os are subjected to a particular form of anti-Black racism hidden under the guise of racial democracy from within the non-Black Latina/o community, and also discusses the myth of a post-racial White dominant group in the United States. She cites a groundbreaking article, "How Race Counts for Hispanic Americans" published by John R. Logan of the Lewis Mumford Center for Comparative Urban and Regional Research. Logan's article is explicitly documented with quantifiable data that demonstrates that racialization affects Latina/os of *obvious* African descent in almost all aspects of their lives.[23] This article elucidates that regardless of educational attainment and job experience, Latina/os of obvious African ancestry still bring in less income than either White or 'Some other race/mixed' identified Latina/os. Gil argues that this phenomenon is related to the deeply entrenched racism in U.S. society, and she rejects many Latina/o claims that race is no longer an issue.

Gil further connects this occurrence to similar circumstances that are also played out in Latin America, and how they are transported even within Latina/o communities living in the U.S.[24] In arguing and presenting this information, blogger Gil is essentially rejecting the notion that both U.S. and Latin American [and as an extension Latina/o], societies are colorblind. She calls upon her fellow Afro-Latina/os and readers, to help our communities unlearn all the ignorance we have been indoctrinated with. Gil ends this entry of her blog with an appeal to a wider audience, proclaiming is, " ... anybody with me?"[25] If the number of online Afro-Latina/os using the internet as a forum of discussion and self-discovery is any measure, then, others are with her.

Reconstructing Latinidad

Throughout many blogs and personal websites, Afro-Latina/os online contribute to a discourse that deconstructs Latinidad which situates *mestizaje*; in essence the light-skinned mestiza of solely Indigenous and European heritage—as the normative imagery of Latina/os in both the United States and Latin America. Popular blogger and sexologist Bianca Laureno stated that, "I identify as a *LatiNegra*, a woman of Color, Afro-Puerto Rican, Black, Other, Caribbean and Latina."[26] By claiming this identity, Laureno is undermining the discourse of the Hispanic-race-as-melting-pot construction [which], in its most extreme form, ignores the *continuing* existence of [I] indigenous or African-descent populations in Latin America, and the same can be argued for its diaspora in the United States. Not everyone identities as *mestizo* or *mulatto*, and indeed, Laureno does not primarily identify as such either. In doing this, Laureno, in the context of Puerto Rico, is also destabilizing the "mythical White *jibaro* imagery represented by Puerto Rican cultural nationalism and [the] search for their Blackness outside the realm of Puerto Ricanness."[27]

Scholar and filmmaker Frances Negrón-Muntaner describes the 'mythical image of the White *jibaro*' as a "nineteenth century, mountain-dwelling White Spanish creolized Puerto Rican" which became the symbol of the elite White nationalist image of Puerto Rican roots, identity, and even as the "Puerto Rican's peoples true (White) soul."[28] Frances Negrón-Muntaner explains further that the 'mythical image of the White *jibaro*' was used for a number of reasons, including; that this representation of Puerto Rico affirmed the 'whiteness' and the "presumed (pure) descendants of the Spanish" and as Arlene Davila writes, the "African contribution to the *jibaro* is never acknowledged or emphasized, as neither is a female gender identity."[29] This image of Puerto Rico, while acknowledging the history of the former peasant culture of Puerto Rico, at the same time, excludes the role of women and the large number of enslaved African descended portions and representations of the island's ancestry.

Another narrative of *Puertorriquenidad* that disrupts the dominant state-sponsored White imagery is that of Black Puerto Rican TV personality and former MTV veejay, Alani "LaLa" Vazquez. On *Latina* magazine's online blog, the TV personality decides to use the internet as a stage to articulate her often 'misunderstood' [or misrecognized], Afro-Latina/o identity. She explains that:

> A lot of people don't realize that I'm Latina, which is fine. One thing about being Latina is that there isn't one look that comes with the territory. I don't expect people to know my cultural background just by glancing at me. I do, however, expect that when I tell people my family is from Puerto Rico, that I will be believed and not accused of trying to be something that I'm not. [Such persons express] … their shock over these realizations for any number of reasons–and common responses are, "You don't look Latina" and "I thought you were Black!" I never said I wasn't Black. *And since when does being Black and being Latina have to be mutually exclusive?* [emphasis added].[30]

Vazquez's articulation of her own identity seems to be a response to those who attempt to deny or question either her Blackness or Puerto Ricaness—it is a response to those who view these two facets of her identity as juxtaposing. This is because of her being racialized as a light-skinned Black woman, and not usually imagined as "some peoples idea of a typical" Puerto Rican—which in the eyes of the media is similar to that of Jennifer Lopez or Ricky Martin.[31] Puerto Rican then, is not normally constructed as Black.[32] Vazquez expresses frustration with society's repeated attempts to marginalize either her 'race' or her 'ethnicity' in ways that seek to erase her Black Puerto Rican body.[33] Accusations of trying to pretend she is something she is not have been leveled at the celebrity, when in actuality—she is both. The particular way she challenges these fundamentally non-Black representations as being the 'typical' look of a Puerto Rico can be understood in the way she proclaims, "and since when does being Black and being Latina have to be mutually exclusive?"[34] In Vazquez' assessment, it becomes obvious that they need not be seen as such, for she, as a Black Puerto Rican, is also an example of what one looks like.

Laureno also disrupts Latinidad that tunes out Blackness by highlighting Latinas of African descent through the grassroots internet-based *Latinegr@s Project*, a grassroots project. Through interviews, history lessons, personal testimonies, and anything else submitters care to share about the African diaspora, everything is shared on one blog entirely dedicated to making *Latinegras* [an alternative term of identification that references Afro-Latina/o heritage] and their experiences visible. In this way, Laureno is expressing a Puerto Rican identity in the U.S. that actively positions Blackness.[35] In addition, she positioned a Black heritage which lays claim to a deliberate and particular identity of Latinidad.

Processes of Afrolatinidad

Many, if not the majority of the Afro-Latina/os using cyberspace to articulate their own conceptions of *Afrolatinidad*, describe at least one way in which an Afro-Latina/o identity was one which they had learned. Moreover, it has been a process in which they came to see their unique experience of both Blackness and Latinidad in the United States as being an Afro-Latina/o one. A '*Latinegr@s Project*' interview with blogger and author Sofia Quintero, a self-described Afro-Latina/Latinegr@, stated that her position as an Afro-Latina [of Puerto Rican and Dominican descent]:

> *Was a process and not a moment* [emphasis mine]. This sense of myself was always there, and one tends to take for granted what is always there, especially if it is accompanied by vulnerability. Still I remember at times being a child and referring to myself as Spanish knowing all the while that this was false. So false that I did not even want it to be true even as I claimed it.[36]

In this way, because of her racialization as a person of color and Spanish speaking, Quintero recognized very early on that 'Spanish' was not fully encompassing or indicative of her ethno-racial identity, experience, and culture. Quintero theorizes that this identity consciousness was not a specific or static 'moment' but rather, a process of becoming. This was a process that was also heavily influenced by her location. Moreover, it was also a process of coming into this idea of an Afro-Latina/o consciousness. Quintero goes on to describe her ethno-racial identity in multifaceted ways that are ultimately summed up as an Afro-Latina. Quintero writes:

> Among countless other things, I am: Afro-Latina, Puerto Rican and Dominican, a Black woman … *hija de la Pura y el Negro*, a feminist, a radical, a cultural activist, a Bronxite … [and though] I tend to use Afro-Latina, I like Latinegr@, too. I also have no problem just being called Black since my Latinidad is a given. To be Latin@ yet claim one's Blackness in a world that is constantly devaluing "Negritude" is, I believe, an act of healing and resistance.[37]

Although indirectly implied in many expressions of Black consciousness within Latinidad, Quintero's testimonial touches on an aspect of *Afrolatinidad* that is, in this case, explicitly stated. This is the concept of *Afrolatinidad* as being an identity that serves to both 'heal and resist.' This is the concept of *Afrolatinidad* [or particular constructed identities] as being both counter-hegemonic and liberating.[38] Her embracing of the ideologies of 'Negritude' is particularly intriguing in that it is a philosophy or world view that singularly rejects the imposed colonial notion that Black is not a component of one's heritage or identity that is worthy of dignity.[39]

There is also a component of *Afrolatinidad* that seems to encompass pride and empowerment of a previously stigmatized ancestry and identity. *New Latina* Blog interviewee and Afro-Puerto Rican Eusebia Aquino-Hughes states:

> I self-identify as a proud Afro-Latina of Puerto Rican/African [descent]. It is an honor for me and many in my family to respect ... our African roots ... and [I] hope that our Latino community does the same .... Our proud African roots have given contributions to our music, foods, arts, language.[40]

The emphasis on ancestral pride here should not be overlooked. The historical legacy of suppressing the African legacy in Latin America has resulted in many Latina/os of African descent denying their African roots.[41]

Aquino-Hughes declares that it is an honor to acknowledge her African ancestry and the contributions that African descended populations have made to the culture of Latin America and their descendants in the United States. In this way, Aquino-Hughes participates in a restoration of dignity and humanity to a people who have historically been denied such.[42] In this way, Aquino-Hughes and others position themselves as being equally and proudly Latina/o and of African descent.

In a similar way, *AOL* blogger, Mariel Concepcion take pride and has a profound acceptance in both her African and Latina/o [Dominican] heritage as components of her identity.

> Depending on where I am in the world, I am considered Latina [because of] my thick Spanish accent—or, because of my "light brown" skin color and the texture of my tresses, Black .... At the end of it all, acceptance comes from within and, [like Zoe] Saldana, I am a Black woman too. I "fit the mold" physically and culturally, and thanks to my African roots which I embrace wholeheartedly, from the inside out.[43]

She also speaks to the ways in which she is racialized as Black, but also marked as Latina because of language use and accent. In addition to a variety of other factors, Concepcion locates both her upbringing in a Spanish-speaking immigrant household and her phenotype as being instrumental to her identity and place. It is in light of these multi-faceted elements of self that she positions herself as a self-described Afro-Latina, who embraces and is proud of both aspects of her ethno-racial identity.

Self-described Afro-Boricua Reggaetonero/rapper and activist Tego Calderón Rosario [known most recognizably as Tego Calderón], is noted for his tremendous influence among many Latina/o youth. Throughout his music and personal life, Calderón regularly proclaims his pride in a Black Latino heritage, and calls for other Black Latina/os to organize and do the same. In an article that was circulated widely online by Afro-Latina/os and non Afro-Latina/os alike, Calderón states:

> Young Black Latinos have to learn their story. We also need to start our own media, and forums and universities. We are treated like second-class citizens …. They have raised us to be ashamed of our Blackness. It's in the language too. Take the word denigrate—*denigrar*—which is to be less than a negro …. This is not about rejecting whiteness rather; it's about learning to love our Blackness—to love ourselves. We have to say *basta ya*, it's enough, and find a way to love our Blackness. They have confused us—and taught us to hate each other—to self-hate and create divisions on shades and features.[44]

By centering Afro-Latina/os in his message, Calderón is performing a counter-hegemonic expression of Black Latina/o identity and presence. He is resisting the dominant narrative in both the U.S. and Latin America which makes and positions Blacks as inferior, serves to make Afro-Latina/os feel "ashamed of our [B]lackness," and calls upon other African descended Latina/os to acknowledge this ancestry, claim it, and learn to take pride and 'love' it instead. By declaring *basta ya* (it's enough), Calderón is plainly stating that it is time to construct an identity that privileges and restores the agency and humanity of those of African ancestry—in all its 'shades and features.'[45]

Narratives of Afro-Latina/o Identity

Another narrative of an Afro-Dominican/Afro-Latina identity that acknowledges Blackness as well as Latinidad is that of aspiring actress and blog interviewee Vianessa Castaños, as she describes what the term Afro-Latina/o means to her and her own concept of identity:

> An Afro-Latina is just what the name implies, someone of Latin (or Hispanic) descent that has a predominantly African ancestry … I usu-

ally just describe myself as Dominican or Afro-Caribbean. I'll occasionally identify with Afro-Latina, but never just 'Latina'... I am 100% Dominican of West African, French, Spanish and Chinese decent. Rumor has it that there is some *Taino* blood in us as well .... It is no secret that racism is deep rooted in our country's history. No one wants to claim to be Black and being called 'negro' is often considered insulting. It makes no sense whatsoever since about 75% of the island is of African descent.[46]

An additional concept of online Afrolatinidad that frequently occurs is the 'outing' of racist ideologies prevalent or expressed in the Afro-Latina/o community—self-identified or not. An 'outing' is actually quite remarkable when one considers that most of these Latin American and Caribbean countries are heralded by many people as being racially harmonious societies [countries without racism]. Castaños describes this racial state of affairs as the ways in which racism is deeply entrenched in the national rhetoric of the country, and how these ideologies have been internalized and reproduced. This racialization of Castaños' body began to be remarked upon by others at a very early age, very likely contributing to her identifying with being an Afro-Latina.

In the following narrative, poet, author, and blogger [and self-described Black Latino] *Latinegro* situates a historical presence of African descended peoples in the Caribbean and Latin America. He offers background information that eventually provides relevance for "why my skin is dark" and why "this identity that I have will always be a part of me."[47] What the author is doing here, like in many other of the narratives provided, is 'outing' the racial ideologies of the region, as well as talking back to a discourse which makes his ancestry invisible in the construction of Latinidad, and as a result, Latina/os in the U.S. *Latinegro* asserts:

I want people to understand that I am very proud to say that I am Afro-Latino. I understand why my skin is dark. I understand the African roots of my culture that includes the music, culture, and religion .... So let me define what *latinegros* are in my own words: Latino Negros can be identified as dark skinned Latinos. Often times they will be referred to as Afro Latinos or Black Latinos. In the various Latino cultures throughout the Caribbean and Latin America, they represent the bottom of the social ladder. They are normally the poor and uneducated. The term Latino Negro is a not a term that is recognized nor used, but it is something I feel best represents what I am in relation to other Latinos. This is who I am.[48]

The writer argues that his racialization as Black has been instrumental throughout his process of navigating Latinidad and claiming *Latinegro*. He also discusses the experiences of Black people throughout the Americas as ignored members of society, and ends by acknowledging both the invisibility and marginalization of his community, and the empowerment of his own self-identification.

Conclusion

Many Afro-Latina/os have used the internet as a site to express and rearticulate their identities. From blogs, to interviews, to online forums and chat rooms, Afro-Latina/os are redefining the identity of people of African descent in the Americas. The world wide web has provided many Afro-Latina/os with an accessible space to freely articulate how they choose to define, discuss, and identify themselves. In the same vein, the online community brings together people throughout the nation who are physically dispersed, yet connected by similar understandings of their ethno-racial selves. They are contributed to a rich discussion occurring online, one people of color have been increasingly using for just such reasons.[49] Afro-Latina/os have re-centered their experience into the larger discourse of African diasporic peoples rearticulating their identities, based upon their own terms.[50] From issues ranging from discrimination, to marginalization, to internalized racism, and historical denial, Afro-Latina/os are simultaneously navigating the complexities surrounding an identity that seeks to claim a fully Black Latina/o identity in all aspects of their social realities.

In the aforementioned narratives, Afro-Latina/os have used the internet as a " … site of incredible cultural consumption and cultural production."[51] The internet has become a platform that many Afro-Latina/os creates spaces of expression and self-definition. Afro-Latina/os online have documented their rich experiences, and produced and maintained narratives of themselves within these sites. In addition, the internet becomes a critical space to develop counterhegemonic identities, and build communities and networks built around these identities. [52] Burnett and Marshall argue that research which investigates online identity and other aspects of cyber culture " … [has] led to a radical deconstructive effect on both identity and culture."[53] What is assuredly evident is that this has been the case of those contributing to the discourse of a transformatively deconstructive consciousness of *Afrolatinidad* online.

The irony here is that many choose white. They are *not* choosing American Indian, or African. Latinos, like the Louisiana Creoles have histories that obfuscate their ethnic multiplicity, linguistic uniqueness, and the everyday realities they experience as people multiracial descent who cannot be categorized as monoethnic/cultural.

Notes

1. Lisa Nakamura. *Digitizing Race: Visual Cultures of the Internet* (Minneapolis: Minneapolis University Press, 2008), 10.

2. Ibid., 13.

3. Yoku Shaw-Taylor and Steven Tuch, *The Other African Americans Contemporary African and Caribbean Immigrants in the United States,* (Lanham, Maryland: Rowman & Littlefield Publishers, 2007).

4. Robert Burnett and P. David Marshall, *Web Theory: An Introduction* (New York: Routledge, 2003), 58.

5. Ibid., 47.

6. Burnett and Marshall, 48-50.

7. Ibid., 77.

8. Ibid., 73.

9. Nakamura, 20.

10. Rob Shield, ed., *Cultures of Internet: Mutual Spaces, Real Histories, Living Bodies* (Thousand Oaks, CA: Sage Publications, 1996), 3.

11. Stuart Hall, "Cultural Identity and Diaspora," in *Theorizing Diaspora*, ed. Jana Evans Braziel and Anita Mannur (Oxford: Blackwell Publishers, 2003), 225.

12. Kimberley Eison Simmons, *Reconstructing Racial Identity and the African Past in the Dominican Republic* (Gainesville: University Press of Florida, 2009), 4.

13. Alicia Anabel Santos [DiosaDominicana], "Response: Don't Dare Call Me Afro-Latino!" April 29, 2010. Weblog entry. *Finding Your Force: A Journey to Love.* http://find ingyourforce.blogspot.com/2010/04/don't-dare-call-me-afrolatino.html.

14. Ginetta B. Candelario, *Black Behind the Ears: Dominican Racial Identity from Museums to Beauty Shops* (Durham, NC: Duke University Press, 2008).

Simmons, 2009.

15. Santos, "Response: Don't Dare Call Me Afro-Latino," 2010.

16. Ibid.

17. Rebecca Lucret [Morenas-Bohio]. "On Not Being Black Enough" *Morena's Bohio.* Weblog Entry. October 15, 2009. http://morenas-bohio.blogspot.com/.

18. Simmons, 2009.

19. Alicia Sanchez Gil [ManifestFreedom], ¿Y tu abuela, donde esta? Weblog entry. *Freedom Fighter: Our Existence is an act of Resistance.* March 13, 2010. http://manifestfree-dom.wordpress.com/2010/03/13/y-tu-abuela-donde-esta/.

20. Sanchez Gil, ¿Y tu abuela, donde esta? 2010.

21. Ibid.

22. Ibid.

23. John R. Logan, Hyoung-jin Shin, and Jacob Stobwell, "How Race Counts for Hispanic Americans," Lewis Munford Center for Comparative Urban and Regional Research, July, 14, 2003.

24. Ibid.

25. Sanchez Gil, ¿Y tu abuela, donde esta? 2010.

26. Bianca Laureno, [LatinoSexuality]. "LatiNegr@s Project: My Testimonio," Weblog Entries. February 14, 2010. http://latinosexuality.blogspot.com/search/label/latine-gros%20project.

27. Jossianna Arroyo, "Roots' or the virtualities of racial imaginaries in Puerto Rico and the diaspora." *Latino Studies* 8 (2010), 198.

28. Frances Negrón-Muntaner, *Boricua Pop: Puerto Ricans and the Latinization of American Culture* (New York: New York University Press, 2004), 216-217.

29. Ibid., 218-219.

30. Alani "Lala" Vazquez, "Personal Essay: Yo Soy Boricua," *Latina*, January 18, 2010. http://www.latina.com/entertainment/celebrity/personal-essay-yo-soy-boricua.

31. Negrón-Muntaner, *Boricua Pop: Puerto Ricans and the Latinization,* 2004.

32. Yeidy M. Rivero, *Tuning out Blackness: Race and Nation in the History of Puerto Rican Television* (Durham, North Carolina: Duke University Press Books, 2005).

33. Ibid.

34. Ibid.

35. Arroyo, " 'Roots' or the virtualities," 2010.

36. Sofia Quintero, interview on Bianca Laureno's '*LatiNegr@s Project*' February 26, 2010. http://latinosexuality.blogspot.com/search/label/latinegrosproject.

37. Quintero, '*LatiNegr@s Project,*' February 26, 2010.

38. Andrew Jolivétte, *Louisiana Creoles: Cultural Recovery and Mixed-race Native American identity* (Lanham, MD: Lexington Books, 2006), 5.

39. Souleymane Diagne, "Négritude," The Stanford Encyclopedia of Philosophy (Summer 2010 Edition), Edward N. Zalta (ed.) http://plato.stanford.edu/archives/sum2010/entries/negritude.

40. Eusebia Aquino-Hughes and Vianessa Castaños, et al. "Afro-Latinas—Finding A Place To Belong" *New Latina*. Weblog Entry. March 20, 2011. http://newlatina.net/afro-latinas-finding-a-place-to-belong/.

41. Godreau, I. "Folkloric 'Others': Blanqueamiento and Celebration of Blackness as an Exception in Puerto Rico." In *Globalization and Race. Transformations in the Cultural Production of Blackness*, eds., K.M. Clark and D. Thomas (Durham, NC: Duke University Press, 2006), 171–187.

42. Lillian Comas-Diaz, "LatiNegras: Mental Health Issues of African Latinas," in *The Multiracial Experience: Racial Borders as the New Frontier*, ed., Maria P. Root (Thousand Oaks, CA: Sage Publications, 1996).

43. Mariel Concepcion. "Am I Black Enough For You? A Latina Talks Race, Ethnicity & Identity." Weblog entry. *The BVX: AOL Black Voices.* March 18, 2010. http://www.the-bvx.com/2010/03/18/am-i-black-enough-for-you-a-latina-talks-race-ethnicity-and-iden/.

44. Tego Rosario Calderón. "Black Pride (Orgullo Negro): Latin America needs its own Civil Rights Movement says the World-Famous Rapper." *New York Post*, February 15, 2007. http://www.nypost.com/seven/02152007/tempo/black_pride_tempo_tego_Calderón.htm.

45. Ibid.

46. Vianessa Castaños, et al. "Afro-Latinas," 2011.

47. Latinegro [Anthony Otero]. "Afro is Latino" Weblog Entry. *Latinegro.* October 12, 2009. http://latinegro.blogspot.com/2009/10/afro-is-latino.html.

48. Ibid.

49. Nakamura, 10.

50. Michelle A. Hays. *I've Been Black in Two Countries: Black Cuban Views on Race in the U.S.* (El Paso: LFB Scholary Publishing, 2009).

51. Burnett and Marshall, 59.

52. Nakamura, 2008.

53. Ibid., 62.

Chapter 14

Louisiana Creoles and Latinidad: Locating Culture and Community

Andrew Jolivette & Haruki Eda

Connecting Latinidad to the Louisiana Creoles might seem like a stretch, but for others, it makes perfect sense. After all, the Creole people of Louisiana who self-identify as multiracial can directly connect their ancestry and culture to the people of France, West Africa, Spain, and to the Indigenous people of the Americas. More importantly, the history of colonialism that created the people of Latin America and the Caribbean is the same social, political, economic, linguistic, and cultural process that produced the Creole culture in the state of Louisiana. This "new" culture, *raza* or *people* came into existence long before the United States achieved independence. Some might argue that the Louisiana Purchase Treaty of 1803, like the Treaty of Guadalupe Hidalgo in 1848, created a division between the Latin-based Creoles of the North and the Latin-based cultures of the South.

The similarities are striking. The 1803 Treaty between France and the United States surrendered fourteen states to the Americans while at the time doubling the size of the country. The Treaty of 1848 surrendered at least seven states to the United States. Both of these treaties created artificial borders that continue to exist to this day. They have negated the rights of the Indigenous people living in these vast territories for centuries, and then through a second colonizing process from the perspective of the "new" raza/people of Louisiana and Mexico (who were the descendants of the Indigenous, the African, and the Latin) the communities and land were once again being divided, sold, and re-constructed in the image of Anglo-America. This is the history that ties the Louisiana Creole to the Latin Diaspora, a term that encompasses a history where cultures intermingled to produce a hybrid people of Indigenous, African, and Latin ancestry, spirituality, language, and culture.

Latinidad: Multiple Intersections

Past and present, Louisiana has always represented the Latin America/ Caribbean of the North. This is evident in the amalgamation of Indigenous-African-Latin based food preparation, the creation of new forms of linguistic communication, the resistance to Anglo-Saxon culture, and in the very transcultural and transnational flow that has always existed between Louisiana and the rest of Latin America and the Caribbean. Scholars of Creole history have traced this transnational, transcultural process of Latinidad by documenting the migratory movement back and forth between Havana, Cuba, Hispaniola (present day Haiti/Dominican Republic), and Mexico (especially to the states of Veracruz and Tamaulipas), in addition to recent work that traces the permanent re-settlement of Louisiana Creoles throughout the Latin Diaspora.[1]

In a contemporary context, some ethnic studies scholars argue that Louisiana Creoles belong more properly within the African or African American Diaspora. The authors of this chapter suggest that Latinos, like Creoles, are both part of a larger African Diaspora and that there are multiple categories within the African Diaspora. There are certainly at least two, if not more, categories within the African Diaspora in the Americas—an Anglo based African Diaspora, and a Latin based African Diaspora. In the Latin based African Diaspora there is the influence of mixed-blood Indigenous, African, and Latin based European cultures. In the Anglo based African diaspora, there is also a mixture. However, it is derived from Anglo traditions, and from very different historical processes that do not include treaty making or nation-to-nation relationships. Thus, for Louisiana Creoles identifying culturally, ethnically, socially, and linguistically with Latinidad, it is about locating culture and community in a specific, rather than a generalized context. According to Lisa Peñaloza, Latinidad is:

> a sensibility and way of being-in-the-world that expresses who one is and what one's culture is about. This quality emanates from a community of very diverse people and is used by them to relate to one another, drawing from their similarities, even as they contest it based on their differences.[2]

This sensibility is what connects Louisiana Creoles and all Latinos to a common culture, community, and collective group history. Despite this common colonial history, there are still obvious debates, tensions, and contestations over both the terminology and the history itself. From an Indigenous perspective, whether mixed-blood or not, we are not, nor have we ever been in a post-colonial moment. Significant decolonization requires a serious reconciliation of not only terminology, but necessitates a deconstruction of the dichotomy between the mixed blood and the Indigenous. Peñaloza explains this complex relationship:

> Born at the multiple intersections of Native American peoples, Europeans, and Blacks, it connotes an amalgam of ritual traditions and values—amor, familia, respeto, compromisos, pasion; that is, love, family, respect, accomplishment, and a passion for living—at once very real, yet imagined, dynamic and organic. The geographical coordinates of its diaspora are no less-complex in pertaining to those of Latin American ancestry in the US and in Central and South American nations, the Caribbean, Spain, and, to a lesser degree, southern Italy and France. Like other social phenomena, it is individually and collectively engineered and reproduced; internally by Latinos/as, and externally, as attributed to us by non-Latinos/as.[3]

Latinidad, then, is about the multiple intersections of different worlds colliding together under a colonial force. While hegemonic and destructive, this force was, and continues to be, a racial project resisted and reshaped by the people themselves, not as passive recipients, but as real actors and agents who have also shaped the outcomes of the 'Americas' that we now call home. In the same way the Indigenous peoples of the Americas continue to exist and resist colonialism, so too do their mixed blood descendants continue to examine the very meaning and definition of community.

While the racial definition of Creoles of Color has changed over time from *gens de couleur libre* (free people of color/Latin) to Creole, to colored, to Black, and now back to Creole again (or one could argue to Afro-Latin), there does exist some form of cultural continuity that persists among Creoles, be it religious, linguistic, or social. There is something that links the cultural experience of multiethnic Latin communities such as Creoles. This is a phenomenon that transcends biological and sociopolitical frameworks articulated by race theories and geographic nationalism. By linking Creoles of Color to a theory of Latinidad and transcontinental diasporic formation, one is able to make connections between the multiple groups that have come to form contemporary Creole consciousness within an Afro-Latin and Indigenous diaspora across the Americas and the Caribbean. Paul Gilroy states:

> Striving to be both European and Black requires some specific forms of double consciousness. By saying this I do not mean to suggest that taking either or both of these unfinished identities necessarily exhausts the subjective resources of any particular individual. However, where

racist, nationalist, or ethnically absolutist discourses orchestrate political relationships so that these identities appear to be mutually exclusive, occupying the space between them or trying to demonstrate
their continuity has been viewed as a provocative and even oppositional act of political insubordination.[4]

In 2011, Creoles are refuting these absolutist notions of identity construction and community location. Gilroy's work is useful in terms of thinking
about the ways in which Louisiana Creoles throughout the United States, Latin
America, and the Caribbean are connected culturally and transnationally to
other multiethnic Indigenous populations. To reduce the relationship of mixed
bloods today to a dichotomy of extremes where you deny the material impact
of colonial interaction is to deny a specific historical process that is continually unfolding. The Louisiana Creole experience in contrast to other Creole
populations throughout the Afro-Latin diaspora has been constructed within
a U.S. specific paradigm for understanding identity as based purely on racial
as opposed to cultural experiences.

These experiences are typically defined within the U.S. context in terms of
"completeness," "totality," and "objectivity." According to James Clifford, "ethnographic truths are inherently *partial*-committed and incomplete. This point is
now widely asserted-and-resisted at strategic points by those who fear the collapse of clear standards of verification. But once accepted into ethnographic art
[daily life experiences], a rigorous sense of partiality can be a source of representational tact [read as representational accuracy].[5] To understand the Louisiana
Creole, this discourse attempts to locate their experiences historically, socially,
and culturally within the contemporary context of Latinidad. Does this suggest that Creoles are themselves Latinos? Not quite. The inference here is that
Creoles who self-identify as multi-ethnic and multi-cultural hybrid people
share a specific colonial experience of ethnic mixing that is uniquely Latin.

The distinct tradition known as Carnival across the Caribbean and Latin
America (known as Mardi Gras in Louisiana) demonstrate how three diverse
populations came together in often painful ways to form something unique to
the Americas. Today, this is captured in the expression of the word Latinidad.
This is why we can also observe similarities in foodways as illustrated with
items such as *chicharrón* from various Latin American countries and *graton*
(cracklin) in Louisiana, in blood sausage or *boudin*, or in King Cake during Mardi
Gras and *Rosca de Reyes* (Mexico)—both baked circular breads with a little
plastic baby Jesus stuffed on the inside. In both traditions, the person who receives the slice with the baby Jesus must bring the tamales or King Cake to the
next celebration. These are but a few examples, and t the similarities are inevitable

given the linguistic, religious, geographic, and cultural similarities of Louisiana Creoles and Latinos. In these traditions, the mutual identities and communities can be located in a sphere of multiplicity not singularity.

Latinidad is a much more encompassing term than Latino, which continues to experience contested meaning within the U.S. and across Latin America. There is no mutual agreement about the best terminology for Latinos or Creoles, and therefore this chapter is about shifting from a simple ethnic/racial category to an epistemological or cosmological definition. This epistemological and cosmological way of being is basically a philosophy of lived experience that speaks to how communities see themselves and the world around them based on who they have been, how they have changed, and who they are becoming under a common ethno-linguistic and culturally specific worldview. This chapter is also about moving beyond borders and spaces that falsely create a sense of singular, monolithic, meanings and socio-political identities.

Louisiana Creoles

To locate Louisiana Creoles within an Indigenous, Afro-Latin framework situates Creoles as members not only of the United States, but more significantly as citizens of the Americas. To continue on a course toward decolonization means to repeatedly stand up to and challenge the current status quo of racial and ethnic arrangements as they currently stand. Latinidad offers the possibility of seeing Creoles and Latinos as distinct ethnic and cultural groups who continue to be at the same time Indians, Blacks, and Latin Europeans. The simplistic and reductionist thinking, that society will see all Creoles or all Latinos as "mixed Blacks" or "Mexican mestizos," does not pass the 'authenticity tests' constructed by racial purists. Nor should Creoles and Latinos see racial/ethnic mixture as an ideal or superior status. Today, if one travels as a Creole/Latino anywhere in the world (including the United States), they will not automatically be read by police, hospitals, or other state institutions as necessarily belonging to the same group. This reality of diversity means that both politically and culturally, Creoles and Latinos must work to decolonize racial thinking within their own communities were one identification is privileged over the others. Acts of resistance and decolonization by Creoles and Latinos vis-à-vis Latinidad must also recognize that these many diverse communities have acted upon the system as much as the system has acted upon their communities:

> The decolonial imaginary remains intangible, unseen, yet quite "real" in social and cultural relationships between the colonizer and the col-

onized, where the ambivalences of power come into play. In other words, one is left to ask, who is really the colonizer and the colonized? Who has agency in this political and cultural arrangement? The difference between the colonial and decolonial imaginaries is that the colonial remains the inhibiting trace, accepting power relations as they are, perhaps confronting them, but not reconfiguring them. To remain within the colonial imaginary is to remain the colonial object who cannot be subject until decolonized. The decolonial imaginary challenges power relations to decolonize notions of otherness to move into a liberatory terrain.[6]

For those both in the United States and Latin America, identification as monoracial (despite a multi-ethnic lived experience), can lead to a denial of how racial mixing impacts individuals regardless of their self-identification as monoracial. In other words, the Dominican who simply identifies as white, despite having Indian and African ancestry, denies that colonization took place. More importantly, they deny that the oppressed do indeed have agency to resist. This is also true for the African American who only identifies as Black, despite Indian ancestry or European ancestry, as well as for the Creek Indian with French and Black ancestry who only identifies as Creek. The human race is a "mixed race." Is identifying with one group truly an act of resistance, or a denial of one's actual lived experience?

Whether one makes a political choice to identify with one group does not change who they are. How they are going to be read in the world is deeply shaped by all of the groups they belong to regardless of what race the society identifies with. For the American Indian who appears white phenotypically, and only identifies as Indian and who participates in cultural, familial, or communal activities (both Native and non-Native), being European does shape who they are and their world view no matter how much they deny that ancestry. The African American in Louisiana who is also German cannot stop being influenced by that experience simply by identifying as one thing over the other. The Salvadorian who recognizes only a nationalist identity as El Salvadorian cannot erase their African and Indian heritage even if it is within their historic and cultural reality. The exchange and interaction has indeed already happened, and is therefore inescapable.

As Louisiana Creoles in 2010 through the current moment locate themselves within the context of Latinidad, they are not attempting to escape historical and cultural realities. They are in fact embracing powerful events that shape not only who they are, but also what they will become in the future. Louisiana Creoles and Latinos as subjective agents in the process of decolonization are actively creating new approaches to locating culture and community. Online social networking spaces such as Facebook have become fertile ground for groups, including *Being Latino* (launched by Lance Rios), and the *I am Creole Network* (created by Elroy EJ Johnson IV). Perhaps one of the most ambitious new efforts taking place in the new media that speaks most directly to decolonization efforts is being led by Christophe Vanderhogan Landry, who is the former Director of the World Studies Institute in Lafayette, Louisiana.

In 2010, Landry led two new efforts that attempted to challenge the status quo of race as it has been constructed within the United States. The first of these efforts, is the "U.S. 2010 Census: Write-in Cajun and Louisiana Creole," which is a measure that encourages Creoles and Cajuns in Louisiana and across the United States to respond "yes" to question 8 on the Census. Responding "yes" to this question (Is the person of Hispanic, Latino, Spanish origin?) would locate Creoles within the Hispanic, Latino, Spanish origin category where they would have the option to fill-in their specific background if not listed. Current options only include the largest Latino/Hispanic groups-Mexican, Puerto Rican, and Cuban. Groups, including the Guatemalans, Chileans, and Dominicans would also have to write in what group they identify with under the Hispanic, Latino, and Spanish cultural/ethnicity categories.

If Landry's census campaign is successful, in the future it could dramatically shift the way that people in the U.S. view ethnic and racial categories. As an act of political mobilization, it could also bring millions of dollars into the Creole community for cultural preservation, bilingual education, health services, employment and other opportunities. In 2000, the Office of Management and Budget (under Directive Fifteen), allowed U.S. citizens to check two or more races on the census. However, for groups such as the Cape Verdeans, Egyptians, Palestinians, and Louisiana Creoles this change still did not allow for recognition of their specific ethnic/cultural groups. This census project ties into Landry's other online organization, "Deracialization: The Liberation of America." According to the Facebook site, it has three primary goals:

> Have the Federal Government of the U.S. officially recognize and acknowledge the evolution and demonstrably harmful effects of Racialization (sub-grouping humans into races), such as the Holocaust, Jim Crow Segregation and American Slavery; 2) Have the Federal Government of the U.S. officially discontinue the practice of racialization in the U.S. on all of its official publications (Censuses, Health certificates, etc); 3) Through common struggles and cultural and ancestral diversity, forge the construction of a new American identity: a deracialized one.[7]

Landry's efforts have been met with resistance. This is similar to the controversy that surrounded the 2000 Census. The changes in the 2000 Census to provide biracial and multiracial families with the two or more races option caused enormous controversy. This controversy centered on the potential decline in population numbers for other groups, such as African Americans, Asian Americans, American Indians, and Latinos.

One of the first posts on the deracialization website is from a subscriber to the page that cites Elizabeth M. Grieco, Chief of the Census Bureau's immigration statistics staff. Grieco said the following about census figures challenging views of race and ethnicity:

> … For example, while 87 percent of Americans born in Cuba and 53 percent born in Mexico identified themselves as white, a majority born in the Dominican Republic and El Salvador, who are newer immigrants, described themselves as neither black nor white. The concept … of race and how we view it culturally has changed. It's a part of not knowing where they fit into how we define race in the United States.[8]

Grieco's analysis of these statistics relates to both Clifford's notion of partial-truth and Perez's comments about the decolonial subject. On the one hand, Latinos are choosing to identify as monoracial whites, and on the other, they appear to refuse categorization with the current confines of the U.S. Census and the black/white racial binary. Louisiana Creoles, Latinos, Arab Americans, and other multi-ethnic populations, whether born inside the U.S. or elsewhere, are slowly, but surely, forcing a collapse of existing notions of race. The question that remains is what will be the political, economic, and cultural impacts of these changes? Who will benefit from any potential changes to the racial status quo?

The challenges to colonial legacies of racial oppression are not new to Louisiana Creoles. When the Anglo-Americans entered Louisiana, they certainly brought their own forms of racial and social designations. In contrast to Latin America, where culture, class, and mixture are the primary determinants of racial and ethnic designation, in Louisiana after the end of Latin (French and Spanish) governance, and since reconstruction, there has been an on-going struggle between Anglo and Latin social and cultural systems. This challenge continues after more than 300 years. Today, with a growing Creole revitalization movement across the United States, it is important to note that current generations of Louisiana Creoles are not tied to the Anglo version of race relations as that of their grandparents' generation. In the same way that Perez articulates a third space for Latinos, so too are Louisiana Creoles reconciling with their multiple identities, as well as social and cultural spaces. Connecting Louisiana Creoles to the concept of Latinidad is not to privilege mestizo or mixed blood over Indigenous or Latin blood over African ancestry. Rather, it is but one way to articulate the specific cultural, geographic, and historic connection between Louisiana Creoles and Latinos of African, Indigenous, and Latin-European ancestry.

In the same way that Louisiana Creoles and other mixed blood people contemplate the 2010 census, so too do Latinos. Designated on the one hand as Hispanics under an ethnicity category, many Latinos are unsure of what to mark for the race category. It seems a great number conflate nationality (Mexican, Peruvian, Guatemalan) as race, while other choose to write-in under some other race, such as mestizo or Chicano/a. The irony here is that many choose white. They are *not* choosing American Indian, or African. However, the majority of Latinos agree that they are treated as whites in their day-to-day lives. The irony here is that many choose white. They are *not* choosing American Indian or African. Latinos, like the Louisiana Creoles, have histories that obfuscate their ethnic multiplicity, linguistic uniqueness, and the everyday realities they experience as people of multiracial descent who cannot be categorized as monoethnic/cultural.

Conclusion

Locating culture and community vis-à-vis Latinidad for Louisiana Creoles and Hispanic populations is about one process, of naming. One could also locate the culture and community of these overlapping ethnic groups through concepts such as Indianization, Indigenismo, Indigeneity or Africanidad, African-ness, or Creolidad. The point here is that there are many names and many sites of resistance for Louisiana Creoles and other Latin-African-Indigenous based cultures in the Americas. To claim the full and exact measure of these histories (though not as socially constructed racial reductions) will be important as these communities continue to grow and reposition majority-minority relations in not just the United States, but throughout the Americas.

As the multiracial population (including Louisiana Creoles, Latinos, American Indians and people of African descent) swells and attempts to overtake a white numerical majority, the question that will remain is one of ideology. How will these multiracial people identify? Will we learn the lessons of previous generations that perpetrated bloodless paper genocide against Indigenous and African people by erasing the history of their existence? Will we deny the diversity among Latinos, including Louisiana Creoles, at the risk of leaving white supremacy intact?

As mixed race populations grow exponentially, it must be understood that the historical and contemporary hybridization of the different groups (Indigenous, African, or Latin) cannot be ignored, erased, or made invisible. Their unique identities have to be preserved. There is unity in numbers. For those who continue to make political arguments for monoracial identification, one might just as forcefully make the case for multiracial identification as a more accurate and unified force against supremacy both in quantity and quality. In practical terms, the youth of today who can see themselves connected to other African, Indigenous, and Latino people might more readily do so if this history, if this knowledge, if this worldview was made available to schools.

For Louisiana Creoles and Latinos, colonization is a historical fact. The Latinidad diaspora would not be here if that process had not begun, and yet we must actively work to decolonize our minds, our hearts, and our communities. In the final analysis, Latinidad in the Americas offers a unique framework for articulating a shared consciousness that facilitates the location of culture and community for Louisiana Creoles and Latinos through our commitment to recognize and embrace the convergence of our histories, cultures, and geographies. In this commitment and recognition of Latinidad, it also becomes possible to create a transformational approach to resistance, decolonization, and liberation.

Notes

1. For discussion of the interactions between Louisiana, Mexico, the Caribbean and other areas in Latin America see the following books: Rodolphe Lucien Desdunes, *Our People and Our History: Fifty Creole Portraits*. Translated and edited by Sister Dorothea O. Mc-Cants (Baton Rouge: Louisiana State University Press, 2001); Carl A., Brasseaux, Keith P., Fontenot, and Claude F. Oubre, *Creoles of Color in the Bayou Country* (Jackson, MS: University of Mississippi Press, 1995); Mary Gehman, "The Mexico-Louisiana Creole Connection" (New Orleans, LA: Margaret Media Publishing, 2001. Online Article, http://www.margaretmedia.com/mexican-la-creoles/info_25.html, accessed April 13, 2010); and Andrew Jolivette, *Louisiana Creoles: Cultural Recovery and Mixed Race Native American Identity* (Lanham, MD: Lexington Books, 2007).

2. Lisa Peñaloza, "Latinidad and Consumer Culture," in *Blackwell Encyclopedia of Sociology,* ed., George Ritzer (Oxford: Blackwell Publishing, 2007), 548–552.

3. Ibid.

4. Paul Gilroy, *The Black Atlantic: Modernity and Double Consciousness* (Cambridge: Harvard University Press, 1993), 1.

5. Clifford, James Clifford, *Writing Culture: The Poetics and Politics of Ethnography* (Berkeley: University of California Press, 1986), 7.

6. Emma Perez, *The Decolonial Imaginary: Writing Chicanas Into History* (Bloomington: Indiana University Press, 1999), 110.

7. Christophe Landry, "Deracialization: The Liberation of America," *Facebook*, http://www.facebook.com/group.php?gid=32475335697&ref=ts, accessed April 13, 2010.

8. Elizabeth Grieco, Department of the U.S. Census, http://www.census.gov, online article from 2007 (Accessed April 13, 2010).

Chapter 15

Stereotypes of Afro-Peruvians Through the Media: The Case of the Peruvian Blackface[1]

Miguel Becerra

From the moment that the first Spanish colonizers arrived to the coasts of Peru in the sixteenth century, they brought with them people from Africa and of African descent mostly to work as slaves. The Spanish crown later gave the colonizers authority to transport more slaves who were initially taken to work in the mines in the highlands. These slaves later ended up along the Peruvian coast, performing mostly agricultural tasks or working as domestic servants. According to Peruvian historian Carlos Aguirre, "slavery reinforced a social, cultural, and mental structure, which condemned blacks to inferior positions and less attractive occupations."[2] After coping with, and fighting against slavery for centuries, Afro-Peruvians achieved freedom in 1854 under the government of Ramón Castilla.[3]

Initially, Afro-descendant slaves were mostly concentrated in Lima, but they eventually moved throughout different parts of the country, mainly along the coast. Even though Afro-Peruvians once composed close to 50% of the population of Lima in the late eighteenth century, today they seem to be an invisible minority in Peru. Today, there are no official statistics regarding this population, since the Peruvian State has not considered differences in race or ethnicity in its censuses since 1940.[4] The numbers concerning the Afro-Peruvian population vary according to the sources. According to some estimates, Afro-Peruvians constitute approximately 5–9% of the total population of Peru.[5] The lack of official statistics about the Afro-Peruvian population accentuates its invisibility.

Racism against Afro-Peruvians

According to a survey carried out by one of the main Peruvian NGOs, *Estudio para la Defensa de los Derechos de la Mujer* (DEMUS, Study for the Defence of Women's Rights), most Peruvians believe that one's ethnicity and/or cultural identity are still significant factors that determine social inequalities in Peru.[6] Although many are aware that racism is present in Peruvian society, this issue affects only the indigenous population, and not necessarily Blacks. One aspect that perpetuates racism against Afro-Peruvians is precisely the invisibility, not only in the sense that the Afro-Peruvian population is an invisible minority, but also in terms of the invisibility of the racism that affects this population. In Peru, the discourse regarding racism usually revolves around the indigenous or Andean population. The fact that Afro-Peruvians are ignored and excluded from this discourse helps perpetuate racism against them; without an awareness of this matter, there is a lack of strategies to counter this issue.

Without a doubt, Afro-Peruvians are still victims of racism, prejudice, and discrimination. This racism comes from society at large, and even from other Afro-Peruvians.[7] Racist (or harmless, according to the one who tells them) jokes and comments against blacks are still common in everyday conversations.[8] Afro-Peruvians are still limited in their occupational opportunities, since in some job advertisements, employers state that the position requires *buena presencia* (good presence), which generally refers to *white* features. Meanwhile, Afro-Peruvians are preferred in other occupations traditionally carried out by blacks, such as doormen, bellboys, or pallbearers.[9] It is moreover uncommon to see individuals who identify as blacks in top positions in firms or in the State in Peru, albeit there are a few exceptions, such as the recent designation of the Afro-Peruvian singer Susana Baca to the position of Minister of Culture. It is common to hear about cases where Afro-Peruvians are denied entry to exclusive night clubs in Lima, where usually a crowd of middle- or upper-class individuals socialize.[10]

Myths still persist that the only contributions of this population have been within the fields of music, cuisine, and sports. Most Peruvians are not aware of Afro-Peruvian contributions to Peruvian society, culture (excluding the field of entertainment), and economy. This includes Afro-Peruvians' participation in the Spanish conquest, the independence movement, and the subsequent wars during the republican period,[11] as well as their contributions to developing new agricultural techniques, and their possible participation in the composition of the first verses of the Peruvian national anthem.[12] Their struggles to obtain their own liberty are also ignored.[13]

The inferior social status and inequalities that Blacks are subject to are not only reflected in the stereotypes and prejudice of Peruvian society, but also in their social and economic conditions. According to a study carried out by Grupo de Análisis para el Desarrollo (GRADE), 35% of Afro-Peruvians live in conditions of poverty and are victims of precarious living conditions in terms of health, nutrition, and education.[14]

There should be some caution when examining these results, since this poverty rate is actually lower than the poverty rate of Peruvians overall (46.6%), a figure that includes the high poverty rate of indigenous people in the *sierra*. It must be stated that Peru is a very diverse country, both in geographic terms and in terms of its population. It has three main geographic regions: the coast, the *sierra* or highlands, and the jungle. As previously mentioned, most Afro-Peruvians live along the coast, a region with a high volume of immigration historically, both from abroad and the rest of Peru. If one compares the poverty rate of Afro-Peruvians with the poverty rate of the indigenous population living along the coast (a region whose standards of poverty are more generous than in the highlands), they are both very similar.[15]

Black people have not historically had a significant political or economic presence in Peru, but they have had a peculiar prominence in Peruvian parody throughout the twentieth and twenty-first centuries. This is demonstrated through advertisements, comic strips, and TV shows, with mainly black people being portrayed as the laughing stock *Other*. It is common to witness jokes about Black people on Saturday night comedy shows or in everyday conversations. Most Peruvians have watched shows like, *JB Noticias, Risas y Salsas, Risas de América,* or *El especial del humor* at some point, which have all included stereotypical portrayals of blacks. These portrayals, which abound in Peruvian television, not only reflect stereotypes about Afro-Peruvians, but they also reinforce them. Stereotypes strengthen the structures of social order and power,[16] thereby maintaining or increasing social inequalities. Most Peruvians have learned to accept these racist portrayals, creating in the words of Peruvian psychoanalyst Jorge Bruce a "tolerance towards intolerance."[17] Because they accept these stereotypes as normal, Peruvians seldom question their accuracy and are often unaware of their harmful consequences.

From Blackface to El Negro Mama

Visual portrayals of black people in Peru have been present for decades, but most Peruvians are unaware that these portrayals have been heavily influenced by blackface portrayals of African-Americans. Stereotypes and portrayals do not appear out of thin air,[18] but are shaped based on previous portrayals and foreign media influenced drastically in molding the portrayals of Afro-Peruvians in the twentieth century.

The influences are obvious in some cases, such as in the portrayals of Afro-Peruvian women in some Peruvian advertisements and products. In the beginning of the twentieth century, one could witness more stereotypical portrayals of Afro-Peruvians in comic strips, and since the mid-twentieth century, these visual representations have exhibited many similarities with those of black characters in U.S. cartoons. The use of blackface makeup to symbolize black skin, like that used in U.S. blackface minstrel plays and television shows was imitated in Peruvian theatre, dance, and television.

The notion of blackface was *exported* from England to the U.S.,[19] and then later *exported* to other countries. Some U.S. minstrel casts performed in Cuba as early as the nineteenth century.[20] U.S. minstrel theatre casts also went on tours throughout South Africa in 1848,[21] and even nowadays, some actors still perform in blackface. In Japan, one can still observe blackface depictions in some food products, like Sanrio.[22] In Mexico, there was a controversy in 2005 (initiated mostly by U.S. black activists) about the release of stamps with the image of a black character called Memín Pingüín, who shows many similarities with the *darky* characters of U.S. cartoons. In other European countries, such as Spain, Great Britain, France, and the Netherlands, one can still see white people who paint their skin black for festivals or photo shoots for major fashion magazines. They also use *darky* characters as logos or mascots to advertise for some products. Peru was no exception to such exploitations. Peruvian comic strips that emerged during the mid-twentieth century were greatly influenced by U.S. cartoons and comic strips, particularly in the case of black characters.[23] The similarities between the physical depictions of black U.S. and Peruvian characters are obvious in the use of excessive dark skin, big eyes, and extremely thick lips highlighted with reddish or whitish colors.

An example of a Peruvian *darky* character is Boquellanta,[24] drawn by Hernán Bartra. Boquellanta was a character that appeared in the popular newspaper *Última Hora* between 1952 and 1954. Secondary characters, like Boquellanta's parents, were never referred to by their names, but simply as *papá*, *mamá*, *negro*, or *negra*.[25] Boquellanta was shown as an ignorant boy who would take advantage of others, even going as far as stealing or appealing to violence. Additionally, he was depicted as someone who always seemed attracted to white women.

Boquellanta was not the only black character that displayed stereotypical attributes similar to those of black characters from the U.S. His mother presented features similar to the U.S. Mammy character: a fat black woman wearing an apron and bandana headscarf. She was portrayed as a dominant woman, but emphasized the stereotypical roles of the uneducated servant who mostly performed domestic chores, such as cooking or doing laundry. His father was depicted as an ignorant criminal and violent drunkard, who was dominated by his wife and, like Boquellanta, was also attracted to white women. The whole family often appeared in violent situations, sometimes attacking each other, and did not display many positive family values.[26]

The similarities between Boquellanta and U.S. *darky* characters were not only physical, but were also displayed in terms of negative features associated with blackness. For example, in one of the comic strips Boquellanta appears washing clothes, as two other white high-class women appear on the background. One of them states, "But … How does 'Boquellanta' know when he has finally washed his hands?" and the other one replies, "It's very easy … When the water doesn't get any dirtier!"[27] This association of blackness with dirtiness is similar to a scene that appears in the 1935 U.S. cartoon *Little Black Sambo*, in which a Mammy-like black woman is washing her black son, as if she was washing clothes, and the water starts to turn black as she washes him. Likewise, the common U.S. stereotype of blacks stealing chickens also appears in a comic strip of Boquellanta (see image below).[28]

Boquellanta was only one of the many black characters present in comic strips in newspapers and magazines in Peru in the mid-twentieth century. As Peruvian curator Carla Sagástegui points out, Peruvian comic strips featured other characters, like Nolicón, Chabike, Tacu Tacu, and Patita, among others, who displayed blackface or *darky* attributes. The influence of U.S. portrayals of blacks was not limited to comic strips. While researching for this chapter and analyzing editions of *Última Hora*, I came across an image of a Peruvian dancer in the October 18, 1952 edition who was wearing blackface makeup and dress, very similar to that of U.S. blackface characters. The footing below the image reads: "Willy Arenaza, national dancer who is increasing his popularity on stage. Arenaza specializes in North American dance." This note indicates the strong influences in Peru from "North American dance," since it tells us several things: that Arenaza specialized in North American dance, that in Peru there was knowledge about blackface shows, and that the person that wrote the caption also considered the blackface portrayal to be derived from the U.S.[29]

Although television did not arrive to Peru until the 1960s, Peruvian audiences had been exposed to images from the U.S. since the 1920s through movie theatres. Since this time, Peruvians preferred movies and shows from the U.S. Both movies and TV shows were shown in movie theatres, among them cartoons by Disney, Warner Brothers, and MGM—some of those very media that presented *darky* characters. These shows would eventually be shown on TV, reaching an even wider audience.

El Negro Mama

In the 1990s, a black character that was to become popular, and later controversial, emerged in Peruvian television. El Negro Mama[30] (a character created by impersonator and comedian Jorge Benavides), parodied a black man who displayed many stereotypical negative traits. This character was presented in 10–25 minute sketches in different shows, like *JB Noticias* and *El Especial del Humor*. El Negro Mama was not performed by an Afro-Peruvian, but by Benavides, who through the use of blackface makeup would pretend to be black. This is the same practice as in early U.S. television during the first half of the twentieth century, and in minstrel shows in the nineteenth century.

Certain stereotypes associated with blacks arise commonly in this show. He is constantly portrayed as an ignorant thief, a dishonest, foul-smelling, ugly, inarticulate liar and rapist. His speech is also exaggerated to make him seem *blacker*. This character usually ends his sketches, after outwitting someone else, with his popular phrase, "Seré negrito, pero tengo mi cerebrito," which could be translated as, "I may be black, but I still have my wily little brain."[31] This statement implies that although blacks are less intelligent than non-blacks, they may still be capable to take advantage of others and get away with it.[32]

Often when someone speaks to him, El Negro Mama cannot understand what the other person is trying to tell him, or he is unable to respond articulately. He also was sometimes portrayed as someone similar to the stereotyped Uncle Tom character from the U.S., as someone unable to stand up for himself. For example, in a sketch where he appears to be interviewed by someone imitating Peruvian TV host and writer Jaime Baily, he seems willing to say anything to please the white interviewer. No matter how much he is ridiculed, he does not radically rebel against others, or question his place in society.

In another episode from the 1990s, in the show *JB Noticias*, El Negro Mama is shown next to the famous Peruvian musician Gian Marco Zignago. As soon as Gian Marco feels the presence of El Negro Mama, he makes gestures indicating that the black character has a foul-smell. Later, as soon as the musician sees him face to face, he reacts in fear, deducing a condition of ugliness, associated in Peru with what is not white or European, or possibly the fear is caused by the fact that he thinks that this black character may rob him, since he was constantly portrayed as a thief.

El Negro Mama emerged when there was a lack of strong black activism, or at least when their actions were not noticeable by most of Peruvian society. Years later, after the fall of the regime of Fujimori, some human right organizations started to have a stronger presence in society. An important step they took was to pressure comedian Jorge Benavides to remove this black character from television, at least temporarily, due to racial sensitivities. However, many Peruvians were not even aware of why this character was removed from screen.

It must be mentioned that this happened during a historical moment that was symbolic for Afro-Peruvians. In 2001, the National Commission for Andean and Amazonian People (CONAPA) was created, and in 2002, the Afro-Peruvian population became part of this commission.[33] The primary representative for Afro-Peruvians was Dr. Jorge Ramírez Reyna, president of one of the main black human rights organizations, the Black Association in Defense and Promotion of Human Rights (ASONEDH). Ramírez Reyna was one of the main activists who engaged in a dialogue with comedian Jorge Benavides to have El Negro Mama removed from television, at least temporarily, in 2002.[34]

Unfortunately, El Negro Mama returned in 2008 with parodies that were updated according to current events or news, like in the episode in which El Negro Mama is shown as the new driver for the President of the United States, Barack Obama. Sometimes, El Negro Mama receives special treatment due to his blackness, or when he is shown representing a black thief who was captured in Lima after a case that received much attention from the press. These roles, as a servant or a thief, did not vary much from the previous roles El Negro Mama played before he had been removed from television.

From Mammy to Ña Pancha

In his work "Tristes querellas en la vieja quinta," Peruvian writer Julio Ramón Ribeyro mentions a "zamba"[35] called Doña Pancha, who the protagonist Memo, refers to as a "*zamba grosera*" (rude zamba) and "*zamba sin educación*" (zamba without education). In this work several racial terms were used to insult this black woman. Likewise, a Peruvian detergent that featured a black woman on its advertisements shared a similar name to that character: Ña Pancha. In 1964, this detergent displayed an ad in the widely read magazine *Caretas*. This ad showed a black woman wearing a white apron and headscarf with red dots, very similar to the traditional red and white Mammy dress. This image persisted for many years in this detergent's advertisements, both in print and on television.[36]

Similar clothing to that which Mammy wore appeared in other portrayals of Afro-Peruvian women in comic strips like Boquellanta and Guayacón, among others, as well as on advertisements for several Peruvian restaurants or desserts. For example, in the Peruvian restaurant Rústica, which has several locations throughout Lima, one can still observe an image of a big black woman with a red headscarf and apron with white dots, just like the Mammy character.

Before the U.S. Mammy character appeared in Peruvian media, black women were usually portrayed differently. For example, in paintings by famous nineteenth century native and foreign-born painters that lived in Peru, like Pancho Fierro and Leonce Angrand (a French painter who lived in Lima), black women were portrayed in a completely different manner, wearing different outfits, and were shown in a more humane way and less like a caricature. If we compare the portrayals and clothing of black women since the mid-twentieth century on to those of Pancho Fierro from the nineteenth century, we will notice the obvious differences.[37]

Racism in the Media

Stereotypes are part of a "collective process of judgment which feeds upon and reinforces powerful social myths,"[38] like the ones of the black man being hypersexual to the point of being a rapist.[39] Such myths exacerbate ethnic suspicion, as the *Other* is portrayed as someone that threatens safety and peace. The myth of the ignorant or less intellectually capable black man portrayed in the media similarly encourages Peruvians to think that blacks are intellectually inferior compared to others. This myth is strengthened by the belief that blacks are only good for sports, music, or dancing, since many of them succeed within these spheres.[40]

These are not the only characteristics associated with blackness. In Peru it is still common to refer to, or portray blacks as cannibals, even though nobody can document cases of blacks eating human flesh in Peru nowadays. In the early twenty-first century, an advertisement for the pizzeria Pastipizza showed Afro-Peruvian comedian Martín Farfán as a cannibal, displaying a bone on his head. This stereotype has been present throughout the years; in comic strips like the ones shown on the newspaper *Última Hora*, one could also find portrayals of blacks as cannibals.[41] The portrayals of cannibals that are not black are practical null in Peru, even though cannibalism has been practiced in different continents throughout the world. The fact that it is only blacks that are associated with this characteristic clearly illustrates the racism that they are subject to.[42]

Nonetheless, racism against blacks through the media is not only about the constant presence of blacks being portrayed with negative stereotypes, but also about the absence of blacks in positive roles, or in other positions such as news anchors or the hosts of shows. The presence of blacks on Peruvian TV is minimal, and in the few occasions in which they do appear, they are usually displayed in the same stereotypical roles.

It is also the case that what is black is not considered aesthetically pleasing; what is considered beautiful is mostly what is seen as *white*. This is clearly expressed in Peruvian advertisements, where the great majority of models or actors/actresses, in the cases of women, men, children, as well as families, are people with *European* traits. It is very uncommon to see a black or indigenous person in these types of advertisements, and as Peruvian psychoanalyst Jorge Bruce stated, this is not shocking for most of the population because Peruvians have assimilated it.[43] Afro-Peruvian activist Jorge Ramírez criticizes these aspects of the media, affirming that "the media is an effective tool of psychological bombarding, which favors the alienation of cultural identity, since through these […] they are defiled in a way we are used to, attacking Afro-Peruvians' human dignity."[44]

The damaging aspect about these portrayals is the internalization, that is, the conviction that the stereotypes are true, and the potential they have to create *reality*. Comedian Jorge Benavides, through his character El Negro Mama, uses certain traits associated with blackness (skin color, features of his lips, hair, eyes, and speech) which are generally exaggerated to make him seem as black as possible, increasing his *Otherness*, and he associates these traits with stereotypes and characteristics that the audience also identifies with blacks. In this manner, he highlights and strengthens stereotypes. The audience sees their beliefs *confirmed* through the repetitive images of blacks with these features, and these stereotypes end up becoming a social *reality*.

As Peruvian scholar, lawyer, and activist Wilfredo Ardito states, Peruvian racism is complex because it not only reflects the rejection of those that are different, but also the rejection of those that are like us. Ardito points out that, "In this manner, unfortunately, racism in Peru is still a victorious ideology: the victims, who are convinced of their inferiority, have internalized it."[45] Another aspect that furthers the proliferation of these portrayals is the way "Peruvian humor" works, and the lack of a politically correct culture in Peruvian society. Peruvian playwright Eduardo Adrianzén states that Peruvian humor is based upon the mockery and ridicule of the shortcomings of others. These shortcomings may range from being too fat, too skinny, poor, ugly, wearing a strange shirt or having a peculiar accent, to being black. He continues:

> Within this context, evidently humor entirely has a racist element,
> of attributing certain characteristics to certain racial biotypes be-
> cause this is what is funny or because this will certainly create laugh-
> ter. Therefore, El Negro Mama uses his supposedly blackness just in
> the same way as others use fatness or speech [...] and uses it as a
> shortcoming.[46]

Jokes are not only presented openly on television, but are also found in everyday conversations among friends or relatives, in schools or workplaces, and in
other sources of entertainment, such as with sporting events or radio.[47]

Response of Peruvian Society

Since the beginning of the twenty-first century, after the fall of the dictatorship
of Alberto Fujimori, some Afro-Peruvian activists and organizations have attempted to counter these racist stereotypes on Peruvian television. However,
there has not been much effort or compromise from other sectors of Peruvian
society to eradicate this sort of racism. Even though black activists have demanded that the Peruvian State cooperate with their efforts to restrict these
portrayals, the State, throughout different governments, have responded that
this is not their responsibility. Rather, they argue that it is responsibility of the
TV channels and the producers of these shows. Government officials claim
that if the State were to intervene, it would be a violation of freedom of speech.
This demonstrates the unwillingness of the Peruvian State to accommodate
the needs of the Afro-Peruvian population. While Peruvians may vary in their
reactions towards these portrayals, most do little to nothing to have these racist
depictions removed from the screen. Many do not see characters such as El
Negro Mama as racist; quite the contrary, many Peruvians think it is funny
and humorous, and a proof of this is the fact that these comedy shows remain
popular.

In this sense, Afro-Peruvian organizations and activists have been the greatest agents in trying to eradicate these portrayals from television. Afro-Peruvian
activist Jorge Ramírez, for example, was primarily responsible for having El
Negro Mama temporarily removed from the screen. Likewise, the organization which Ramírez leads, the Black Association for the Defense and Promotion of Human Rights (ASONEDH), protested the portrayals of blacks on
some TV commercials, such as the Good Year Tire commercial that compared
tires with the lips of a black person. After his complaint, which made it to international stances, this commercial was removed.[48]

More recently in 2010, Monica Carrillo, the President of the Afro-Peruvian organization the Center for Afro-Peruvian Studies and Empowerment (LUNDU), protested El Negro Mama and attempted to have this character, once again, removed from television. Comedian Jorge Benavides, the creator and impersonator of El Negro Mama, responded that "El Negro Mama represents a good man with values," and accused Carrillo of being racist because she only focused on the character s negative attributes, not on the positive ones.[49]

The countervailing pressures were so great that Frecuencia Latina, the channel in which this character was being shown, decided to remove this character from its broadcast on April 8, 2010, but days later, channel representatives announced that El Negro Mama could return at any moment. He did go back on screen weeks later. Ironically, after this incident, the movement in favor of this character appeared to be stronger than the one attempting to have him removed. In a survey in the online version of El Comercio, 86% of the readers indicated that they agreed with having this character stay on television because it is not racist, while 13% said he should be removed, and that it is racist.[50] Facebook users started to create Facebook groups in favor of and against El Negro Mama, but the groups in favor had more members than those against him. Carrillo stated afterwards that she was harassed and threatened.[51] While the Ethical Court of the National Association of Radio and Television ordered that Frecuencia Latina should issue an apology to the Afro-Peruvian community,[52] black activists were not satisfied with this apology.

Conclusion

According to representatives of one of the main Afro-Peruvian organizations, the Center of Ethnic Development (CEDET), racist expressions displayed in the media are no more than the surface of a complex issue. By assigning racist roles, aesthetic patrons, and expressions with racist content, the media actually nourishes the growth of racism. Likewise, the media influences society in a direct but invisible manner, promoting negative values about blacks and encouraging blacks to assume them.[53]

Several factors in Peruvian society have led to the proliferation and perpetuation of these racist portrayals. The ethno-racial hierarchy, present since colonial times, placed Afro-Peruvians as one of the populations at the bottom of the social order, encouraging negative stereotypes about blacks. Likewise, foreign racist portrayals of blacks also shaped perceptions of Afro-Peruvians. Moreover, the Afro-Peruvian population remains largely invisible. Peru lacks a strong black movement and a culture that promotes social consciousness about the negative consequences of these portrayals. Consequently, Peru provides a propitious environment for the endurance of negative portrayals and jokes about blacks on Peruvian media. In other countries, such jokes and portrayals would probably cause wide outrage if they occurred today.

On November 28, 2009, the Peruvian State, in a historic, although mostly symbolic gesture, apologized officially to the Afro-Peruvian population for the "abuse, exclusion, and discrimination" it had suffered throughout Peruvian history. This is an important first step demonstrating that the Afro-Peruvian population is finally emerging from invisibility. Nevertheless, this apology has not been accompanied by any concrete actions by the State to change Afro-Peruvians' condition of human rights or living conditions. Although in certain aspects some progress has been made, as these types of portrayals show, there is still a long road ahead. As long as Peruvian audiences accept this humor and ignore its harmful consequences, racism will persist. It is time for Peru to take humor seriously.

Notes

1. This chapter is based on the author's M.A. thesis, which won the award for the best M.A. thesis in Latin American & Iberian Studies at University of California, Santa Barbara in 2010.

2. Carlos Aguirre, *Breve historia de la esclavitud: una herida que no deja de sangrar* (Lima: Fondo Editorial del Congreso del Perú, 2005), 70 [Unless otherwise noted, all translations are my own].

3. It is often the common perception of many Peruvians that blacks achieved freedom thanks to the righteousness of a benevolent *caudillo*, ignoring the role of Afro-Peruvians fighting for their own rights. However, as Carlos Aguirre points out, there were several factors that led to the abolition of slavery in Peru, among them, the essential participation of blacks in order to gain freedom. The belief in the benevolence of Castilla is also expressed through some Afro-Peruvian songs, such as a popular one that states, "¡Que viva mi papá, que viva mi mamá ... que viva Ramón Castilla que nos dio la libertad!" See Carlos Aguirre, *Agentes de su propia libertad: Los esclavos de Lima y la desintegración de la esclavitud, 1821–1854* (Lima: PUCP, 1995).

4. The census of 1940 was the only Peruvian census during the twentieth century that requested information about *race*. The question was formulated in the following manner: "Race: Are you white, Indian, black, yellow, or mestizo?" Martín Benavides and Martín Valdivia, *Metas del milenio y la brecha étnica en el Perú.* (Lima: GRADE, 2004), 3.

5. José Luciano and Humerto Rodríguez Pastor, "Peru," in *No Longer Invisible: Afro-Latin Americans Today* (London: Minority Rights Group, 1995), 276.

6. Jorge Bruce, *Nos habíamos choleado tanto—psicoanálisis y racismo* (Lima: Editorial Universidad San Martín de Porres, 2007), 26.

7. Wilfredo Ardito, "Cuestión de autoestima," *La insignia.* March 30, 2008. http://www.lainsignia.org/2008/marzo/ibe_024.htm (February 21, 2008).

8. In Peru it is common to hear comments, phrases, or jokes about blacks, such as, "White man running: athlete. Black man running: thief." "White man with wings: angel. Black man with wings: bat." "Blacks only think until midnight." "He is a refined black man/woman." "She's pretty ... but black."

9. Historically, having blacks carry one's coffin was seen as a sign of prestige and honor for the deceased and his family. See Calvin Sims, "For Blacks in Peru, There's No Room at the Top." *The New York Times*, August 16, 1996.

10. This situation is slowly changing, since racial discrimination is nowadays legally penalized in Peru.

11. Aguirre, *Breve historia de la esclavitud*, 186.

12. See analysis by Juan José Vega in *La estrofa del "largo tiempo-" y los negros del Perú* (Lima: Instituto Sanmartiniano del Perú, 1999).

13. See the history of the abolition of slavery in Peru by Aguirre in *Agentes de su propia libertad*.

14. The method used in this study was through surveys carried out in 10 focal groups in regions with a high rate of individuals that identified as blacks. The interviewees were individuals who self-identified as "negros," "mulattoes," or "zambos." Benavides and Valdivia. *Más allá de los promedios*, 11.

15. Benavides and Valdivia. *Más allá de los promedios: Afrodescendientes en América*

298 15 · STEREOTYPES OF AFRO-PERUVIANS THROUGH THE MEDIA

Latina, 9.

16. Michael Pickering, *Stereotyping: The Politics of Representation* (New York: Palgrave, 2001), 3.

17. Bruce, *Nos habíamos choleado tanto*, 75.

18. Pickering, *Stereotyping: The Politics of Representation*, 8.

19. John Strausbaugh, *Black Like You*. (New York: Penguin Group, 2006), 63.

20. The following U.S. minstrel shows were shown in Cuba: La esencia de Virginia in 1870, Los negritos del norte and Los negritos musicales de Mississippi in 1877. Jill Lane, *Blackface Cuba* (Philadelphia: University of Pennsylvania Press, 2005), 117.

21. Coon Carnival Cape Town. May 14, 2011. http://web.archive.org/web/20051027061922/http://www.africapetours.com/Coon+Carnival.htm.

22. John Greenwald and Kumiko Makihara, "Japan Prejudice and Black Sambo," *Time*. June 24, 2001.

23. Carla Sagástegui, *La historieta peruana 1: los primeros 80 años (1887–1967)*, (Lima: Galería ICPNA, 2003), 30–33.

24. Play on words mocking the protuberance of this character's lips. In Peru it is common to make fun of physical characteristics of blacks, such as their lips. Boquellanta is a shortened version of '*boca de llanta*,' which translated means 'tire-like mouth.'

25. In these comic strips, as in current Peruvian society, the word "negro" would often appear next to a denigrating adjective, such as "*negro desgraciado*," "*negro sinvergüenza*," "*negro bruto*," among others.

26. Hernán Bartra, Boquellanta. *Última Hora*, November 6, 1952, 12.

27. *Última Hora*, June 16, 1953, 12.

28. Hernán Bartra, Boquellanta. *Última Hora*, April 16, 1953, 12.

29. *Última Hora*, October 18, 1952, 12.

30. The origin of the name of this character is not clear, but every time that this character says the word "Mama," he speaks in an exaggerated way, using a very stereotypical speech, emphasizing the blackness of this character. The word "Mama" is a feminine word, whereas the character is a man. In different comical characters in Peruvian television, there is an ambiguity of genders. For example, the characters La Paisana Jacinta and La Chola Chabuca, both represent indigenous women, but are played by male comedians (Jorge Benavides, the same comedian that interprets El Negro Mama, also interprets La Paisana Jacinta and Ernesto Pimentel interprets La Chola Chabuca).

31. Due to language and cultural differences, it is difficult to accurately translate this phrase. The words "negrito" and "cerebrito" are the diminutives of the words "black" and "brain" in Spanish. It is probable that the common use of diminutives in the Spanish spoken in Peru has influences from the Quechua use of "cha."

32. El Comercio, *Organización afroperuana insiste con el retiro del 'Negro Mama' de la TV*, April 26, 2011, http://elcomercio.pe/espectaculos/748328/noticia-organizacion-afroperuana-insiste-retiro-negro-mama-tv (July 19, 2011).

33. This commission later became *the Instituto Nacional de Pueblos Andinos, Amazónicos y Afro-peruanos* (INDEPA). Jorge Ramírez, *Racismo, derechos humanos e inclusión social: afrodescendientes en el Perú* (Lima: Instituto Internacional de Relaciones Públicas y Comunicaciones, 2006), 201–202.

34. This comedian did not stop portraying Afro-Peruvian characters completely. He created a new character, impersonating the former head coach of the Peruvian national soc-

cer team and a former soccer star, Julio César Uribe, who is Afro-Peruvian. This character was called "Jeta Jeta Uribe," *Jeta* is the term sometimes used to refer to a black person's lips, emphasizing its size and thickness. This character displayed many similar physical attributes and personality traits as El Negro Mama.

35. Wolfgang A. Luchting. "Zambas y zambos en la obra de Julio Ramón Ribeyro." *Socialismo y participación.* Número 31, 1985, 65–73. Whereas the term "zambo/a" referred to the offspring of an indigenous and black person during colonial times, this term is now often used as an alternative term to "negro/a" in Peruvian society.

36. Caretas, 1964.

37. Pancho Fierro. Puesto de chicha y picante.

38. Pickering, *Stereotyping*, 48.

39. In some sketches El Negro Mama is shown as a rapist who is waiting for another man to fall asleep in a cell or in a hospital to take away and rape him.

40. According to Afro-Peruvian activist Jorge Ramírez, this fact also causes some Peruvians to believe that there is no racism against blacks, since some of them have been able to participate, succeed, and receive public recognition from the rest of society due to their talents within these fields. Jorge Ramírez, interview by author, on June 27, 2008.

41. *El Comercio*, the main Peruvian newspaper, had to issue an apology to Afro-Peruvians due to an advertisement shown on TV for their supplement on healthy diets, where they showed a tribal family of black cannibals ready to eat a human. They also had to remove this advertisement from television.

42. Commercial of Peruvian pizzeria Pastipizza. The actor in the advertisement is Martín Farfán.

43. Bruce, *Nos habíamos choleado tanto*, 75.

44. Ramírez, *Racismo, derechos humanos e inclusión social*, 85–87.

45. Ardito, "Cuestión de autoestima."

46. Eduardo Adrianzén, interview by author, March 26, 2009.

47. Wilfredo Ardito, blog Reflexiones Peruanas Nº 250: *Es sólo una broma …* June 1, 2009. http://reflexionesperuanas.blogspot.com/2009_06_01_archive.html (June 20, 2009).

48. Ramírez, *Racismo y derechos humanos e inclusión social*, 79.

49. El Comercio, *Explotó: Jorge Benavides acusó de discriminadoras a organizaciones afroperuanas*, June 17, 2010, http://elcomercio.pe/espectaculos/496457/noticia-exploto-jorge-benavides-acuso-discriminadoras-organizaciones-afroperuanas (June 18, 2010).

50. El Comercio, *Jorge Benavides: "El Negro Mama representa a un hombre bueno y con valores,"* March 28, 2010, http://elcomercio.pe/espectaculos/453276/noticia-jorge-benavides-negro-mama-representa-hombre-bueno-valores (August 10, 2011).

51. BBC Mundo, *Amenazas en Perú por "El Negro Mama,"* May 2, 2010, http://www.bbc.co.uk/mundo/cultura_sociedad/2010/05/100502_peru_negro_mama_lundu_racismo_g.shtml (July 10, 2010).

52. El Comercio, *Frecuencia Latina debe pedir disculpas a comunidad afroperuana por personaje 'Negro Mama,'* December 3, 2010, http://elcomercio.pe/espectaculos/678534/noticia-frecuencia-latina-pedir-disculpas-comunidad-afroperuana-personajenegro-mama (December 4, 2010).

53. CEDET *El estado y el pueblo afroperuano: balance y propuestas del proceso afroperuano ante los acuerdos de la Conferencia Regional de las Américas.* (Lima: CEDET, 2005), 56.

Chapter 16

Afro-Mexican Queen Pageants: NGOs and the (Re)Construction of Blackness

Jorge Gonzalez

In May of 2008, a Los Angeles Mexican newspaper *El Oaxaqueno* dedicated for the first time half its front cover to the Afro-Mexican presence in the city of Pasadena, California, headlining: "Afro-Oaxaqueños en California."[1] This newspaper included a short article that referenced the annual participation of the Afro-Mexican music/dance group *El Baile de los Diablos* (Dance of the Devils) and the annual festival known as *la Guelaguetza*. The article shed light on some of the reasons as to why members of this community decided to create the first U.S. based Afromexican NGO in Pasadena, California called Afromexicana. Ultimately, the article discussed how since 2002, Afromexicana's main goal[2] has been to strategize around the issue of obtaining visibility[3] within the Oaxacan indigenous (Mixtec and Zapotec) and Mexican-American or Chicano/a community in Los Angeles.

The organizational goals of Afromexicana, similar to other Oaxacan ethnic organizations,[4] are not only to preserve cultural traditions of Afro-Mexicans abroad but more importantly to create fundraisers in order to send economic remittances back to their marginalized hometown communities known as *Los Pueblos Negros*[5] (The Black Villages) in Costa Chica; in the case of Pasadena the community has direct ties to Jose Maria Morelos, Oaxaca (a headquarter of the Black Social Movement). Hence, it is within the process of sending cultural and economic remittances that this author has come to the following conclusion: AMQPs are a fine example of how AFRICA invents and manipulates the performance and aesthetics of public space to construct black ethnic consciousness within *costeño* culture.

This author first became familiar with this topic in 2004 while enrolled in the Native American Studies program at the University of California at Davis. As a result of preliminary findings, some pertinent questions arose: What are the missing "ethnic" characteristics that disqualify Afro-Mexicans as an ethnic group? How are AMQPs mirroring internal and external politics of representation? To what extent are the state and civil associations (NGOs), specifically the civil association AFRICA, transforming the meaning and contours of blackness in Oaxaca and Pasadena?

I became aware of an AMQP in 2004 while in an attempt to grasp how Afro-Mexican NGO's (Mexico Negro[6] and AFRICA[7]) in Costa Chica were organizing in order to accomplish a common mission. The goal of these two organizations was to take responsibility for civil actions in their respective town/municipalities in order to bring awareness, give representation, and make visible the Afro-Mexican population in Oaxaca and Guerrero. This in turn led to an examination of how civil associations such as Mexico Negro and AFRICA, at the regional, state, national and international level, were fulfilling civil duties at a grassroots level. In the process, I came across the first primary source which highlights the existence and invention of the first AMQP: an online photo blog of a queen pageant on AFRICA's website.[8] Ultimately, this gives testimony to the *1ra Reyna Afromestiza* (1st Afromestiza Queen) in the town of Jose Maria Morelos in the municipality of Huazolotitlan; one of the so-called five black villages in the area. The picture captured the 2004 AMQP Denise Reina Medina wearing a red dress and a golden crown, holding a Mexican flag, while riding on a parade float with other Afro-Mexican young girls. Her description is that of a *morena* queen pageant that Laura A. Lewis describes in her article titled, "'Afro' Mexico in Black, White, and Indian":

> ... a young woman who looks neither "too" black nor "too" Indian [waving the] Mexican flag for a *crowd* that through speeches *link* San Nicolas (a black town) to the nation ....[9]

Moreover, on the side of the parade float, there hangs a banner reading *Reyna Afromestiza* surrounded by a frame of African motifs. The naming of the queen pageants thus became a marker as to how the black movement began ethnicizing blackness.

More interestingly, that same picture of Denise was eventually used in DIGEPO's (General Population Department of State) 21st front cover magazine issue released in 2008.[10] This edition also became the first one dedicated to the African descent population residing in Costa Chica, Oaxaca. Hence, at this juncture in my research a question arose: Why out of all of the pictures that could have been used to represent the Afro-Mexican population in Costa Chica, Oaxaca was the photo of a queen pageant symbolically relevant? At a macro-level, how were young women tied to the idea of visibility and representation within the ideals of multiculturalism and the nation? Despite the facts that pointed to the relevance of ethnic queen pageants, I was not fully convinced about how they were becoming a phenomenon until the NGO Afromexicana in Pasadena, CA organized their very own pageant in April of 2009 titled "*Reyna de la Primavera*" (Queen of Spring). It was at this precise moment of this investigation that I realized how queen pageants, or rather inter-ethnic performances of multiculturalism and pluralism in Mexico, could be used as an ideal performance space to explain Afro-Mexican identity politics. Indeed, according to Anita Gonzalez in her latest book titled, *Afro-Mexico: Between Myth and Reality*, performance spaces in Afro-Mexican communities play a crucial role as they help "… clarify and articulate their history [or identity] through embodied expression."[11]

The aim of this chapter is to explain why and how AMQPs in Costa Chica can serve as a window to understand Afro-Mexican identity politics in correlation with social movements. Using ethnographic (interviews and participant observation) and archival data, as well as other preliminary findings, the chapter demonstrates how ethnic queen pageants serve as effective identity reconstructive spaces and ideal platforms to reclaim citizenship. First it is argued that these pageants serve to perform cultural/ethnic differences or conundrums of Afro-Mexican identity within *costeño* culture. Second, the pageants serve to construct or imagine a black collective consciousness, and bring visibility to the "black villages" which will allow NGOs to practice civil rights in Mexico. Furthermore, the chapter examines the socio-historical background on the ethnicization of blackness[12] in Mexico, and the conception of the Afro-Mexican social movement since 1997; which is the official birth of the movement and is integral to this study.

I also explain how ethnic queen pageants in Costa Chica and Pasadena, CA correlate to the transnational current agendas of NGOs both in Costa Chica (Mexico Negro and AFRICA) and Pasadena, CA (Afromexicana). Hence, the goal of this chapter is to explore the symbolism of AMQPs both culturally and within their socio-historically context. In doing so, I address the following questions: how is the performance of queen pageants mirroring ethnic-racial politics of black identity in Costa Chica? And under what premises is the civil association AFRICA interested in manipulating the space and performance of them. In contrast, I conclude by explaining the transnational relevance of queen pageants between Pasadena, California and the Afro-Mexican community of Jose Maria Morelos, Oaxaca.

The Ethnicization of Blackness in Mexico

In 1951, anthropologist Gonzalo Aguirre Beltran's published the first ethno-historical publication, titled *Cuijla: esbozo etnográfico de un pueblo Negro,* of a black village named Cuajinicuilapa (back then Cuijla), in the state of Guerrero. His detailed studies would help trace, resynthesize, and contemporize the African legacy in México by bringing to the surface unprecedented numbers and origins of imported African ethnic groups. Yet, simultaneously, Aguirre Beltrán reported that the remaining afrodescedants left in the country were in the verge of being "absorbed" into the Mestizo race. Thus his assertions were made using afrocentric 'ethnic' parameters—which he adopted as a student at Northwestern University under the guidance of anthropologist Melville Herskovits—to measure African physical and cultural traits; also known as the "African Thesis" periodization.

According to the scholarly consensus,[13] back then, Mexican anthropology was consolidating the nation using indigenous ethnic groups as a model of study to understanding politics of difference. Based on his findings, Aguirre Beltrán, who since 1946 had already been director of the INI (National Indigenous Institute), declared that "Afromestizos" could *not* be differentiated as a collective (ethnic) group and as a result they were not rendered into national legislation Aguirre Beltrans' work romanticized, essentialized, minimized, and generalized the Afro-Mexican identity.[14] Indeed, because he went as far as to say that Afromestizos could *not* be differentiated as an (ethnic) group,[15] these assertions would eventually be rendered into nation-state legislations. Specifically, Aguirre Beltran made these assertions after becoming director of the National Indigenous Institute (INI).

Despite Aguirre Beltrans' shortcomings in not being able to grasp the intraraciality and interethnicity of Afro-Mexicans, his research continues to be prominent in the literature because no work has synthesized the black colonial and post-independence experience in Mexico as accurate. Indeed, his groundbreaking contribution to the historical ethnic make-up of Mexico would eventually inspire multiple scholars[16] to follow a similar line of work. And as a consequence, an entire wave of government initiatives flourished, thereby fulfilling national and international conventional agendas. However, as a counter effect of these processes, a bottom-up Afro-Mexican social movement, known as *El movimiento de los pueblos negros* (The Movement of the Black Villages), would eventually surge to reassert blackness, thus, using the ethnicization of blackness as a tool to highlight cultural difference as opposed to *racial* difference. Hence, in the following paragraphs, I discuss how the civil association Mexico Negro (since 1997) and more so AFRICA (since 2007) in Costa Chica, eventually redefined and become the main cultural promoters or arbitrators of difference in the ethnicization process.

In 1989, UNESCO launched a program throughout the Americas and the world to help synthesize the transatlantic African diaspora. As a result, in Mexico, under the National Council for Culture and the Arts (CONACULTA), a government initiative project initiated titled *Nuestra Tercera Raiz. presencia de las culturas africanas* ("Our Third Root: The Presence of African Cultures"). The program was established and directed by Afromexicanist (Historian) Luz Maria Martinez Montiel.[17] From this project alone multiple micro projects (i.e. photo exhibits, Afromexicanist Conferences, a documentary,[18] book article compilations, music festivals and museums)[19] later branched from—specifically in 1992 with the commemoration of the 500 years "discovery" of America. Interestingly, however, these processes of finding the African legacy in Mexico would only be interested in carving out *afro*-ethnic or folkloric elements (i.e. afrodescendant music such as *Son Jarocho, La Chilena,* gastronomy, religious practices, etc.) in Mexico.

By 2003, the program functioned under the umbrella of General Direction of Popular Cultures (DGCP), directed by Guillermo Bonfil-Batalla—who since 1988 had an interest to "bring attention to *afromestizos* & afromexicanos [in order to] shed light to their contributions to [Mexico's] ethnicity and culture."[20] However, in agreement with anthropologist Sagrario Cruz-Carretero, despite their efforts of "rescuing" the historical legacy of Africans in Mexico they failed to address issues of "racism and discrimination [that] are serious issues in Mexico compared to other countries such as the United States or South Africa, thus diminishing the importance of taking measures to confront them."[21] The Third Root project has not taken a social-political stance to make visible the marginalization and invisibility of black communities. The projects launched under its umbrella have simply attempted to recognize African contributions to national culture and capture the cultural expressions of the African legacy. The project attempts to ethnicize blackness in the national imaginary by romantically demarcating their racial and not necessarily cultural difference. In addition, these processes fail to discuss "affirmative action, compensatory measures, and public policies to place black identity and inclusion at the heart of national culture."[22]

No project spearheaded by the Third Root Project captures government efforts to ethnicize Afromestizos better than the first and only *Museo de las culturas Afromestizas Vicente Guerrero* (Afromestizo Museum Vicente Guerrero),[23] established in 1999 in Cuajinicuilapa, Guerrero. Unlike any other project, this interactive small museum, composed of a photo exhibit, dance costumes, masks, musical instruments, and *redondos* ("African" mud round houses) located outdoors, offered for the first time a space for local black costeños to reimagine their "Afromestizaje." While there is sufficient visual material that

educates them to their history of slavery, there is hardly anything that con-
temporizes their Black Costeño inter-ethnicity. As a result, there is a low attendance
of locals to the museum. According to Laura A. Lewis, in large respect this is
because there is a "lack of interest in [African] heritage, in part because of their
migration experiences and global restructuring, and in part because, as they
see it, they are 'Mexicans' for whom the past is not only *not* African, but gone."[24]
Overall, the establishment of the museum raises the following question: For
whom and under what rubric was the Afromestizo Museum designed?

Unsatisfied by the Third Root national project's lack of political drive and,
more importantly, by the precipitous migration of Afro-Mexicans to the US,
towards the end of the twentieth century, in March 1997 NGO Mexico Negro
would host their first on-going annual *Encuentro de los Pueblos Negros* (Meeting of Black Villages) at El Ciruelo, Oaxaca (a black village in the municipality of Pinotepa Nacional). This event would not only congregate various
representatives from twenty-five Costa Chica communities, but also draw a crowd
of 350 attendees—most of them foreign scholars. This event signified the
birth of the grassroots black movement in Mexico. As Afro-Mexican anthropologist Bobby Vaughn asserts: "the very use of the [imagined towns] *Pueblos Negros* (Black Villages) … signaled a certain contestation of dominant ways
of denying blackness."[25] If one traces the propaganda material (i.e. posters,
banners, and leaflets) generated by the encounters, one could also come to
the conclusion that to a certain degree, the ethnicization of blackness was
being adopted and modified as a mechanism to help (re)construct collective
black consciousness.

For instance, the background flyer image of the 1st Meeting of Black Villages is one of Tony Gleatons' photographs—that appeared in the 1992 "Mexico Negro" photo exhibit sponsored by the Third Root project.[26] The image
portrays a dark skinned young boy, dressed in a white loose robe, with a serious stare away from the camera. This image resembles what Afro-Mexicanist Laura
A. Lewis refers to an "unambiguous racism that construes blackness as a 'prim-
itive' and unwelcome blot on the national landscape."[27] Nonetheless, images
such as this one pay testimony to the early bold use of the ethnicization of blackness in the Mexico Negro. Although the imagery or art selection used by organizers in more recent propaganda material to promote their annual Meeting
of Black Villages or other related events has changed significantly, according to
my preliminary research, it continues to highlight "several ideological conflicts
that are emblematic of the difficulty in politicizing blackness in Mexico."[28]

Fourteen years after the first meeting of black villages—which have strategically taken place in different black communities[29] both in Oaxaca and Guerrero—two recurring issues are central in the black social movement's agenda:

"absence of a juridical frame that can recognize the identity and *diversity* rights of [Afro-Mexicans]"[30] and the inclusion into the Oaxacan CENSUS of the Afro-Mexican population residing in Costa Chica. While these advances of recognizing the black population continue pending, in the state of Guerrero, for instance, the town of Cuajinicilapa has already been recognized as the first "Municipio Negro" (Black Municipality) at the federal level. This recognition came during the term (1999–2005) of governor of Rene Juarez Cisneros. In all of Costa Chica, in order to nationally visibilize the Afro-Mexican population there has yet to be a consensus among government council programs (CONAPO,[31] CONAPRED,[32] CDI,[33] INEGI[34]) regarding how to best implement a ethnic-racial category in the CENSUS to determine who autoidentifies and autodenominates as "*Negr@.*" Hence, without an official headcount of the Afro-Mexican population, which takes into consideration the unique *cultural characteristics* of their communities, the institutionalization of specific public policies and reforms that grant recognition cannot be conceived.

In summary, ever since Article 16 was modified in Oaxaca in 1998, granting same equal rights to "Afro-Mexicans" as Indigenous ethnic groups, it has given black civil associations some political leverage. According to Afro-Mexican scholar Sagrario Cruz-Carretero, this became the first legal victory on behalf of the black social movement in the state of Oaxaca.[35] Though what is vague about the revision of this article is the wording:

> The state of Oaxaca has a pluriethnic composition, sustained by the majority of indigenous peoples. This law recognizes the following indigenous villages, *amuzgos, cuicatecos, chatinos, chinatecos, chocos, chocholtecos, chontales, huaves, ixcatecos, mazatecos, mixes, mixtecos, triques, zapotecos and zoques.* This law will also protect Afro-Mexican and Indigenous communities, *regardless of state of origin or temporary or permanently*, qualify equally to the same rights under this law.[36]

Based on this reform, Afro-Mexicans subsequently became technically Oaxacas' seventeenth ethnic group. The main problem, however, is that is presumes not only that blacks do not reside in Oaxacan territory but also as an "ethnic community" they must advocate for their rights under indigenous policies. According to Costa Chica sociologist Odile Hoffman, what explains this social inequality or the *delay* to implement adequate public policies for Afro-Mexicans is the "lack of estimation instruments and statistic description of the 'Afromestizo ethnic group.'"[37] Henceforth, in order to demand collective rights and government funding the black social movement is using the political language of "*usos y costrumbres*," which are framed around indigenous traditions, thus leaving no option for civil associations but to ethnicize blackness in unprecedented ways.

Fourteen years after the first encounter, one recurring issue that continues to play a central role in Mexico Negro A.C.'s agenda is the Mexican government's failure to implement into their CENSUS the Afro-Mexican population residing in Costa Chica. The reason is that in order to nationally and legislatively make the Afro-Mexican population visible, there is yet to be a consensus among government officials regarding what grants ethnic legitimacy to this minority sub-group in Costa Chica. Moreover, as Afromexican activist Israel Reyes Larrea states, there is an "absence of a juridical frame that can recognize the identity and *diversity* rights of [Afro-Mexicans] that have derived in public political applications not adequate for the characteristics and necessities of the [Black Villages] which find themselves in a marginalized and vulnerable position."[38] Indeed, when new reforms in Mexico's multicultural and plural-ethnic paradigms (affirmative action policies) were enacted in 1998 (through Article 2 of the Mexican Constitution), they were *only* framed to measure ethnic differences or *usos y costrumbres* (everyday uses and customs) in indigenous communities, and *not* in Afrodescedant towns. Based on this exclusion and invisibility, there is a lack of work opportunities, schools, health facilities, and road infrastructures. These are just some of the basic human and citizenship rights that did not arrive to the black villages of Costa Chica.

According to sociologist Odile Hoffman, what explains this social inequality, or *delay*, is the lack of estimation instruments and statistic description.[39] Unlike indigenous people who can more easily be distinguished by their indigenous customs and physiognomy, Afro-Mexicans can be typified by their gastronomy, Spanish language accent, regional jobs, traditional dances, and everyday customs. Henceforth, the ongoing negotiation processes occurring between NGO Mexico Negro A.C. (or AFRICA A.C.), government pilot programs (Secretary of Government (SEGOB), the National Institute of Statistics (INEGI)) and PUMC (University of UNAM Multicultural Program) attempt as a first step to negotiate an ethnic label, to denominate a name category which can best represent the Afrodescendant population in the CENSUS.[40]

The shifting point in Afro-Mexican identity politics occurred in 2001, when Article 16 became enacted in Oaxaca, Mexico granting equal rights to "Afro-Mexicans" as Indigenous people.[41] What is technically dysfunctional and fundamental about the description of this legislation is that all *ethnic* communities are fully responsible in claiming these rights. Since the only way to demand collective rights and government funding is to use the political spiel of "*usos y costrumbres*" based on the ethnic differences framed around indigenous traditions, it forces Afro-Mexican NGO's to ethnicize blackness in unprecedented ways, thus creating a controversy when Afrodescendants are asked or questioned about their race and responding with ambiguity about labeling their identity.[42] In other words, in order for Afro-Mestizos or Afro-Mexicans to claim collective rights, they are left with no other option but to utilize classic indicators (for example, Spanish accent, music/dance, dress codes, and traditional social organization), that differentiates them from Indigenous groups and mestizos.[43] They leave no option for Oaxacan based organizations such as NGO AFRICA A.C. but to compromise with public policies or actions in order to revitalize, impose, and *invent* ethnic differences; since, as aforementioned, no statistical INEGI head countdown exists to make large claims.

De Afro-Mexicanos a Pueblos Negros (From Afro-Mexicanos to The Black Towns) was the first book compilation spearheaded by the movement. It was released in 2009 as a result of the first Afro-Mexican forum from July 21–22, 2007 which took place in Morelos; headquarters of AFRICA Leading the opening forum were members of Mexico Negro, AFRICA, and PUMC-UNAM (UNAM's Nation Multicultural Program) as well as an Afro-Colombian activist Carlos Rua. According to the national newspaper *La Jornada* (published July 24, 2007), more than one hundred representatives of multiple organizations (i.e. *ECOSTA, Revista Fandango, Museo Regional de las Culturas Afro-mestizas, Barca-Costa, Ojo de Agua*) from Veracruz and Guerrero attended.[44] Unlike the annual encounters of black villages, that primarily consists of round table discussions and all day activities, the objective of the open forum was to methodologically resynthesize, crystallize, and strategize previous works for the constitutional recognition—under article 2 of the Mexican constitution—of black villages living inside and *outside* Mexican territory.

The village representatives were also to discuss the politics of obtaining a headcount by the national U.S. Census. According to my preliminary research, no event organized by the movement of black villages has generated more commotion than this Afro-Mexican forum.[45] This might have had to do with AFRICA's (Alliance for the Strengthening of Indigenous and Afromexican Community Regions) grassroots vision, and the strong collaborative efforts with government pilot programs and egalitarian alliance with the indigenous movement.[46] In respect to obtaining public visibility, foment collective consciousness, and generate funding, AMQPs have become a recent phenomenon to accomplish these goals both at the regional and enclave abroad scale.

Arbitrating Ethnic Difference through AMQPs

This author attended the AMQP titled *Reyna de la Primavera* (Queen of the Spring), which was organized by NGO Afromexicana in April of 2009 at

Pasadena, CA, for two central reasons. The first was because of the pageant organizers, founders, and members of the NGO Afromexicana, Martin Aleman and Arturo Herrera. They were key Afromexican activists in Costa Chica (prior to their migration to Pasadena, CA) between 2000 and 2008. Both of their oral histories regarding the awakening of the movement of the black villages and the role Queen Pageants play in Costa Chica, were crucial to fulfill the gaps of my preliminary research. Second, I needed ethnographic data to support my hypothesis: Afro-Mexicans in Pasadena, CA, unlike Laura A. Lewis's ethnographic findings[47] in North-Salem, North Carolina, are experiencing a similar process of constructing and imagining black identity as in Costa Chica. The following paragraphs offer a thorough assessment of my preliminary findings regarding AMQPs, as well as a comparative study between those in California and Costa Chica. The goal is to underscore how selecting a Queen Pageant creates the ideal processes and the novel space for a black ethnic identity to "emerge and transform in contraposition, juxtaposition, and correlation with other ethnic identities as well as with other kinds of cultural identities."[48]

According to the historiography[49] of beauty/queen pageants, in general, there seems to be a consensus that underlines their feminine subjectivity of racial landscapes, embodiment of cultural ideals, and the institutionalization of social and economic hierarchies. More importantly, the power of the queen pageant to create a space for self-definition within the refashioning of the collective identity is also recognized. As will be explained later in the chapter, with the case of Afromexican NGO's manipulating the performance of Queen Pageants in Costa Chica or in Pasadena, CA, they can also help fund-raise, channel demands of citizenship, and intersect blackness within the rubric of *mestizaje*, *Latinidad*, *Chicanidad*, or *Mexicaness*. Queen Pageants can provide a theoretical framework on how space, bodies and performance can then transform into a "novel assemblage of memory"[50] where categories of race, ethnicity, and culture can overlap within their blackness and Mexicaness. According to Juliet Hooker, this kind of overlapping simply mirrors practices of *multicultural liberalism* in Latin America were "some combination of remedies [are] designed [in order] to overcome racialized oppression and to accommodate cultural difference."[51]

Based on preliminary research, Queen Pageants in Mexico have been an understudied phenomenon. However, in the case of Costa Chica, Gloria Lara in her article, "The Resource of Ethnic-Racial Difference in the Logics of Political Inclusion. The Case of Pinotepa Nacional," makes reference to a historical account when the first *Afromestiza* Queen was selected to participate in the patriotic festivities of 2002 in the municipality of *Pinotepa Nacional*. According to her findings, the municipality governor at the time was promoting interculturality and because of that, a committee was put together in order to select the first Afromestiza pageant. Although Lara's work is limited in providing names or describing the processes, she does in fact explain how Queen Pageants—as civil actions—in Costa Chica are central to canonizing ethnic differences. They serve as an underway to highlight global economic and cultural shifts, and appropriate ethnic symbolic elements as instruments of action and legitimization.[52]

Considering that Queen Pageants have served as vehicles to canonize citizenship demands, since 2004, NGO AFRICA A.C. have taken the initiative to manipulate their infrastructure. And in the process, the aesthetic nuances and name ambivalence embodied in the queen finalist underscores how the pageant is subjective to the movement of the black villages. For instance, in 2004 the queen pageant Denise Reina Medina was referred to as the *Reyna Afromestiza* (Afromestiza Queen). Her queen pageant attire was simple, and the overall performance would carry a patriotic theme.[53] But in 2010, the Queen Pageant Eva Donicio would be referred to as *Reyna Negra* (*Black Queen*), and her dress will be painted with African motifs as well as be escorted by the regional Afro-Mexican dance *El Baile del Diablo*.[54] More importantly, however, is the discourse commemoration that she delivered with the assistance of AFRICA A.C. in her presentation at the Huazolotitlan carnival:

> In name of the Black Villages, from the municipality of Santa Maria Huazolotitlan, and in representation of AFRICA A.C., I crown you Queen of the 2010 carnival. And we commence you to strengthen the activities in which in turn allow us to gain the national recognition for the rights of the black villages of Mexico. And also, we want to take the opportunity to thank the committee of culture in our municipality for granting us, the town of Jose Maria Morelos, the opportunity to give the black race representation in the event. And we hope this is not the last time we participate in the Huazolotitlan festival. Let this moment repeat itself to interweave these two cultures (mixtec and black) that form part of our municipality.[55]

After the introduction, the AMQP then proceeded by stating that, "It is an honor to represent our Black Village of our Municipality. And I will work in the strengthening of our cultures and, more importantly, in the official national recognition for the rights of the black villages."[56] Essentially, NGO AFRICA A.C. is using the platform of Queen Pageants to voice their demands regarding the official national recognition of Black Villages in Costa Chica. In retrospect, her naming as Black Queen and repetition of the name Black Villages sheds light on how in 2007, as previously discussed, the movement officially declared itself the movement of the black villages rather than Afromestizo or Afromexican.

In the case of Pasadena, CA, the spring queen pageants have a different function. This is based on the sociological context within which they exist. Unlike constructing a politically driven performance for municipality representatives and attendees, the NGO Afromexicana is more concerned with fundraising and collecting economic remittances to help the black villages in Costa Chica. Indeed, one of their main fundraising strategies is taking semi-professional studio pictures of the pageant, and then selling them at church events (a.k.a. *kermeses*). Indeed, based on the data collected in 2009–2010, part of the proceeds goes into buying the queen pageant finalist a laptop and the rest were placed into a bank account. Since 2009, the spring queen pageants have taken place at a warehouse driveway where they mass produce *quinceañera* dresses—amongst low income communities in Pasadena.

According to Martin Aleman, secretary and main founder of the NGO, the pageant serves as a large "*pachanga*" (*party*) to fundraise, support the youth, and create alliances. Thereby, the intention behind the pageant is not necessarily to generate ethnic differences.[57] "It is the opposite," he stated. Supporting this statement, he mentioned the difficulties that Afro-Mexicans confront in the US in comparison to Costa Chica. He also stated, "With the economic and psychological hardships we confront here as undocumented workers, not to say the estimated four hundred black *costeños*, we seek in these gatherings a sense of belonging and comfort." Moreover, after asking him, why then organize through queen pageants and not through some other cultural mediums? He responded: Before becoming [the NGO] Afromexicanos, I attempted to gather [Afro-Mexicans] to a music/dance performance, regarding the Music/Dance of the Devils, but I did not have a good turnout. Costeños in the US seem to be more distracted by the American Dream and therefore begin to forget about their roots. Besides the fact that Queen Pageants play a role within the high school system and patriotic festivities in Costa Chica, the idea of a queen pageant was pitched by a lady in the community that showed up to one of our monthly meetings. After hearing her out we all agree to organize one. And since then, it has become our number one benefit event of the year.[58]

Aleman's responses then allowed me to grasp how Queen Pageants were in fact culturally symbolic among *costenos* as well as how they function as ideal mechanisms to generate economic remittances in order to strengthen the movement of the black villages. In 2010, when attending the spring queen pageant for a second time, Arturo Herrera (Vice-President of Afromexicana), as a host of the event, would overtly emphasize through the microphone where the $7,000 dollars of that evening proceeds were going, as well as the $50,000 dollars collected over the years. He also overtly repeated through the speaker system: "all the money collected this evening would be soon sent over to [the black villages] in Costa Chica in order to purchase a full medically equipped ambulance. So far we are $18,000 dollars away from reaching our goal."[59]

Conclusion

This chapter has shown how Black ethnic formation in everyday politics of representation of institutional multiculturalism play out in Oaxaca. The stories in the chapter complicate assessments of ethnic-racial politics/relationships of indigenous and black communities. After eight years of tracing the birth and the development of the Afro-Mexican social movement, the author found that AMQPs are symbolic of the wider process of the making of black political subjects and subjectivities. On the one hand, they exemplify how in the ethnicization process NGO have had to comply with the dominant standards of prosperity/modernity. AMQPs help arbitrate difference and re-negotiate intra-ethnic identity thereby creating a platform and an ambivalent space to construct an imagined black identity within the paradigm of multicultural or mestizo Mexico. In the context of Pasadena, CA, it helps give visibility amongst the Oaxacan and Mexican-American population as well as fundraise unlike any other event.

The lack of head count statistics on the black population residing in Costa Chica, Oaxaca thus far continues to be a barrier towards obtaining ethnic group "authenticity" and political agency. Without demographic statistics, civil associations are unable to make specific lawsuits to the state. Since 1998, however, under new multicultural and anti-discriminatory reforms that helped recognize, institutionalize and regulate ethnic difference—thus placing Afro-Mexicans as Oaxaca's seventeen ethnic group—Black NGOs have a certain political leverage to negotiate and challenge institutional recognition. Leading these negotiations and helping arbitrate Afro-Mexican ethnic difference in Oaxaca as cultural promoters since 2007 has been the civil association AFRICA. Helping fundraise and establishing new forms of obtaining visibility abroad is the organization Afromexicana in Pasadena.

Furthermore, there is no doubt that if the black social movement continues using similar tactics to work cohesively and construct collective political consciousness in Black Costeño communities, more costeños will begin to deconstruct everyday negative connotations of blackness and begin to accept their African heritage. As this chapter argues, the manipulation of the media, space and performance in public actions, is crucial for the revindication, restructuring, reimagining and reconceptualization of being an African descendant in Mexico. Considering that the national ideologies encouraging "whitening" through miscegenation are embedded in ethnic queen pageants, such as *La Reyna America/Fiestas Patrias* in Costa Chica, there is then no option but for Afro-Mexican NGOs to produce their own normative versions of cultural difference. The classic ethnic (indigenous) parameters designed in Mexico's early anthropology—fabricated by integrationist theory—have been problematic when measuring blackness in Costa Chica because they create a dichotomy between Indigenous and Blackness.

The ultimate problem was that investigators tend to reproduce and transmit stereotypes of (in)difference. These indigenous-based ethnic paradigms leave no option for black civil associations but to mark or hyphenate cultural difference in unprecedented ways. Yet, from a macro perspective, regarding the similar techniques Black NGOs develop around negotiating ethnic representation in Latin America's era of anti-discriminatory reforms, they should also be viewed as "*self-generated* strategies for negotiating official multicultural models whose categories do not always readily recognize Afro-descendants and that may continue to conceal persistent racial hierarchies."[60] Ultimately, these on-going gradual processes not only reaffirm success on behalf of the movement to negotiate ethnic political legitimacy and challenge Mexico's multicultural and multiethnic policies, but also highlight early stages to implement adequate public policies in Oaxaca's legislation.

Notes

1. "Afro-Oaxaqueños en California," *El Oaxaqueño*, 9 May 2008, front page.

2. Afromexicana's main objectives as an NGO are the following: 1) Identity: To show our identity, who we are, where we came from and where we go. 2) Culture: Rescuing our culture and regional traditions and / or preservation. 3) Education: To educate our communities in all daily aspects that affect thousands of people. 4) Economy: how to get funds to help our people. 5) Health: Keep the level of safety without infection. 6) Organizations: continue to organize in order to have more control of our future (Info taken from main website www.afromexicano.com, May of 2010).

3. According to the newspaper and a personal interview with Marin Aleman (founder of Afromexicana), the Afro-Mexican population residing in Pasadena, CA estimates around 400–600.

4. See the following work relating to Transnationalism in *Mixtec* (Oaxacan Indigenous) communities: Matínez Novo 2006; Stephen, Lynn 2007.

5. *Los Pueblos Negros, as the black social movement resfers to them,* consists of African descent communities—excluded from the state/national census and yet to be legitimately recognized by the state—remnant of colonial *palenques* (maroon communities) and *haciendas*. The Black Villages in Oaxaca can be considered an *imagined* community, since what defines these communities as black is determined based on cultural customs rather than phonotypical differences. Moreover, according to socio-anthropologist Luis Campos Munoz the black villages are composed of several inter ethnic-racial identified afrodescendants villages (i.e. El Ciruelo, Collantes y Corralero, Jose Maria Morelos) that form part of municipalities (*pueblos*) such as: Pinotepa Nacional, Huazolotitlan, Jamiltepec and San Pedro Tutupec. The total population of Afrodescendants, according to his is approximately 40,000 2008. *Relaciones interétnicas en pueblos originarios de México y Chile.* Providencia, (Santiago de Chile: Universidad Academia de Humanismo Cristiano).

6. Mexico Negro A.C. was founded in 1997, as a result of the first encounter of Black Villages in El Ciruelo, Oaxaca, Costa Chica. The organization is composed of multiple scholars, activists, and state officials throughout Mexico and abroad. Their mission is to obtain national recognition for all afrodescedants residing in Oaxaca and Guerrero by writing demands to the government.

7. AFRICA's acronym stands for: *Alianza para el fortalecimiento de las Regiones Indígenas y Comunidades Afromexicanas (Alliance for the Strengthening of Indigenous and Afromexican Community Regions).* The organization was founded in 2002 and primarily focuses in promoting and preserving black cultural manifestations using the arts (radio, annual cultural events (i.e. AMQPs), photography, painting workshops, etc.) as a medium to bring regional, state, national and international visibility.

8. Back in 2006 they were known as *Colectivo* AFRICA, and ran an online photo blog called *Imagenes de la Costa Chica* (Images of Costa Chica)—directed by founding member of the organization Israel Reyes Larrea. Website: http://africacimarron.multiply.com/photos/album/6/DENIS ... Nuestra-Reina-Negra (Accessed July 12, 2012).

9. Laura A. Lewis. 2009. "Afro' Mexico in Black, White, and Indian". (eds.) Vinson, Ben, and Matthew Restall. *Black Mexico: race and society from colonial to modern times.* Albuquerque: University of New Mexico Press. Pgs. 183–201, 188.

10. DIGEPO. Abril 2008. Oaxaca Poblacion Siglo XXI. *Revista de la Direccion General*

de Poblacion de Oaxaca:Afrodescendientes. Ano 8. Numero 21.

11. Gonzalez, 3.

12. I will use this term in agreement with Eduardo Restrepo's use and interpretation; in regards to how he applies it with the case of Afro-Colombiano's: "The ethnicization of blackness […] implies a particular articulation of memories and identities in the politics of representation of alterity. The ethnicization of blackness involves a specific '*imagined (black) community*' both within and beyond the nation. Therefore, […] not an euphemism for race, but that to understand the particular inscriptions of blackness as an ethnic group one has to *problematize* the 'racial discourse' assumed by most scholars in the study of blackness" (2004:698). "Ethnicization of Blackness in Colombia: Toward de-recializing theoretical and political imagination." Cultural Studies Vol.18, No.5, 698–715.

13. See: Lewis 2000, Vaughn 2001–2009; Hoffman 2006–2007, Campos Muñoz 1998/2008.

14. Odile Hoffman underscores that Aguirre Beltrán's shortcomings began "the moment he catalogued certain practices as 'black', even 'African', and assimilate certain practices, or assembling multiple practices, to one collective identity arbitrarily named 'black' by the investigator" Hoffman, Odile. 2006. *Negros y Afromestizos en Mexico: viejas y nuevas lecturas de un mundo olvidado.* Revista Mexicana de Sociologia 68, num. 1:103–135, 117.

Laura A. Lewis also argues that Aguirre Beltrán's assimilationist views were grounded on his perception that "post-independence national statistics that omitted blacks and mulattoes reflected a *biological* disappearance, for they had 'blurred into' (Aguirre Beltrán, 1970: 12) the process of mestizaje (race-mixing) that came to characterize the new nation" Laura A. Lewis, "Blacks, Black Indians, Afromexicans: The Dynamics of Race, Nation, and Identity in a Mexican Moreno Community (Guerrero)." *American Ethnologist.* Num. 27. Vol. 4, 2000, 898–996.

15. See: Gonzalez Aguirre Beltran. 1989 [1958]. Cuijla: esbozo etnográfico de un pueblo negro. Mexico City: Fondo de Cultura Económica, 7.

16. For Gastronomy see Torres 1995, *corridos* or *afromestizo* ballads see McDowell 2000: Ramsay, 2004: Ruiz 2004, alternative medicine see Cardenas, 1997: Bristol, 2007, linguistics Githiora, 2008, identity politics, see Vaughn 2001–2009, Lewis, 2000–2009, Campos Munoz, 1998–2008.

17. Inspired by Aguirre Beltran's work, in 1974 Dr. Montiel lays the groundwork for what would unfold to multiple government state projects pertaining to the African presence in Mexico known as: "Afroamerica." In 1987 she was responsible for the first slavery exhibit in Veracruz. Between 1988 and 1989, as director of Direction of Popular Cultures she organized eight international Afroamerican conferences. In effect, with the sponsorship of CONACULTA, four major book compilations on Afro-Mexico were printed. Moreover, she is known for being a faculty of the Letters & Science program at UNAM and founder of the African and Afroamerican studies.

18. See: Rebollar, Rafael. 1994. *La Tercera Raiz.* Mexico. CONACULTA: Video.

19. For pictures and more information see: http://www.nacionmulticultural.unam.mx/Portal/Izquierdo/INVESTIGACION/Afroamerica/afro_anteced.html (Accessed May of 2012).

20. Source: Personal Translation, www.nacionmulticultural.unam.mx (Accessed July 2012).

21. Sagrario Cruz Carretero. 2006. *The African presence in Mexico: from Yanga to the present.* Chicago, IL: Mexican Fine Arts Center Museum, 40.

22. Vinson, Ben and Matthew Restall, *Black Mexico: Race and Society from Colonial to Modern Times* (Albuquerque: University of New Mexico Press, 2009), 224–231, 227.

23. Initiatives to open a museum in Cuaji began as early as 1995. Meetings between INAH, DIGEPO, Our Third Root Project and a local civil association called *Comite de Museo Comunitario Cuijla* (CMCC was established in 1995) took place as early as 1997. The museum was curated by Luz Maria Martínez Montiel and is directed by CMCC. (Eduardo Añorve's Website, http://eltapanqo.blogspot.com/search/label/afromestizos (Accessed September 2011).)

24. Laura A. Lewis, "Home Is Where the Heart Is: Afro-Latino Migration and Cinder-Block Homes on Mexico's Costa Chica," *South Atlantic Quarterly*, Fall 2006, Vol. 105. Issue 4, 2006, 802.

25. Bobby Vaughn, "The African Diaspora through *Ojos Mexicanos*: Blackness and Mexicanidad in Southern México," The *Review of Black Political Economy*. 33 (1): 2005, 49–58, 129.

26. For full collection of exhibit see: Tony Gleaton, *Africa's Legacy in Mexico* (Washington, D.C.: Smithsonian Institution Traveling Exhibition Service, 1993).

27. Laura A. Lewis. "Modesty and Modernity: Photography, Race, and Representation on Mexico, Costa Chica (Guerrero) 1," *Identities: Global Studies in Culture and Power*, 11 (4), 2004, 279.

28. Bobby Vaughn, "Afro-Mexico: Blacks, Indigenas, Politics, and the Greater Diaspora," in *Neither enemies nor friends: Latinos, Blacks, Afro-Latinos* eds., Dzidzienyo, Anani, and Suzanne Oboler (New York: Palgrave Macmillan, 2005), 129.

29. Oaxaca: El Ciruelo, 1997, San José Estancia Grande, 1998, Collantes, 2000, Santiago Tapextla, 2001, San Nicolás, 2002, Santo Domingo Armenta, 2003.

30. Israel Reyes Larrea, *Costumbres y tradiciones de los pueblos negros de la Costa Chica de Oaxaca. Oaxaca: Secretaria de Cultura del Gobierno de Oaxaca;* Personal translation, 2008, 17.

31. Acronym stands for: *Consejo Nacional de Población* (National Council of Population).

32. Acronym stands for: *Consejo Nacional de Prevención contra la Discriminación* (National Council for the Prevention of Discrimination).

33. Acronym stands for: *Comisión Nacional para el desarrollo de los Pueblos Indígenas* (National Commission for the Development of Indigenous Communities; known before as INI).

34. Acronym stands for: *Insituto Nacional de Estatisticas y Geografia* (National Institute of Statistics and Geography).

35. Cruz Carretero, Sagrario, *The African presence in Mexico: From Yanga to the Present* (Chicago, IL: Mexican Fine Arts Center Museum, 2006), 42–43.

36. *El Estado de Oaxaca tiene una composición pluricultural, sustentada por la mayoría de pueblo indigenas. Esta ley reconoce a los siguientes pueblo indigenas amuzgos, cuicatecos, chatinos, chinatecos, chocos, chocholtecos, chontales, huaves, ixcatecos, mazatecos, mixes, mixtecos, triques, zapotecos and zoques. La ley reglamentaria protegerá a las comunidades afromexicanas y a los indígenas pertenecientes a cualquier otro pueblo procedente de otros Estados de la República y que por cualquier circunstancia, residan dentro del territorio del Estado de Oaxaca* (Personal Translation, www.digepo.oaxaca.gob.mx).

37. Hoffman, Odile, "Negros y Afromestizos en Mexico: viejas y nuevas lecturas de un

mundo olvidado," *Revista Mexicana de Sociologia* 68, Num. 1: 2006, 103–135., 115.

38. Vaughn, 2007.

39. Hoffman 2006: 115.

40. In April of 2010, an online newspaper published an article regarding a conference that attempted to find a consensus amongst the black villages on how to categorize Afro-Mexicans on the census. See: http://www.oaxacadigital.info/portal/index.php?option=com_content&view=article&id=6027&catid=39&Itemid=55. Also, for related video footage, see Youtube video at: http://www.youtube.com/watch?v=sMB7Agqxpf8.

41. Article 16, circumscribed under the Law of Rights of Indigenous Communities and Villages, of the constitution of Oaxaca reads: "The state of Oaxaca has a pluriethnic composition, sustained by the majority of indigenous villages. This law recognizes the following indigenous villages, *amuzgos, cuicatecos, chatinos, chinatecos, chocos, chocholtecos, chontales, huaves, ixcatecos, mazatecos, mixes, mixtecos, triques, zapotecos and zoques*. Afro-Mexican and Indigenous communities, regardless of state of origin or temporary or permanently, *qualify* equally to the same rights under this law." (Personal Translation, www.digepo.oaxaca.gob.mx).

42. Besides my personal ethnographic preliminary research since 2004, a series of ethnographic publications prove the complexity of this matter. See Laura A. Lewis 2000–2012; Bobby Vaughn 2001–2009; Odile Hoffman 2006–2007; Gloria Lara 2007; Luis Muñoz Campos (1998/2008).

43. Hoffman 2006: 115.

44. Misael Habana de los Santos, July 2007. "*Exigen reconocimiento a los derechos de los pueblos negros.*" La Jornada de Guerrero: (http://www.lajornadaguerrero.com.mx/2007/07/25/index.php?section=sociedad&article=012n1soc).

45. For multiple newspaper articles see: Perez Pineda, Edgar. 2007. "*Llaman a reivindicar a los pueblos negros.*" La Jornada de Guerrero. (http://www.lajornadaguerrero.com.mx/2007/03/20/index.php?section=sociedad&article=012n1soc); Mendez, Mario. 2009. "*De Afromexicanos Pueblo Negro.*" Periodico Opinion. Pinotepa Nacional. Septiembre 2009, 6.

46. See: De la O, Margena y Fracisca Meza, "*Comienzan los preparativos para la convención indigena y afromexicana*" La Jornada de Guerrero. (http://www.lajornadaguerrero.com.mx/2009/04/23/index.php?section=sociedad&article=006n2soc).

47. Laura A. Lewis's findings, beginning with her first publication regarding Afro-Mexican identity politics in U.S. (2006) to her latest publication, titled "'Afro' Mexico in Black, White, and Indian" in 2009, has underscored that Afro-Mexicans from San Nicolas, Costa Chica currently residing in North-Salem, North Carolina show now signs of embracing or cultivating black identity.

48. Restrepo, 2002: 41.

49. See: Barnes, 1994; Cohen/Wilk/Stoeltje, 1996; Hooks, 1999; Banet-Weiser, 1999; Rogers, 2003; King-O'Riain, 2006; Daniel, 2007.

50. Restrepo, 2009:711.

51. Hooker 2009: 136.

52. Lara, 104.

53. For picture see: http://africacimarron.multiply.com/photos/album/6/DENIS … Nuestra_Reina_Negra#photo=2.

54. For picture see: http://africacimarron.multiply.com/photos/album/144/CARNAVAL_HUAZOLO_2010#photo=3. And for Youtube video footage see: http://www.youtube.

com/watch?v=90d7Q9F393o&feature=related (Accessed May 31, 2010).

55. Personal Translation of speech taken from transcribed audio content from a youtube video see: http://www.youtube.com/watch?v=2kJdlt4cAYQ. (Taken May 31, 2010); Angustia Torres Diaz, member of AFRICA A.C.

56. Ibid. Eva Donicio, 2010 Black Queen of the Black Village.

57. Interview conducted April of 2009 at Pasadena, CA.

58. Ibid. Martin Aleman, 2009 Secretary of Afromexicana.

59. Interview conducted April of 2010.

60. Kwame Dixon and John Burdick, eds., *Comparative Perspectives on Afro-Latin America* (Gainesville, FL: University Press of Florida, 2012.), 278.

Contributors

Aaron, Ashley D., M.A. is currently a Lecturer in the Department of Africana Studies and is Affiliated Faculty in the Race and Resistance Studies Program at San Francisco State University, in the world's only College of Ethnic Studies. Her teaching and research interests include Afro-Latina/o American history, identity, and culture, Black liberation movements in Latin America and the Spanish Caribbean, Histories of Peoples of Color in the U.S, Critical Pedagogy, and Family Studies.

Adekunle, Julius O., Ph.D. is Professor of African History in the Department of History and Anthropology, Monmouth University, New Jersey. He is the author of *Culture and Customs of Rwanda* (Greenwood Press, 2007); co-editor of *Color Struck: Essays on Race and Ethnicity in Global Perspective* (University Press of America, 2010); and co-editor of *Democracy in Africa: Political Changes and Challenges* (Durham, NC: Carolina Academic Press, 2012). Julius has contributed numerous articles and essays to edited volumes and texts on the subject of African history and culture.

Alzouma, Gado, Ph.D. is Associate Professor of Anthropology at the School of Arts and Science, American University of Nigeria (AUN), Yola. He did his undergraduate and graduate studies in France between 1981 and 1987 and later completed a Ph.D. in anthropology from Southern Illinois University, Carbondale, USA. His research and publications focus on information and communication technologies for development (ICT4D) as well as globalization and identities. Before joining AUN, he taught sociology and anthropology courses for twelve years in Abdou Moumouni University of Niamey, Niger. He also worked as coordinator, evaluation, at the International Development Research Center in Dakar, Senegal, and as a research fellow in the Global Media Research Center of Southern Illinois University, Carbondale. He is the author of many articles in internationally renowned academic journals.

Becerra, Miguel, M.A. had his B.A. in Sociology from California State University Bakersfield, where he focused on issues related to racism. He developed interest in Afro-Peru while pursuing his M.A. in Latin American & Iberian Studies in University of California, Santa Barbara. His interest in Afro-Peruvian history and culture began during his trips to his homeland Peru, and through his passion for Afro-Peruvian music. His research focused on racism against blacks, analyzing it through the media, and studying it from a historical perspective.

Caddoo, Cara, is an instructor of American Studies at the State University of New York at Old Westbury and a Ph.D. student in American history at the Graduate Center, City University of New York. She is currently completing her dissertation on black film exhibition and production in the early twentieth century United States.

Combs, Barbara H. Ph.D. teaches at the University of Mississippi, where she has a joint appointment in Sociology and Southern Studies. She has a Ph.D. in Sociology from Georgia State University and a law degree from Ohio State. Her dissertation, "The Ties That Bind: The Role of Place in Racial Identity Formation, Social Cohesion, Accord, and Discord in Two Historic, Black Gentrifying Atlanta Neighborhoods," reflects her larger interests in place, urban spaces, and community building. Her dissertation research was funded by a Doctoral Dissertation Research Grant from the Department of Housing and Urban Development. She is also the recipient of a dissertation year fellowship award from the Southern Regional Education Board. Currently, she is working on a manuscript about the 1965 Selma to Montgomery Voting Rights Marches. The book is under contract with Routledge.

Cook Bell, Karen holds her Ph.D. in U.S. history with specialization in slavery and emancipation from Howard University. She is currently Assistant Professor of History at Bowie State University and has also engaged in postdoctoral study at Johns Hopkins University. Her publications on slavery, emancipation, and the African Diaspora have appeared in the *Georgia Historical Quarterly*, the *Journal of African American History, U.S.-West Africa: Interaction and Relations* (University of Rochester Press, 2008), *Before Obama: A Reappraisal of Black Reconstruction Era Politicians* (Praeger, November 2012), and *Slavery and Freedom in Savannah* (work in progress).

Daniel, G. Reginald, Ph.D., Professor, Department of Sociology, University of California, Santa Barbara teaches courses exploring comparative race and ethnic relations, particularly in terms of multiraciality. He has numerous publications that explore this topic. These include his books *More Than Black? Multiracial Identity and the New Racial Order* (2002), *Race and Multiraciality in Brazil and the United States: Converging Paths?* (2006), *Racial Identity and the Brazilian Novelist: The Life and Writings of Machado de Assis* (2012), and his chapter "Race, Multiraciality, and Barack Obama: Toward a More Perfect

Union?" (2009). In June 2012, Daniel received the Loving Prize, which commemorates the June 12, 1967 Loving v. Virginia decision that removed the last laws prohibiting racial intermarriage. It is awarded annually to outstanding artists and community leaders for inspirational dedication to celebrating and illuminating the mixed racial and cultural experience.

Eda, Haruki is a doctoral student of sociology at Rutgers, The State University of New Jersey. He holds a B.A. in sociology from San Francisco State University, and he is expected to receive a M.Sc. in Gender, Development and Globalization from the London School of Economics and Political Science. He is the author of "Intimate Agency: A Radical Sexual Revolution" in *Gender and Love,* edited by Noemi de Haro García and Maria-Anna Tseliou (2012). His current project examines the Orientalist representations of North Korea in the Western media.

Gonzalez, Jorge, M.A., completed his undergraduate at University of California, Davis in 2006 double majoring in Spanish and Native American Studies with a minor in Chicano Studies. He completed graduate school from 2009–2012 at University of California, Santa Barbara in Latin American and Iberian Studies. While in graduate school, Gonzalez received the Best Graduate Student Paper Competition at the CILAS Conference at UCSD in 2011. To find more information related to his topic of interest visit the FACEBOOK-Afromexico group.

Iromuanya, Julie is both a scholar-critic and creative writer. "Passing for What?: The Marrow of Tradition's Minstrel Critique of the Unlawfulness of Law" appears in Charles Chesnutt Reappraised: Essays on the First Major African American Writer. Her fiction appears, or is forthcoming, in *The Kenyon Review*, *Passages North*, the *Cream City Review*, and the *Tampa Review*, among other journals. Iromuanya earned her doctorate at the University of Nebraska-Lincoln and was the inaugural Herbert W. Martin Fellow in Creative Writing at the University of Dayton. She is Assistant Professor of English at Northeastern Illinois University in Chicago.

Johnson, Andre E., Ph.D. serves as chair of the department of Christianity and Culture and as the Dr. James L Netters Professor of Rhetoric and Religion and African American Studies at Memphis Theological Seminary. In addition to his academic titles, he also currently serves as Senior Pastor of Gifts of Life Ministries, in Memphis Tennessee and is the editor of the blog Rhetoric Race and Religion.

Jolivette, Andrew, Ph.D. is Associate Professor and chair of American Indian Studies at San Francisco State University. He is the author of *Cultural Representation in Native America* (2006), *Louisiana Creoles: Cultural Recovery and Mixed Race Native American Identity* (2007), and *Obama and the Biracial Factor: The Battle for a New American Majority* (2012). Dr. Jolivette is currently working on a new book, *Indian Blood: Mixed Race Gay Men, Transgender People, and HIV*. He is the board President of and a national speaker with Speak Out, the Co Chair of the GLBT Historical Society Board, and serves as board vice chair with the DataCenter for Research Justice. Dr. Jolivette is an IHART (Indigenous HIV/AIDS Research Training) Fellow at the University of Washington in Seattle.

Kretsedemas, Philip is Associate Professor of Sociology at UMass-Boston. His current work focuses on US immigration policy and immigrant racialization. He has co-edited books on these subjects for Greenwood/Praeger and Columbia University Press. Some of his journal articles have appeared in American Quarterly, International Migration and Stanford Law and Policy Review. He is also the author of The Immigration Crucible: Transforming 'Race,' Nation and the Limits of the Law (Columbia University Press, 2012). Forthcoming books with Routledge include *Migrants and Race in the US: Territorial Racism and the Alien/Outside* and the co-edited volume, *Migrant Marginality: A Transnational Perspective.*

Okpeh, Jr., Okpeh Ochayi Ph.D. is Reader/Associate Professor of African history and Deputy director Centre for Gender Studies at the Benue State university, Makurdi, Nigeria. He is also consultant on Gender and development studies. He has authored/co-authored and edited/co-edited many books including *Gender, Power and Politics in Nigeria* (Makurdi: Aboki Publishers, 2007); *Population Movements, Conflicts and Displacements in Nigeria* (Trenton, New Jersey: Africa World Press, 2009). He is the editor, Journal of globalization and International Studies.

Streets, Barbara F., Ph.D., L.P., is an Assistant Professor at SUNY-Oswego in the Department of Counseling and Psychological Services, where she teaches *Race, Class and Gender in Counseling and Psychology*. She also teaches counseling practicum and trauma courses. She is a Board Certified Fellow in African Centered /Black Psychology. She is also a New York State licensed psychologist and an AFAA certified aerobics instructor. Barbara Streets has presented at national conferences and published articles on cultural immersion and multicultural competency. Her other areas of interest include multicultural counseling, college students, mental health outreach programming and wellness management.

Williams, Hettie V. has taught survey courses in U.S. history, world history, and upper division courses on the history of African Americans at the University level for more than a decade. She has published various entries and essays for several encyclopedias and two edited volumes. She has written a text on the American civil rights movement entitled *We Shall Overcome to We Shall Overrun: the Collapse of the Civil Rights Movement and the Black Power Revolt* (2009), and an edited volume with Julius O. Adekunle titled *Color Struck: Es-*

says on Race and Ethnicity in Global Perspective (2010). Currently, Hettie is a lecturer of African American history in the Department of History and Anthropology at Monmouth University. Her latest research is an edited volume with G. Reginald Daniel tentatively titled *Race in the Age of Obama: Toward a More Perfect Union?* (University Press of Mississippi, forthcoming, 2013).

Index